AF760048

Post-Crisis Growth and Integration in Europe

Catching-up Strategies in CESEE Economies

Edited by

Ewald Nowotny

Governor, Oesterreichische Nationalbank, Austria

Peter Mooslechner

Director, Economic Analysis and Research Department, Oesterreichische Nationalbank, Austria

Doris Ritzberger-Grünwald

Head of the Foreign Research Division, Oesterreichische Nationalbank, Austria

Edward Elgar

Cheltenham, UK • Northampton, MA, USA

© Ewald Nowotny, Peter Mooslechner and Doris Ritzberger-Grünwald 2011

All rights reserved. No part of this publication may be reproduced, stored in a retrieval system or transmitted in any form or by any means, electronic, mechanical or photocopying, recording, or otherwise without the prior permission of the publisher.

Published by
Edward Elgar Publishing Limited
The Lypiatts
15 Lansdown Road
Cheltenham
Glos GL50 2JA
UK

Edward Elgar Publishing, Inc.
William Pratt House
9 Dewey Court
Northampton
Massachusetts 01060
USA

A catalogue record for this book
is available from the British Library

Library of Congress Control Number: 2011925775

MIX
Paper from responsible sources
FSC® C018575

ISBN 978 0 85793 290 7

Typeset by Servis Filmsetting Ltd, Stockport, Cheshire
Printed and bound by MPG Books Group, UK

Contents

Contributors

Ignazio Angeloni, Advisor to the Executive Board, European Central Bank, Germany

Bas B. Bakker, Head of the IMF's Emerging Europe Regional Division, International Monetary Fund, Washington DC, USA

Marek Belka, President, Narodowy Bank Polski (Central Bank of Poland), Poland

Håkan Berg, Head of Baltic Banking, Swedbank, Sweden

Stephen G. Cecchetti, Economic Adviser and Head of Monetary and Economic Department, Bank for International Settlements, Switzerland

Vítor Constâncio, Vice President, European Central Bank, Germany

Attila Csajbók, Deputy Head of Financial Stability, Magyar Nemzeti Bank (Central Bank of Hungary), Hungary

Jože P. Damijan, University of Ljubljana; Institute for Economic Research, Ljubljana, Slovenia; LICOS, KU Leuven, Belgium

María Teresa Fábregas Fernández, Deputy Head of Unit, European Commission, Belgium

Jarko Fidrmuc, Economist, Oesterreichische Nationalbank (Central Bank of Austria), Austria

Joseph F. Francois, Johannes Kepler Universität, Linz; The Vienna Institute for International Economic Studies, Vienna; and CEPR, London

Vladimir Gligorov, Senior Economist, The Vienna Institute for International Economic Studies, Austria

László Halpern, Institute of Economics, Hungarian Academy of Sciences (IEHAS) and CEPR

Seppo Honkapohja, Member of the Board, Suomen Pankki (Central Bank of Finland), Finland

Michael Hysek, Managing Director, Head of Banking Supervision at the Austrian Financial Market Authority, Austria

Boštjan Jazbec, Central Bank of the Republic of Kosovo and Faculty of Economics, University of Ljubljana, Slovenia

Albulenë Kastrati, Central Bank of the Republic of Kosovo, Kosovo

Júlia Király, Deputy Governor, Magyar Nemzeti Bank (Central Bank of Hungary), Hungary

Corinna Knobloch, Economist, Financial Stability Department, Deutsche Bundesbank (Central Bank of Germany), Germany

Črt Kostevc, University of Ljubljana; Institute for Economic Research, Ljubljana, Slovenia

Mihály András Kovács, Deputy Head of Monetary Strategy and Economic Analysis, Magyar Nemzeti Bank (Central Bank of Hungary), Hungary

Leslie Lipschitz, Director, IMF Institute, Washington DC, USA

Michael Loufir, Head of Emerging Markets Research, National Bank of Greece S.A., Athens, Greece

Reiner Martin, Head of Section – Convergence and Structural Analysis, European Central Bank, Germany

Kieran Mc Morrow, European Commission, DG ECFIN, Brussels, Belgium

Peter Mooslechner, Director of the Economic Analysis and Research Department, Oesterreichische Nationalbank (Central Bank of Austria), Austria

Joachim Nagel, Member of the Executive Board, Deutsche Bundesbank (Central Bank of Germany), Germany

Ewald Nowotny, Governor, Oesterreichische Nationalbank (Central Bank of Austria), Austria

Cristian Popa, Deputy Governor, Banca Națională a României (Central Bank of Romania), Romania

Doris Ritzberger-Grünwald, Head of the Foreign Research Division, Oesterreichische Nationalbank (Central Bank of Austria), Austria

Werner Röger, European Commission, DG ECFIN, Brussels, Belgium

Dariusz K. Rosati, Professor, Warsaw School of Economics, Poland

Andrzej Stopczyński, Managing Director, Polish Financial Supervision Authority, Poland

Andreas Treichl, Chief Executive Officer, Erste Bank Group, Austria

Marko Voljč, Chief Executive Officer, Central and Eastern Europe and Russia, KBC Group

Boris Vujčić, Deputy Governor, Hrvatska narodna banka (Central Bank of Croatia), Croatia

Paul A. Wachtel, Stern School of Business, New York University, USA

Julia Wörz, Foreign Research Division, Oesterreichische Nationalbank (Central Bank of Austria), Austria

Preface

Although the crisis which started in 2008 does not seem to have been overcome yet and the economy is still struggling as this book goes to press, it is time to make a first analysis. In this vein, this book tackles the highly relevant question of 'What next?' with a special focus on the catching-up process in Central, Eastern and South-Eastern Europe (CESEE). Do we have to change all our conceptual frameworks, all our models and all our forecasts, or did the crisis merely put a temporary halt to developments, so that things will proceed in the future more or less as they did in the past? This is not only a serious academic concern but a question of high immediate relevance also for policy-makers and private investors, for central bankers and commercial ones, and for regional developers and other agents.

Specifically, the book covers four main topics, each dealing with the post-crisis scenario from a different angle. The first part deals with the very fundamental question of whether post-crisis growth is going to be the same as pre-crisis growth. Will we see structural breaks in the growth models? Or was the crisis a mere outlier? Given the new, less favourable external environment, many economists expect recovery to be sluggish and catching-up to slow down. In addition, consolidation necessities will dampen growth prospects. Fiscal debt increased in all CESEE countries as a result of the crisis, although public debt levels were still lower in CESEE than in the euro area.

But slightly dampened growth rates will also have some positive side-effects. Before the crisis, current account deficits had widened as a result of excessive consumption growth and a credit boom that was also supported by foreign currency loans. These unfavourable and unhealthy developments have come to an end, or will at least be restricted in the future. As a result the economies in the region will now hopefully embark on a much more sustainable growth path.

Eastern Europe's substantial convergence with Western Europe will continue to be driven by total factor productivity growth. The crisis will, however, result in lastingly lower levels of productivity growth and reduced investment-to-GDP ratios in CESEE, thus slowing down future convergence. By contrast, lower EU-15 growth as a result of the crisis will partially offset this effect in the medium to longer run.

The second part of the book deals with policy challenges in the CESEE region and beyond, with a special focus on monetary policy on the one hand and with a particular focus on three countries – Poland, Romania and Croatia – on the other hand. On these three countries readers will find an in-depth analysis by high-ranking representatives of the respective national central banks. In short, the message is that Poland benefited from its policy of flexible exchange rates, which contributed to its impressively good growth performance, whereas in Romania flexible inflation targeting failed to prevent the build-up of external imbalances. Nor was nominal appreciation successful in containing soaring prices, neither in the pre-crisis boom period nor beyond. While price stability is only a minor issue for most CESEE central banks at the time of writing, the main focus of their attention has shifted to appropriate credit growth and sound financial stability – in the region in general and in Croatia in particular.

In a historical comparison, the recent financial crisis has changed the views about central banking, bringing prudential and regulatory issues to the forefront. As outlined by Paul Wachtel for the United States in particular and for central banks in general (see Chapter 10), the role of central banks may even have broadened, and the new role for central banks foresees that financial sector stability will have more weight in policy considerations. Or, to put it differently, central banks will have to integrate financial sector stability into their price stability focus.

The third part of the book deals with the new role of financial integration, growth financing and exports. In this respect the role of capital, financial deepening (what is still to be done in this respect?) and regulatory requirements are debated. Capital inflows and exports were the two main drivers of CESEE economic growth in the past. Both factors are heavily dependent on what shape the highly advanced economies are in. Following the financial crisis, capital inflows, as well as internal and external demand, have fallen substantially, which has in turn raised the question of whether we were witnessing a possible structural decline in capital inflows and, if so, what would be its long-term growth impact. The guess is that capital will no longer flow into the CESEE region at the levels seen before the crisis, as investors are likely to have become more risk-averse in general, or they may diversify their risks more broadly and shift some of their portfolios to other emerging market regions. Exports will not fully recover as long as external demand is sluggish, and the full recovery of external demand is in turn highly dependent on the economic shape of the euro area countries.

Analytical results show that exports and the stock of foreign direct investment (FDI) in the CESEE region are positively related to industrial production, and thus to economic growth. These findings imply, first, that the CESEE countries should make determined efforts to remain attractive locations for inward FDI and to enhance their export prospects, and, second, that the reduction of portfolio investment inflows appears to be unproblematic from a long-term growth perspective. Overall, the aim is to become more independent; as the countries become more advanced, more impetus is going to come from their domestic sectors.

The fourth and final part of the book deals with challenges for the banking sector in the CESEE region. Given Austria's exposure this question is of special relevance from an Austrian perspective, which is also provided in this book. Interestingly, the banking sector in the CESEE region was not affected as adversely as the Western banking sector. Being less sophisticated and less deleveraged was definitely an advantage in the crisis situation. At the same time, the banking sector was and still is dominated by foreign banks in some countries, as a result of which the financial sector was affected at least indirectly in several countries.

Strengthening competitiveness and sustainability are major points. Therefore it is no surprise when international institutions are claiming that banks need to clean up their balance sheets before the revitalization of lending and any economic recovery will gain momentum. This is even more relevant as significant changes in the legal and supervisory frameworks are in the offing for banks. The new frameworks will, among other things, be better equipped to capture risks, contain more stringent capital requirements and strengthen cross-border supervisory cooperation. To stabilize and broaden the base of financial development in CESEE, the Vienna Initiative will concentrate on the establishment of local currency capital markets in which banks should participate. Yet banks themselves seem to be rather sceptical about these developments and rather hesitant to change their business model, as it was very successful in the past.

Summing up, CESEE has survived the crisis reasonably well. Growth prospects have become less favourable, but catching-up has not come to a standstill. Still, rethinking will need to occur in several economic fields and adequate policy instruments will need to be adopted. As the initial major shock has faded away relatively quickly, resistance to change has increased and persistence tendencies have resurfaced, so that it will take time for changes to be effected and to materialize. But all in all we are confident that the necessary adjustments are going to be implemented, on both the macro and the micro level, in the medium term.

PART I

Catching-up and growth prospects after the crisis

1. Challenges to European economic integration

Vítor Constâncio

This chapter will focus on the challenges to the process of European economic integration in the aftermath of the global turmoil. The financial crisis has exposed widely held views on large domestic and external imbalances as having several shortcomings, which has led to an overall reassessment of the associated risks.

With regard to the process of European economic integration, the financial crisis has undermined the staunch belief in a 'development model', whereby low-income countries in Central, Eastern and South-Eastern Europe (CESEE) could achieve rapid growth simply by: (i) engaging in market-oriented reforms; (ii) liberalizing trade; (iii) having access to foreign capital markets via debt flows and foreign direct investment (FDI); and (iv) allowing the entry of foreign banks. The associated growing imbalances were judged as temporary phenomena associated with the catching-up process.

I will argue in the following that this development model should not be abandoned, but refined, as the push towards market reform has engendered significant benefits. However, the global crisis has shown that economic convergence in Europe should not be viewed as an automatic process. In fact, stability-oriented policies and careful risk management should accompany and support convergence efforts. With this in mind, I will focus on the following three aspects, which highlight the role of policy in ensuring a sustainable development model:

1. a review of the growth experienced in CESEE countries in order to determine if any general lessons can be drawn;
2. the role of the foreign banking sector in CESEE countries, which, despite having been beneficial overall for the catching-up process, may have contributed to increasing domestic imbalances in some countries;
3. the establishment of a new macro-prudential and regulatory framework in the European Union.

1 THE EXPERIENCE OF GROWTH IN THE CESEE REGION

Before the global financial crisis erupted, the CESEE region was experiencing an economic boom, with rapid GDP growth that could be attributed to domestic and international factors.

The widespread and enduring process of convergence of living standards and prices towards euro area levels prompted considerable optimism about the future. Market-oriented reforms were a key feature of the development model that was followed in almost all EU CESEE countries from the mid-1990s, spurring productivity gains and access to foreign technology and capital. In most non-EU countries in the region, typically the catching-up process also gained speed later. There was mounting evidence of a link between these market reforms and long-term growth.[1]

However, developments in the region were not homogeneous: over time a growing number of countries showed increasingly visible signs of vulnerability. In particular, over the past decade several countries recorded a deterioration in their current account deficits and price competitiveness indicators. To a large extent, these developments were viewed as having been predicted by economic theory and were thus often downplayed. The explanations generally advanced to explain these developments were as follows:

- Capital is expected to flow 'downhill' to countries where the rate of return is higher. From an inter-temporal perspective this appears to be a reasonable argument. Tapping foreign savings and accumulating external debt allows a country to finance investment, smooth consumption, import technological know-how and expand the ability of the export sector to penetrate foreign markets. The trade deficit is eventually expected to turn into a surplus as exports rise and imports of capital goods decline, leading to a gradual stabilization and eventually to a fall in external debt.
- Based on economic theory, a country is expected to experience real exchange rate appreciation during the catching-up phase. This point is typically expressed in terms of the Balassa–Samuelson effect or equilibrium exchange rate analysis, suggesting that prices may converge to euro area levels if fundamentals improve. This benign assessment was also reinforced by pointing to rising export market shares, which were seen as evidence that overall competitiveness might even have improved.

While these and similar arguments had their appeal, in a sub-set of countries inflation and current account imbalances reached such high levels that an orderly self-adjustment mechanism seemed increasingly unlikely. Nevertheless, access to international capital markets continued without disruption and the cost of external financing remained low, thus contributing to rapid credit growth. The risk of economic overheating was also fuelled by low or, in some cases, negative real interest rates. It was particularly challenging to deal with these phenomena in countries that had fixed exchange rate regimes, given the lack of an autonomous monetary policy.

On the eve of the global financial crisis, different countries had accumulated different degrees of external and internal imbalances. Taken as a whole, most of the CESEE region was characterized by a sizeable contribution of private consumption to growth and an increasingly negative contribution of net exports.[2] The underlying causes of the shift from the tradable sector to the domestic sector were rather country-specific. In some cases, it was related to foreign funding, through bank lending or FDI, while in others, the main underlying factor was domestic, in the form of rising government spending or a domestic credit boom. As a result of both external and domestic forces, in some countries the situation appeared out of control: inflation even surged to double digit levels, wages increased far above gains in labour productivity and there were remarkable increases in asset prices, notably in housing markets.

Let me now turn to the global financial crisis, which has made it clear that the risks associated with growing imbalances such as those described above cannot be neglected. In fact, after some initial resilience, the CESEE region was affected by the crisis particularly strongly, even though it was not directly exposed to US markets.

As access to international capital markets was impaired, countries that were most in need of external financing experienced larger welfare losses. A number of economies in Central and Eastern Europe were affected less seriously, but recessionary forces were stronger in the Baltics and South-Eastern Europe, suggesting that it was the countries with the larger imbalances that were typically most affected. In countries with fixed exchange rates with limited room for manoeuvre through monetary policy, the adjustment process proved even more challenging. In the absence of nominal exchange rate flexibility, prices and, in particular, wages eventually had to be adjusted downward amid rapidly rising unemployment.

Looking back at what has happened since the crisis hit the region, it can be seen that a considerable stabilization effort has taken place. National and, in some cases, international responses prevented the crisis from having a more disruptive impact, as the prevailing exchange rate regimes were preserved and the banking sector showed considerable resilience.

Indirectly, unlimited liquidity provision by the European Central Bank (ECB) to banks established in the euro area helped to secure funding to the region. The policy response to the crisis also varied significantly depending on the scope for manoeuvre on both the fiscal and the monetary front. Fiscal policies have been tightened in some cases, financial conditions have stabilized and there are now clear signs of a recovery in economic activity in most countries.

However, the impact of the global crisis and the years of exuberance proved very costly, leading to a general sharp contraction in national output and a corresponding steep rise in unemployment. Moreover, the ongoing deleveraging process, the need to repair household and corporate balance sheets, tighter bank credit standards, as well as rising long-term unemployment could all slow the pace of the catching-up process in many CESEE countries in the coming years. In the most severe cases, the process of unwinding external vulnerabilities is still underway.

Although the crisis has not undone the progress achieved on convergence over the past two decades and past reforms have helped the stabilization effort, important lessons should be learned. The good parts of the development model pursued so far should be retained. Countries in the region should not lose their appetite for structural reform and progress on enhancing labour market flexibility, improving the business environment and preserving free access to trade and financial markets. There is still a fundamental need to increase productivity and promote innovation, as well as raise capital and labour participation. At the same time, the crisis has clearly revealed that the catching-up process must go hand in hand with macro and financial-oriented policies, while specific challenges remain for countries that maintain hard pegs, which require adequate support measures.

2 THE ROLE OF THE FOREIGN BANKING SECTOR IN CESEE COUNTRIES

Let me now turn more specifically to the 'parent bank' model in CESEE. At a broader level, it is still controversial whether international financial integration and foreign banks have an unambiguously positive effect on economies that are in the process of catching-up.[3]

On the one hand, it is argued that the presence of foreign banks in the region has ensured the availability of credit to the real economy and improved the efficiency of the financial intermediation process. In addition, the lending activities of foreign banks appear to be more resilient to local shocks than those of domestic banks.[4] It has also been found that the region's resilience to capital outflows is related to a high level of financial integration and the presence of foreign banks.[5]

On the other hand, other observers have argued that financial stress originating in EU parent banks may have been transmitted to the CESEE region during the early stages of the crisis.[6] Some also hold the view that parent banks from Western Europe were fuelling local credit booms and encouraged the use of unhedged foreign currency borrowing.[7]

As the crisis erupted, region-specific arrangements made CESEE countries more resilient to the risk of sudden stops in capital inflows: under the umbrella of the International Monetary Fund (IMF), the European Bank for Regional Development (EBRD) and the EU, the European Bank Coordination Initiative – also known as the 'Vienna Initiative' – enabled a dialogue between parent banks, home and host supervisors, and relevant governments. This initiative, in which the ECB participated as an observer, ensured that parent banks kept their exposure to CESEE countries with large imbalances. Together with a strong commitment on the part of home governments backing parent banks and thus indirectly the CESEE region, the Vienna Initiative helped to maintain confidence in the banking sectors across the region. It has in fact become a vehicle for public–private sector coordination which could serve as a promising model for overcoming the problems associated with collective action.

However, from a policy perspective, a number of challenges lie ahead. In particular, it is important to assess the extent to which parent banks may have contributed indirectly to financial stability risks via lending in foreign currency.[8] Lending in foreign currencies to the non-financial private sector is not an entirely new phenomenon in Europe, and in most countries of the region such activities account for a significant proportion of the total lending by banks. In some countries, lending in foreign currencies has led to a substantial build-up of currency mismatches on private sector balance sheets. The increasing share of foreign currency in total lending in countries in the CESEE region, in particular euro-denominated lending but also loans denominated in Swiss francs and Japanese yen, was accompanied by a strong expansion in overall credit amid strong inflows of foreign capital attracted by expectations of dynamic economic convergence.

Let me briefly elaborate on the implications of high dependence on foreign currency lending. At the turn of 2008–09, all countries with flexible exchange rate regimes experienced rapid depreciations of their currencies vis-à-vis the euro. This inflated the local currency value of foreign currency loans, and thus weighed on private sector balance sheets. However, low market interest rates on foreign currency loans mitigated, to some extent, the increase in the debt-servicing burden of borrowers. In an environment of rising interest rates on foreign currency loans, this could have affected a significant proportion of the private sector and could have posed a systemic financial stability risk in countries where foreign currency loans accounted for a large share of total domestic lending. In addition, the major role played by foreign currency lending has posed some challenges for the conduct of monetary policy. In particular, the existence of a large stock of loans denominated in foreign currency has weakened the ability of monetary policy to influence the economy through the interest rate channel. Furthermore, central banks might have become hesitant to alter their policy stances in the light of the possible adverse implications for financial stability stemming, for example, from a downward pressure on the exchange rate.

A number of countries in the region have made attempts to address the risks related to rapidly expanding foreign currency lending to unhedged borrowers. As standard policies aimed at decreasing interest rate differentials and developing domestic funding markets might take too long to achieve this goal, some countries in the region have introduced different monetary policy, regulatory and administrative measures[9] to address the risks stemming from increased foreign currency lending. Practical experience with these measures reveals that their effectiveness has been somewhat limited for a variety of reasons. In particular, persistently wide differentials between interest rates on loans in domestic currency and those in foreign currency have fostered demand for foreign currency loans, while shortages of domestic savings denominated in local currency together with intense bank competition underpinned their supply.[10] In fact, as parent bank financing continued to be mainly denominated in foreign currency, local subsidiaries avoided currency mismatches on their own balance sheets by lending in foreign currency. In addition, when domestic lending in foreign currency was made more costly, it was circumvented by cross-border lending. Recently, authorities in some European countries (for example, Austria and Hungary) have introduced stricter measures to limit further increase in foreign currency lending to domestic households. These measures are mostly of an administrative nature and set limits on customer eligibility to obtain a loan in foreign currency. However, these measures do not preclude domestic customers in these countries from obtaining foreign currency loans directly from banks domiciled in other countries.

It appears, therefore, that the issue of foreign currency lending requires a supranational approach – at least at the EU level. More generally, in order to make the financial system less prone to crises and ensure long-term sustainable growth, we are setting a broader policy agenda for the EU as a whole by means of Basel III and the creation of a new macro-prudential supervisor in the EU.

3 BASEL III AND MACRO-PRUDENTIAL POLICY IN THE EU

During the recent crisis several gaps in the regulatory and supervisory framework for financial institutions were revealed. It became apparent that the quality and quantity of the capital base of many financial institutions were insufficient to withstand severe shocks. In addition, the abundant liquidity that characterized the financial system in the years preceding the crisis suddenly disappeared, exposing several institutions to liquidity shortages. To avoid a complete financial meltdown, governments provided an unprecedented amount of financial support and central banks had to significantly increase their provision of liquidity during the initial stages of the crisis.

These events led to many different policy responses, resulting in a major overhaul of the regulatory and supervisory framework. Under the aegis of the G-20, a tremendous amount of work has been done by the Financial Stability Board and the Basel Committee to reform the regulatory and supervisory framework in order to address the core causes of the crisis. A major component of this reform was the revision of the Basel II framework with the aim of strengthening the capital base of banks and introducing stricter liquidity risk requirements and an absolute leverage ratio.

3.1 The Revision of Micro-prudential Regulation – Basel III

The agreement reached on the Basel III framework in 2010 and its full endorsement by the Group of Central Bank Governors and Heads of Supervision is an important piece of work that delivers on global financial reform and constitutes a cornerstone of the new regulatory system.

The five main elements of the new framework are as follows. First, under the new definition of regulatory capital, both the quality and the consistency of the capital base will be improved. As a general principle, all regulatory capital instruments should have loss-absorbing capacities. This will help to ensure that sufficient high-quality capital is available when it is most needed, namely at times of stress. Particular emphasis will be placed on the core elements of Tier 1 capital. Tier 2 capital elements will be simplified, and existing Tier 3 capital will be abolished. Enhanced disclosure requirements will further improve the transparency of the capital structure of banks. Overall, I am confident that stricter conditions for what should count as regulatory capital will contribute to restoring confidence in the ability of banks to weather future periods of stress. This in itself will substantially reduce the probability of future banking crises, thus improving long-term economic and social welfare.

Second, the introduction of counter-cyclical capital buffers should protect the banking sector from periods of excessive credit growth. As witnessed during the crisis, the build-up of excessive credit levels in an economic upturn is often followed by large losses on this outstanding credit when economic conditions deteriorate. These losses may in turn have a destabilizing effect on the banking sector. The buffering mechanism consists of two elements. First, a capital conservation buffer range – equal to 2.5 per cent of risk-weighted assets and made up of Tier 1 common equity – would be established above the minimum. The second element, still under development at the time of writing, consists of the possible extension of the buffer range up to an additional 2.5 per cent in periods of excessive credit growth (known as a 'counter-cyclical buffer'). An important additional benefit of this measure would be that it might mitigate the credit cycle.

As a complementary measure to improving the quality and quantity of the capital base, the third element of the framework consists of strengthening the risk coverage of the capital framework by revising the prudential rules on securitization and trading book activities, and by putting forward proposals for the revision of the counterparty credit risk framework. This would imply higher risk weights and thus result in higher capital requirements for these activities.

Fourth, the planned introduction of a non-risk-based leverage ratio should serve as a credible supplementary measure to the risk-based requirements to contain the build-up of excessive leverage and address model risks associated with the risk-based capital framework.

Last, but not least, since it constitutes a building block in the new framework, is the development of a liquidity risk framework aimed at improving banks' resilience to liquidity shocks. The liquidity risk framework consists of two main measures: a short-term measure (liquidity coverage ratio) establishing a minimum level of high-quality liquid assets to withstand severe stress over a one-month period and a long-term measure (net stable funding ratio) designed to ensure that the maturity structures of assets and liabilities are better matched, requiring banks to fund long-term assets with more stable types of liability. Work is underway on the important details and precise calibration of these ratios.

All of these new measures, which will be introduced over the agreed transition period, should not have any unduly severe implications for the national banking system and will thus support the nascent economic recovery.

3.1.1 Further work ahead

Although the agreement on Basel III constitutes a robust conceptual framework, much remains to be done. Aside from the ongoing introduction of counter-cyclical buffers, more work also needs to be carried out on other important elements of the framework.

In this respect, the potential implications of the leverage ratio and the liquidity risk framework still need to be assessed. An observation period has therefore been agreed upon in order to carefully monitor the potential implications for certain banking sectors, business models and the real economy. Full use of the observation period should be made to identify any such implications and to prevent the new measures from having any unintended consequences.

Furthermore, since the leverage ratio is largely based on accounting information, the accounting standard-setters should strengthen their efforts to eliminate existing accounting differences. This is essential in order to ensure a level playing field.

Work is also still underway on ensuring the loss-absorbency of all regulatory capital at the point of non-viability. The Basel Committee has also decided at the level of Governors and Heads of Supervision that systemically important financial institutions will be required to have a higher loss-absorbency capacity than the other institutions that are subject to Basel III. To achieve this, banks are permitted to use new instruments such as 'contingent capital' or bail-in bonds, which raises some issues. First, on a general level it is necessary to assess whether these instruments can really provide a feasible funding alternative and foster a robust investor response. If this is deemed the case, the precise features of these instruments will need to be determined. Key design features include the event that would trigger the conversion of the instrument, as well as the conversion price and ratio.

I should like to stress that a strengthened regulatory framework is necessary, but is in itself not an adequate policy response. Consistent implementation and application of Basel III at the global level is of the essence to ensure a level playing field and to avoid regulatory arbitrage causing any disruption in the future. In this respect, I would like to underline the importance of adhering to the agreed transition period, which was based on the outcome of the impact assessments[11] and country-specific considerations. In addition, it should be highlighted that any market pressure to accelerate the implementation of Basel III would be detrimental to the overall objective of the regulatory reform package and might compromise the economic recovery.

3.1.2 Potential impact of Basel III

It is expected that banks engaged in different business activities will be affected differently by the Basel III framework. The consensus view among market participants seems to be that the new stricter capital requirements will have a substantial impact on universal banks, mainly as a result of the limits imposed on the recognition of minority interest and the application of most regulatory adjustments to and deductions from common equity Tier 1 capital. As a consequence, banks that have significant holdings in other financial institutions and insurance companies will most probably have to adjust to the new rules either by strengthening their capital base or by revising their business activities. In this context, given the sizeable share of large, internationally active universal banks in the region, the potential impacts of the new measures on the financial systems and economies in CESEE have to be carefully explored and assessed.

3.2 The New Macro-prudential Framework – ESRB

In parallel with the revision of the micro-prudential framework, extensive work is being carried out at the regional, country and global levels on developing consistent macro-prudential policy frameworks. The financial crisis has illustrated the importance of having an effective macro-prudential oversight function to safeguard financial stability by proposing timely policy responses. Macro-prudential oversight taking a system-wide perspective should complement micro-prudential supervision, allowing the relevant authorities to assess and address potential systemic risks.

The European Systemic Risk Board (ESRB) has been entrusted with responsibility for macro-prudential oversight at the EU level, alongside other initiatives at the national and international levels in this field. Under the new legislation, the ECB has been entrusted with providing the ESRB with a Secretariat, as well as logistical, administrative and analytical support. Similar frameworks were also created in the United States and the United Kingdom with the close involvement of their respective central banks.

The macro-prudential oversight function of the ESRB is aimed at linking systemic risk analysis with appropriate policy responses to address potential risks identified as material. It therefore comprises both an analytical and a policy component. The analytical part focuses on identifying, measuring and assessing the impact of potentially systemic risks, while the policy part entails the calibration of policy instruments that could be implemented to address the identified risks or mitigate their consequences.

More specifically, the first task of the ESRB will be to identify systemic risks. This will require a broad and deep information basis, aided by a wide range of tools to process the relevant data. Important ingredients for analysis include market intelligence, rigorous monitoring of financial stability indicators and financial market and economic developments at large. It is important at this initial stage to cast the net as wide as possible to ensure that no risk is overlooked. This type of analysis could be supported by early warning models and indicators based on current data on financial or macro variables in order to identify early on where imbalances may be building up.

Its second task will be to assess the severity of the risks identified and to evaluate the ability of the financial system to absorb shocks. In this context, macro stress-testing models can be used to assess the resilience of the financial system, as can contagion and spillover analysis to evaluate propagation mechanisms and their potential impact on the financial sector or the real economy.

Finally, the ESRB will use the outcome of the risk assessment for possible risk warnings or policy recommendations, which will need to be concrete and well targeted.

The ESRB will be in a good position to perform all of these tasks and to address in a timely fashion potential systemic risks, such as those related to the rapid expansion in foreign currency lending to unhedged borrowers in the CESEE region. Addressing the problem at the EU level will allow different measures to be implemented on a consolidated basis, thus addressing all of the relevant financial sector players active in the region, ensuring that macro-prudential policy across the EU is consistent and minimizing cross-border and cross-sectoral policy circumvention.

In short, the establishment of the ESRB will introduce a new policy function at the EU level with great potential for enhancing the ability of European and national authorities to safeguard the stability of the EU financial system as a whole. It is recognized that the design and implementation of this new EU macro-prudential policy function pose a considerable challenge. However, with the necessary preparations, which are currently underway in close cooperation with all involved parties, the ESRB is assured a smooth start in 2011.

To sum up, the crisis has revealed that the catching-up process in CESEE countries must go hand in hand with prudent macro and financial sector policies, and this lesson also applies to all countries in the EU. The achievement of high rates of growth cannot be detached from stability-oriented policies and careful risk management. To this end, policy makers will be engaged in the task of designing coherent policy frameworks for some years to come.

NOTES

1. See Falcetti et al. (2005).
2. See Gardó and Martin (2010).

3. See Agénor (2003).
4. See ECB (2010) and De Haas and van Lelyveld (2010).
5. See Herrmann and Mihaljek (2010).
6. See Popov and Udell (2010).
7. See EBRD (2009).
8. See, for example Brown, Kirschenmann and Ongena (2010).
9. Examples of these are: (i) a differentiation between minimum reserve requirements on bank liabilities in domestic and foreign currency; (ii) higher risk weights and provisioning rates on loans in foreign currency; (iii) restrictions on loan-to-value and payment-to-income ratios; and (iv) tighter eligibility criteria for borrowers to obtain a loan in foreign currency.
10. See, for example, Luca and Petrova (2008) and Rosenberg and Tirpák (2009).
11. See Basel Committee on Banking Supervision (2010a).

REFERENCES

Agénor, P.-R. (2003), 'Benefits and costs of international financial integration: theory and facts', *The World Economy,* **26** (8), 1089–118.

Basel Committee on Banking Supervision (2010a), 'An assessment of the long-term economic impact of stronger capital and liquidity requirements'.

Basel Committee on Banking Supervision (2010b), 'Assessing the macroeconomic impact of the transition to stronger capital and liquidity requirements'.

Brown, M., K. Kirschenmann and S. Ongena (2010), 'Foreign currency loans – demand or supply driven?', CEPR Discussion Paper, No. 7952.

De Haas, R. and I. van Lelyveld (2010), 'Internal capital markets and lending by multinational bank subsidiaries', *Journal of Financial Intermediation*, **19**, 1–25.

EBRD (2009), *Transition Report 2009*, London: EBRD.

ECB (2010), 'Financial stability challenges in EU candidate countries – financial systems in the aftermath of the global crisis', ECB Occasional Paper Series, No. 115.

Falcetti, E., T. Lysenko and P. Sanfey (2005), 'Reforms and growth in transition: re-examining the evidence', EBRD Working Paper Series, No. 90.

Gardó, S. and R. Martin (2010), 'The impact of the global economic and financial crisis on central, eastern and south-eastern Europe – a stock-taking exercise', ECB Occasional Paper Series, No. 114.

Herrmann, S. and D. Mihaljek (2010), 'Determinants of cross-border bank flows to emerging markets – new empirical evidence on the spread of financial crisis', BIS Working Paper Series, No. 315.

Luca, A. and I. Petrova (2008), 'What drives credit dollarization in transition economies?', *Journal of Banking and Finance,* **32**, 858–69.

Popov, A. and E.F. Udell (2010), 'Cross-border lending and the transmission of financial distress during the crisis of 2007–2008', ECB Working Paper Series, No. 1203.

Rosenberg, C. and M. Tirpák (2009), 'Determinants of foreign currency borrowing in the new member states of the EU', *Czech Journal of Economics and Finance*, **59** (3), 216–28.

2. A forward-looking view on catching-up strategies from an Austrian angle

Ewald Nowotny[1]

As is well known, the period since 2008 has been characterized by the global financial crisis. In its early stage, the crisis had been confined to advanced economies, as local and foreign banks in Central, Eastern and South-Eastern European economies were holding only a negligible amount of so-called toxic assets. Yet excessive risk-taking eventually put the financial system as a whole under serious stress, which in turn had an adverse impact on the world economy.

The CESEE economies were particularly affected by output declines. These were also caused by accumulated vulnerabilities in the region, especially the credit boom (Backé and Wójcik, 2008; Fidrmuc and Hainz, 2010) and foreign currency lending in many countries (Dvorsky et al., 2010). The output loss, with average GDP decline amounting to –3.5 per cent in new EU member states and around –4 per cent in all CESEE countries in 2009 (IMF, 2010), was deeper than had been expected. The CESEE region did, however, recover fairly quickly in 2010.

Therefore, as indicated in the title, this chapter is forward-looking, dealing with catching-up strategies after the crisis. The beginning of 2010 actually featured developments which were better than expected and fuelled the hope that the crisis was already passing away. Nearly all CESEE countries (with the exception of Bulgaria and Romania) were expected to grow during 2010 (Schreiner et al., 2010). This growth in most cases is fuelled mainly by restocking and external demand. At the same time, the forecasts for 2011 and 2012 remain modest. The growth prospects are still fragile and there are some downsize risks. The growth path will be above the EU average, but below the pre-crisis trend for the coming years.

After the positive trend in the first half of 2010, we are beginning to see the light at the end of the tunnel at the time of writing, but we still have much to do. The previous output declines have to be taken as an incentive to reduce vulnerabilities in the region and to continue economic and structural reforms. Fiscal stabilization will represent an extraordinary challenge for the next few years. Fiscal debt increased in all countries in 2008 and 2009. Prior to the crisis, the new member states had a relatively low level of public debt (37.4 per cent of GDP), but this level increased by nearly 10 per cent of GDP on average in 2009 alone (IMF, 2010). As in other countries of Europe, this indicates the predominant role of automatic stabilizer effects for fiscal developments during the crisis. Allowing these automatic stabilizer effects to work made sense, but it is also necessary to reduce deficits and debt levels as soon as macro-economically possible. So although this level is still lower than the public debt of the euro area (forecast of the EU Commission of autumn 2010 for 2011: 87 per cent of GDP), we have to return to a sustainable growth path. The new member states will have to increase their efforts in order to stabilize public finances and fulfil the Stability and Growth Pact. We have to use every possibility of financial stabilization, while at the same time keeping in mind also the global fragile growth prospects.

Exchange rate developments represent another important challenge. We have seen a high degree of volatility, with the euro and the Swiss franc gaining strength. This has also important implications for CESEE economies where both the euro and the demand from euro area countries play an overwhelmingly important role. Exchange rate appreciations may have negative implications for Europe's external – but indirectly also for its internal – trade and debt structures.

The development of CESEE has important implications for the Austrian economy due to strong linkages through trade and FDI. We have strong and healthy relationships especially with our Western neighbours, but we are also part of the Central European family. Actually, Austria has made effective use of its geographic location during the two decades since the fall of the Iron Curtain. It has become one of the most important investors in the neighbouring Central European countries. Despite the recent financial crisis, Austria increased its market shares especially in Central Europe, for example in countries like Slovenia and Slovakia which have adopted the euro (Ritzberger-Grünwald and Wörz, 2010).

During the financial crisis, Austria's links to CESEE economies have been seen as a potential source of vulnerability for the Austrian economy, especially with regard to Austrian banks investing intensively in CESEE. These concerns did not materialize, however – not least because of the Vienna Initiative, which brought together the parties involved in home–host country discussions, public–private sector dialogues and conversations with and among banks, and has thus come to be an example of successful crisis management (Berglof, 2009).

In the banking sector, international regulations have been revised as part of the Basel III agreement. The Oesterreichische Nationalbank and the Austrian Financial Market Authority (FMA) participated in these preparations from the beginning. The new regulations will ensure improved financial stability. However, there are also potential risks related to these regulatory changes. Some banks in our region are characterized by relatively low capitalization. This will imply for some banks the need to strengthen their capital base or else to retrench on financing activities. It is in the self-interest of economic policy authorities in this region to be aware of the close relationships between bank capitalization, lending activities and economic growth.

The CESEE region is, of course, not a homogeneous region, but as a whole it has weathered the storms of the past years quite well, especially with regard to questions of financing sustainability – questions that unfortunately dominate the discussion in other parts of Europe.

It should also be underlined that the euro has clearly contributed to the financial stability of the CESEE region. During the financial crisis, the euro has kept and improved its position as a global currency (ECB, 2010). In addition, the euro has acted as a shelter not only for the participating countries, but also for a broader European region, as has been impressively documented in *The Euro and Economic Stability: Focus on Central, Eastern and South-Eastern Europe* (Nowotny et al., 2010). Thus, the European Union has shown its ability to make important decisions also during hard times. While the European Union is based on the equal treatment principle, we have also learned to put special emphasis on the sustainability of economic policies and on the developments in the real economy of individual countries.

Let me conclude and stress that catching-up strategies after the crisis represent an important policy challenge for the next few years. Having successfully braved the storms of the worst financial and economic crisis of post-war history, the EU and the euro have been and will continue to be an important anchor of growth in a broader European region.

NOTE

1. Jarko Fidrmuc, of the Oesterreichische Nationalbank's staff, contributed to these remarks.

REFERENCES

Backé, P. and C. Wójcik (2008), 'Credit booms, monetary integration and the new neoclassical synthesis', *Journal of Banking & Finance*, **32**, 458–70.

Berglof, Erik (2009), 'The crisis has changed the EBRD', EBRD Blog, posted on 7 May.

Dvorsky, S., T. Scheiber and H. Stix (2010), 'Real effects of crisis have reached CESEE households: euro survey shows dampened savings and changes in borrowing behavior', *Focus on European Economic Integration*, Q2/10, Vienna: Oesterreichische Nationalbank, pp. 79–90.

ECB (2010), *The International Role of the Euro*, Frankfurt: ECB, http://www.ecb.int/pub/pdf/other/euro-international-role201007en.pdf.

Fidrmuc, J. and C. Hainz (2010), 'Default rates in the loan market for SMEs: evidence from Slovakia', *Economic Systems*, **34** (2), 133–47.

IMF (2010), 'Regional economic outlook: Europe, building confidence', Washington DC: IMF, http://www.imf.org/external/pubs/ft/reo/2010/eur/eng/ereo1010.pdf.

Nowotny, E., P. Mooslechner and D. Ritzberger-Grünwald (eds) (2010), *The Euro and Economic Stability: Focus on Central, Eastern and South-Eastern Europe*, Cheltenham, UK and Northampton, MA, USA: Edward Elgar.

Ritzberger-Grünwald, D. and J. Wörz (2010), 'Wechselkurse und österreichischer Aussenhandel', FIW Policy Brief No. 5, Research Centre International Economics, Vienna.

Schreiner, J. et al. (2010), 'Developments in selected CESEE countries', *Focus on European Economic Integration*, Q4/10, Vienna: Oesterreichische Nationalbank.

3. Re-establishing growth after the crisis – lessons from the Nordic countries

Seppo Honkapohja[1]

1 INTRODUCTION

The financial crisis that started in 2008 led to a very big recession and also seems to have longer-term consequences for the international economic environment. The recession has resulted in large output gaps, that is, differences between actual and potential output. Re-establishing growth requires, as a first stage, closing of the output gaps.

It is also clear – though current information is not so precise – that potential output and growth have also been affected by the crisis and recession. The second stage in the process for catching-up by the CESEE economies must then focus on growth prospects on the supply side, that is, potential output.

The first part of this chapter discusses the experience from earlier financial crises, using the 1990s crisis in the Nordic countries – that is, in Finland and Sweden (and also partly Norway), one of the biggest crises in advanced economies since the 1970s – as a 'case study'. This case is worth considering because the crisis resolution in the Nordics was successful and thus some general lessons can perhaps be learned. The second part of my remarks addresses some ideas and principles that the CESEE countries may want to consider when they reformulate their catching-up processes after the current crisis.

2 THE NINETIES CRISES IN THE NORDIC COUNTRIES

The fundamental reason for the financial crises of the Nordic countries lies in the financial liberalization in the 1980s. This process created a boom and overheating situation and led to large increases in real estate

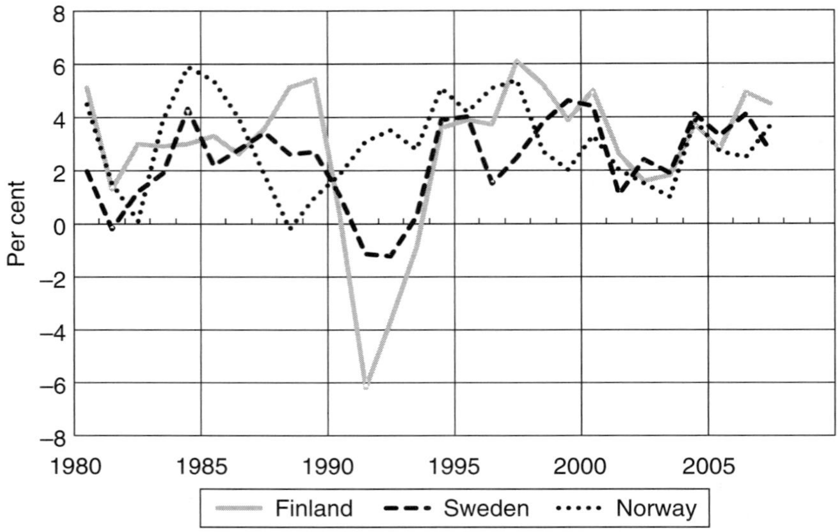

Source: Eurostat and IMF.

Figure 3.1 Real GDP growth

and stock prices. To a significant degree the boom was financed by financial inflows from abroad, as indicated by the current account deficits.

The Nordic crises are classic examples of financial crises. There was a combined banking and currency crisis, a recession which was quite deep except in Norway, a big rise in unemployment, and a rapid increase in public debt, which was gradually brought under control. Figures 3.1–3.3 illustrate the main features of the Nordic crises.[2]

Figure 3.1 shows the developments in GDP growth. Both Finland and Sweden experienced rather long periods of negative growth in the early 1990s, whereas Norway had an earlier recession in late 1980s, caused to a large extent by the decline in oil prices in 1986. The Norwegian crisis was less severe than the Finnish and Swedish crises. The recession in Finland was far deeper than the one in Sweden. This was due to the breakdown of the Soviet Union, which led to a collapse of Finnish trade with the Soviet Union.

Figure 3.2 indicates that all three countries experienced significant current account deficits. They were particularly persistent in Finland, while Norway had acute developments only for a couple of years because of the lower oil prices. In Sweden current account problems were clearly smaller than in the other two countries. All three countries had major banking problems as indicated by the loan losses relative to lending, which

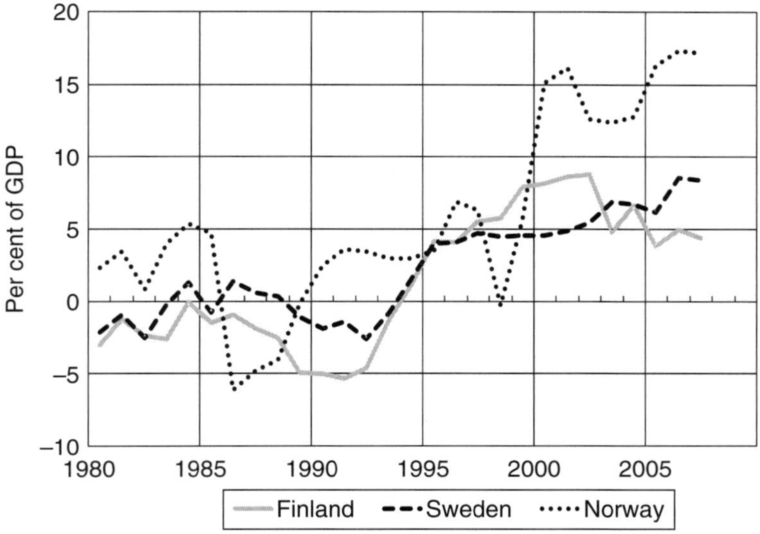

Source: European Commission.

Figure 3.2 Current account

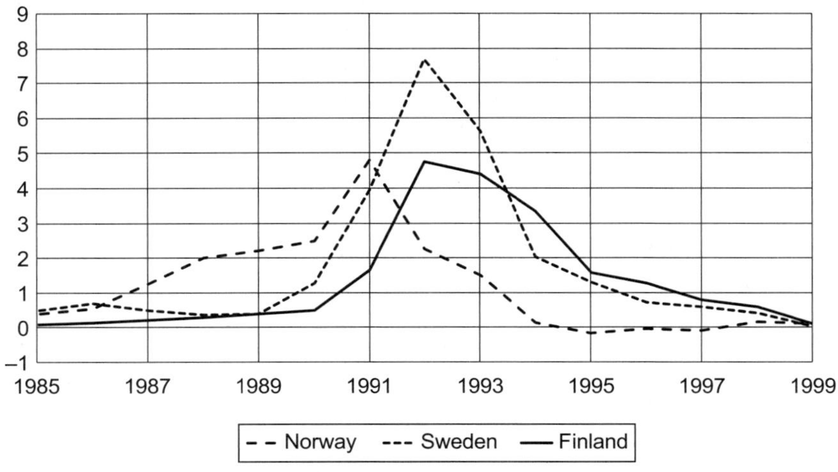

Source: Central banks.

Figure 3.3 Loan losses/lending in the Nordic countries' banking sector 1985–99 (in per cent)

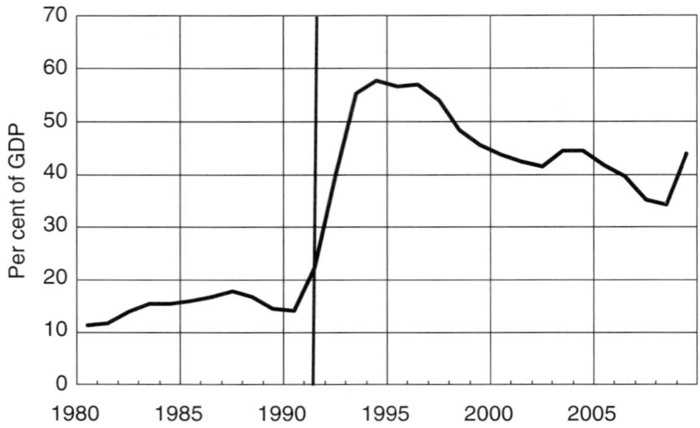

Source: Statistics Finland.

Figure 3.4 Public debt to GDP in Finland

are shown in Figure 3.3. I will not discuss the resolution of the banking crises any further, given space constraints.[3]

Public debt also shot up in Finland and Sweden. In Figure 3.4 only the Finnish data are shown. The build-up of debt was very rapid and it took over ten years to reduce the public debt–GDP ratio from nearly 60 per cent to about 35 per cent. The development of public debt was qualitatively very similar in Sweden. Norway did not have any public debt problems because of its large oil tax revenues, which were largely placed in a national wealth fund. The proceeds from the fund contributed to the public sector funding.

3 WHY DID FINLAND AND SWEDEN RECOVER SO WELL?[4]

The Nordic crises are sometimes viewed as examples in which policies to resolve the financial crisis worked well.[5] What were the reasons for this? Recovery from the deep crises in Finland and Sweden indeed proceeded exceptionally well. Both countries are fairly small and homogeneous societies in which crisis response was relatively rapid and politically widely accepted (though unsurprisingly there were some initial demonstrations and strikes).

The short-term macroeconomic response to close the output gap consisted of three main spheres of action. First, the competitiveness problem had to be resolved. This involved reforming the exchange rate regime from fixed to floating exchange rates. Currencies depreciated and, in addition, other measures such as freezes or strict limits on nominal wage increases were introduced.

Second, it was important to re-establish the credibility of the monetary policy regime. The two countries introduced inflation targeting some months after the floating of their currencies. Finland later decided to apply for membership in the euro area and joined the area at its inception. Sweden instead 'opted out' and adopted a regime of inflation targeting, an independent central bank, and a floating exchange rate. In Sweden this regime is still in place today.

The third element in initiating recovery was the design of fiscal strategies with gradual consolidation. Both Finland and Sweden ran big deficits during the crisis but gradually tightened the public budgets as recovery from the crisis proceeded.

The supply-side policy response to re-attain persistent growth in potential output focused on the fundamental factors behind economic growth. Even in the recession the countries did not sacrifice on education spending, technology policy or R&D. The recovery period involved very major structural change with high-tech industries, especially in the field of information and communications technology (ICT), taking leading roles in the economy. We now look at these elements in more detail.

Figure 3.5 shows the relative roles of capital deepening and total factor productivity (TFP) growth in the growth of labour productivity in Finland.[6] It is evident that the IT and high-tech revolution in the 1990s increased the role of TFP in the growth process. TFP growth has also been the main driver of growth in many CESEE countries in the past decades. The economies of CESEE countries are diverse, so that in some countries – notably those in Central Europe – medium- to high-tech sectors have a significant role in the economy, while this is less so in other CESEE countries. This suggests that for these countries TFP growth as the driver of the catching-up process partly reflects a more general modernization and change in the economy and not just the increased importance of high tech.[7]

Continuing with the factors behind the recovery of the growth process in the Nordic countries, another important factor was the continuous improvement in the quality of the labour force. Figure 3.6 shows that in Nordic countries the older age cohorts in the 1990s were significantly less educated than younger age cohorts. A further familiar force was the high level of R&D spending, of which an increasing share was carried out by the private sector. Figure 3.7 makes a comparison

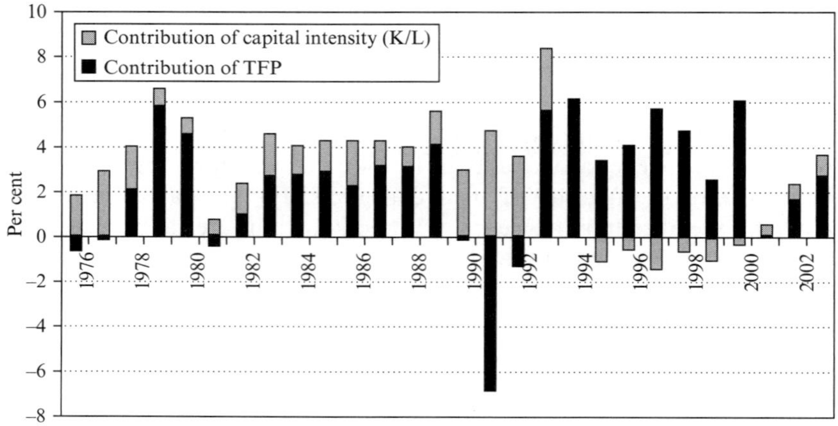

Source: Tuottavuuskatsaus 2004, Statistics Finland, National Accounts.

Figure 3.5 Role of capital deepening and TFP growth in labour productivity growth

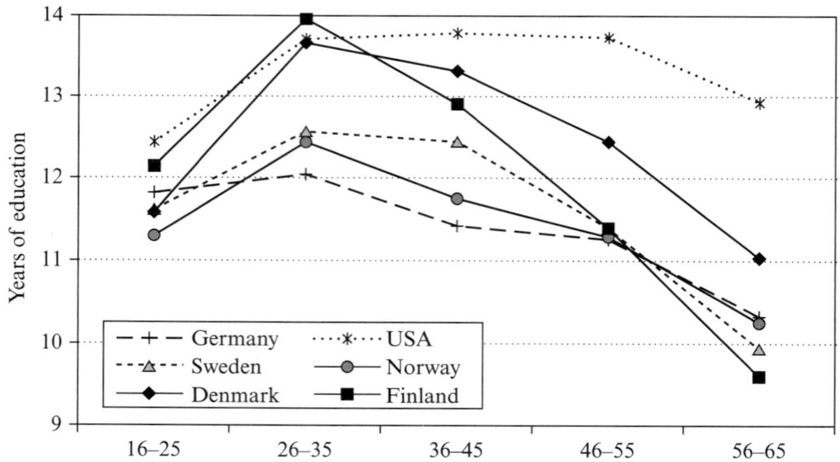

Source: adapted from Honkapohja et al. (2009).

Figure 3.6 Education attainment by age cohort in the 1990s

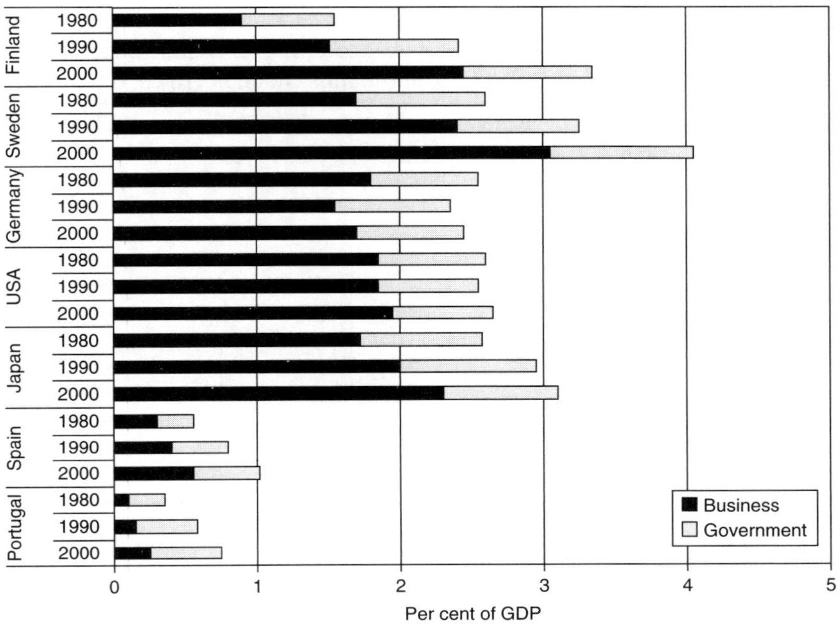

Source: OECD.

Figure 3.7 R&D spending in selected countries

of R&D spending in Western countries for this period. It shows that Finland and Sweden had the highest R&D spending relative to GDP among the OECD countries. Moreover, these ratios have increased very rapidly in recent decades.

Finally, it must be pointed out that Finland and Sweden were also lucky in that the recovery from crisis coincided with the ICT revolution. Both countries had exceptionally important large players in this sector, Nokia in Finland and Eriksson in Sweden. To illustrate the importance of ICT in the growth process, Table 3.1 shows for Finland, Sweden and the US a growth-accounting exercise in which ICT capital is distinguished from non-ICT capital. The contribution of ICT capital to growth in Finland and Sweden is almost as high as in the US for the period 1995–2004.

Table 3.1 Growth accounting with ICT capital

	GDP growth	Contributions to GDP growth by			
		ICT capital growth	Non-ICT capital growth	Labour growth	TFP growth
FINLAND					
1995–2000	4.9	0.7	0.1	1.0	3.0
2000–04	2.3	0.6	0.3	−0.3	1.7
SWEDEN					
1995–2000	3.5	0.8	0.4	0.7	1.7
2000–04	2.1	0.4	0.2	−0.4	1.9
USA					
1995–2000	4.2	0.9	0.6	1.3	1.5
2000–04	2.4	0.6	0.4	−0.3	1.7

Source: Groningen Growth and Development Centre, Total Economy Growth Accounting Database.

4. RESTARTING THE CATCHING-UP PROCESS IN CESEE COUNTRIES

I now move to consider some aspects of catching-up prospects for the CESEE countries. Figure 3.8 shows the growth rates for selected CESEE countries that are also EU members (Slovakia is not included in the data). The figure shows that, first, the period 2000–07 was on the whole remarkably successful for these countries though some countries did have sub-periods of slow growth. The second point to notice is that the recession has in general been deep but short-lived as most of these countries have turned round toward positive growth. Some countries have already reached positive growth. In other countries GDP continues to decline, though with smaller rates than in 2008–09. In general, the recovery is still weak and positive growth is modest so far. The global crisis is by no means over. It can also be noted that there are differences between the countries. Remarkably Poland did not experience any decline in the level of GDP.

In assessing prospects for catching-up, it is important to start with the general economic environment for CESEE countries. Their economic situations are challenging. Uncertainties and risk perceptions remain high both domestically and internationally, which makes financing conditions difficult in comparison with the pre-crisis period. Deleveraging of debt and

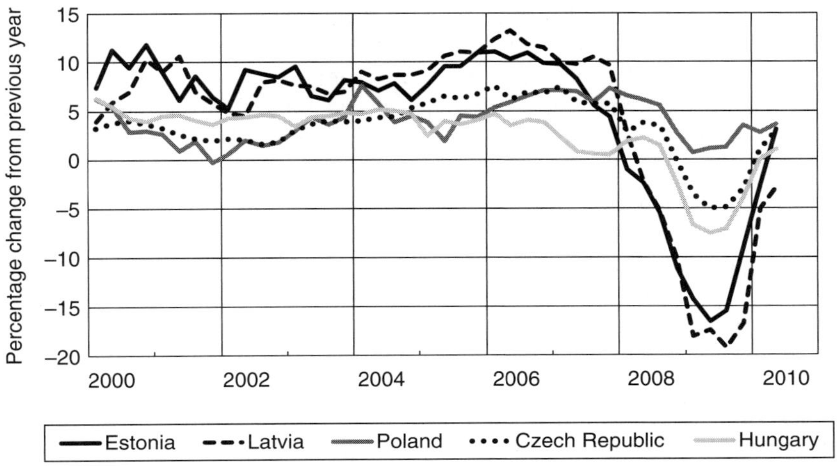

Source: Eurostat.

Figure 3.8 GDP growth in selected CESEE countries

higher saving rates for households have been going on for some time and this will continue into the future. Fiscal positions have worsened. Some countries are faring reasonably well in this respect, whereas fiscal problems are difficult in some other countries.

The international environment for CESEE countries is and probably continues to be difficult. Trend growth in Western Europe is forecast to be slower than before the crisis, and the crisis itself is far from over. On the financial side the current picture is mixed. Uncertainties in connection with the sovereign debt crisis continue and their resolution will be slow even in best scenarios, as indicated, for example, by the Finnish data in Figure 3.4. On the other hand, it appears that the international reform of financial architecture is proceeding and this will probably bring new stability to financial systems. If so, the coming reforms will provide guidance to strengthening the financial systems in the CESEE countries. Such a development would in the longer term mean improvement in financing conditions for companies and households.

At the time of writing, there are big tensions in the international financial system, including the exchange rate regimes. For CESEE countries, the ongoing uncertainties may well lead to some rethinking about the choice of the exchange rate regime. One possibility is to remain outside the euro area and continue with a flexible or fixed exchange rate regime. The other possibility is to continue with an objective to reach membership in the euro area.

The choice of exchange rate regime is a perennial classic topic in international finance, and there are no simple answers to the choice. Interestingly, Finland and Sweden provide a revealing comparison. Finland decided to join the Eurosystem, whereas Sweden opted for a floating currency and inflation targeting as the monetary policy regime. Both countries have done well in the period from the mid-1990s to the start of the current crisis. The comparison does not yield an unambiguous 'winner'.

Restarting the catching-up processes has two main parts.[8] First, it is important to focus on closing the output gap that the recession has created. Second, attention must be directed at potential output growth, so that the closing of the output gap does not lead to bottlenecks and overheating.

In the next few years, the CESEE countries must try to close the output gap and get their GDP close to potential. Several CESEE countries had big saving–investment gaps before the crisis and relied heavily on capital imports to finance investment. In the future higher saving rates are likely to help in closing the saving–investment gaps. More generally, financing of investment will probably have to rely more on domestic sources even if there appears to be some recovery in FDI.

A major challenge for many CESEE countries lies in the public sector, where deficits and build-up of debt can create problems. Though circumstances vary a lot between countries, it is important in my opinion to focus on fiscal improvements in all countries. A high level of effectiveness in government activities and support for growth should be emphasized in public fiscal policies. Clear fiscal programmes that address concerns about fiscal sustainability should be instituted. For example, in the 1990s the Nordic countries introduced the practice of fiscal guidelines that cover the whole electoral cycle. Political credibility and stability are essential here.

Finally, I would like to note that sufficient focus on unemployment is important also from the growth perspective. High long-term unemployment means that, on average, labour skill levels are probably in decline, which has negative effects on growth.

Looking at the supply side, an educated labour force is a strengthening factor for many CESEE countries. Education can facilitate structural change from low-tech to medium- and high-tech industries, which will speed up economic growth.

More generally, it is important to emphasize that the CESEE countries are open economies, and for such countries the main drivers for success lie in the international competitiveness of the economy. EU membership or close links to EU countries from non-members have been and will be very beneficial. It follows that maintaining cost competitiveness is the main key to success. This means control of costs and, equally importantly, ensuring ongoing growth in productivity. Figure 3.9 illustrates the development of

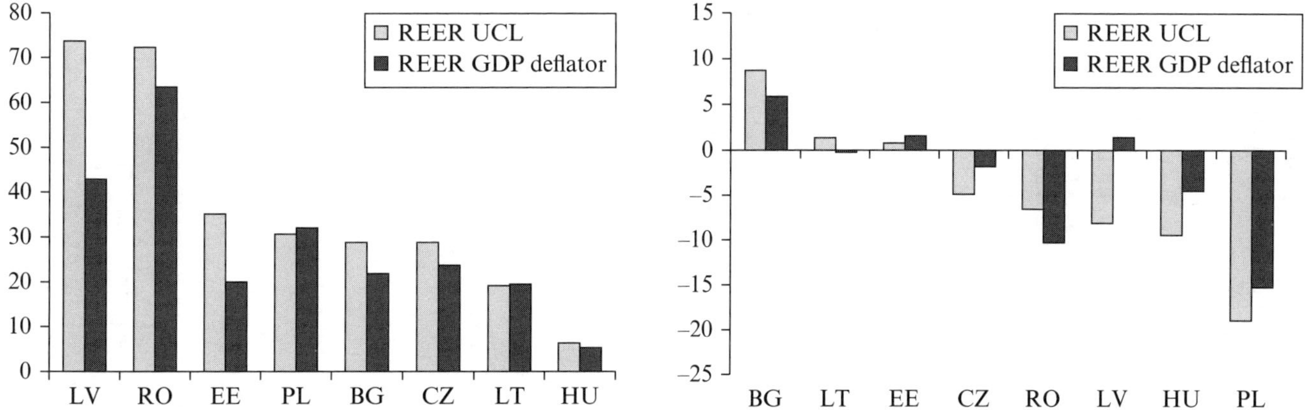

(a) Cumulative change (%) 2004–08

(b) Year-on-year % change, 2008–09

Source: Ameco and European Commission.

Figure 3.9 Real effective exchange rates in selected CESEE countries the real effective exchange rates (REER) for selected CESEE countries. The crisis years have in fact made it possible for many of these countries to improve cost competitiveness, which has reversed the trend of worsening competitiveness before the crisis.

In a somewhat longer-term perspective, it is also important to ensure that the economic and political environment is conducive to continuation of structural change in the CESEE economies. Crises provide a good opportunity for reform. The current global crisis may well have initiated significant changes in the comparative advantages of countries in the international arena. Countries must find ways to adapt to such new and changing situations.

NOTES

1. The views expressed are my own and do not necessarily reflect those of the Bank of Finland. I am grateful to Harri Hasko for comments and assistance.
2. See Honkapohja et al. (2009), Englund (1999) and Steigum (2004) for overviews of the crisis in Finland, Sweden and Norway, respectively.
3. See Honkapohja (2009) for a detailed overview of the Nordic banking crises in the 1990s and how they were managed in the three countries.
4. See Honkapohja et al. (2009) for a thorough discussion of the Finnish recovery from the crisis.
5. See, for example, Allen and Gale (1999, 2007).
6. Total factor productivity measures the part in productivity growth that cannot be attributed to explicit productive factors. Thus, TFP growth contains the reasons for productivity growth that are independently measured. Growth accounting computations differ in their lists of measured productive factors. For example, Table 3.1 incorporates IT capital as an explicit factor of production, whereas in Figure 3.5 the contribution of IT capital is not measured.
7. See, for example, Backé et al. (2010) for data on the structural differences between the CESEE countries. The paper also contains an important comparison between CESEE and Latin American countries.
8. See Landesmann (2010) for a related discussion of the ways to re-initiate the catching-up processes for CESEE countries.

REFERENCES

Allen, F. and D. Gale (1999), 'Bubbles, crises, and policy', *Oxford Review of Economic Policy*, **15** (3), 9–18.

Allen, F. and D. Gale (2007), *Understanding Financial Crises*, Oxford: Oxford University Press.

Backé, P. et al. (2010), 'How did the global financial crisis affect the CESEE region and Latin America? A comparative analysis', *Focus on European Economic Integration*, Q1/10, pp. 49–66.

Englund, P. (1999), 'The Swedish banking crisis: roots and consequences', *Oxford Review of Economic Policy*, **15** (3), 80–97.

Honkapohja, S. (2009), 'The 1990's financial crises in Nordic countries', Bank of Finland Research Discussion Paper 5/2009.

Honkapohja, S. et al. (2009), *Economic Prosperity Recaptured: the Finnish Path from Crisis to Rapid Growth*, Cambridge, MA: MIT Press.

Landesmann, M.A. (2010), 'Which growth model for Central and Eastern Europe after the crisis?', FIW Policy Brief, No. 4.

Steigum, E. (2004), 'Financial deregulation with a fixed exchange rate: Lessons from Norway's boom–bust cycle and banking crisis', in T.G. Moe, J.A. Solheim and B. Vale (eds), *The Norwegian Banking Crisis*, Norges Banks Skriftserie/Occasional Papers No. 33, pp. 23–75.

4. Catching-up prospects after the crisis for the EU's CESEE region

Kieran Mc Morrow and Werner Röger[1]

The CESEE region,[2] as well as the EU-27 as a whole, has been deeply affected by the global economic and financial crisis that erupted in 2008. In the wake of the crisis, policy makers are asking whether the CESEE growth model will have to be fundamentally adapted to address the inadequacies which have emerged. This chapter tries to provide some answers to these questions by assessing the growth and catching-up performance of CESEE as a whole, as well as its individual members, in the ten years leading up to the crisis and comparing this with the likely growth trajectory for these countries over the coming decade up to 2020.

The chapter is structured as follows: Section 1 provides a short overview of the type of factors to be considered when thinking about the medium- to long-term growth and catching-up prospects of a region such as CESEE. Section 2 assesses the degree of convergence achieved in the ten-year period leading up to the crisis, with Sections 3 and 4 looking at the impact of the financial crisis on the underlying growth capacity of the CESEE region as well as providing an assessment of post-crisis prospects up to 2020. Finally, Section 5 gives some concluding remarks.

1 SOME RESULTS FROM THE CONVERGENCE LITERATURE

Various theories exist concerning the speed with which less developed economies develop over time, and whether, or when, they converge to the income levels of the most advanced economies. Some economists, such as Romer (1986 and 1990) and other advocates of the new endogenous growth theories, are quite pessimistic regarding the likelihood of convergence occurring even over long periods of time since productive technology is, in their view, of the increasing – rather than the more normally assumed decreasing – returns-to-scale variety, which means that global technology leaders tend to retain the lead over extended periods of time due to knowledge spillovers or learning-by-doing effects. At the other end of the scale are economists such as Sachs and Warner (1995), who are quite optimistic concerning the potential for catching-up, provided the policy framework is adequate.

Between these two extreme views and most common in empirical analysis – and also used in the production function (PF) approach underlying this chapter (see D'Auria et al., 2010) – is the Solow (1956) neoclassical growth framework, which predicts what is referred to as 'conditional' convergence. The theory suggests that convergence does occur but not necessarily to the same higher level of income, since the growth potential of countries differs essentially because of differences in respective savings rates and population changes. The theoretical support for this view is provided by endogenous growth models and, in particular, by models of poverty traps.[3]

Given the wide choice of models, the empirical evidence naturally becomes a major deciding factor in terms of which model to use for any long-run growth analysis. In overall terms, the neoclassical view would appear to have enjoyed the greatest degree of support in the literature. There is in fact now widespread empirical acceptance that 'conditional' convergence does occur across countries. Typical of this line of research is a 1992 study by Mankiw et al. which showed, using cross-country regression analysis, that the neoclassical growth model could explain nearly 80 per cent of the differences in international standards of living, using just three explanatory variables, namely population growth rates, savings rates and an indicator of human capital.

In addition, papers by Barro and Sala-i-Martin (1991), Islam (1995) and Sala-i-Martin (1996), amongst many others, all found evidence for 'conditional convergence' for 'developed economies' including the EU, with rates of convergence of 2 per cent per annum being typical for these studies. With regard to the debate on openness and growth, a number of studies, such as Sachs and Warner (1995) and Ben-David (1996), using a modified neoclassical framework, found strong evidence of per capita income convergence for open economies with strong trading links, a scenario which is typical of the EU as a whole, as well as Japan and, more recently, a number of the CESEE economies.

2 CATCHING-UP OF THE CESEE REGION PRIOR TO THE CRISIS (1998–2007)

CESEE as a group experienced a strong and sustained process of real convergence over the years 1998–2007, with potential growth rates well in

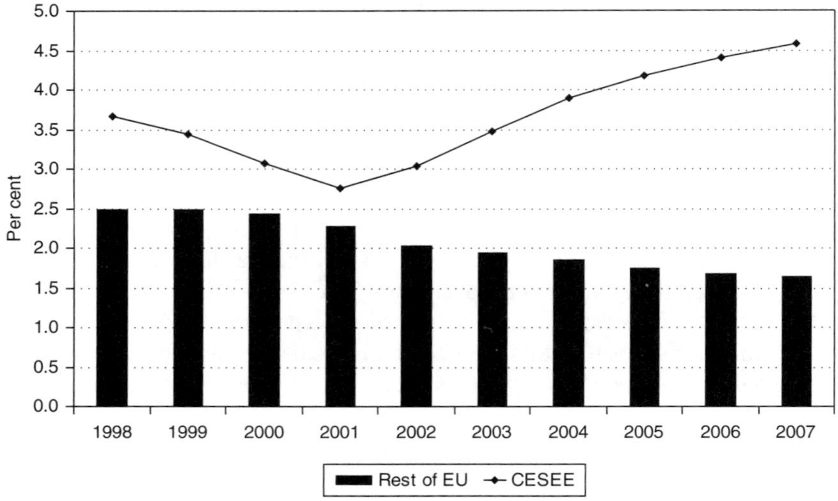

Source: Commission services and authors' calculations.

Figure 4.1 Potential growth rates, CESEE versus the rest of the EU, 1998–2007

excess of the rest of the EU over the period as a whole. In fact, as made clear in Figure 4.1, the out-performance of the CESEE group of countries accelerated over the period, with the initial gap in potential growth rates of about 1¼ percentage points giving way to gaps of 2–3 percentage points over the period 2004–07.

With regard to the components of growth (Table 4.1), virtually all of the CESEE countries had lower contributions to growth from labour over the pre-crisis period because of lower population growth but also less favourable trends in the employment rate. All of the seven CESEE countries, reflecting their catching-up status, had contributions from capital which were substantially higher than in the rest of the EU, in fact more than double the EU-20 contribution rate. Rather encouragingly, this capital accumulation pattern was also replicated with respect to total factor productivity (TFP) trends, with the contribution from TFP running at nearly three times that of the rest of the EU. The only exception to these patterns at the individual CESEE country level was Hungary, with its catching-up process over the period being focused on a greater use of the factors of production, labour and capital, rather than on stronger efficiency gains in the form of higher TFP growth.

Table 4.1 Potential growth and its components, 1998–2007 (per cent change)

	Total	Contributions to potential		
		Labour	Capital	TFP
Bulgaria	3.9	0.3	1.7	1.8
Czech Republic	2.9	−0.4	1.3	2.0
Hungary	3.6	0.6	2.1	0.8
Poland	4.0	−0.2	1.8	2.4
Romania	3.1	−1.0	1.6	2.4
Slovakia	4.3	−0.4	2.2	2.4
Slovenia	3.8	0.2	2.3	1.3
CESEE	3.7	−0.4	1.8	2.3
EU-20	2.0	0.4	0.8	0.8

Source: Commission services and authors' calculations.

Table 4.2 Potential and per capita growth rates and levels, 1998–2007

	Potential growth (% change)	Total population growth (% change)	Per capita income growth (% change)	GDP per capita relative to EU-20 (PPP EU-20 = 100)	
				1998	2007
Bulgaria	3.9	−0.8	4.8	24.7	33.8
Czech Republic	2.9	0.0	2.9	62.8	71.1
Hungary	3.6	−0.2	3.8	47.2	57.2
Poland	4.0	0.0	4.0	40.9	50.7
Romania	3.1	−0.5	3.6	25.6	31.1
Slovakia	4.3	0.0	4.3	45.8	58.4
Slovenia	3.8	0.2	3.6	67.9	81.3
CESEE	3.7	−0.2	3.9	39.8	48.9
EU-20	2.0	0.5	1.6	100	100

Source: Commission services and authors' calculations.

With respect to the pace of income convergence, Table 4.2 shows per capita income growth rates for the CESEE countries and for the EU-20. The region as a whole strongly boosted their income levels relative to the rest of the EU, with GDP per capita levels in CESEE rising from roughly 40 per cent of EU-20 levels in 1998 to 49 per cent in 2007.

3 IMPACT OF THE FINANCIAL CRISIS ON CESEE GROWTH

The crisis has already had a dramatic impact on actual GDP growth rates in the CESEE region, with growth slowing considerably in 2008, followed by a contraction of 2¾ per cent in 2009 and, on the basis of the Commission's spring 2010 forecasts, an expected growth rate substantially below potential in the 2010–11 period. A review of the literature on past financial crises, including the experiences of countries such as Finland, Sweden and Japan in the early 1990s, points to the following factors as important influences on the evolution of the different components of growth in the post-crisis period.

Labour A lot of the research work in this area suggests that the length of the downturn in the aftermath of the crisis is pivotal in determining the extent of any damage to an economy's underlying labour potential. A long and deep recession may cut the potential labour force by discouraging some workers from seeking a job and by reducing migration flows. Moreover, the potential labour supply could be damaged if the crisis heightens the political pressure to delay reversing a number of short-term, crisis-related, measures in the recovery phase (for example, a temporary increase in unemployment benefits) or to implement policies to curb the growth in labour market participation rates (for example, early retirement schemes). Finally, in the case of a prolonged recession, long unemployment spells may cause a permanent destruction in human capital, leading to a rise in the non-accelerating wage rate of unemployment (NAWRU) – due to so-called 'hysteresis effects'– and further losses in the potential output level.

Capital The financial crisis can also reduce potential output in the short and medium term through its adverse impact on investment. The downward pressure on investment results, firstly, from increases in risk premia on loans to firms and households due to shifts in attitudes towards risk; secondly, from the more cautious lending behaviour of banks resulting from, amongst other things, credit constraints; and thirdly, from a correction to more 'normal' investment levels following the over-investment pattern of the 'boom' period (generated, on this occasion, by bubbles in both the financial and housing markets). Given the unprecedented financial market problems, the impact on capital is unlikely to be limited to price and volume effects – there is also a distinct risk that an impaired capital allocation system may result not only in a more anaemic investment trend during recovery but also in a less than optimal reallocation of capital resources to aid the crucial restructuring process.

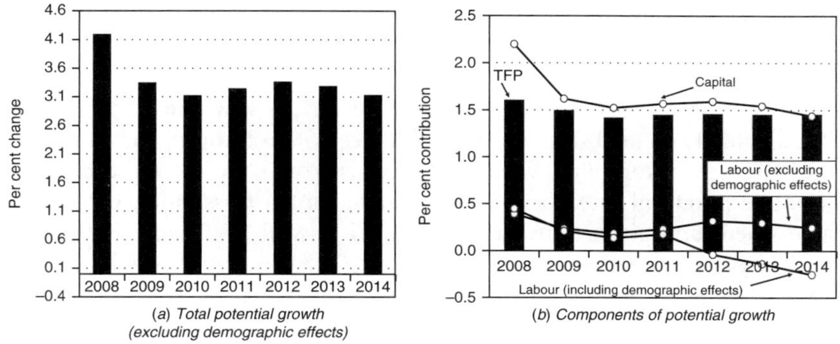

Source: Commission services and authors' calculations.

Figure 4.2 CESEE potential growth rates and their labour (including and excluding demographics), capital and TFP components, 2007–14

TFP Theory does not give a clear answer as to what the expected impact of the crisis on long-run TFP might be. While a number of mechanisms tend to dampen TFP in the immediate aftermath of a crisis, downturns can have a positive TFP impact as they can induce a process of essential restructuring and cleansing in the economy. Consequently, ex ante, the expected effect of the crisis on TFP is ambiguous, with a range of specific factors making any definitive assessment of the fallout from the current crisis particularly uncertain. These factors include, firstly, the need to allow for the initial downward-level shifts in TFP associated with industrial restructuring, with some industries (for example, financial services and construction) likely to experience permanent reductions in the level of their activities as a result of the crisis; secondly, the difficulty in estimating realistic capital obsolescence rates; thirdly, the uncertainties regarding the financial crisis impact on R&D spending and on the financing of R&D; fourthly, the extent to which the crisis results in scarce resources being locked into relatively unproductive activities; and finally the possibility of a crisis-induced shift away from the relatively high TFP growth manufacturing sector towards services.

As can be seen from Figure 4.2, potential growth in CESEE countries has declined by about 1 per cent and is projected to remain lower over the medium term. Lower potential growth essentially reflects a decline in the investment rate and consequently a reduction in the capital contribution.

4 GROWTH SCENARIOS FOR THE CESEE REGION UP TO 2020

Section 3 has suggested that, as with the EU as a whole, the financial crisis is likely to lead to permanently lower potential output levels in the CESEE region, compared with the pre-crisis growth path, with some small negative potential growth rate effects also being a possibility. Given this assessment and given that ageing populations will be an additional drag on EU growth, particularly in some of the CESEE countries, what would constitute a reasonable scenario for growth for the CESEE and EU-20 country groupings over the coming decade? Section 4.1 gives an overview of the baseline growth scenario, with Section 4.2 highlighting a number of possible challenges in realizing this scenario.

4.1 Baseline Scenario Suggests that Convergence is Set to Continue

For the baseline scenario, the broad features of which are laid out below in Table 4.3 and Figures 4.3 and 4.4, we have adopted the following set of assumptions:

- Short to medium term (2011–14): the outlook for individual CESEE and EU-20 countries for this period is based on the Commission services' spring 2010 short-term forecasts up to 2011 as well as a three-year, medium-term, extension covering the period up to 2014.
- Long run (2015–20): for the labour input projections for the period 2015–20, we employ the economic and budgetary consequences that the EPC's Ageing Working Group established ageing populations to have up to 2060 in 2009.

On the basis of these assumptions, Table 4.3 shows, for CESEE as a whole, that potential growth rates are close to double those of the rest of the EU. The differences in per capita income growth rates are even greater (2.8 per cent versus 1.1 per cent). Achieving these much higher per capita income growth rates would result in a significant closing of the income gap, with GDP per capita in the CESEE region growing from 55 per cent of EU-20 levels in 2011 to 63 per cent in 2020. When one compares this performance with the pre-crisis decade discussed in Section 2, one sees that the pace of income convergence is broadly similar over the post-crisis decade up to 2020, at least at the aggregate level.

With respect to the specific drivers of growth over the coming decade, Figure 4.3 shows the predicted CESEE and EU-20 trends for productivity and labour input. Regarding productivity, the pace of growth in CESEE

Table 4.3 Potential and per capita income growth rates and levels, 2011–20

	Potential growth 2011–20 (% change)			Total population growth (% change)	Per capita income growth (% change)	GDP per capita relative to EU-20 (PPP EU-20 = 100)	
	Total	Productivity	Labour input (hours)			2011	2020
Bulgaria	1.6	2.4	−0.8	−0.5	2.2	37.8	41.1
Czech Republic	2.6	3.0	−0.4	0.1	2.4	75.3	84.6
Hungary[1]	0.8	1.1	−0.3	−0.1	1.0	57.3	56.4
Poland	3.3	3.4	−0.1	0.0	3.3	59.3	70.7
Romania	2.4	2.9	−0.5	−0.2	2.6	35.4	40.1
Slovakia	3.8	3.9	−0.1	0.0	3.8	66.4	83.6
Slovenia[1]	1.2	1.5	−0.3	0.1	1.1	84.8	84.1
CESEE	2.7	3.0	−0.3	−0.1	2.8	54.8	62.8
EU-20	1.5	1.3	0.2	0.3	1.1	100	100

Note: 1. The relatively low growth rates for Hungary and Slovenia are strongly driven by the TFP growth rates produced by the official production function methodology. This methodology uses a HP filter based approach to produce trend TFP. The alternative trend TFP estimation method, using a Kalman Filter for the 'old' EU-15 member states, would give TFP growth rates for Hungary and Slovenia which are ½–¾ of a per cent higher.

Source: Commission services and authors' calculations.

will be roughly double that of the rest of the EU, with high rates of capital deepening in part being driven by the less than favourable labour input developments.[4] In addition, TFP growth rates will average around 1½ per cent annually in CESEE compared with rates which are expected to be at least a ½ of a per cent lower in the rest of the EU. Ongoing restructuring efforts, as well as the greater scope for efficiency gains in the CESEE region, are expected to help sustain this relatively respectable pace of TFP growth. Regarding labour input developments, Figure 4.3 highlights the fact stressed earlier that the CESEE countries as a group are facing a dramatically difficult decade due to shrinking labour forces, with an expected average negative contribution to growth from labour of –0.3 per cent over the next ten years, compared with an ongoing positive contribution in the rest of the EU of 0.2 per cent. In addition, as Figure 4.3 underlines, this average ¼ of a per cent negative contribution to CESEE growth from labour is expected to widen sharply over time, with the expected drag on growth being closer to ¾ of a per cent by 2020.

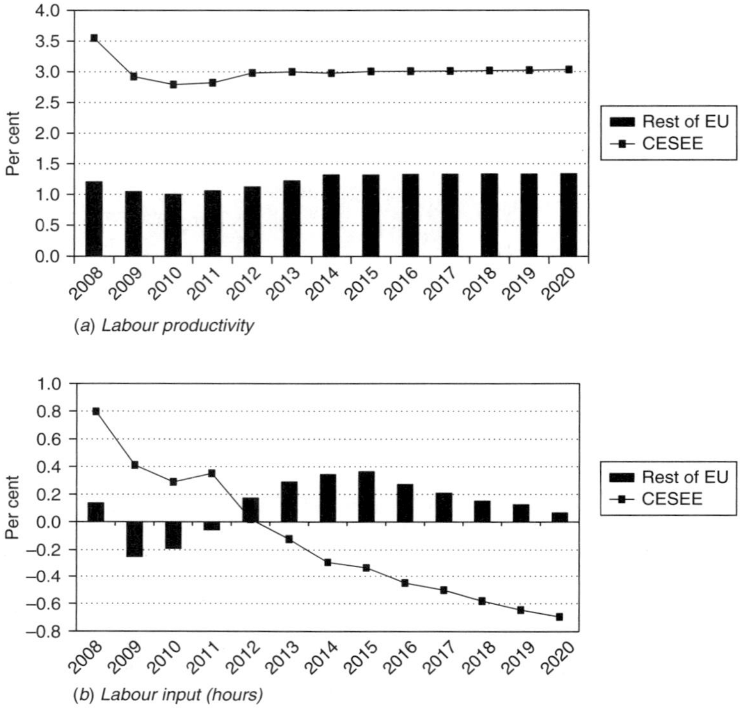

Source: Commission services and authors' calculations.

Figure 4.3 Productivity and labour input growth rates, CESEE member states versus the rest of the EU, 2008–20

4.2 Convergence Challenges Should Not However Be Underestimated

Whilst the baseline convergence performance of the CESEE region discussed in Section 4.1 appears satisfactory, this should not hide the fact that catching-up is expected to occur against a background of lower overall growth rates in both CESEE and the rest of the EU. In addition, whilst the baseline view of convergence is a relatively sanguine one, a closer look at some of the underlying TFP, capital and labour market trends which are driving CESEE's catching-up prospects suggests that the convergence process may in fact be quite fragile. This viewpoint is supported by the evidence shown in Figure 4.4, with the following points highlighting the relatively optimistic nature of the baseline scenario for the CESEE grouping relative to that for EU-20:

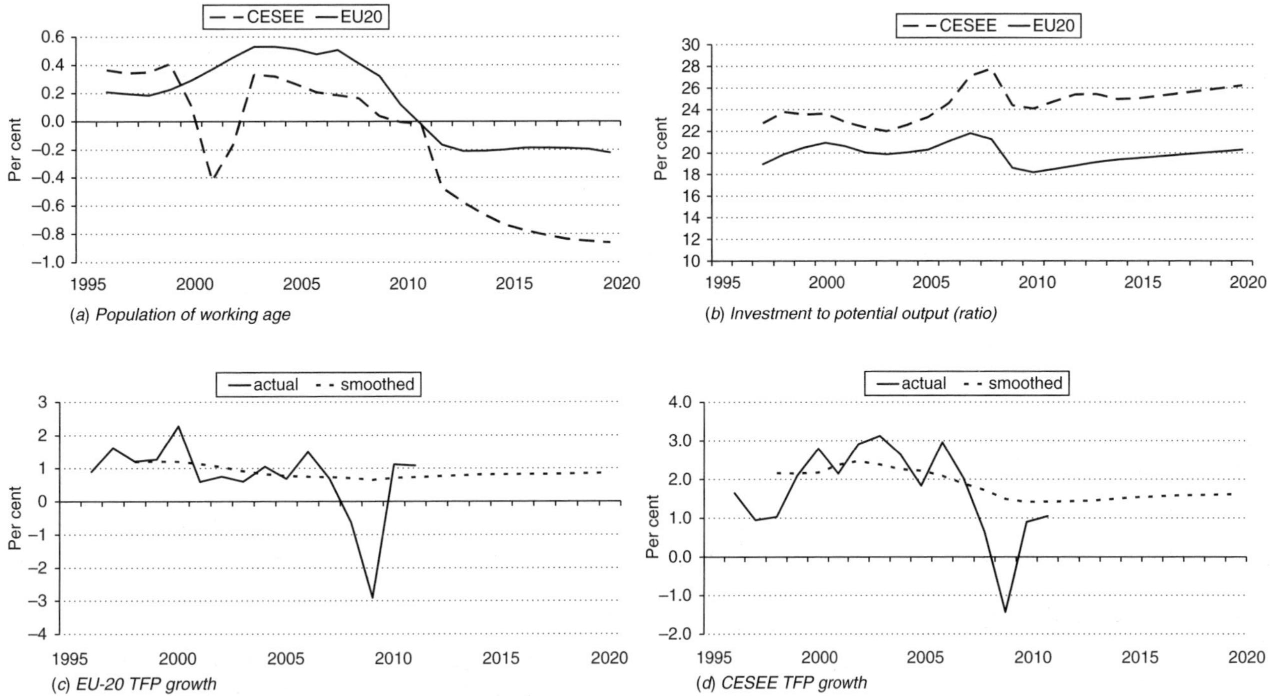

Source: Commission services and authors' calculations.

Figure 4.4 Drivers of growth, CESEE versus EU-20

- Eurostat's 'EUROPOP–2008' population projections suggest that the negative drag on growth emanating from changes in the population of working age in CESEE will be substantially greater than in EU-20 over the coming decade, compared with 1998–2007.
- Regarding investment trends, given that the pre-crisis investment 'bubble' in CESEE was arguably larger than in EU-20, it might have been more prudent to assume an investment-to-GDP ratio in 2020 which is lower than that used in the baseline.
- Figure 4.4 also shows that the pace of recovery in actual TFP in CESEE may not warrant a trend growth rate scenario of 1½ per cent over the period to 2020. It could easily be argued that a figure of closer to 1 per cent would be more appropriate.

5 CONCLUDING REMARKS

Catching-up prospects for CESEE as a whole over the period to 2020 are expected to compare relatively favourably with the progress achieved in the pre-crisis period, with CESEE income levels rising by 8 percentage points to reach 63 per cent of those of the EU-20 by 2020. However, despite the expected progress in convergence, the catching-up process may be quite fragile, with optimistic assumptions for some of the key drivers of growth, underlining the need for caution. In addition, convergence will also take place against an EU-wide background of lower sustainable rates of growth, as the initial financial crisis induced contraction in potential output and the expected slow medium- to long-term recovery process will inevitably lead, in the absence of an adequate policy response, to a less healthy aggregate supply-side position in the EU as a whole. Lower levels and growth rates of potential output over the period to 2020 will be mainly driven by permanently higher borrowing costs leading to below-trend tangible and intangible investment rates as well as higher structural unemployment rates. The medium-term cumulative loss in the underlying growth potential of the CESEE region is expected to be similar to that for the rest of the EU, although this aggregate-level performance masks much larger individual CESEE country losses, which in some cases are likely to approach those of the Baltic economies.

Despite differences in the degree to which countries will be affected by the crisis, virtually all of them will be forced to consider a range of structural reform measures aimed at boosting their underlying supply-side potential. This process will necessitate an assessment of the relative effectiveness of a range of measures linked to improving the functioning of their product and labour markets, as well as specific initiatives in the knowledge and innovation domains. Given the crisis-induced urgency for reform, as well as the ongoing large scope for further catching-up in CESEE, the region as a whole should use the framework provided by the 2020 programme as an additional impetus for bold policy action. This is particularly pertinent for some individual countries since although the aggregate-level picture for CESEE may compare favourably with the rest of the EU, this is patently not the case for a number of individual CESEE countries which will require sustained efforts over many years to get back onto a higher, more sustainable, growth path.

NOTES

1. The views expressed in this chapter are those of the authors and do not necessarily represent those of the European Commission.
2. The CESEE region is made up of seven EU member states, namely Bulgaria, the Czech Republic, Hungary, Poland, Romania, Slovakia and Slovenia.
3. This new body of theoretical work on multiple equilibria predicts the formation of 'convergence clubs' or different poles of attraction (with member countries converging towards each other and diverging away from other different clubs), with the polarization of the distribution into 'twin peaks' of rich and poor countries. In these new models, the dynamic system is characterized by multiple, locally stable, steady-state equilibria (see, for example, Quah, 1995 and 1996).
4. Capital deepening refers to the change in capital intensity in an economy. For example, an increase in capital deepening means that capital inputs are growing faster than labour inputs, resulting in an increase in the amount of capital available per worker/per hour worked.

REFERENCES

Barro, R. and X. Sala-i-Martin (1991), 'Convergence across states and regions', *Brookings Papers on Economic Activity*, No. 1, 107–82.

Ben-David, D. (1996), 'Trade and convergence among countries', *Journal of International Economics*, **40**, 279–98.

D'Auria, F. et al. (2010), 'The production function methodology for calculating potential growth rates and output gaps', Economic Papers 420, July, European Commission.

Islam, N. (1995), 'Growth empirics: a panel data approach', *Quarterly Journal of Economics*, **110** (4), 1127–70.

Mankiw, G., D. Romer and D. Weil (1992), 'A contribution to the empirics of economic growth', *The Quarterly Journal of Economics*, **107** (2), 407–37.

Quah, D. (1995), 'Empirics for economic growth and convergence', CEP Discussion Paper, no. 253, pp. 27–59.

Quah, D. (1996), 'Twin peaks: growth and convergence in models of distribution dynamics', *Economic Journal*, **106** (437), 1045–55.

Romer, P. (1986), 'Increasing returns and long run growth', *Journal of Political Economy*, **94** (5), 1003–37.
Romer, P. (1990), 'Endogenous technological change', *Journal of Political Economy*, **98** (5), S71–102.
Sachs, J. and A. Warner (1995), 'Economic convergence and economic policies', NBER Working Paper no. 5039.
Sala-i-Martin, X. (1996), 'Regional cohesion: evidence and theories of regional growth and convergence', *European Economic Review*, **40** (6), 1325–52.
Solow, R.M. (1956), 'A contribution to the theory of economic growth', *Quarterly Journal of Economics*, **70** (1), 65–94.

5. Growth prospects in the EU-10 member states after the crisis

Dariusz K. Rosati

1 INTRODUCTION

After having recovered from the transformational recession in the early 1990s, the countries of Central and Eastern Europe have been growing fast, gradually reducing income gaps between them and the more affluent countries of Western Europe. The rapid catching-up process has been fuelled by trade and financial integration as well as legal and institutional harmonization in the context of EU accession. But the global financial and economic crisis of 2008–09 hit the region particularly hard, with most countries suffering substantial falls in output levels, generally more severe than in Western Europe. Also, the subsequent recovery seems rather slow and hesitant.

This chapter addresses the issue of growth prospects after the global crisis in ten Central and Eastern European countries that joined the EU in 2004–07 (EU-10). The purpose of the chapter is twofold. First, the chapter aims at explaining the phenomenon of rapid growth in EU-10 before the crisis and the subsequent massive fall of output during the crisis. Second, the chapter tries to answer the question whether economic growth will resume quickly and what changes in policies are needed, both in EU-10 and at the EU level, in order to make this process quick and sustainable. It is shown that between 2000 and 2008 economic growth in all EU-10 followed a specific pattern (although with individual variations), based on large inflows of foreign capital supported by trade, financial and institutional integration within the EU. These inflows have strongly accelerated growth but also contributed to the emergence of various economic imbalances, which made most of EU-10 extremely vulnerable to external shocks. The policy recommendations for the post-crisis period are therefore focused on eliminating these imbalances while preserving the growth-enhancing elements of the growth model followed before the crisis.

2 CATCHING-UP IN EU-10 IN 2000–09

The economic performance of EU-10 after the mid-1990s, and especially after the slowdown in 2001–02, has been remarkable. All countries of the region registered consistently very high growth rates, with even double-digit rates in some of them. Figures 5.1 and 5.2 show the changes in GDP per capita levels in EU-10 relative to EU-15 between 2000 and 2009. The new member states managed to reduce the income gap on average by 10–15 percentage points before the crisis hit in 2009. As could be expected, poorer countries (Bulgaria and Romania) considerably outperformed more affluent countries (Slovenia and the Czech Republic). The figures also show that EU-10 are quite diversified in terms of GDP per capita – in 2008 the incomes levels in the more advanced countries of the region were roughly twice as high as in the less advanced countries.

The hypothesis that the speed of catching-up depends inversely on the initial income level is well established in the real convergence literature. The growth rates of poorer countries, as the standard explanation goes, can be accelerated thanks to large productivity gains that can be obtained through higher technology import and imitation. For a poor country it is easy to implement standard technologies that are being discontinued and replaced by more advanced ones in developed countries. When incomes levels rise, this exercise becomes more and more difficult, as more up-to-date technologies are required, which are more difficult to import or imitate. Hence, imports and imitation are gradually replaced by innovation, but GDP growth dynamics in the process inevitably slow down.

The speed of convergence can be measured with a standard equation on conditional convergence (see, for example, Barro, 1991; Barro and Sala-i-Martin, 1991, 1992; Mankiw et al., 1992), where y(t) is the level of per capita GDP in period t (in PPS), and λ is the speed of convergence towards a steady state level y^*. The convergence hypothesis can therefore be formulated as follows:

$$\ln(y(t)) - \ln(y(0)) \approx [1 - \exp(-\lambda t)]\,[\ln(y^*) - \ln(y(0))] \quad (5.1)$$

Rearranging terms and denoting: $a = [1 - \exp(-\lambda t)]\,[\ln(y^*)]$, and $b = \exp(-\lambda t)$, one obtains:

$$\ln(y(t)) = a + b\ln(y(0)) \quad (5.2)$$

This equation has been estimated for the cross-section of 27 EU member countries for 1999–2008, and the values obtained for the structural

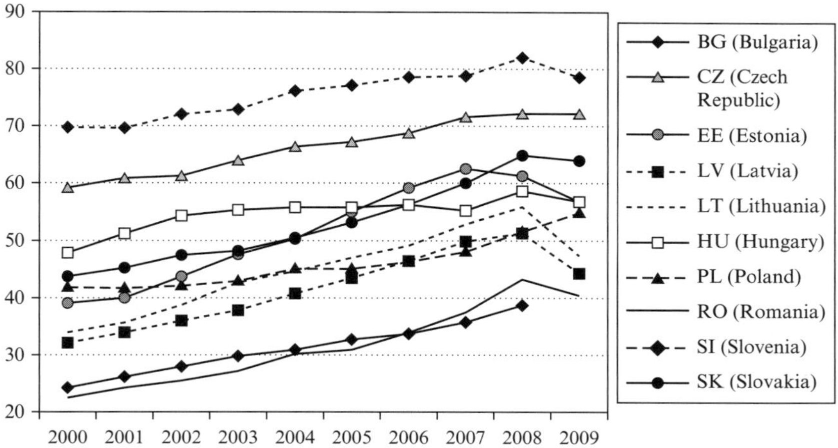

Source: Author's calculations based on Eurostat data.

Figure 5.1 GDP per capita in EU-10 (in PPS) in 2000–09, EU-15 = 100

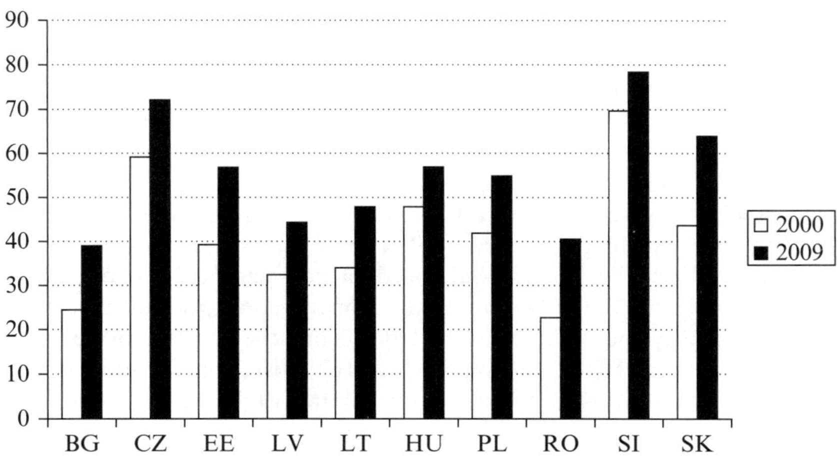

Source: Author's calculations based on Eurostat data.

Figure 5.2 GDP per capita in EU-10 (in PPS) in 2000 and 2009, EU-15 = 100

Table 5.1 EU-10, the average speed of convergence to EU-15 GDP/capita levels, 1999–2008 (per cent of the initial income level), and the estimated number of years to reach the average EU-15 level (λ = 1.81 per cent)

Country	% p.a.	No. of years
Bulgaria	4.75	53
Czech Republic	2.00	18
Estonia	3.79	32
Hungary	1.73	32
Latvia	3.21	46
Lithuania	3.48	41
Poland	2.79	33
Romania	6.01	50
Slovenia	1.20	14
Slovakia	3.94	25

Source: Author's calculations based on Eurostat data.

parameters are: a = 1.836, b = 0.834. Substituting into $b = \exp(-\lambda t)$, one obtains λ = 0.00181, which implies an average speed of convergence to the steady state (from the initial level) of around 1.8 per cent per annum.[1] Note, however, that this is an average for the whole sample; for the EU-10 group the speed of convergence can be assumed to be much higher, because their income levels are lowest among all EU member countries. Taking the growth rates used for preparing Figures 5.1 and 5.2, the average convergence speed values estimated for EU-10 are as shown in Table 5.1.

With the gradual reduction of the distance in income levels between EU-10 and EU-15, the speed of convergence is expected to decline systematically. Assuming the convergence process is driven (on average) by the value of λ (1.81 per cent), the number of years to reach the average EU-15 income level is still substantial for most of the catching-up countries (see the second column of Table 5.1). But it is unlikely that the convergence performance of 1999–2008 can continue in future. First, with the initial income levels in EU-10 higher in 2010 than in 1999, the speed of convergence will be slower by definition. Second, it can be demonstrated that future growth will take place under different, and generally less favourable, conditions, and that the growth mechanism which was so successful in the past decade cannot be continued unchanged.

3 THE INTEGRATION GROWTH MODEL (IGM)

The economic performances of all EU-10 in 2000–08 displayed a number of striking similarities which made the growth path of these countries different from those of other groups of emerging economies. Apart from generally high growth rates, the new EU member states have run large current account deficits, financed with massive capital inflows in the form of FDI, portfolio investment and bank credits. In fact, both the ratio of foreign capital inflows to GDP and the ratio of current account deficit to GDP were higher for Central and East European countries than for any other emerging economies group worldwide (IMF, 2010; WIIW–Bruegel, 2010). These large capital inflows allowed EU-10 countries to increase domestic credit, sometimes at dizzying rates, and finance rapidly expanding domestic expenditures. On the external trade side, the EU-10 countries took advantage of the unrestricted access to the European single market and increased their exports considerably, albeit at lower rates than imports.

The key factor behind this remarkable foreign-capital-financed growth has been economic integration with the EU (for example, WIIW–Bruegel, 2010; European Commission, 2009). Since the end of the 1990s, EU-10 have been already well integrated with the core EU in terms of trade, production links and investment flows. During the accession process in the run-up to full EU membership further liberalization took place, including free movement of capital, and, after the accession, largely free movement of people was achieved. In parallel, EU-10 have harmonized their legal and institutional systems to the EU norms and standards, completing this institutional integration process at the moment of accession. Since accession, practically all remaining barriers to trade, investment and finance have been removed.

This integration process created a unique environment for EU-10. Their economies became an integral part of the EU Single Market, both as new centres of export expansion and a target for foreign imports and capital inflows. The free access to the huge European market, combined with a relatively well-educated and inexpensive labour force, geographical proximity and low domestic taxes, has encouraged foreign companies to come and invest in EU-10. Moreover, the institutional convergence and the adoption of the *acquis communautaire* contributed to strengthening macroeconomic stability and policy predictability in EU-10, and resulted in reduced risk premia that have made these economies even more attractive for foreign investors.

This extremely favourable economic environment had a number of important (and not always well-understood) implications. High rates of returns on investment in EU-10, resulting from relative capital scarcity

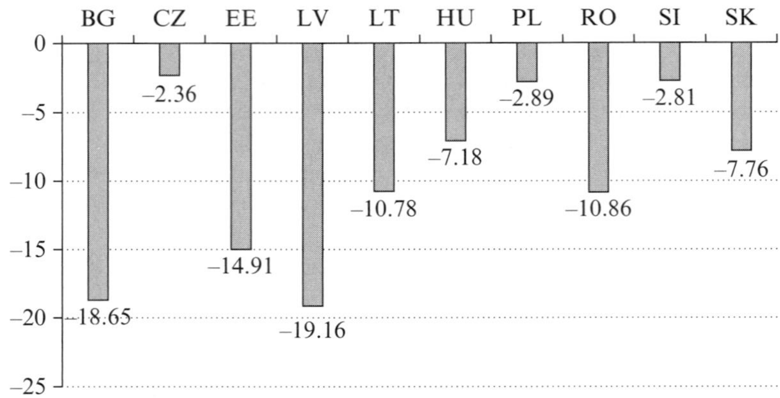

Source: Author's calculations based on Eurostat data.

Figure 5.3 Current account balance in EU-10, per cent of GDP, annual average for 2004–07

and limited savings, attracted foreign capital into production and service sectors. Reduced macroeconomic and commercial risk helped to lower nominal market interest rates, driving down the real rates close to zero or even into negative territory. Financial integration was further strengthened with foreign banks taking over large chunks of domestic banking systems in EU-10 and providing necessary liquidity to sustain rapid expansion of domestic credit. The lower cost of capital and abundant bank capital inflows have practically removed constraints on access to capital in these countries.

This specific growth model, based on trade, financial and institutional integration with the EU and, through it, also with global markets, has been essential to ensure rapid growth and continuous catching-up in EU-10. But it also contributed to building up growing imbalances making EU-10 economies increasingly vulnerable to shocks, including capital flow reversals and sudden changes in market sentiment (Berglof et al., 2009; Darvas, 2010).

First, in most of the countries current account deficits widened sharply, reaching in some cases levels well exceeding 10 per cent of GDP (Figure 5.3). To the extent these deficits were financed by inflows of bank capital and debt investments, the EU-10 economies became vulnerable to exogenous shocks. Practically all EU-10 countries, except Poland, Slovenia and the Czech Republic, were in a state of deep and unsustainable external disequilibrium.

Second, the pace of domestic credit expansion was clearly excessive. In 2004–07 the annual rates of credit growth to the private sector in EU-10 varied from 25–30 per cent for Poland, Slovenia and the Czech Republic

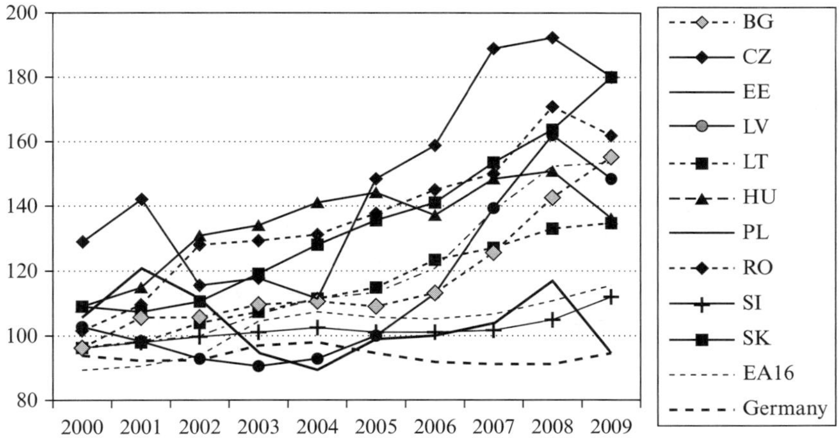

Source: Author's calculations based on Eurostat data.

Figure 5.4 Real effective exchange rates in EU-10, euro area and Germany (deflated by ULC, 1999 = 100)

up to 50–60 per cent for Romania, Latvia and Lithuania. Even though the levels of private debt were still relatively low, the speed with which credits accumulated had a number of negative consequences. The massive and indiscriminate domestic credit flows led, under generally lax and sometimes weak banking supervision, to adverse selection, high indebtedness and increased risk of default in the private sector, as many borrowers did not meet standards of prudent lending. In addition, a growing popularity of foreign exchange denominated credits, with growing exchange rate risk, increased the existing imbalances.

Third, the allocation of new capital was suboptimal. Domestic credits were mostly directed into financing real estate, construction and other service sectors, where real interest rates were low or negative (because of higher inflation in non-tradables), rather than into financing the development of tradable sectors. A very similar pattern was followed by FDI, which also concentrated in specific domestic services (mostly trade and distribution, financial services, housing and real estate, and telecommunication), with only scant presence (especially in smaller economies) in export-oriented, productive sectors.

And fourth, massive capital inflows and the fall in risk premia put upward pressure on domestic currencies, leading to substantial real appreciation. Figure 5.4 shows that the impact was very substantial in practically all countries irrespective of the foreign exchange regime adopted, except for Poland and Slovenia. The figure shows that between 2000 and 2007 the real effective exchange rate appreciated in most countries by 30–50 per cent (and by as much as 90 per cent in Romania). This must have seriously weakened the competitive position of export sectors in many EU-10 countries, especially vis-à-vis their key export market (Germany) and the euro area as a whole.

Domestic policies in EU-10 did not respond adequately to these accumulating imbalances. Banking regulation and supervision in most countries did not react to excessive credit emission and the deteriorating quality of bank loans. Governments did little or nothing to cool down growing domestic demand or to strengthen tradable sectors. In many countries, rapid economic growth and increased inflows of EU funds weakened the political appetite to undertake necessary structural reforms (public finances, pensions, labour markets). Complacency and short-termism took hold.

One important factor that increased vulnerability of EU-10 was that trade and financial openness, and the resulting high dependence on foreign capital inflows, was not accompanied by a sufficient increase of macroeconomic credibility. Having been fully integrated financially with the rest of the EU, the EU-10 countries have not gained the same level of credibility enjoyed by the euro area member countries. Financial markets have not regarded them as belonging to the same risk category, which was reflected by investment ratings generally lower by several notches than for the euro area countries, even though the EU-10 'fundamentals' (debt and deficit levels, growth rates) were generally much stronger than those of many euro area members. As a result, not only were bond yields in EU-10 systematically higher by 100–300 basis points than in the euro area, but also financial investors were much more sensitive to any change in market sentiment. While it was not a serious problem in 'good times' (although it increased the cost of public and private borrowing), it became a serious shortcoming when the crisis started.

This asymmetry was largely ignored not only in the countries concerned but also at the EU level. While insisting that EU-10 remove all restrictions on international capital movements and open up fully to the risks of global financial flows, the EU did not provide any sort of substitute protection mechanism that would, at least partly, shield EU-10 from the unwanted implications of sudden capital reversals. The result was that while being fully integrated with global financial markets, as were the euro area countries, the EU-10 countries have been much more exposed to the vagaries of international capital flows. The unwanted consequences of this status inequality have been felt painfully during the crisis.

4 THE CRISIS

The crisis of 2008–09 immediately revealed all the vulnerabilities of EU-10 (see, for example, EBRD, 2009; World Bank, 2009). The falls in output in this group of countries were generally larger (with the notable exception of Poland) than in the 'old' member states. In a sense, this was surprising, because EU-10 economies were generally believed to be flexible enough, and their banking systems were not contaminated by the 'toxic assets', such as US mortgage-backed securities. The cumulative fall in output between the third quarter of 2008 and the second quarter of 2009 was between 13 per cent and 18 per cent for the Baltic states, and between 5 per cent and 10 per cent for the rest (except for Poland), well exceeding the cumulative fall for the euro area (4.4 per cent) and for the EU-27 as a whole (4.5 per cent). Countries with floating exchange rates have also experienced substantial depreciations, sometimes raising concerns about the overall sustainability of their currencies (for example, between August 2008 and February 2009 the Romanian leu weakened nominally by 28 per cent, the Hungarian forint by 35 per cent, and the Polish złoty by 46 per cent). A sudden stop of capital inflows (partly because of liquidity problems of mother banks, and partly because of an increase in overall uncertainty) blocked new credit emission and entailed a massive adjustment on the demand side.

The crisis has also demonstrated that EU-10 are not a homogeneous lot. While the countries concerned share a common history, have followed similar paths of integration with the EU and embraced a broadly similar growth model, they differ in many important respects, such as the size of their economies and domestic markets, economic structure and – crucially – economic policies pursued (Berglof et al., 2009). The Baltic countries (Estonia, Latvia and Lithuania) and the Balkan countries (Bulgaria and Romania) have clearly been less stable economically, more vulnerable and, consequently, suffered deeper recessions. In the Baltic–Balkan countries real appreciation under fixed exchange rates (except Romania) led to large current account deficits, while massive financial inflows produced unsustainable credit expansion. The Central European countries (the Czech Republic, Hungary, Poland, Slovakia and Slovenia) have been economically more stable, thanks to much smaller imbalances. Export sectors were more robust, current account deficits limited, exchange rate regimes flexible (except for Slovenia and Slovakia after their accession to the euro zone in 2007 and 2009, respectively), and domestic credit growth more moderate. As a result, the necessary demand adjustments were smaller and the output recession in the Central European group was milder during the crisis.

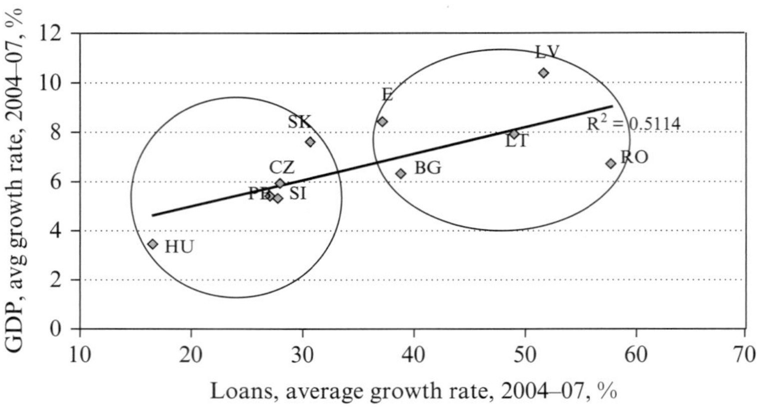

Source: Author's calculations based on Eurostat data.

Figure 5.5 Average growth of credit to economy in 2004–07 and average GDP growth in 2004–07, per cent

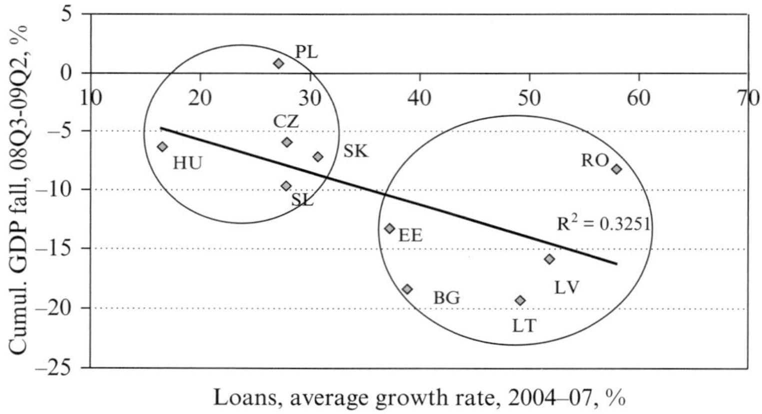

Source: Author's calculations based on Eurostat data.

Figure 5.6 Average growth of credit to economy in 2004–07 and cumulative GDP fall in recession, per cent

Figures 5.5 to 5.8 show the pre-crisis and during-the-crisis behaviour of output as a function of the pre-crisis rate of domestic credit expansion (Figures 5.5 and 5.6) and as a function of the pre-crisis current account deficit (Figures 5.7 and 5.8) in the two groups of countries. As can clearly

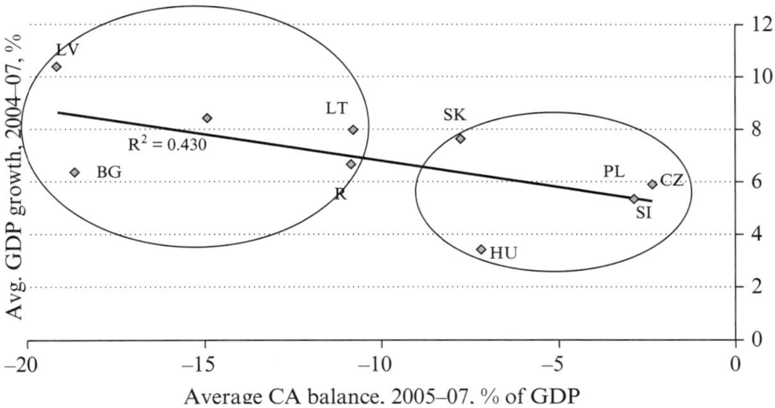

Source: Author's calculations based on Eurostat data.

Figure 5.7 Average current account deficit in 2005–07 and average GDP growth in 2004–07, per cent

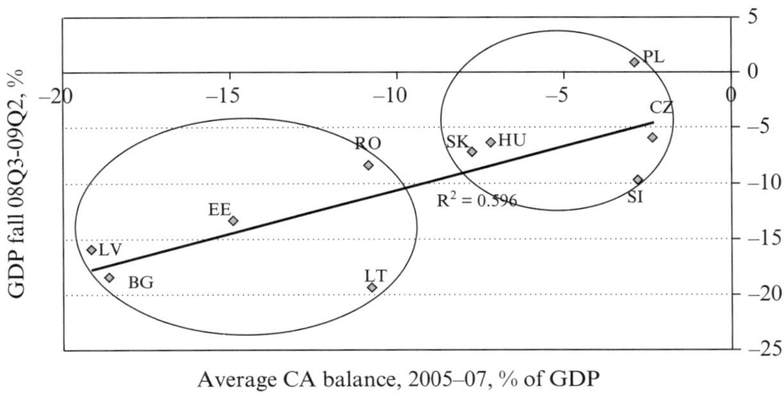

Source: Author's calculations based on Eurostat data.

Figure 5.8 Average current account deficit in 2005–07 and cumulative GDP fall in recession, per cent

be seen, the build-up of large domestic and external imbalances in the pre-crisis period contributed to the deeper recession during the crisis (see, for example, Ghosh, 2009).

The dependence of pre-crisis GDP growth rates on the speed of domestic credit expansion and on the size of current account deficit is statistically significant (coefficients R (square) are 0.43 and 0.51, respectively) and valid for all EU-10 countries (although with variations between the countries concerned and generally much higher for Baltic and Balkan countries). Clearly, a return to the same level of dependence in the post-crisis period is not possible. Therefore, growth patterns in EU-10 will have to be modified if growth is to be sustainable.

One important factor that impacted the depth of the recession has been the foreign exchange regime. Countries with fixed exchange rates (Bulgaria, Estonia and Lithuania followed a currency board regime; Latvia had a fixed exchange rate) suffered much larger declines in output and have more difficulties in returning to a stable growth path (see below). This is not surprising. The initial imbalances simply grew much larger in those countries, partly because no adjustment was possible in the pre-crisis period and partly because under fixed exchange rates currency risk was limited (or plainly non-existent), which attracted more capital inflows and allowed for faster expansion of domestic credit. Moreover, when the crisis hit, the 'fixers' could not (actually, did not want to) devalue, which of course entailed larger losses in output.

5 WILL RAPID GROWTH RESUME QUICKLY IN EU-10?

The answer is 'no', and for various reasons. First, because the integration growth model, which was so successful in achieving high growth dynamics in 2000–07, cannot be continued in an unchanged form, and some important changes are needed to reduce its dependence on unstable capital flows and to scale down the imbalances involved. Second, in the medium term growth in EU-10 will be hampered by new barriers and constraints on the domestic side, as well as by a less favourable external environment.

That growth is not returning to the pre-crisis elevated levels can be seen from the most recent Eurostat statistics on GDP changes. Figure 5.9 plots data on GDP quarterly changes on a yearly basis to the third quarter of 2010. It can be seen that recovery in EU-10 is sluggish and nowhere near the pre-crisis highs. While the growth rates between 2006 and mid-2008 have been broadly between 5 per cent and 10 per cent annually, the growth rates in 2010 do not exceed 5 per cent, and in the most affected countries are still in the negative territory. Of particular concern is the visible slowdown of the recovery in the second and third quarters of 2010, which may signal that investors and consumers anticipate some barriers to growth that are likely to emerge soon.

On the domestic economy side, things will not return to 'normal' any time

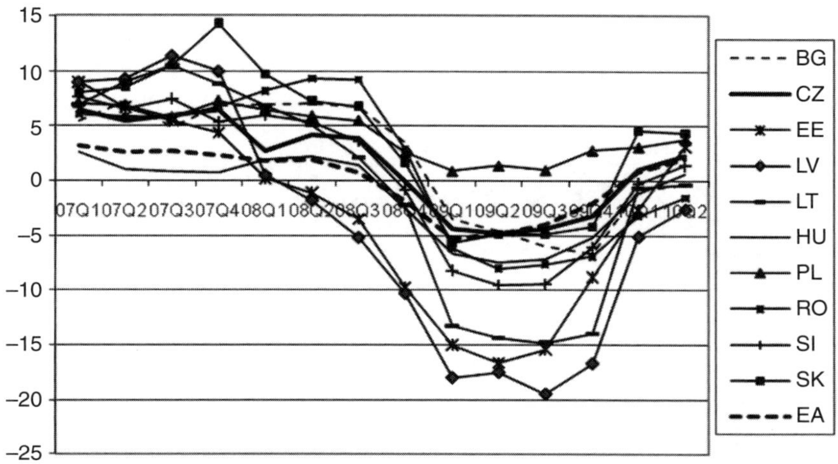

Source: Author's calculations based on Eurostat data.

Figure 5.9 Quarterly GDP changes in EU-10 and the euro area, per cent

soon. First, risk perception will stay higher because of budgetary problems, gloomy export perspectives and overall increased uncertainty in EU-10. This means capital inflows from abroad will be lower and domestic credit conditions tighter. The actual credit squeeze will be even more restrictive because of the limited availability of foreign currency denominated loans, so popular in the pre-crisis period (in countries like Hungary, Latvia and Romania the share of foreign currency loans to households exceeded 75 per cent of total loans). Banks are likely to gradually reduce the share of those loans to the private sector, both because of increased awareness of the exchange rate risk involved and because of the continuously high cost of swap transactions necessary to refinance foreign exchange loans.

It will take time to restore the international competitiveness of most of the EU-10 economies, especially those with fixed exchange rates. With no devaluation option at hand, and with low inflation levels likely to continue in the euro area, the countries concerned will have to go through a prolonged period of wage deflation combined with large-scale reallocation of resources from housing and financial services into productive uses. Unless exports gather momentum, imports will have to be cut, as financing the gaps in the balance of payments will be much more difficult. Any additional external financing will come at a higher cost and in limited amounts.

The balance of payments constraint will be somewhat less rigid for countries with flexible exchange rate regimes. When the crisis hit in 2008, their

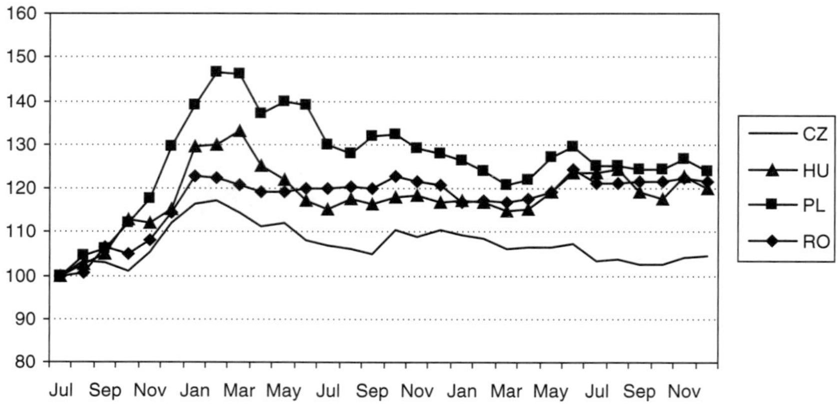

Source: Author's calculations based on Eurostat data.

Figure 5.10 Nominal exchange rates in the Czech Republic, Hungary, Poland and Romania, July 2008 = 100 (units of national currencies per euro, end of period)

currencies depreciated substantially in nominal and real terms, cushioning the impact on the real sector. Although the currencies have strengthened since then, in none of these countries have the exchange rates returned to the pre-crisis levels. At the end of 2010 the euro nominal exchange rates in Hungary, Poland and Romania were still 20–25 per cent higher than in July 2008 (see Figure 5.10). This may be a factor supporting export growth and helping efforts to reduce current account deficits.

Deleveraging of the private sector (enterprises and households alike) will be a drag on growth for the years to come. Servicing and repaying excessive debts, under stagnant or diminishing incomes, will necessarily put a brake on growth of domestic demand in most EU-10 countries. A similar impact will come from the burst speculative bubbles in the housing and real estate sectors. Unfortunately, the government sector will be unable to step in and compensate for the loss of private demand. As in most of the countries where budget deficits are already high and governments struggle to bring growing public debts under control, there is only very limited scope for Keynesian-type fiscal stimulation.

Also the external environment will be less favourable for resuming rapid growth in EU-10. First, potential growth rates will drop in EU-15 and in the euro area, mainly because of the serious drop in investment in 2008–10. Ample spare production capacity and a low confidence level will reduce the pace of investment in new technologies. This will translate into slower demand growth in EU-15, with negative implications for exports from EU-10. Second, many banks in the EU still struggle with inherited bad loans and are still short of capital. Their balance sheets are still loaded with some risky assets, such as government bonds of the most indebted euro area countries. Moreover, the new wave of banking and financial market regulations (chiefly Basel III and the measures proposed by the Financial Stability Board) will put additional pressure on banks to consolidate their capital base and follow more prudent credit policies. This will inevitably reduce the resources available for EU-10 countries – capital inflows are starting to recover but it will take a long time before they can exceed the pre-crisis levels.

The on-going crisis in the euro area, and especially the debt problems of peripheral euro countries, will reduce the scope for fiscal stimulation. Faced with massive deficits inside and the need to provide funding for rescue programmes for ailing member countries, and under the rigours of excessive deficit procedures (imposed on 24 out of the 27 EU member countries, as of end-December 2010), the EU countries will be very reluctant to spend more. Moreover, fiscal austerity applied across Europe will most probably translate into less resources in the EU budget, which is an important source of funds for investment in EU-10.

Slower exports to EU markets can only be partly compensated by higher export sales to third countries. Global competition is likely to get stronger – not only because emerging economies, such as China, India, Brazil and Turkey, will try to retain, or increase, their export market shares, but also because one can expect a shift towards more exports from developed countries, especially from the US and the EU. In general, in the context of rebalancing the global economy, more countries will have to sell more on exports, and EU-10 will have to adjust to this new situation.

In this new environment, economic growth in the EU-10 countries will remain moderate. However, the performances of individual countries will differ, depending on their starting positions, inherited rigidities and policy responses. Given the extent of current imbalances and the existing scope for adjustment (flexible versus fixed exchange rates, fiscal positions), economic growth will most probably return sooner and be more sustainable in the group of Central European countries, whereas it will remain weaker in the group of Baltic and Balkan countries.

6 CONCLUSIONS: WILL THE IGM BE SUSTAINED?

No doubt, the integration growth model has been a source of much success for EU-10 countries. Trade, financial and institutional integration with the EU allowed them to grow fast in 2000–07, reducing income gaps between them and the more affluent EU-15 countries. This remarkable economic performance came to a sudden stop during the crisis of 2008–09, with most EU-10 countries suffering big losses of output. As argued above, some important reasons for this unexpectedly severe recession have been linked to the IGM model embraced by EU-10, and in particular its financial integration part.

Economic theory tells us that international integration is growth-enhancing because its static and dynamic effects bring about gains from trade, specialization, large-scale production and increased investment. Integration also allows for faster technological progress and removes constraints on capital. All these advantages have been tested positively in Central and Eastern Europe. There is no reason to give up these benefits, stop integration or even go into reverse. Integration should continue in EU-10.

But lessons from the recent crisis show that there are some risks involved in the IGM and that smart policies are needed to neutralize them. The first priority is to reduce the potential for imbalances and bubbles that can be unwanted side effects of free capital movements. The measures that can discourage excessive and volatile financial flows include more flexible exchange rate regimes (to increase currency risk and fend off speculative flows) or fixed rates with exit options, better financial regulation and, perhaps, well-designed fiscal measures that make financial transactions costly (for example, Tobin-tax-type charges). As these instruments, however, can still be insufficient to change trends in times of 'irrational exuberance' or irrational panic, imposing strict prudential micro-regulation, raising lending standards and strengthening banking supervision may be key to preventing credit-financed bubbles.

On the structural front, the need to control unit labour costs and maintain international competitiveness throughout the business cycle requires changes in the labour markets to make them more flexible. Fiscal reforms aimed at reducing inefficient social transfers and gradually shifting the burden of taxation towards indirect taxes should be combined with structural reforms of pension systems, including extending retirement age and promoting larger and longer active participation in labour markets. One possibility to restore international competitiveness without necessarily going through a painful wage deflation is to reduce red tape and other bureaucratic and administrative costs for companies. In general, more resources should be spent on education, innovation and entrepreneurship, in order to make EU-10 economies more flexible, dynamic and competitive.

A separate issue concerns the adoption of the euro by EU-10 countries (apart from Slovenia, Slovakia and Estonia, which are already lucky members of the euro area). Given the recent series of sovereign and banking crises in the euro zone, the idea of joining the club may raise some doubts, and may even be regarded as bizarre by sceptics. Yet there should be no change of plans. There is a vast body of economic literature that consistently demonstrates that euro adoption would be beneficial for EU-10 (see, for example, IMF, 2005; Darvas and Szapáry, 2008).[2] These theoretical conclusions are also confirmed by the experience of Slovenia and Slovakia (it is too early to say anything on Estonia). Apart from the standard benefits suggested by the early version of the optimum currency area theory, such as the elimination of transaction costs, joining the euro zone would reduce the cost of capital, eliminate risk of currency crises and strengthen the political position of EU-10 within the EU.

Also, contrary to what some pessimists (especially from across the Atlantic) say, there is no danger that the euro zone will fall apart. First, such a break-up does not make economic sense, because it would not solve any of the underlying problems of the 'weak' countries (they would go bankrupt the very moment the break-up was announced, and not only would they still have to make tough reforms to restore competitiveness and credibility but also they would lose access to multilateral assistance under the European Financial Stabilization Facility, which they are covered by now), and it would impose costs on the 'strong' countries (relative currency appreciation, heavy bank losses and reduced exports). Second, the political costs of the break-up would be enormous, as it would practically mean a failure of the European integration project, with all the ramifications. Plainly, the euro zone will not fall apart because it is in nobody's interest.

Of course, it does not mean that the euro zone is in good shape. It badly needs reforms to strengthen fiscal discipline, increase policy coordination and improve competitiveness. These reforms have already started and will be continued, because the alternative is much worse. And an improved and more stable euro area remains an even more attractive destination for Central and Eastern European countries.

NOTES

1. For the period 1992–98 Rosati (2004) found that for a sample of EU-14 and eight prospective member countries the speed of convergence was actually negative ($\lambda = 0.0012$).
2. For instance, in a recent study by the Polish central bank on the economic effects of Poland's accession to the euro zone the net benefits are estimated at 0.7 per cent of GDP annually over a ten-year period (NBP, 2009).

REFERENCES

Barro, Robert J. (1991), 'Economic growth in a cross section of countries', *Quarterly Journal of Economics*, **106** (May), 407–43.

Barro, Robert J. and Xavier Sala-i-Martin (1991), 'Convergence across states and regions', *Brookings Papers on Economic Activity*, No. 1, 107–82.

Barro, Robert J. and Xavier Sala-i-Martin (1991), 'Convergence', *Journal of Political Economy*, **100** (April), 223–51.

Berglof, Erik et al. (2009), 'Understanding the crisis in emerging Europe', EBRD Working Paper, No. 109.

Darvas, Zsolt (2010), 'Central-Eastern Europe and the Economic Crisis: Policy Lessons Learnt', Bruegel, Brussels, January, mimeo.

Darvas, Zsolt and Gyorgy Szapáry (2008), 'Euro area enlargement and euro adoption strategies', European Economy Economic Papers, no. 304, European Commission, Brussels.

EBRD (2009), *Transition Report 2009*, London: European Bank of Reconstruction and Development.

European Commission (2009), *Five Years of an Enlarged EU: Economic Achievements and Challenges*, Directorate for Economic and Financial Affairs, Brussels.

Ghosh, Swati (2009), 'Credit crunch or weak demand for credit?', *EU10 Regular Economic Report*, Washington, DC: World Bank, October, 37–44.

IMF (2005), *Adopting the Euro in Central Europe*, Washington, DC: International Monetary Fund.

IMF (2010), *World Economic Outlook*, Washington, DC: International Monetary Fund, April.

Mankiw, G., D. Romer and D. Weil (1992), 'A contribution to the empirics of economic growth', *The Quarterly Journal of Economics*, **107** (2), 407–37.

NBP (2009), Report on full membership of Poland in the third stage of the Economic and Monetary Union, National Bank of Poland, Warsaw (in Polish).

Rosati, Dariusz K. (2004), 'The impact of EU enlargement on economic disparities in central and eastern Europe', in Michael A. Landesmann and Dariusz K. Rosati (eds), *Shaping the New Europe: Economic Policy Challenges of European Union Enlargement*, Palgrave Macmillan, pp. 275–314.

WIIW–Bruegel (2010), *Whither Growth in Central and Eastern Europe? Policy Lessons for an Integrated Europe*, by Torbjoern Becker et al., Bruegel Blueprint Series, vol. XI, Brussels, November.

World Bank (2009), *EU10 Regular Economic Report*, Washington, DC: World Bank, October.

6. Neoclassicism in the Balkans

Vladimir Gligorov

European post-socialist transition has followed the neoclassical strategy of growth, the key proposition of which is that an open economy supports the catching-up process of growth by attracting foreign investments. From a policy point of view, this strategy comes in two versions: one strategy calls for implementing whatever policies support foreign investments, and the other strategy postulates that policies need to make sure that FDI-driven growth is sustainable. In practice, policy-makers have typically applied a broad mixture rather than one or the other strategy for growth. In a stylized form, however, it can be argued that the Balkan economies and policy makers have neglected the sustainability aspect of the neoclassical model of growth. As a consequence, disequilibria have developed that have made them extremely vulnerable to external shocks, as became evident in the crisis that emerged in 2008. That has put the whole process of transition to the test.

In this chapter, the neoclassical model of transition will be briefly described; the development of macroeconomic disequilibria will be reviewed; the effects of the crisis will be set out; and the risks and the prospects that the region is facing will be commented on.

GROWTH AND SUSTAINABILITY

If a small, developing economy liberalizes, that is, adopts a free trade regime and allows cross-border financing (with or without certain restrictions), foreign investments should flow into that economy, driven by a higher marginal productivity of capital in that economy. Whether this happens in practice clearly depends on the underlying risks of investments, which depend on stability factors, on transaction costs of various types, and on sustainability; that is, on the long-term policy mix. The latter comes into play because FDI inflows lead to trade and current account deficits, which increase foreign debt, so the rate of growth of foreign debt needs to be sustainable. That in turn means that current account deficits need to diminish over time and perhaps turn into surpluses if foreign debt is to be kept at a sustainable level. So, sustainability requires FDI to support the growth of tradable goods in order to support exports, hopefully faster than imports over time.

In addition to the need to deal with the sustainability of external balances, the neoclassical model of growth entails two other macroeconomic problems. The first stems from the fact that foreign investments are driven by the productivity differential, that is, are labour-saving. As a consequence, employment may decline after liberalizations and may stay depressed over an extended period of time. That is because the labour market will develop significant structural disequilibria both on the supply and on the demand side. In the short run, there may also be cyclical unemployment, but most of the labour market problems will be structural and will be connected with the changing structure of demand for skills and with the need to improve the supply of human capital. Thus, this model of growth may lead to prolonged periods of low employment and high unemployment and inactivity.

Finally, FDI-led growth will require institutional changes and changes in the fiscal system. The latter will present the fiscal authorities with a dilemma because they need to decrease the tax burden and reduce public expenditures at the same time as depressed labour markets put significant pressure on social security and other public spending which is needed to support the structural changes in the product and labour markets. That may create the need to run fiscal deficits to cover restructuring costs, which may yet again raise the issue of sustainability, in this case of fiscal balances.

Clearly, problems of sustainability of emerging macroeconomic imbalances will be alleviated if growth is strong enough. Basically, if the rate of growth is higher than the rate at which either foreign debt or public debt is increasing, the sustainability of external and fiscal balances will not present a problem. In addition, fast growth is the surest way to get employment to increase and once it also leads to higher wages that will support the social pressure stemming from unemployment and inactivity. Obviously, these are interrelated issues and fast growth may not be sustainable due either to the problems in allocation of investments or to distributional effects. In the case of the former, growth may be due to bubbles that may look sustainable for some time though they can eventually prove not to be so.

Hence the crucial role economic policies and structural adjustments play in this context. The process of FDI-led growth needs to be supported by the development of relative prices that will support the sustainability of transitory imbalances. Given the nature of the strategy for growth, the exchange rate has to carry the bulk of the sustainable development of the macroeconomic disequilibria. That also means that monetary policy will have to be quite active because of the need to safeguard price stability. Finally, given structural problems in the labour market, appropriate income policies need to be adopted even if labour market institutions are conducive to market setting of wages. Given significant needs for social security and wage pressures that are going to arise in a fast-growing economy, fiscal considerations together with the need to support competitiveness will necessitate active income policies.

Thus, the neoclassical model of growth can support fast growth and catching-up in incomes and development if the right policies are in place to ensure the sustainability of the emerging macroeconomic imbalances. Trade and current deficits need to be reduced over time, employment needs to start to increase, and fiscal policies need to be both sustainable and supportive of growing efficiency. In order to achieve that, relative prices – the exchange rate, the interest rate, the wage rate, and the tax rate – need to adjust so as to support the equilibrating processes. In other words, growth needs to be sustainable in the short as well as the long run.

THE BALKAN TRANSITION

In the first decade or so of the new millennium, the Balkan countries have gone through a transition process that is very much in the spirit of the neoclassical model of growth. Obviously, the process started much earlier in Greece, but some of the characteristics of the disequilibria are the same in the whole region. Reliance on foreign investment has led to the existence of higher and often widening current account deficits and growing foreign debt volumes. Also, structural deficiencies in the labour markets have been strongly exposed, with employment levels falling in a number of countries and unemployment remaining often at very high levels for an extended period of time. Finally, social security systems have remained under constant pressure, with fiscal systems feeling the strain and the tax burden tending to be higher than is conducive to a good business climate.

What can account for this apparent failure of neoclassicism in the Balkans? Looking at growth performance, the record in the first decade of this century has certainly been encouraging. The average growth rate has been above 5 per cent per year in most Balkan countries. At those growth rates, most of the disequilibria looked sustainable. In practically all countries, the public-debt-to-GDP ratio was either stable or declining and similar tendencies could be observed in the case of foreign debt. Even in the cases where the foreign-debt-to-GDP ratio has been increasing, most of the debt was private and was not seen as unsustainable at the prevailing growth rates.

In tune with that, risks to investment in the region were declining before the crisis. That was helped by the fact that most of the banks are under foreign ownership and are considered to be sound and beyond negative influences by the local authorities. Hardly any studies found worrisome bubbles developing in the real estate markets, though there was clearly inflation in the tourist areas (for example, in Croatia, Montenegro and Greece). Other indicators of macroeconomic instability were not worrisome, either, with inflation either subdued or declining throughout the region and the central banks accumulating high volumes of foreign reserves that enabled them to support the prevailing exchange rate regimes and rates.

Finally, despite wide and widening external imbalances, export growth rates were accelerating, so the prevailing opinion was that it was just a matter of time until these gaps would start to be closed and that the external balances would prove to be sustainable. Here, comparisons were made with the other transition economies mainly in Central Europe and the Baltic in order to suggest that neoclassical transition was proving to be successful and sustainable in the Balkans too. Indeed, there were some indications of change toward more sustainable growth in a number of respects.

However, the recovery of the tradable sector was relatively slow or stalling in a number of cases, especially in the case of industrial production. In some countries, budding re-industrialization processes seemed to be taking hold. Coastal countries, however, displayed an increased reliance on tourism and on the development of the services sector. That was coupled with fast-rising prices of real estate, often supported by credits or direct investments from abroad. There is no doubt that incomes were improving, and there were also some modest, and in some cases not so modest, improvements in the labour markets. All that created the sense of rather favourable economic development throughout the region.

The persistent problem was external disequilibrium. In the run-up to the crisis, the current account deficits of the region as a whole increased rather sharply. Not only did the gap between investments and savings tend to increase, but the share of savings in GDP continued to fall during most of the high-growth period. So, borrowing from abroad and surging consumption growth contributed to the development of sustainable external imbalances. With that, the region became vulnerable to a sharp setback.

Why did the neoclassical model of growth fail to self-correct the widening current account and trade deficits? The main reason is misallocation of foreign investments given inadequate policies. Usually, weak fiscal policies are blamed for the development of unsustainable external and internal balances. However, public debts were either stable or falling in terms of GDP.

The key imbalance was that of the balance of payments, which would put the primary blame on inappropriate exchange rate or monetary policies.

Indeed, most of the Balkans are on fixed exchange rates or rely on monetary policies that are supported by managed exchange rates. Fixed exchange rates or managed floats are typically adopted with a view to stabilizing prices and often also with a view to supporting exports. This is often associated with the mercantilist model of growth, as practised by the newly industrialized Asian states. The strategy is to fix the exchange rate at a low level and to adjust domestic consumption to that level. If the exchange rate is initially undervalued, and if private and public consumption is constrained to levels that do not cause the exchange rate to become ultimately overvalued, that policy mix will support exports as well as investment in the tradable sectors. Moreover, it will support higher domestic savings and often fuel capital outflows. The crucial aspect of this development strategy is the ability to control domestic consumption, private as well as public – which means that the authorities need to have the ability to formulate and implement appropriate income policies. If income policies fail or cannot be implemented, the fixed exchange rate will stoke inflation or fuel imports as a consequence of growing incomes and the loss of competitiveness. In any case, trade deficits will be the rule and without either exchange rate correction or some way to control wages and incomes in general, the tradable sectors will lose out to investment in services and in non-tradable sectors. Over time, that may prove to be unsustainable, and the neoclassical virtuous circle of FDI and growth through industrialization will fail.

Now, adopting appropriate income policies has typically been hard in the Balkans for many different reasons. Thus, wages are kept down or indeed kept up through relatively high unemployment. And, in fact, in the cases in which employment has improved, that was mostly due to the growth of the services sector. In transition, liberalization and privatization have led to mediocre improvement in industrial production and slow if any improvement in agricultural production, but with fast expansion of services. In some cases, these were exportable services, for example, in tourism. In other cases, transport and construction saw significant improvements due to both public and private investments out of relatively cheap credit lines. Credit accessibility improved markedly as these economies opened up and the banking and financing sectors were improving fast, mostly supported by banks and investment firms from the EU. So, in some sense, everything conspired toward the generation of unsustainable external balances. But, the root causes were the fixed and overvalued exchange rates as well as wage and income inflation, which looked conducive to private credit expansion.

SUDDEN DECLINE

The development being unsustainable, some kind of an adjustment was going to happen anyway. A number of countries looked set for various types of adjustments – among those certain candidates were Greece, Serbia, Croatia, Montenegro and Bulgaria. The developments in Romania looked more sustainable and the same is true for small Balkan countries like Macedonia and Albania, while Bosnia and Herzegovina and Kosovo are special cases because of their high reliance on aids, grants and other transfers, especially remittances.

The crisis, however, did not come in the form of the typical sudden stop of foreign finance, but in the form of a decline of foreign finances due to the global banking crisis. The effects were pretty similar, nonetheless. More open economies and those that export more saw a sharper decline in GDP. Similarly, countries relying on real estate investments and with overgrown construction sectors saw a significant decline in domestic demand and also experienced prolonged liquidity problems. Some countries could mitigate these effects by increasing public spending either because they were able to secure IMF financial support or because they had accumulated some money while they had run fiscal surpluses (Montenegro and Bulgaria). The headline crisis was that of Greece, but that is a case that does not fit into a story about transition economies. Also, Greece is a country with significant fiscal problems, which is otherwise not characteristic of the Balkan region.

The decline of GDP was quite strong, on average, with some countries doing better than others. Serbia, a rather closed economy, did better than Croatia, Romania, Bulgaria or Montenegro, and the small economies like those of Albania, Kosovo and Macedonia also did better. However, none of these countries is showing significant improvement at the time of writing even though they are in the third year of the crisis.

In fact, there are still strong effects in the labour markets. The decline in employment has been quite strong throughout the region and is continuing. Having in mind that employment was low even at the best of times before the crisis, this is certainly going to be the main problem in the years to come. These adverse developments in the labour markets are combined with declines in real wages and incomes, which also have adverse effects on public revenues and thus on public spending. The region as a whole will have to watch carefully how it spends public money because revenues will continue to recover only slowly and borrowing possibilities are limited. Thus, there is no doubt that the crisis will have an enduring effect on the whole region and will certainly be felt for the next few years.

NEW BEGINNING

The crisis has truncated the neoclassical model of growth. To the inherited disequilibria it has added problems with public finances. So, the region has ended up with high foreign debts, low employment and high unemployment, underdeveloped production structures and ill-conceived fiscal systems. On top of that, growth prospects are conditional on structural reforms that will take time to conceive and implement. Thus, growth prospects are rather dim in the medium run and growth is needed for the solution of all inherited disequilibria but also for social and political sustainability.

What can policy and structural reforms aim at? One basic constraint is the preference for fixed exchange rates, or rather for foreign money, in the region. That ties the hands of monetary policy and of income policy too, at least to a large extent. Fiscal policy will not have very much space either, as public obligations will be large in the context of low employment and significant social challenges.

That leaves structural policies. The aim will have to be to increase the competitiveness of the Balkan economies in order to resume foreign investments, but this time around into tradable goods rather than into services. With that, consumption will have to take the back seat, with savings being necessary to service the accumulated debts. Far-reaching institutional reforms will also be needed in practically all markets, but also in social and public services. All that will take time and significant sacrifices.

Therefore, the medium-term prospects are more for reforms than for growth, in the optimistic scenario.

CONCLUSION

The neoclassical model of growth is successful only if supported by appropriate policies. Those policies must not start from the premise that it suffices to implement FDI-friendly reforms. They have to be such as to improve efficiency in allocation and to support the sustainable distribution of income. The authorities in the Balkans failed to design appropriate policies and transformed temporary disequilibria into unsustainable ones. Those mistakes have been exposed in the crisis and will have to be corrected in the post-crisis period. That will have to be done while growth is slow or stagnant and under political and social uncertainty. However, given long-term commitments and preferences, there is no workable alternative to the FDI-led growth model, hopefully with a strengthened policy mix and more solid institutional frameworks.

7. Unlocking growth potential in the Balkans

Boštjan Jazbec and Albulenë Kastrati

1 INTRODUCTION

The financial crisis that started in 2008 and whose impact on world financial markets is still unresolved also affected the less developed economies in the CESEE region, formerly known as transition economies. The crisis response of those countries, which have more or less successfully joined the European Union or are intensively involved in the accession process, depended primarily on the extent of the reforms they have been able to introduce during the last 20 years of the transition process. Following in the footsteps of the most successful erstwhile transition economies in terms of their economic development and proximity to euro adoption, today's less developed economies of the EU region are able to leap over the early stages of the transition process as observed almost 20 years ago.

However, it seems that the factors which largely determined the success of the transition process at the time have diminished in importance as it has become obvious that macroeconomic stabilization and financial liberalization are not enough to maintain higher growth rates.

The South-Eastern European (SEE) countries[1] have been late-comers to the process of EU accession. The region was plagued by political and war conflicts, which slowed down the pace of structural reform. Being geographically landlocked was also unconducive to faster economic revival and higher economic growth. Lying next to Greece, the most problematic of the EU member countries in terms of economic stability and financial fragility in recent years, the only EU country in the region is Bulgaria, which joined the EU in 2007. The aim of this chapter is to examine the growth potential of the SEE countries also with regard to the effects of the financial crisis in the EU. We will show that the financial crisis in the EU and particularly in Greece did affect the financial systems in the SEE countries. However, slow economic revival and lower than expected growth rates in the region cannot be attributed to the macroeconomic developments and fragile financial systems in those countries alone. On the contrary, as will be shown, most countries have been successful in implementing reforms and enhancing the macroeconomic framework and have opened up their financial sectors, thus paving the way for economic revival. Yet the crucial point is that these economies lack the institutional setting which would support the investment demand needed to generate economic growth.

The second section of this chapter discusses the transition process of the last 20 years. In hindsight it is obvious that macroeconomic stabilization and financial liberalization are not sufficient determinants of economic growth in less developed economies. The third section presents the macroeconomic developments in the region, pointing out the similarities despite different monetary and exchange rate regimes implemented to stabilize the economies. Financial sector development in the region is presented in Section 4. It is shown that the financial crisis did affect the SEE countries although they retain sufficient access to financial sources to support economic growth. Potential sources of economic catch-up of the region are presented in Section 5. Section 6 concludes.

2 WHAT HAVE WE LEARNED IN THE LAST 20 YEARS OF TRANSITION?

At the outset of transition, experience with the process of economic transformation was limited. Western expertise and experience with structural reforms in developing countries served as guidance, with the Latin American countries providing the blueprint for the design of macroeconomic stabilization programmes, despite the substantial differences in starting points.

What economists knew *a priori* about restructuring and transformation was that inflation stabilization was necessary for growth to resume. However, the striking problem at the beginning of transition was the enormous fall in output, ranging from 30 to 50 per cent, accompanied by high inflation. Although transition encompasses a wide horizon of institutional and political changes to stabilize and restructure ill-designed economies, the key economic concerns at the time were inflation and output performance. Apart from the fact that the countries shared the challenge of transforming their economies from a centrally planned to a market-oriented framework, the common objective of curbing inflation rates which were mitigating the success of all other reforms transformed the rather mixed setting of structural changes across the region into a uniform process of transition.

While the Central and Eastern European countries adopted different exchange rate regimes, they all experienced real appreciation as well as large capital inflows in a relatively short time span. Although capital inflows were not a key concern at the beginning of transition, the relevance of the presence of foreign capital in transition economies was driven home just after the first shock of political and economic transformation had gradually vanished. Those economies that were fast to restructure and privatize state and social entities were among the first to enjoy the positive effects of fresh foreign capital. While the surge in foreign capital inflows was associated with new problems in terms of pressure on external competitiveness, it seems that negative effects of capital inflows were mainly offset by early growth recovery. In contrast, those economies that were slow in adopting reform measures and attracted foreign capital mainly by selling government debt to finance increasing budget deficits suffered from balance of payments and financial crises.

The choice of fundamental macroeconomic policy in the design of stabilization programmes was even more pronounced in those transition economies that seriously tackled fiscal reform. Fiscal policy in transition economies not only entails control over the budget deficit but also involves the issue of reducing the role of the government. However, tackling inflationary pressure was not the only area of action needed to bring transition economies on to the right track of transformation and restructuring toward market economies. The need for action was widely recognized in six areas (Fisher et al., 1996):

- macroeconomic stabilization
- price liberalization
- trade liberalization and current account convertibility
- enterprise reform (especially privatization)
- creation of a safety net
- development of the institutional and legal framework for a market economy, including the creation of a market-based financial system.

There were a few authors[2] in the 1990s who emphasized the importance of building the institutional arrangements, since there is a danger of informal institutionalization that fills the systemic vacuum. One cannot separate one area of action from the others. However, sound macroeconomic stabilization was necessary for the success of all other reforms, since it forced some state enterprises to contract as a consequence of implementing hard budget constraints and pushed people into a new private sector. In some respects, economic reforms in transition economies can be compared to reforms introduced in Latin American countries

(Bruno, 1992). However, the extent of institutional reforms required in transition economies was much greater and demanded the change of fundamental characteristics of the institutional legacy of the centrally planned regime.

3 MACROECONOMIC DEVELOPMENTS IN SOUTH-EASTERN EUROPE

The SEE economies are struggling to reach their growth potential after 20 years of political turmoil and uncertain economic developments. Being geographically far from the EU common market, if one does not take into account the relatively modest trade flows with Greece and Bulgaria, the SEE countries are mostly left on their own in the process of reinvigorating their economic development. As will be shown, the essence of the problem lies in the lack of appropriate development of the market institutions, which restricts the effects of the initial positive macroeconomic stabilization and microeconomic liberalization.

All six SEE countries are small and open economies which operate different monetary and exchange rate policies in order to achieve macroeconomic stabilization. Bulgaria opted for a currency board while Macedonia introduced tightly managed floating similar to the regime Slovenia introduced in the 1990s. Albania and Serbia undertake inflation targeting, which implicitly presupposes free floating of the domestic currency; nonetheless, one can observe fairly systematic central bank intervention in both countries. The tiniest of the SEE countries, Montenegro and Kosovo, chose to unilaterally adopt the euro, given the unfavourable conditions prevailing at the time they declared independence.

Despite these differences, all SEE countries have experienced similar price developments in the last ten years, with Serbia reporting the highest degree of volatility but all other SEE countries being able to curb their inflation rates below 5 per cent, which makes their macroeconomic environment relatively stable. It is rather instructive to say that despite differences in monetary regimes all countries in the region have faced very similar if not almost identical price developments in their economies. Confusion about the most appropriate monetary or exchange rate regime which was so legitimate 20 years ago has lost its strength during the course of transition in other more developed transition economies. It seems that the choice of the monetary or exchange rate regime was rather arbitrary and prone to particular circumstances at the time of the transition process. Trade openness and a substantial presence of foreign-owned institutions in the financial sector limit the operational scope of different monetary or exchange rate regimes and reduces them to following the autonomous flows of trade and capital into and out of these economies. Corner solutions in the design of the monetary or exchange rate policies are therefore adjusted to the point that one can hardly differentiate among different regimes, proving the tendency of the central bank to be rather discretionary in the conduct of monetary policy (Calvo and Reinhart, 2002).

The cases of Montenegro and Kosovo strengthen that argument even further by deliberately surrendering the option of quasi-independent monetary policy and opting to unilaterally adopt the euro. Without their own monetary policies, price developments in those countries are closely mimicking inflation rates in the neighbouring countries.

As will be shown below, some SEE countries have even experienced deflation in the last few years. Price developments in the SEE countries largely mirror the prices of imports. Most countries import food, final products and machinery, which are all sectors that were greatly hit by the recent financial crisis. The structure of imports in SEE countries also corresponds to the general level of development and the prevailing predominance of the low-value-added sectors. Exports include mostly base materials and mineral products, with the exception of Serbia, where manufactured goods dominate, and Albania, which has specialized in exporting textiles. Relatively low-value-added exports and imports of high-value products also contribute substantially to chronic current account deficits. Although recent import price developments contributed to bringing down inflation rates in these economies, developments in the balance of payments are less favourable in the medium and long run. See Table 7.1 for the structure of imports and exports in the SEE countries.

To further strengthen the argument that SEE countries exhibit similar developments in real and financial sectors, a short presentation of each individual country follows.

3.1 Kosovo

Kosovo unilaterally adopted the euro as legal tender in 2002. Consequently, the Central Bank of the Republic of Kosovo (CBK) is not a member of the euro zone, does not conduct a monetary policy of its own and is not a lender of last resort.

Economic growth (Figure 7.1(b)) was mainly generated by higher private consumption and public investment, largely financed by banking sector loans, remittances, foreign assistance, and considerable increase of budget expenditures. With the adoption of the euro facilitating foreign trade, Kosovo achieved great progress in terms of keeping inflation close to euro area levels (Figure 7.1(a)). Being mainly an import-based

Table 7.1 The structure of exports and imports in selected countries (in per cent)

Kosovo	Macedonia	Albania	Bulgaria	Serbia	Montenegro
Mostly exports:	*Mostly exports:*	*Mostly exports:*	*Mostly exports:*	*Mostly exports:*	*Mostly exports:*
Base metal (50)	Iron & steel (26)	Textiles (35)	Non-ferrous metals (37)	Manufactured goods (33)	Aluminium (41)
Mineral products (15)	Clothing (20)	Minerals (30)	Clothing (36)	Food (16)	Iron and steel (13)
Vegetables (6)	Food and beverages (14)	Construction mat. & metals (19)	Energy resources (5)	Machinery (15)	Beverages, alcohol, vinegar (6)
Mostly imports:	*Mostly imports:*	*Mostly imports:*	*Mostly imports:*	*Mostly imports:*	*Mostly imports:*
Mineral products (17)	Machinery & transport equip. (24)	Machinery (20)	Machines & tools (43)	Machinery (25)	Machines & mech. equipment (12)
Machinery (14)	Mineral fuels (16)	Food & beverages (18)	Food (32)	Manufactured goods (20)	Mineral fuels (8)
Food & beverages (13)	Food (11)	Construction mat. & metals (15)	Textiles (27)	Mineral fuels (18)	Iron and steel products (5)

Sources: Central banks of the respective countries.

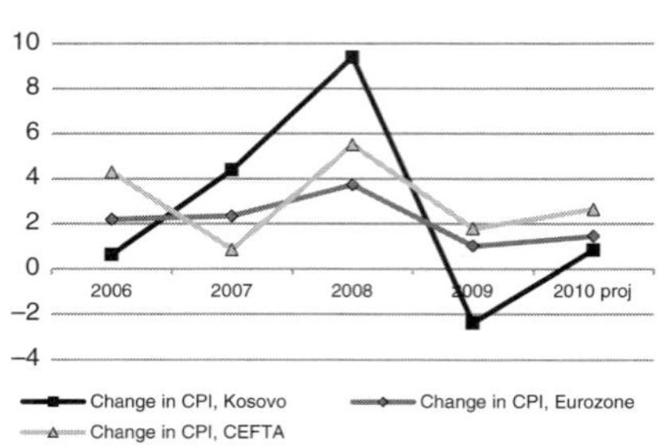

Source: WEO April 2010, IMF.

(*a*) *Inflation, average consumer prices*

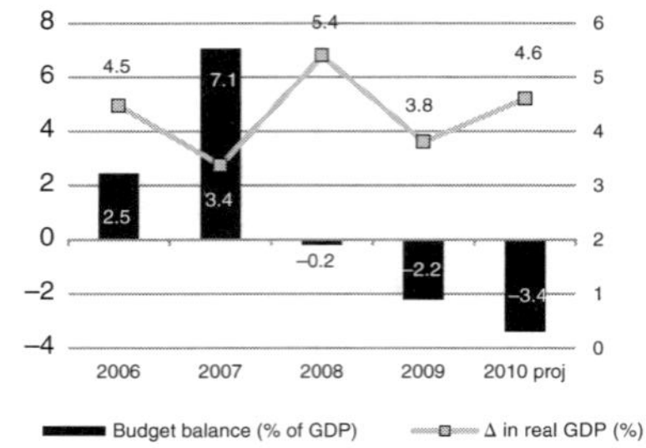

Source: WEO April 2010, IMF.

(*b*) *Real growth and budget balance*

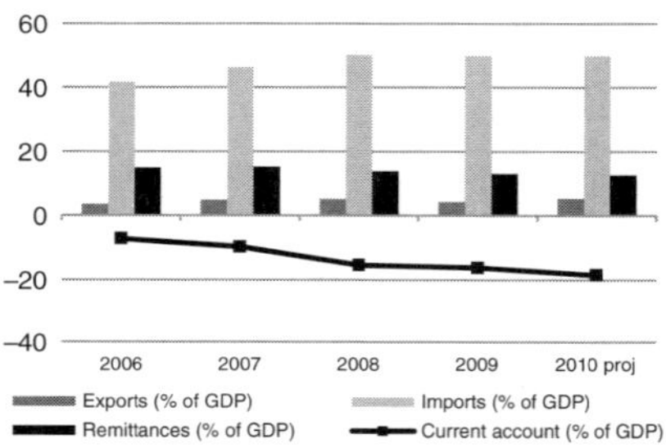

Source: CBK (2010).

(*c*) *Current account, in per cent of GDP*

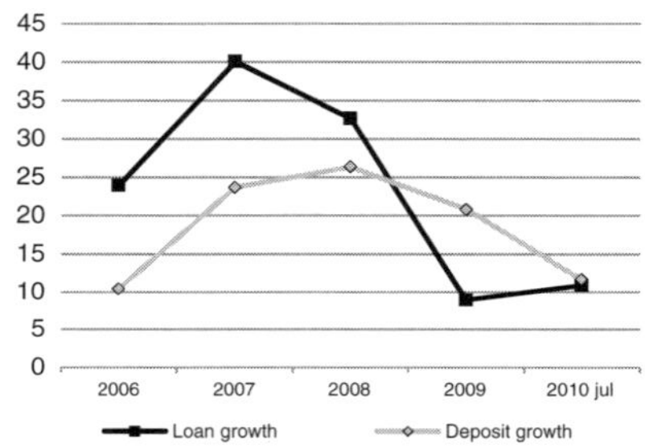

Source: CBK (2010).

(*d*) *Deposit and loan growth, in per cent*

Figure 7.1 Kosovo

economy, inflation in Kosovo closely reflects import price developments. The export base is low but with positive trends (Figure 7.1(c)). EU and Central European Free Trade Area (CEFTA) countries account for around 74 per cent of Kosovo's trade, with exports going primarily to Italy (around 30 per cent) and Germany (around 4 per cent), and imports coming primarily from Germany (around 13 per cent) and Greece (around 5 per cent). Remittances to Kosovo comprise around 14 per cent of GDP. Around 64 per cent of remittance inflows come from the euro area, mostly from Germany.

The financial sector of Kosovo is almost fully euroized (around 96 per cent of deposits and loans) (Figure 7.1(d)), therefore it is not exposed to exchange rate risk or the need to guarantee central bank liabilities. Hence, besides central bank's monitoring and risk assessment of the banking sector, most of the burden of safeguarding the financial stability falls on the fiscal authorities.

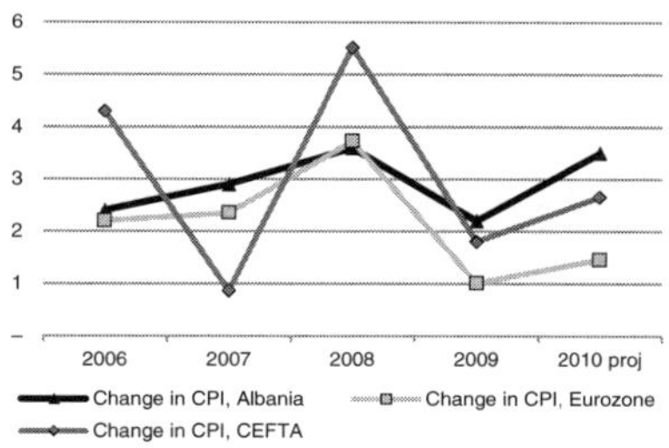

Source: WEO April 2010, IMF.

(*a*) *Inflation, average consumer prices*

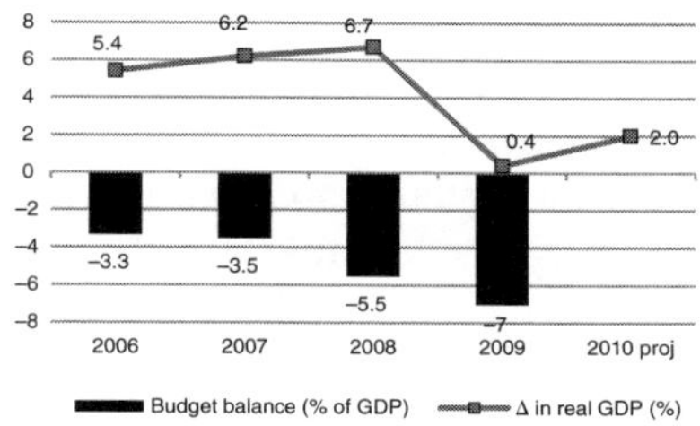

Source: WEO April 2010, IMF.

(*b*) *Real growth and budget balance*

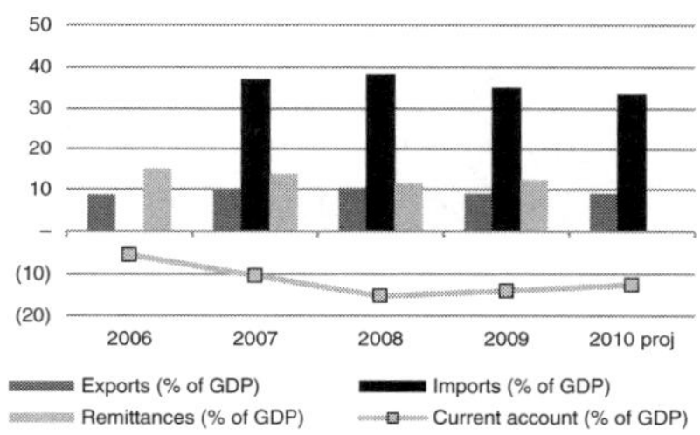

Sources: INSTAT and WEO April 2010, IMF.

(*c*) *Current account, in per cent of GDP*

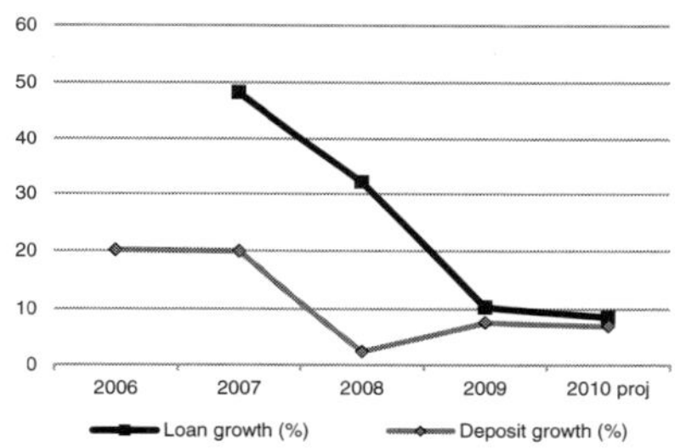

Sources: BoA (2010) and country report, IMF (2010).

(*d*) *Deposit and loan growth, in per cent*

Figure 7.2 Albania

3.2 Albania

Albania uses a flexible exchange rate regime combined with inflation targeting (Figure 7.2(a)), which has served in absorbing the external shocks of financial crisis and proved to be an asset in the current uncertain environment, while keeping real growth at positive levels (Figure 7.2(b)).

Euroization in Albania is mainly favoured by FDI inflows, trade, remittances and credit lines. Albania is one of the region's countries highly exposed to Greece and Italy through significant trade, remittances and financial sector. The main trading partners of Albania are EU countries (around 67 per cent), notably Greece and Italy. Recently, the decline in Greek and Italian demand negatively impacted the Albanian exports, as well as imports. However, trade in Albania is mainly import-based (Figure 7.2(c)). Moreover, given rising unemployment in Greece in and Italy, host to the largest share of the Albanian emigrants, Albania recorded a sharp decline in remittances during 2008 and 2009.

Another strong link between Albania and Greece is through the banking sector (Figure 7.2(d)).

Greek bank subsidiaries and branches account for one quarter of the banking system and have the lowest capital and liquidity buffers in the system. Greek banks in Albania have witnessed deposit withdrawals during recent economic problems in Greece. However, following the IMF and EU programme with Greece, Greek banks in Albania are recording deposit growth.

3.3 Macedonia

The Macedonian denar is quasi-pegged to the euro with a view to keeping prices stable (Figure 7.3(a)). Conservative measures adopted by the National Bank of the Republic of Macedonia (NBRM) in 2009 (raising banks' liquidity and reserve requirements) put Macedonia among the countries with the tightest monetary policy in the region. The rationale for the measures,

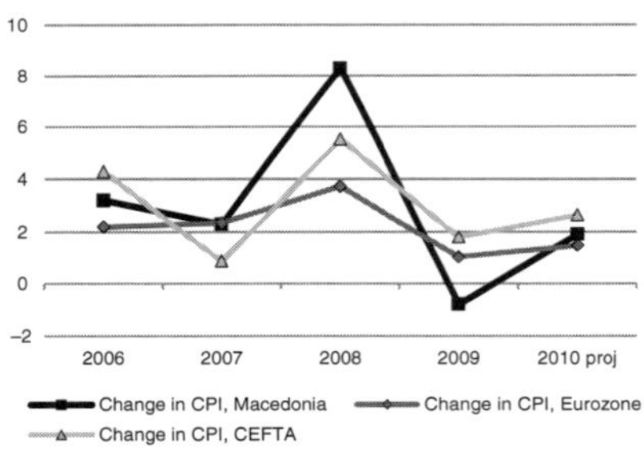

Source: WEO April 2010, IMF.

(*a*) *Inflation, average consumer prices*

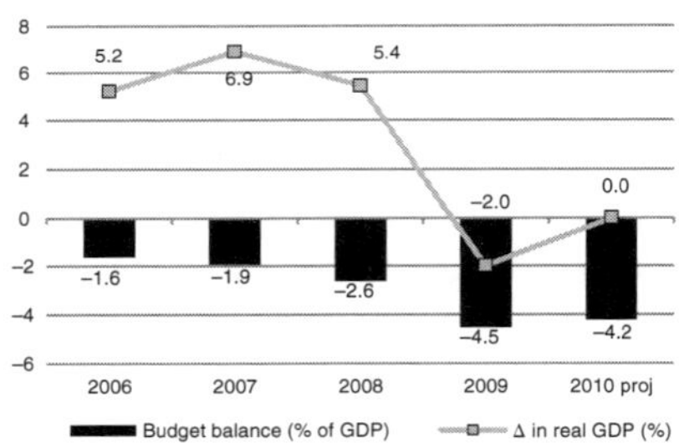

Source: WEO April 2010, IMF.

(*b*) *Real growth and budget balance, in per cent*

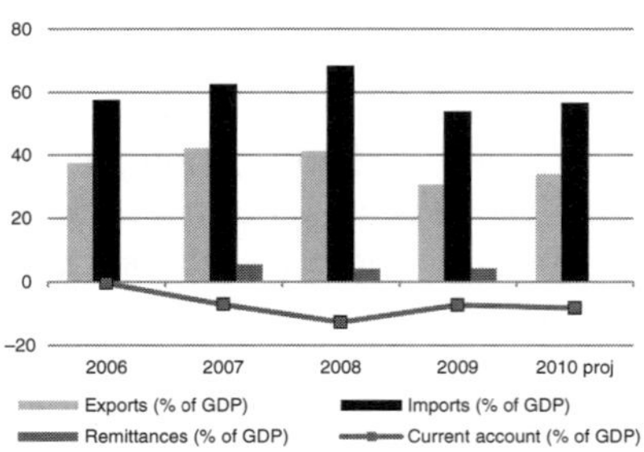

Source: NBRM (2010) and WEO April 2010, IMF.

(*c*) *Current account, in per cent of GDP*

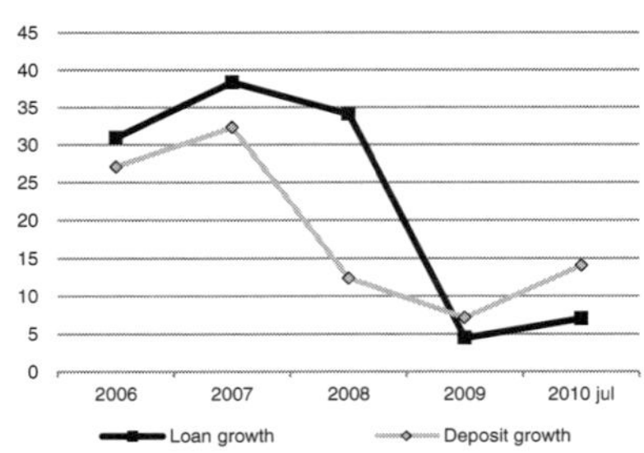

Source: NBRM (2010).

(*d*) *Deposit and loan growth, in per cent*

Figure 7.3 Macedonia

whose impact on growth was relatively small (Figure 7.3(b)), was to maintain the peg with the euro and secure continued access to foreign reserves.

Macedonia experiences a relatively high current account deficit (Figure 7.3(c)). Recently, potential adverse effects may have come from trade with EU countries, since Germany, Greece, Bulgaria and Italy alone account for 45 per cent of exports and 31 per cent of imports. In the first part of 2010 Macedonia recorded a fall in exports to Greece, while imports were increasing. The recent Greek crisis may impact Macedonia's trade deficit with Greece adversely. In addition, Macedonia has the smallest share of remittances to GDP (around 5 per cent), however with a stable trend.

Macedonia has a small banking system with limited reliance on external financing or investments (Figure 7.3(d)). One of Macedonia's biggest banks (Stopanska Banka) is a subsidiary of a Greek bank. Nevertheless, the Macedonian banking sector appears to be stable and well positioned. Around 30 per cent of the banking sector is euroized. In 2009 and in early 2010 the government issued bonds with high interest rates and low risk, which created more favourable conditions for banks to invest in bonds rather than crediting the economy.

3.4 Bulgaria

Bulgaria has a euro currency board, with a final goal of euro area membership. The currency board has served Bulgaria in anchoring inflation and keeping fiscal deficit at moderate levels.

High inflation during 2006–08 (Figure 7.4(a)) was a consequence of high capital inflows, which raised credit growth and boosted domestic demand. This was mirrored by higher prices and wages (though the lowest in the EU). Nevertheless, when the global crisis erupted, Bulgaria was hit by a sharp decline in capital inflows, impacting domestic demand and budget revenues. Consequently, Bulgaria's economy fell 5 per cent after years of economic growth (Figure 7.4(b)). Bulgaria felt the effects of the crisis mainly in 2009, with the recession of trading partners hitting exports and declining domestic demand decelerating imports (Figure 7.4(c)).

Bulgaria trades mostly with EU countries (62 per cent of exports and 53 per cent of imports), above all with Greece (Bulgaria exports around 9 per cent from and imports around 5 per cent from Greece).

In 2009, loans issued in euro comprised 57.9 per cent, while deposits were 58.7 per cent of the total (Figure 7.4(d)). Greek banks' assets account for around 16 per cent of total banking sector assets. However, existing capital buffers are pretty sufficient to absorb counter-cyclical increases in non-performing loans (NPLs) and provisions. Moreover, the Bulgarian National Bank (BNB) has advised banks to fully retain their profits in Bulgaria.

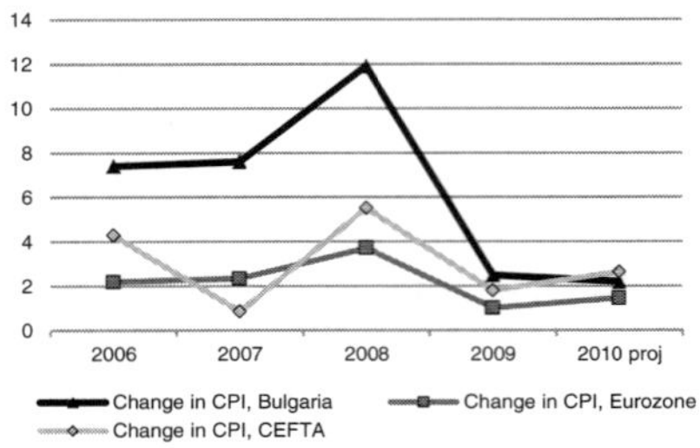

Source: WEO April 2010, IMF.

(*a*) *Inflation, average consumer prices*

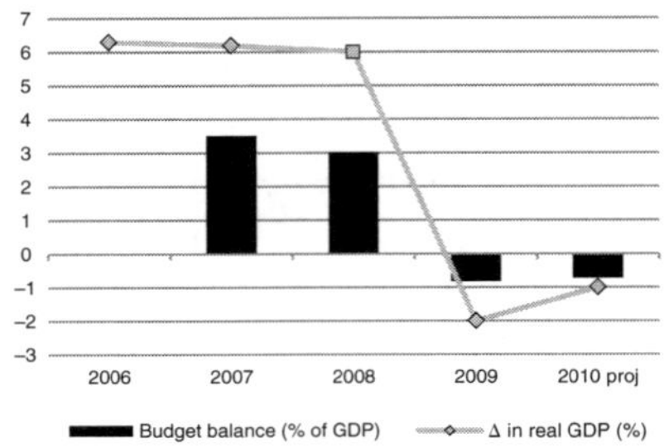

Source: WEO April 2010, IMF.

(*b*) *Real growth and budget balance, in per cent*

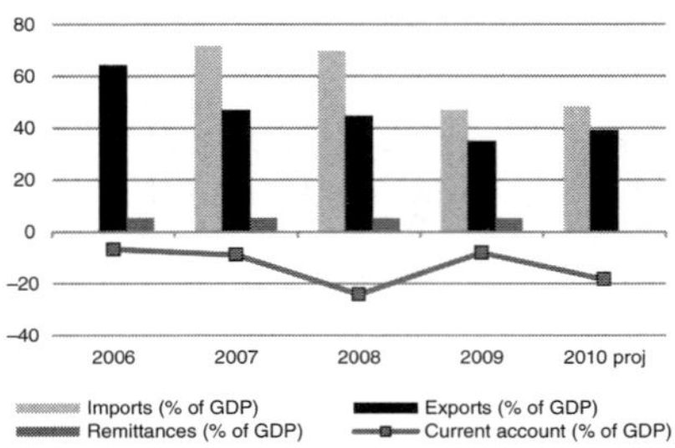

Sources: BNB (2010); WEO April 2010, IMF and World Bank.

(*c*) *Current account, in per cent of GDP*

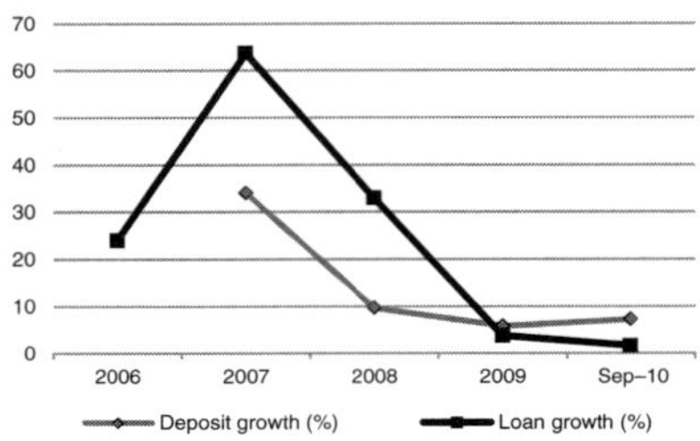

Source: BNB (2010).

(*d*) *Deposit and loan growth, in per cent*

Figure 7.4 Bulgaria

3.5 Serbia

Serbia pursues managed floating, which enables the National Bank of the Republic of Serbia (NBRS) to intervene to keep prices stable and foreign reserves at adequate levels. Serbia uses interest rates as its main monetary policy tool.

Average inflation during the 2000s was the highest in the region (Figure 7.5(a)). Generally, Serbia has inherited the lack of trust in the dinar following hyperinflation in the 1990s, which tended to cause high inflationary expectations. Moreover, establishing dinar confidence was hardly possible considering the expansionary monetary policies of the NBRS aimed at financing high current account deficits (Figure 7.5(c)) and buying foreign reserves. Entering the IMF financial programme in 2009 helped Serbia stabilize inflation considerably.

Serbia trades with EU countries (54 per cent of exports and 55 per cent of imports) rather than CEFTA countries (31 per cent of exports and 8 per

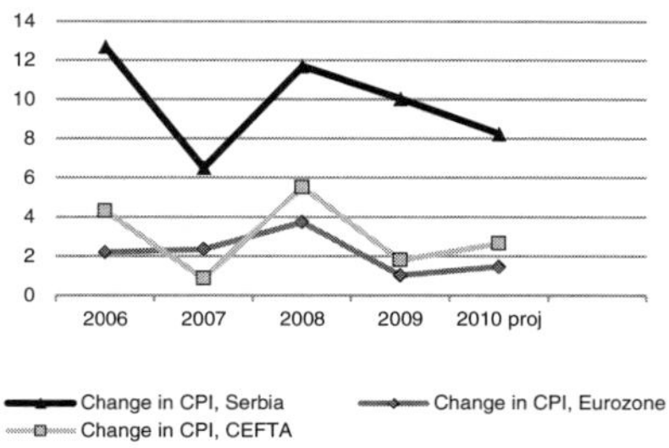

Source: WEO April 2010, IMF.

(*a*) *Inflation, average consumer prices*

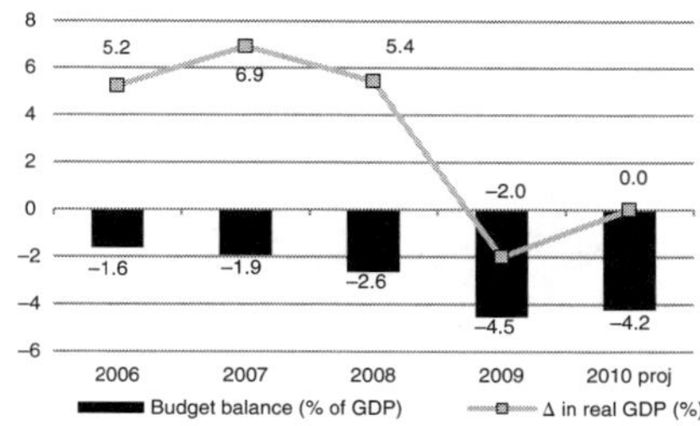

Source: WEO April 2010, IMF.

(*b*) *Real growth and budget balance, in per cent*

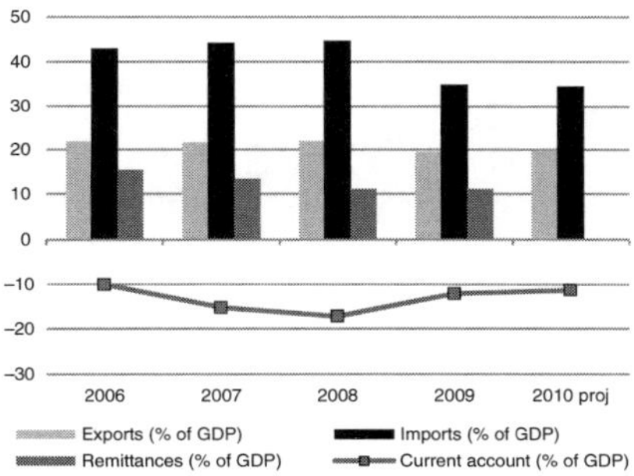

Source: WEO April 2010, IMF.

(*c*) *Current account, in per cent of GDP*

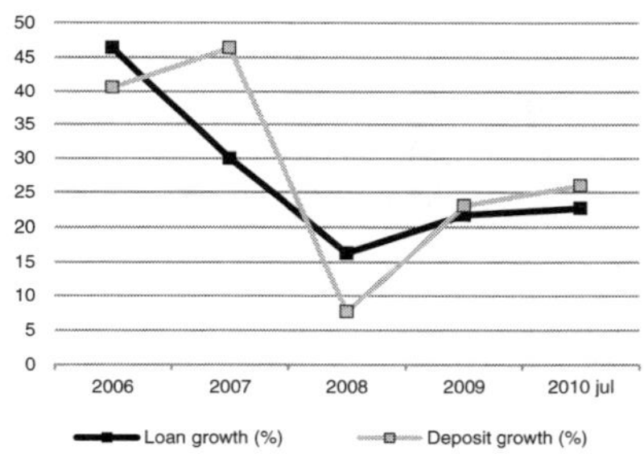

Source: NBS (2010).

(*d*) *Deposit and loan growth, in per cent*

Figure 7.5 Serbia

cent of imports). Like Bulgaria, Serbia enjoyed fast economic growth prior to the global crisis (Figure 7.5(b)). In late 2008 the global crisis hit Serbia through a trade contraction, a sudden decline of the capital inflows and household deposit withdrawals. Serbia's banking sector (Figure 7.5(d)) is highly euroized. There are four Greek bank subsidiaries in Serbia, which account for around 14 per cent of total assets.

3.6 Montenegro

Montenegro used to use the Deutschmark (DM) heavily in the private sector and the banking sector. Now the euro serves as legal tender. While mirroring regional patterns, average inflation during the 2000s appears to exceed regional levels up to 2009 (Figure 7.6(a)). Like other countries in the region, Montenegro is heavily linked with EU countries through trade and capital flows. More than 50 per cent of Montenegro's exports go into

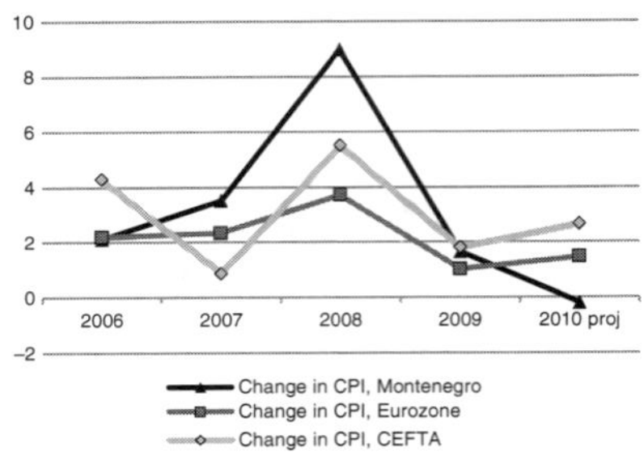

Source: WEO April 2010, IMF.

(a) Inflation, average consumer prices

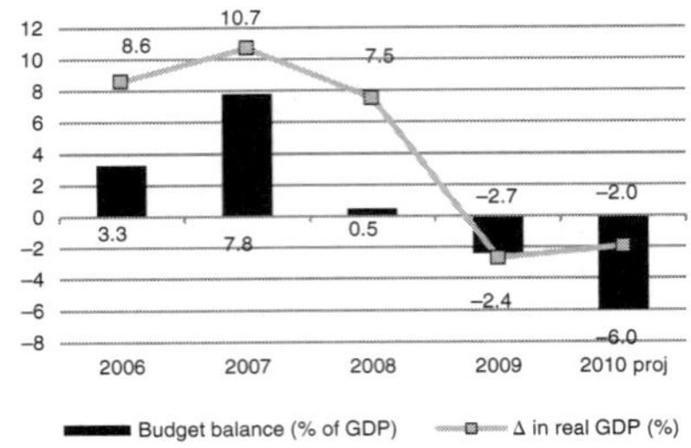

Source: WEO April 2010, IMF.

(b) Real growth and budget balance, in per cent

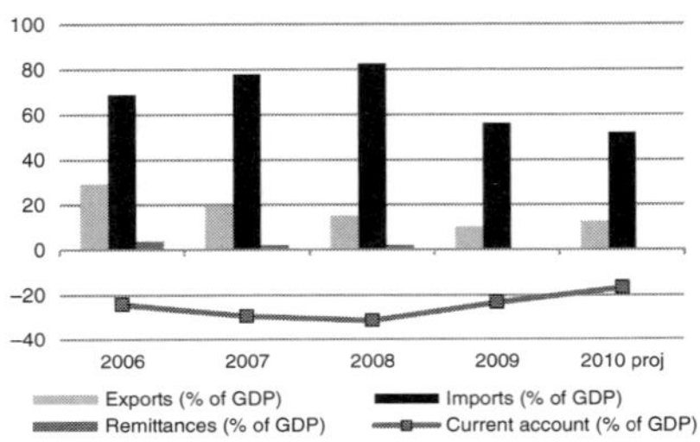

Source: Country Report, IMF (2010).

(c) Current account, in per cent of GDP

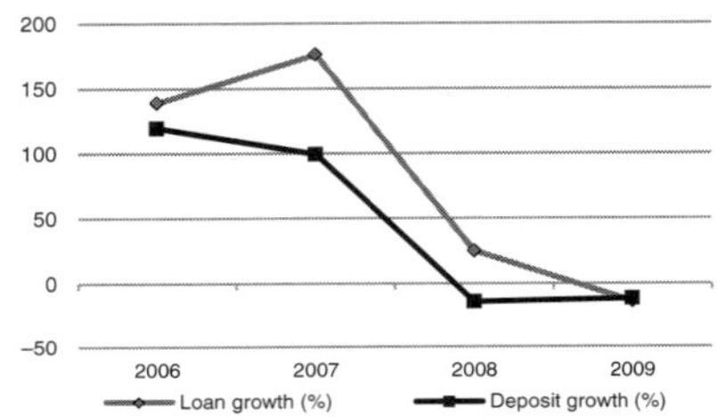

Source: Country Report, IMF (2010).

(d) Deposit and loan growth, in per cent

Figure 7.6 Montenegro

the EU, primarily to Greece (22 per cent) and Italy (12 per cent), while 41 per cent of imports come from Serbia and 31 per cent from EU countries. The decline in exports during 2010 also reflected adverse external circumstances (including recent developments in Greece, one of Montenegro's biggest importers).

Large FDI inflows boosted by independence contributed to strong economic growth (Figure 7.6(b)), and the growth levels of credit to the domestic sector reached very high levels soon after independence. Yet the financial crisis hit the economy severely. The current account deficit (Figure 7.6(c)) and private sector debt rose, while loan quality deteriorated and banks suffered deposit withdrawals (Figure 7.6(d)), pushing the economy into negative growth territory. While euroization was useful in anchoring expectations, Montenegro lacked the tools to control massive credit growth or FDI inflows. Moreover, expansionary monetary policy in the euro area clashed with the macroeconomic problems of Montenegro, and fiscal policies, as the only tool left to control money supply and banking sector, were already loose. Therefore, considering the impact of the shocks, Montenegro's economy weakened more than other countries in the region.

4 DEVELOPMENTS IN THE FINANCIAL SECTOR

Despite different monetary and exchange rate regimes across the region, developments in the financial sectors have been similar. The financial crisis which originated in the USA and later spread to the EU did not affect the countries in the region directly. The main avenues of contagion were declining sources of financing given diminishing foreign direct investments and dwindling remittances. Consequently, loan growth decreased substantially, which decelerated domestic demand and lowered economic growth. Interest rates remained at relatively high levels averaging around 14 per cent for loans and around 5 per cent for deposits.

The economic growth decline in the SEE countries has been associated with the rise of unemployment and the considerable decline of international trade and capital inflows. Starting from low levels of economic development, the declines in economic growth are likely to be greater in the SEE countries than in the advanced economies where the crisis actually originated. By 2010, real economic activity was expected to revive slowly in the advanced economies, while economic recovery in the SEE countries is still uncertain and at most gradual. In the financial sector, contagion from the world financial crisis has been limited because the traditional banking models prevail in the area, with literally no exposure to toxic assets. Nonetheless, loan growth in all SEE countries has decreased as banks started to cut loans by introducing new lending policies, thus increasing their lending rates, partly as a reaction to rising non-performing loans (Kosovo, Albania and Montenegro), while others (Serbia and Macedonia) raised lending rates to protect their currencies from substantial depreciation. Although higher lending rates contributed to a slowdown of domestic demand, it will be claimed later that higher interest rates have not been a dominating factor in determining developments in aggregate demand in these countries.

While all SEE countries aspire to enter the EU, they are already linked to the EU through the ownership of their banking sectors, as shown in Table 7.2. There are only two EU countries in the region: Bulgaria and Greece, which is also the country that is for the time being the most problematic in terms of its macroeconomic stability. Greek banks are present in four of the SEE countries: Albania, Macedonia, Serbia and Bulgaria, which might be a point of concern in terms of financial stability in these economies.

Table 7.2 The structure of ownership of the banking sector (in per cent)

Description	Kosovo	Macedonia	Albania	Bulgaria	Serbia	Montenegro
Foreign ownership	91.5	93.1	93.6	83.9	75.3	84.5
Domestic ownership	8.5	6.9	6.4	16.1	24.7	15.5

Sources: EBRD *Transition Report 2009* and central banks of the respective countries.

One obvious consequence of the financial crisis was an increase in deposit interest rates, confirming the hypothesis that banks aggressively started to look for sources from domestic households. The effect of financial and economic turmoil in Greece was most pronounced in Bulgaria, where the presence of Greek banks is the highest in the region. Contrary to other countries in the region, lending interest rates also increased in Bulgaria jointly with a significant increase in deposit interest rates. This development was not observed in other SEE countries, where only deposit interest rates were raised to strengthen domestic sources of financing. Because of larger domestic sources of financing together with restrictive lending policies due to economic uncertainties, the banking sectors in the SEE countries turned out to be net capital exporters. This is primarily true for Kosovo and Albania, where banks have been experiencing excess liquidity problems in recent years. That might come as a surprise as these are also the least developed countries in the region. Hence the conclusion that it is not necessarily the development of the financial sector which affects the growth potential in these countries, and that one should look at other factors determining SEE growth.

The SEE countries have been affected by the global crisis, not through financial contagion but through lower demand in most EU trading partners and declining global commodity prices. The financial markets in SEE countries have suffered indirectly through the decline of FDI, remittances, and bank lending to the private sector. Therefore, the decline of economic growth is likely to be greater in the SEE countries than in the advanced economies where the crisis really originated. However, one should not overlook other factors determining the growth revival in the SEE countries, as explained below.

5 GROWTH POTENTIALS IN THE SEE COUNTRIES

As has been shown, the SEE countries have established macroeconomic stability and pursued financial market liberalization as suggested by early reformers in Central and Eastern European countries. They all chose the monetary and exchange rate regimes which appeared to be most suitable. They all opened up their financial sectors to foreigners with the intention of raising integration with financial markets and primarily because those sectors hardly existed before. Most countries started to export to EU markets extensively, although the structure of their exports still reflects a relatively low level of economic development. As argued before, the export structure of these economies contributed substantially to less preferable economic development in recent years, as raw material prices helped to bring down inflation rates in the SEE countries but negatively affected current accounts.

Also, dependency on EU export demand negatively affected growth dynamics in the region. Table 7.3 presents intra-regional trade flows which are relatively weak and request further explanation. Namely, although landlocked, the countries in the region trade among themselves relatively little. With similar export structures, they do not regard their trade patterns as complements but rather compete with each other on primarily EU markets. Regional cooperation is further restricted by pending political problems which prevent these economies from fully exploiting their growth potentials.

However, it is the lack of institutional development in the region that one may blame for the lack of stronger economic growth revival. Although one could argue that the SEE countries have been successful in establishing macroeconomic stability and proceeded prudently with microeconomic liberalization and privatization, it is important to acknowledge that they have not been successful in developing the institutional market economy framework necessary to support further economic growth, namely establishing property rights, protecting the rule of law, and especially creating the capacity to enforce existing contracts.

Table 7.4 presents the ranking of the SEE countries according to the World Bank *Doing Business 2010* study, which provides a tentative answer to the question why the SEE countries lack the power to grow faster. Namely, private investors in the region are not protected by the institutional settings in these countries, which prevents them from increasing their exposure to the region. This is even more important in times when world financial markets are more cautious about supporting new investments in relatively riskier environments.

For the time being, the SEE countries exhibit relative macroeconomic stability despite unfavourable developments in the current account and fiscal balances. Most of the financial sector is foreign owned, which helps to maintain the financial stability in those economies, notwithstanding the temporary effects of the financial crisis. However, the economic revival

Table 7.3 Matrix of the trade of the selected countries as a share of the total, unless otherwise indicated

	Kosovo	Macedonia	Albania	Bulgaria	Serbia	Montenegro
Kosovo	Exports=4.6% of GDP Imports=47.6% of GDP	Exp (KS→MKD)=9.6% Imp (KS→MKD)=15%	Exp (KS→Al)=13.5% Imp (KS→Mac)=3.2%	Exp (KS→Blg)=2% Imp (KS→Blg)=2%	Exp (KS→SR)=1.6% Imp (KS→SR)=11.1%	Exp (KS→MNG)=1.5% IMP (KS→MNG)=0.6%
Macedonia	Exp (MKD→KS)=7.5% Imp (MKD→KS)=0.2%	Exports=37.1% of GDP Imports=59.7% of GDP	Exp (MKD→AL)=2.9% Imp (MKD→AL)=0.5%	Exp (MKD→BLG)=8.8% Imp (MKD→BLG)=4.8%	Exp (MKD→SR)=18% Imp (MKD→SR)=7.8%	Exp. (MKD→MNG)=1% Imp (MKD→MNG)=0.03%
Albania	Exp (AL→KS)=6.7% Imp (AL→KS)=0.6%	Exp (AL→MKD)=2.8% Imp (KS→MKD)=2.0%	Exports=9.5% of GDP Imports=35.8% of GDP	Exp (AL→Blg)=0.7% Imp (AL→Blg)=1.4%	Exp (AL→SR)=3.0% Imp (KS→SR)=3.5%	Exp (AL→MNG)=3.4% Imp (KS→MNG)=03%
Bulgaria	Exp (BLG→KS)=n/a Imp (BLG→KS)=n/a	Exp (BLG→MKD)=2.1% Imp (BLG→MKD)=3.2%	Exp (BLG→AL)=0.5% Imp (BLG→AL)=0.05%	Exports=45.8% of GDP Imports=59.2% of GDP	Exp (BLG→SR)=2.1% Imp (BLG→SR)=3.2%	Exp (BLG→MNG)=2.1% Imp (BLG→MNG)=3.2%
Serbia	Exp (SR→KS)=3.5% Imp (SR→KS)=0.03%	Exp (SR→MKD)=4.6% Imp (SR→MKD)=2.2%	Exp (SR→AL)=1.4% Imp (SR→AL)=0.1%	Exp (SR→BLG)=2.5% Imp (SR→BLG)=2.1%	Exports=20.9% of GDP Imports=40.2% of GDP	Exp (SR→MNG)=4.6% Imp (SR→MNG)=2.2%
Montenegro	Exp (MNG→KS)=7.4% Imp (KS→KS)=0.1%	Exp (MNG→MKD)=0.5% Imp (KS→MKD)=1.4%	Exp (MNG→AL)=0.5% Imp (KS→AL)=1.4%	Exp (MNG→BLG)=2.8% Imp (KS→BLG)=0.0%	Exp (MNG→SR)=24.9% Imp (KS→SR)=41.2%	Exports=17.3% of GDP Imports 67.6% of GDP

Source: Created by the authors based on the IMF World Economic Outlook Database (April 2010), World Bank data, and central banks of respective countries.

Table 7.4 Doing business in the SEE countries, 2010

	Ease of doing business rank	Starting business	Con-struction permits	Empl-oying workers	Registering property	Getting credit	Protecting investors	Paying taxes	Trading across borders	Enforcing contracts	Closing business
Macedonia	5	2	14	9	14	11	3	1	9	19	22
Bulgaria	10	12	11	8	12	1	7	12	17	21	11
Montenegro	15	18	19	6	24	11	6	19	8	26	5
Albania	18	11	22	16	17	4	2	18	11	22	27
Serbia	19	15	23	14	21	1	15	17	13	23	21
Kosovo	22	27	24	4	16	11	27	6	19	27	2

Source: World Bank, *Doing Business 2010*.

of these economies is substantially dependent on the development of market institutions aimed at protecting the rule of law and the efficiency of market-based institutions and processes known in developed economies. Table 7.4 shows that the SEE countries rank lowest in terms of enforcing contracts among 27 countries in Eastern Europe and Central Asia. While most of them rank higher in other categories according to the World Bank study, it is the legal framework of doing business that seems to be detrimental to experiencing higher investment demand in the region at the time of writing.

6 CONCLUSIONS

According to the general understanding of the transition process, the SEE countries should exhibit higher economic growth rates. They have all brought down inflation rates and imposed macroeconomic stability. The financial sectors in the region operate according to international standards and practices. Moreover, the health of the financial sectors is better than in other Central and Eastern European countries and it does not seem to deteriorate despite financial sector difficulties in the parent banks. Although interest rates are high in the region, the reasons for the higher interest rates lie in the higher risks perceived by the financial sector. Those risks are mainly associated with weak legal protection of banks and other financial institutions in the enforcement of existing business contracts.

For those reasons one could conclude that the SEE countries seem to lack the institutional support to generate higher economic growth. Although most of those economies exhibit positive growth rates, mainly generated by public investment, it is important to acknowledge that higher growth rates can only be achieved by higher private and foreign direct investment. For that to happen, the SEE countries should develop credible institutional and legal frameworks, which would protect investors willing to invest in the region, both private domestic and international investors. What seemed to be taken for granted in other transition economies might take longer to develop in the SEE countries. However, one cannot expect those countries to benefit from relatively stable financial sectors unless the institutional and legal environment is developed.

NOTES

1. Albania, Macedonia, Bulgaria, Kosovo, Serbia and Montenegro.
2. Wyplosz (1999) and Kolodko (1999).

REFERENCES

Bank of Albania (2010), Financial Stability Report 2009, Tirana: BoA.

Bruno, Michael (1992), 'Stabilization and reform in Eastern Europe: a preliminary evaluation', *IMF Staff Papers*, **39** (4), 741–77.

Bulgarian National Bank, Monthly Bulletin; various issues from 2008 to 2010, Sofia: BNB.

Calvo, Guillermo and Carmen Reinhart (2002), 'Fear of floating', *The Quarterly Journal of Economics*, **117** (2), 379–408.

Central Bank of Montenegro, Quarterly Report, various issues from 2008 to 2010, Podgorica: CBM.

Central Bank of the Republic of Kosovo, Monthly Statistics Bulletin, various issues from 2008 to 2010, Prishtina: CBK.

European Bank for Reconstruction and Development, Transition Report, various issues from 2006 to 2009, London: EBRD.

Fisher, Stanley, Ratna Sahay and Carlos A. Vegh (1996), 'Stabilization and growth in transition economies: the early experience', *Journal of Economic Perspectives*, **10** (2), 45–66.

Institute of Statistics of Albania (2010), Balance of Payments, Tirana: INSTAT.

International Monetary Fund (2010), World Economic Outlook, Washington, DC: IMF.

International Monetary Fund (2010), IMF Country Report Albania, Washington, DC: IMF.

International Monetary Fund (2010), IMF Country Report Bulgaria, Washington, DC: IMF.

International Monetary Fund (2010), IMF Country Report Kosovo, Washington, DC: IMF.

International Monetary Fund (2010), IMF Country Report Macedonia, Washington, DC: IMF.

International Monetary Fund (2010), IMF Country Report Montenegro, Washington, DC: IMF.

International Monetary Fund (2010), IMF Country Report Serbia, Washington, DC: IMF.

Kolodko, Grzegorz W. (1999), 'Ten years of postsocialist transition: lessons for policy reforms', The World Bank Policy Research Working Paper, No. 2095, April.

National Bank of the Republic of Macedonia (2009), Financial Stability Report for the Republic of Macedonia in 2009, Skopje: NBRM.

National Bank of the Republic of Macedonia, Quarterly Report, various issues from 2006 to 2010, Skopje: NBRM.

National Bank of the Republic of Serbia, Statistical Bulletin, various issues from 2006 to 2010, Belgrade: NBRS.

World Bank (2010), *Doing Business 2010*, Washington, DC: The World Bank.

Wyplosz, Charles (1999), 'Ten years of transformation: macroeconomic lessons', paper presented at the World Bank's 11th Annual Bank Conference on Development Economics, Washington, DC, 28–30 April.

8. The catching-up experience of the Western Balkans – the cases of Serbia, FYR of Macedonia and Albania

Michael Loufir

Although they effectively started their transition to free-market economies almost at the same time – at the beginning of the new millennium – the Western Balkan countries (WBC, comprising Albania, Bosnia and Herzegovina, Croatia, the Former Yugoslav Republic (FYR) of Macedonia, Montenegro, and Serbia) and the Eastern Balkan countries (EBC, comprising Bulgaria and Romania) have experienced quite different catching-up processes.

Before the global crisis, WBC were slower to catch up to the EU-27 average than EBC. However, when the global crisis emerged, WBC proved to be better placed than EBC to withstand all but the severest of external shocks, thus catching up faster to the EU-27 average than EBC. The purpose of this chapter is to present the factors that explain the different catching-up speeds of WBC and EBC in the pre-crisis period and the post-crisis period. Evidence provided here is limited to those countries in which the National Bank of Greece Group has a strong presence, namely Albania, FYR of Macedonia and Serbia from among the WBC segment and the two EBC, Bulgaria and Romania.

1 BEFORE THE GLOBAL CRISIS: WBC SLOWER TO CATCH UP, FROM A LOWER BASE

Unlike their neighbours in Central and Eastern Europe, both WBC and EBC had experienced slow progress in their transition to free-market economies in the 1990s, due to, *inter alia*, political instability and stop-and-go economic policies. However, at the start of the new millennium, a turnaround story gained momentum, underpinned by restored political stability, the implementation of prudent economic policies, significant progress on institutional and structural reforms, a restructured and privatized banking system, and prospects of EU integration.

It is worth noting that, in the first half of the past decade, the health and performance of the banking sector in all WBC and EBC had improved significantly. This was the result of the implementation of the standard mantra of bank reforms, including the restructuring and privatization of state-owned ones – with a large share going to foreign owners – the closure of insolvent banks, non-performing loan write-offs, the adoption of new prudential regulations and tighter supervision. As a result, on the eve of the global crisis, both WBC and EBC banking sectors were relatively well regulated and supervised, highly capitalized, quite profitable, and fairly liquid. It is important to understand that a large part of the banks' operational improvement is due to the large share of foreign ownership, which brought capital, technical expertise and competition into the system. In fact, for WBC as a whole, foreign investors control 43 banks out of a total of 50 banks and about 75 per cent of banking assets. A notable example is Albania, where foreign investors control 14 out of 16 banks and about 95 per cent of banking assets. The banks' improved performance also reflects the acceleration in financial intermediation that has taken place since 2001, with loans to the private sector and to households growing by an average annual rate of 35 per cent and 64 per cent, respectively, between 2001 and 2008 in WBC – against 49 per cent and 89 per cent in EBC.

As a result, WBC macroeconomic fundamentals have improved significantly, with average annual GDP growth of 5.2 per cent between 2002 and 2008 (see Figure 8.1) compared with 6.3 per cent in EBC and 1.7 per cent in the euro area. At the same time, the inflation rate had declined to single digits for the first time since the beginning of the transition to a market economy, standing at 6.8 per cent at end-2008 compared with 10.1 per cent at end-2002; the fiscal deficit had narrowed to a historical low of 3 per cent of GDP at end-2008; and the debt-to-GDP ratio had declined to 33.7 per cent at end-2008 from 67.6 per cent at end-2002.

The only cloud on the horizon was a widening current account deficit, which had reached a worrying level of 17 per cent of GDP at end-2008 (see Figure 8.2). However, the current account deterioration, in certain ways, suggests that WBC have been victims of their own success, as booming domestic demand reflects buoyant consumption and investment, supported by a far more active privately owned banking system. Further support for this more benign interpretation is the fact that the bulk of the current account shortfall was comfortably covered by FDI inflows

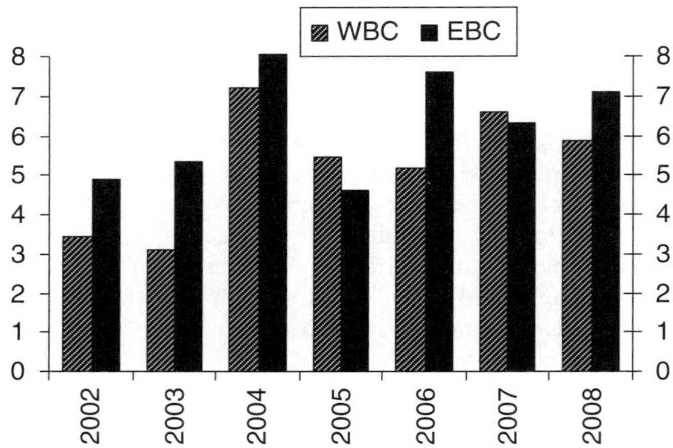

Source: Author's calculations based on national statistics.

Figure 8.1 Real GDP (year-on-year % change)

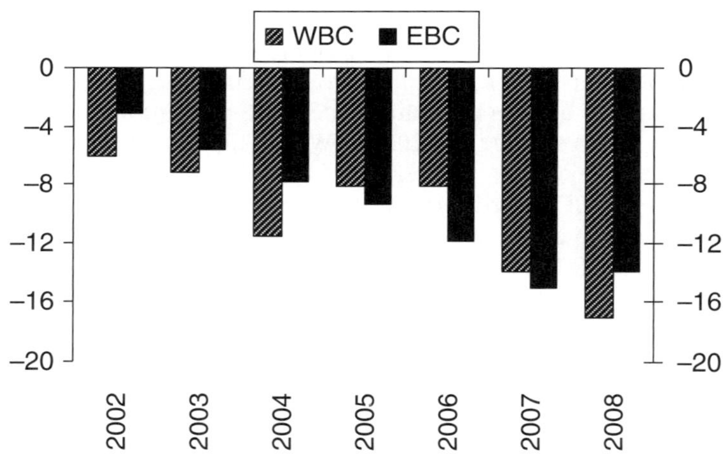

Source: Author's calculations based on national statistics.

Figure 8.2 Current account deficit (% of GDP)

(around 60 per cent), including a large share of greenfield investments. More importantly, FDI inflows to WBC have embarked on a strong upward trend since 2002, with FDI per capita of EUR 225 in 2008 compared with EUR 62 in 2002.

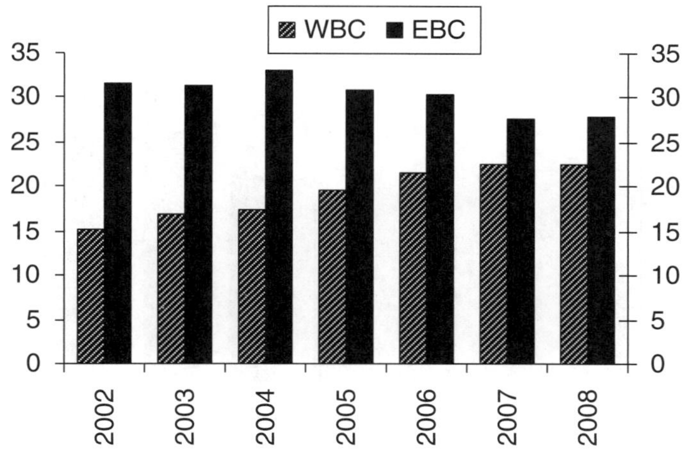

Source: Author's calculations based on national statistics.

Figure 8.3 Exports (% of GDP)

However, despite this impressive performance, WBC remain underdeveloped, as their average GDP per capita (EUR 4,047) was far below that of EBC and the EU-27 average (EUR 6,138 and EUR 25,100, respectively). Even when adjusted by purchasing power standards, WBC GDP per capita stood at only 34.6 per cent of the EU-27 average at end-2008, while that of EBC amounted to 46.4 per cent of the EU average.

WBC growth, while peaking during the period 2002–08, remained below that of EBC in that period. This was the result of, *inter alia*:

1. a low degree of openness and a weak export base (see Figure 8.3)
2. a relatively weaker credit impulse (see Figure 8.4)
3. relatively weaker capital inflows (see Figure 8.5)
4. relatively slower appreciation of the local currency in real terms (see Figure 8.6).

These factors had boosted domestic demand, but not as much as in EBC, and had led to less pronounced external imbalances and therefore to a moderate increase in the external-debt-to-GDP ratio (see Figure 8.7).

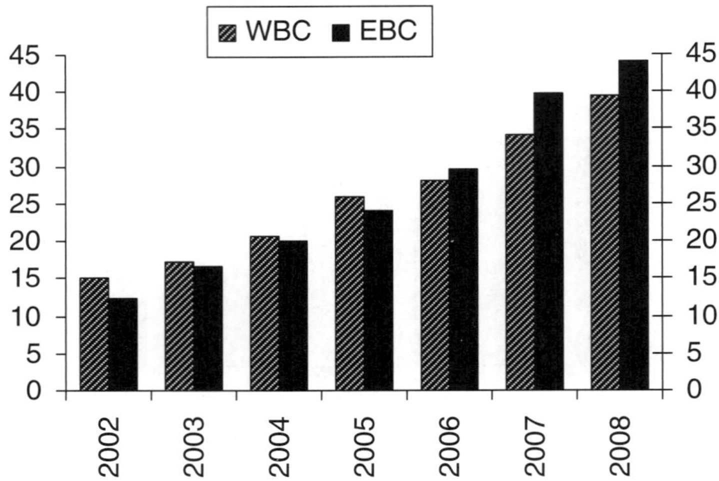

Source: Author's calculations based on national statistics.

Figure 8.4 Loans (% of GDP)

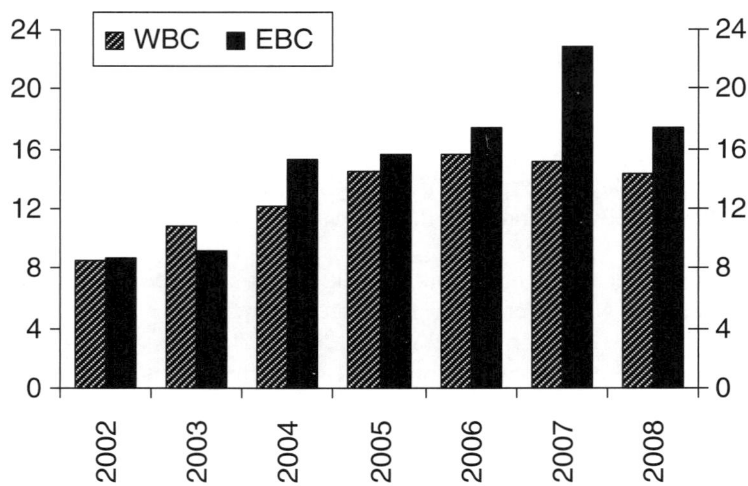

Source: Author's calculations based on national statistics.

Figure 8.5 Net capital inflows (excluding IMF, % of GDP)

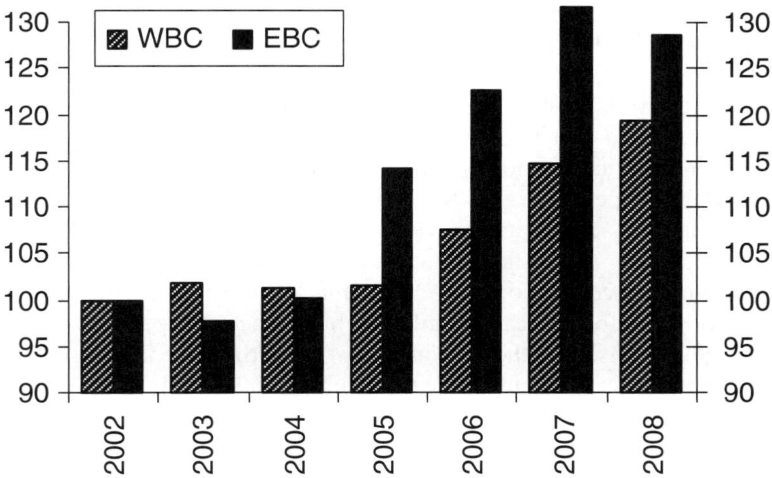

Source: Author's calculations based on national statistics.

Figure 8.6 CPI-based REER (2002 = 100)

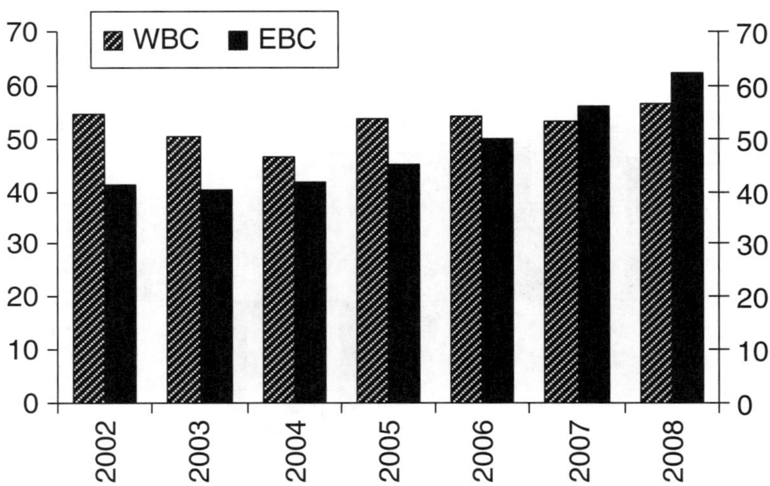

Source: Author's calculations based on national statistics.

Figure 8.7 External debt (% of GDP)

2 SINCE THE START OF THE GLOBAL CRISIS: LESS OF A BOOM AND LESS OF A CRASH

The international environment changed drastically for the worse, following the collapse of Lehman Brothers in September 2008, with a sharp drop in international trade, scarce and expensive external financing and a weakening appetite for emerging market assets. Against this backdrop, WBC economic activity has proved to be more resilient than that of EBC (see Figure 8.8), as the factors considered to act as a brake on a rapid catching-up process before the crisis, mainly the low export base and relatively weak foreign capital inflows, have since dampened the impact of the global crisis on these economies. Note that the fallout from the global financial crisis would have been substantially greater for WBC had they not already systematically implemented structural changes as part of their European orientation in recent years. Nonetheless, the international financial crisis presents an opportunity for far-reaching adjustment of the imbalances that characterize these economies, including unsustainable current account deficits and high rates of inflation.

The average growth rate in 2009–10 is estimated to have been nil for WBC (0.1 per cent), despite a sharp drop in exports (see Figure 8.9), and to have stood deep in the red for EBC (–4.3 per cent). WBC resilient economic activity reflects, *inter alia*:

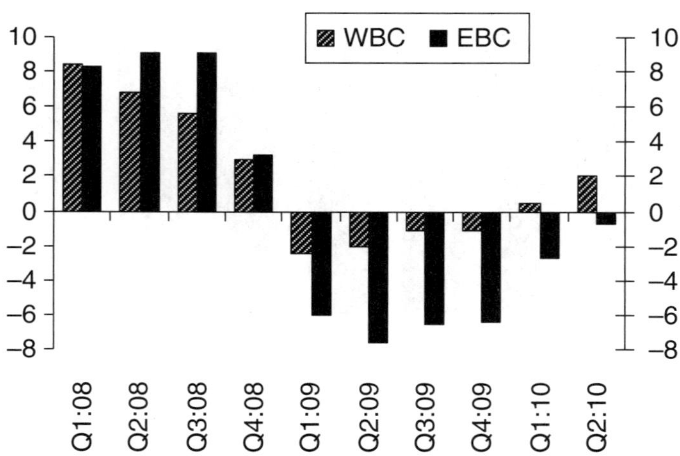

Source: Author's calculations based on national statistics.

Figure 8.8 Real GDP (year-on-year % change)

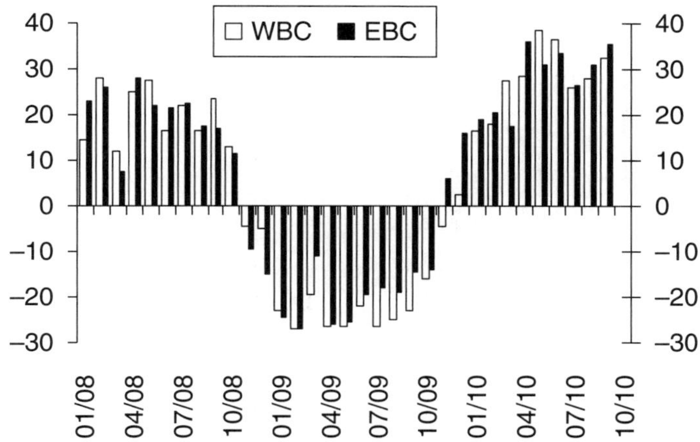

Source: Author's calculations based on national statistics.

Figure 8.9 Exports (year-on-year % change)

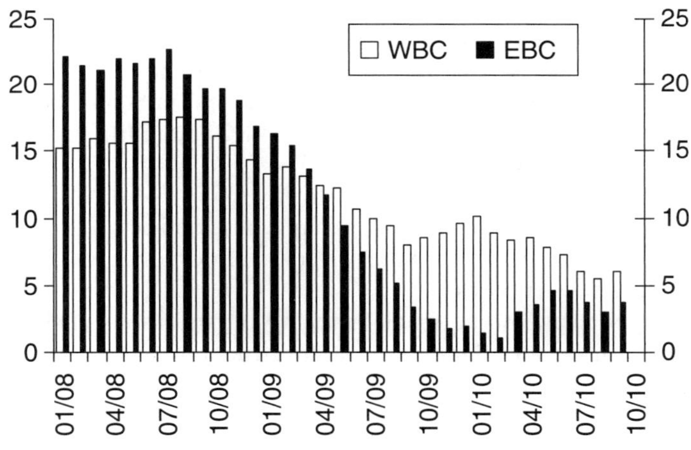

Source: Author's calculations based on national statistics.

Figure 8.10 Net capital inflows (excluding IMF, % of GDP)

1. relatively robust capital inflows (see Figure 8.10);
2. still robust, albeit decelerating, credit expansion (see Figure 8.11), despite tight liquidity conditions and credit standards, due to the banks' concern to maintain their asset quality and capital adequacy

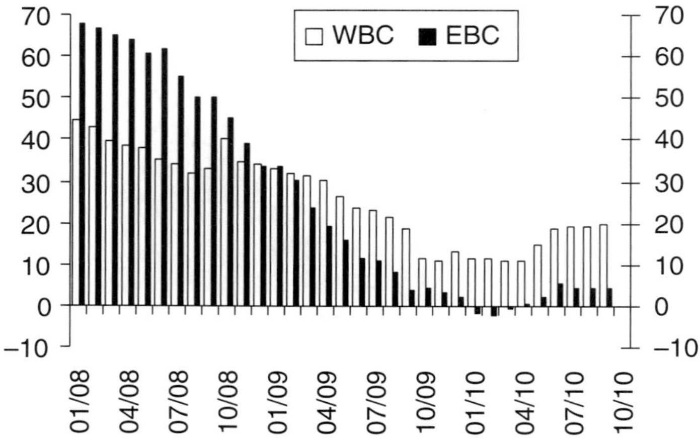

Source: Author's calculations based on national statistics.

Figure 8.11 Loans (year-on-year % change)

in a stressed operating environment. WBC lending growth slowed to 20.7 per cent year-on-year in October 2010 from 33.3 per cent in September 2008 while EBC lending growth plunged to 2.8 per cent year-on-year in October 2010 from 50 per cent in September 2008. It should be noted, however, that both WBC and EBC banks remain solvent, well capitalized and profitable.

3. accommodative fiscal policy;
4. counter-cyclical monetary and exchange rate policies;
5. the good shape of the banking system – a traditional Achilles heel of emerging market crises;
6. the support of international financing organizations (IMF, World Bank, European Bank for Reconstruction and Development, European Investment Bank).

3 REAL NEED TO ACCELERATE REFORMS FOR A FASTER CATCHING-UP PROCESS

Looking forward, WBC's faster catching-up process, observed since the start of the global crisis, is set to continue in the coming years, as these countries are still poorer, but competitive and with a prospect of EU membership.

This will be underpinned by, *inter alia*, their closer EU integration. Recall that:

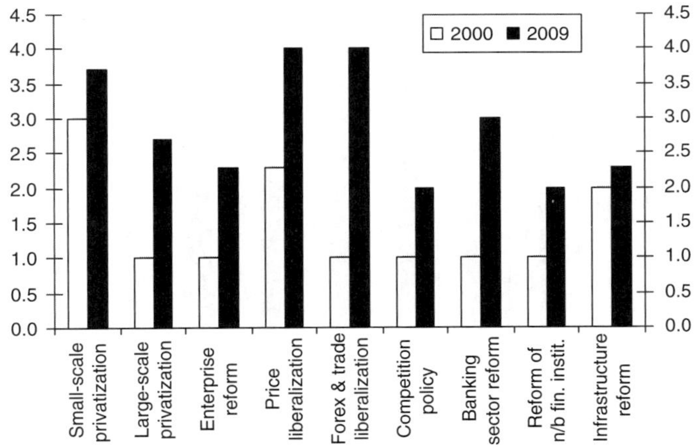

Source: EBRD, *Transition Report 2009*.

Figure 8.12 Serbia – EBRD transition indicators

1. FYR of Macedonia is a candidate country. It was granted the status of candidate to EU membership by EU leaders in December 2005 and is waiting for a date for the start of entry negotiations.
2. Albania is a potential candidate country. It signed a Stabilisation and Association Agreement (SAA) with the EU, one step ahead of the start of EU accession negotiations, in June 2006.
3. Serbia is a potential candidate country. It signed an SAA in April 2008.

The EU membership process is expected to be long and difficult, but it is set to provide the much needed anchor for policy and reform. Indeed, on the fronts of institutional, economic and structural reform, substantial progress has been made; but more has to be done (see Figures 8.12–8.16).

EU-related reforms, along with the already attractive business environment, should make WBC a prime location for FDI and a 'convergence play'. Indeed, the business climate in WBC is very attractive. Wages are about 15 per cent of those in Western Europe, corporate tax rates are less than half of those in Western Europe (10 per cent in Albania, Bulgaria, FYR of Macedonia and Serbia) and labour markets are relatively more flexible.

The still underpenetrated WBC banking sectors should also support a faster catching-up process, as they are healthy and have a huge growth potential. Indeed, despite the impressive lending growth in the past

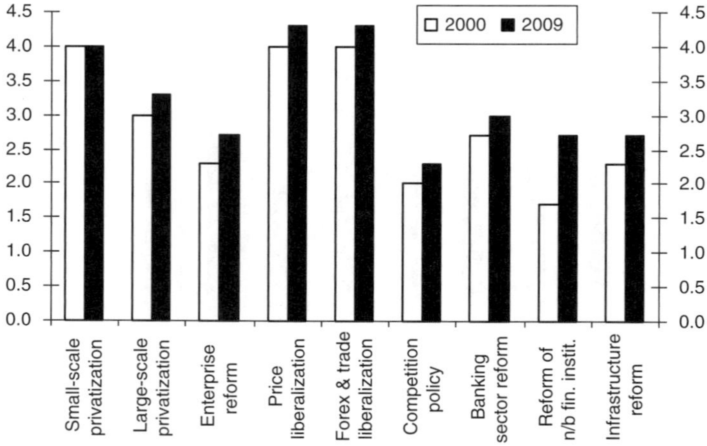

Source: EBRD, *Transition Report 2009*.

Figure 8.13 FYR of Macedonia – EBRD transition indicators

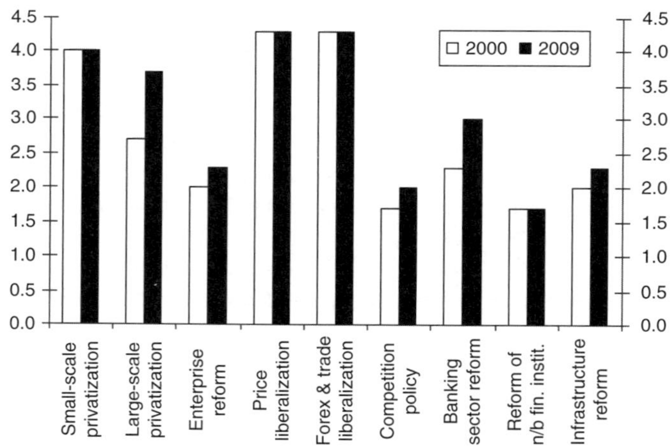

Source: EBRD, *Transition Report 2009*.

Figure 8.14 Albania – EBRD transition indicators

decade, the loan-to-GDP ratio stood at only 47.6 per cent in October 2010, compared with 120 per cent in the euro area. The comparable ratio for retail lending was 16.3 per cent of GDP, compared with 56 per cent in the euro area. WBC banks' relatively strong reliance on domestic financing

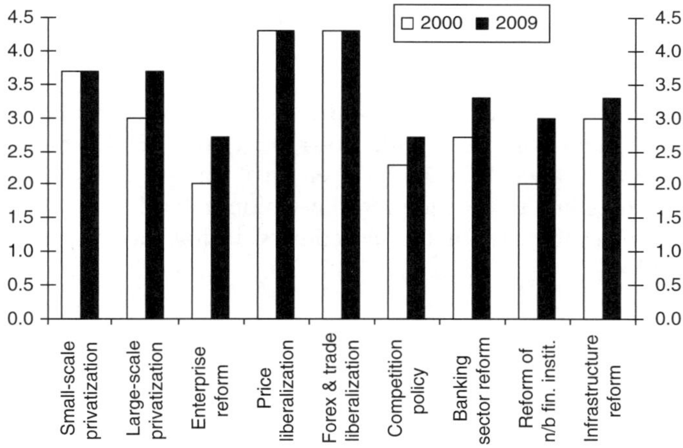

Source: EBRD, *Transition Report 2009.*

Figure 8.15 Romania – EBRD transition indicators

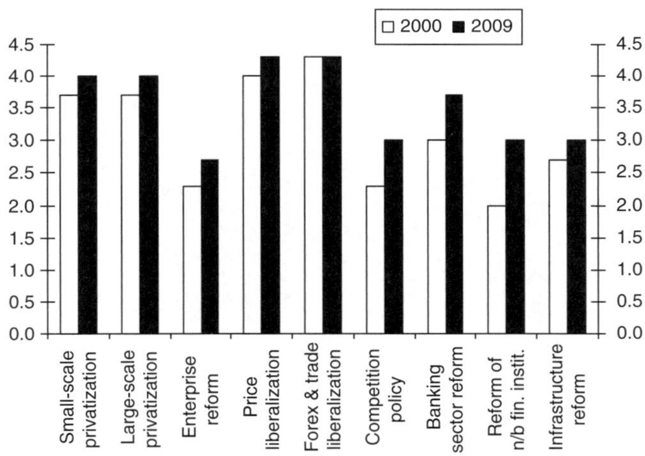

Source: EBRD, *Transition Report 2009.*

Figure 8.16 Bulgaria – EBRD transition indicators

to fund credit expansion should also keep loan volume growth for WBC in the mid-teens – more than in EBC, but well below a 'red hot' pace of circa 35 per cent between 2001 and 2008. It is worth noting that among WBC Albania has the highest lending growth potential, due to abundant liquidity – the loan-to-deposit ratio is around 60 per cent, giving Albania plenty of room for manoeuvre to increase lending without resorting to external financing.

That said, economic activity in WBC should grow at around its potential of 5 per cent compared with 3.5–4 per cent in EBC and 1.5–2 per cent in the euro area. It could be even stronger. Indeed, the European Commission estimates that joining the Union will add up to 1 per cent extra growth each year for the newcomers during the first ten years of membership.

PART II

Policy challenges in the CESEE region and beyond

9. Monetary policy and financial stability: what's ahead for Central and Eastern Europe

Stephen G. Cecchetti[1]

This chapter describes the monetary policy and financial stability challenges facing Central and Eastern Europe (CEE) after the crisis. I will begin with a description of the current global monetary policy environment and its effects on emerging market economies. Following this, I will briefly comment on ongoing regulatory reforms and their potential impact on credit supply. And finally, I will turn to what this all means for monetary policy and financial stability in Central and Eastern Europe.

My main message is that monetary policy in this region is in a period of transition. Existing policy frameworks have performed relatively well during the crisis. Contrary to widespread expectations, there have been no currency collapses and no banking crises. And, at the time of writing, the recovery is proceeding gradually and inflation is low.

That said, the landscape for monetary policy and financial stability in other emerging market economies (EMEs) has changed considerably over the past few years. Having weathered the severe financial stress and the impact of a steep decline in global demand, emerging markets in Asia and Latin America are once again confronting issues similar to those they faced before the bankruptcy of Lehman Brothers in September 2008. Capital flows are back and policy makers are focusing on managing the consequences of these inflows – as well as the inflows themselves.

Although the challenges faced by Brazil, Korea or Thailand may seem remote, I will argue that policy makers in the CEE region need to prepare as their turn is likely to come. And, when capital inflows return, it will be important that authorities are able to rely on existing monetary policy frameworks. This will mean resisting spillovers from policies pursued by other EMEs, while fighting the tendency toward distorting policies such as foreign exchange intervention and capital controls.

With that as a background, let me now turn to describing briefly the current global monetary environment. Over the past few months it has become clear that growth performances in the global economy are diverging.

GLOBAL MONETARY CONDITIONS AND EMERGING MARKETS

The US and Japanese economies have weakened, with growth rates in the United States falling from 2.7 per cent on average in the first half of 2010 to 2 per cent in the third quarter (advance estimate), and in Japan from 4.2 per cent to 3.9 per cent over the same period. Meanwhile, many euro area and emerging market countries have continued to expand, albeit at a slower pace than earlier this year. For instance, growth in Germany slowed from 6 per cent in the first half of 2010 to 2.8 per cent in the third quarter, while in the BRIC countries and Korea growth has fallen from a rate in excess of 8 per cent to an average of 6.5 per cent.

In response, the United States and Japan recently embarked on a further round of monetary easing. The Federal Reserve has announced additional measures of quantitative easing, buying a further US$600 billion of assets to June 2011. Meanwhile the Bank of Japan has entered into what it has labelled comprehensive monetary easing, which includes the establishment of an asset purchase programme and a commitment to keep the call rate between zero and 0.1 per cent until price stability is in sight.

In anticipation of these moves, long-term bond yields in the G3 economies declined; in the United States, for instance, by 25 basis points between mid-September and early October, before returning recently to their early August levels; and in Japan by about 25 basis points since early September.

The combination of high growth in the emerging markets and further easing of monetary policy in the advanced economies has reinforced what were already strong portfolio investment flows. Looking at Figure 9.1, we see that flows to emerging Asia, in the left-hand panel, strengthened to over US$20 billion in the third quarter and about US$17 billion in just six weeks of the fourth quarter (that is, to 10 November). The bulk of these inflows went to Asian equity funds. At the same time, net portfolio flows to Latin America, in the right-hand panel, increased to nearly US$10 billion per quarter in the third quarter and so far in the fourth quarter.

Interestingly, this same phenomenon has not manifested itself in CEE; at least, not yet. In Figure 9.2(a) we see that the Czech Republic, Hungary and Poland have together received less than US$2 billion in portfolio inflows since September 2010. Russia and Turkey, in Figure 9.2(b), are

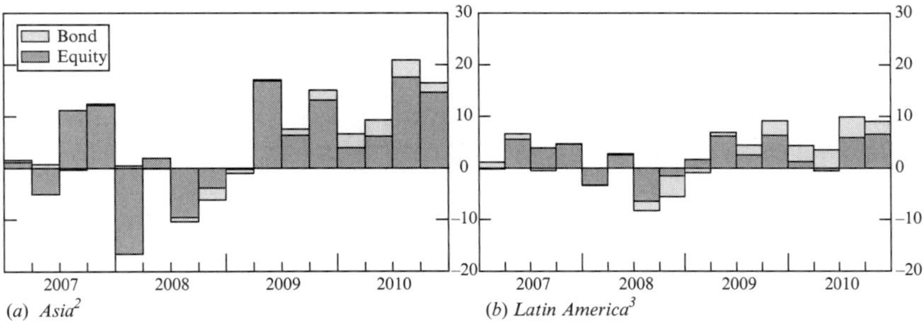

Notes:
1. Sums of weekly data up to 10 November 2010; sums across economies listed.
2. China, Chinese Taipei, Hong Kong, India, Indonesia, Korea, Malaysia, the Philippines, Singapore and Thailand.
3. Argentina, Brazil, Chile, Colombia, Mexico, Peru and Venezuela.

Source: EPFR.

Figure 9.1 Net flows into emerging market equity and bond funds[1] *(US$ billion)*

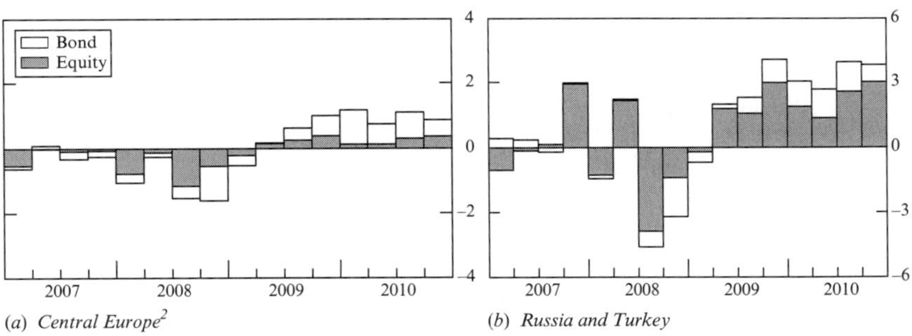

Notes:
1. Sums of weekly data up to 10 November, 2010; sums across economies listed.
2. The Czech Republic, Hungary and Poland.

Source: EPFR.

Figure 9.2 Net flows into CEE equity and bond funds[1] *(US$ billion)*

exceptions, having received over US$4 billion in the third quarter and another US$4 billion in just six weeks of the fourth quarter.

In trying to assess these flows, it is important to keep in mind that interest rate differentials are normally a symptom of strong economic

Table 9.1 Cross-border bank lending to emerging market economies[1] *(US$ billion)*

	2007	2008	2009	2009		2010	
				Q3	Q4	Q1	Q2
Total EMEs	512	128	−149	−62	68	116	95
Asia[2]	111	−59	11	8	47	72	48
Hong Kong and Singapore	140	42	−48	−35	32	40	40
Latin America[3]	61	22	−19	−7	6	17	15
CEE[4]	125	107	−39	−8	−2	−9	0
CIS[5]	75	16	−53	−20	−14	−4	−8

Notes:
1. External loans of BIS reporting banks (on the residence basis) vis-à-vis individual emerging market economies; exchange rate adjusted changes in gross amounts outstanding. Does not include changes in reporting banks' holdings of emerging market securities.
2. China, Chinese Taipei, India, Indonesia, Korea, Malaysia, the Philippines and Thailand.
3. Argentina, Brazil, Chile, Colombia, Mexico, Peru and Venezuela.
4. Total of 10 new EU member states from Central and Eastern Europe, South-Eastern Europe (including Turkey).
5. Russia, Ukraine and Kazakhstan.

Source: BIS, locational banking statistics.

fundamentals. For instance, with nominal policy rates between 6 and 11 per cent, and inflation between 4 and 6 per cent, real policy rates in Brazil, China and Russia are currently between 1 and 6 per cent, compared with negative policy rates in the United States and the euro area. As noted at the outset, these countries have very high growth rates, projected at 5–10 per cent this year and only slightly lower next year. We would expect the neutral real interest rate in a country – the policy rate that equates aggregate demand with potential output – to be roughly in line with the growth rate of per capita output. So, higher growth means higher real interest rates. And higher real interest rates translate into higher capital inflows.[2]

We can see this in the cross-border lending data as well. Looking at the BIS data in Table 9.1, note that cross-border bank lending to emerging Asia, adjusted for exchange rate changes, was US$120 billion in the first half of 2010 – that is the sum of the two numbers in the far right columns of the second row of Table 9.1. This was higher than the US$111 billion in the whole of 2007, itself a historical peak for external bank lending to the emerging markets. Cross-border bank lending to Latin America has also

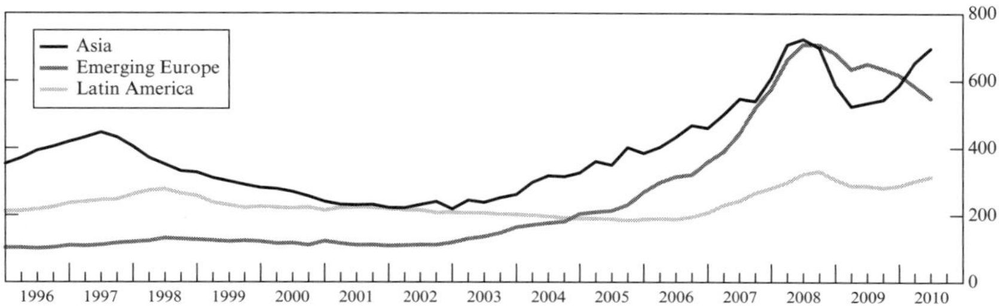

Source: BIS, locational banking statistics.

Figure 9.3 External loans of BIS reporting banks vis-à-vis emerging market regions (amounts outstanding at end-of-quarter, US$ billion)

returned to the peak levels seen in 2007 – US$32 billion in the first half of 2010 versus US$61 billion for the whole of 2007. Finally, after declining steadily for over two years, cross-border bank lending to CEE is now steady.

Turning from flows to stocks of external financing, Figure 9.3 shows that emerging Asia, the black line, and Latin America, the light-grey line, have returned to almost the pre-crisis peaks of US$725 billion and US$330 billion, respectively. Looking at the dark-grey line in Figure 9.3, we can see that the exposure of advanced economies' banks to CEE countries has fallen by US$160 billion since its pre-crisis peak, and seems unlikely to increase any time soon. While the rough equality of the Asian and CEE lines in Figure 9.3 may be surprising, the rationale is simply that Asians have developed local currency bond markets, reducing their overall demand for bank loans, while corporates in this part of the world have not.

Needless to say, these large capital inflows create a number of challenges for policy makers. To see these, we can look, in turn, at equity prices, bond yields and exchange rates.

Starting with equity prices, we can see in Figure 9.4 that in eight of the 16 cases plotted here equity prices went up by 15–30 per cent from August to October! To see this, note that the data in the lines in Figure 9.4 are all normalized at 100 on 2 August 2010. Given the limited supply of domestic equities in most of these countries, and generally underdeveloped financial markets in many EMEs, strong increases in foreign demand have given rise to concerns that equity price bubbles are developing. And, rising equity prices are putting strong pressures on aggregate demand and consumer prices in a number of Asian and Latin American countries, as well as in Turkey.

(*a*) *Asia* (*b*) *Latin America* (*c*) *Other EMEs*

Note: 1. Indices are computed from local currency prices.

Sources: Bloomberg; Datastream.

Figure 9.4 Equity prices[1] *(2 August 2010 = 100)*

Turning to bond yields, inflows are driving up prices of fixed income instruments. So, long-term domestic bond yields are falling in many EMEs. While more pronounced in some countries than in others, the trend is definitely evident in Figure 9.5. Analysts' commentaries have linked these developments more or less directly to foreign investors' demand for emerging market local currency bonds. For instance, at the end of July 2010, foreign investors held 27 per cent of Indonesia's local currency government debt, compared with 16 per cent a year earlier. It is worth noting that in some countries – including Brazil, Korea, Malaysia, Peru, the Philippines and Thailand – local currency long-term bond yields declined despite increases in short-term policy rates; a phenomenon that is eerily similar to what happened in the United States in the early part of the last decade.

Turning to exchange rates, capital inflows have been, unsurprisingly, accompanied by currency appreciations. And, given the importance of exports as a source of growth in many EMEs, this has created concerns. At an abstract level, currency appreciation is what we should expect. And, it should not really be a problem. Solid economic fundamentals should be reflected in strong and appreciating exchange rates. And, to the extent that neighbouring countries' exchange rates – those of export competitors – are appreciating as well, the effect of dollar depreciation should be less of an issue. In practice, however, concerns about exchange rate volatility induced by the inflows and the loss of export revenues at a time when the outlook for growth in major advanced economies is uncertain have led policy makers in many EMEs to resist exchange rate appreciation for both political and economic reasons. That said, we can see in Figure 9.6, on the left-hand side, that the CEE countries, following their strong free-market instincts, have let their exchange rates adjust much more – both up and down – than other EMEs.

Turning to the specific policy responses to the capital inflows, EMEs have raised interest rates, albeit cautiously; intervened in the foreign exchange markets, sometimes substantially; employed macroprudential tools in an effort to address the perceived build-up of asset price bubbles; and in some cases instituted outright capital controls.

Starting with the first, we have seen interest rates rise by a quarter to half a percentage point in Southeast Asia since the start of 2010, 2½ percentage points in India and 1¼–2 percentage points in Latin America.

Next, there is foreign exchange intervention. Figure 9.7 compares the most recent data with those in July 2009. Increases in Korea, Brazil, Thailand and Mexico are significant – more than US$50 billion in some cases – increases in the order of US$1 billion per week! That said, reserve accumulation in Asia and Latin America has clearly been

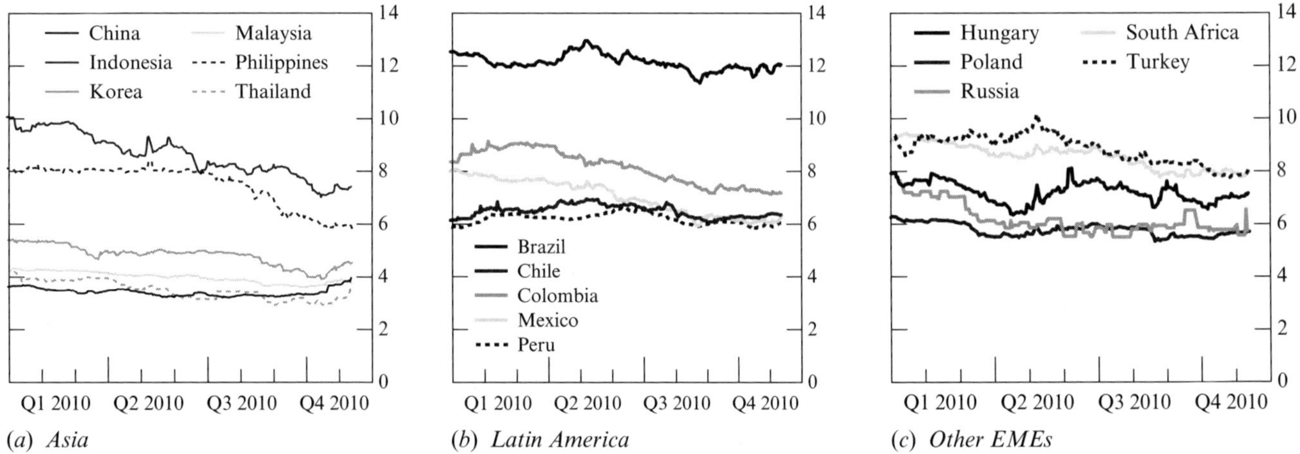

Note: 1. Ten-year government bonds; for Brazil, 3-year; for Chile, 9-year; for Turkey, 2-year.

Sources: Bloomberg; national data.

Figure 9.5 Local currency bond yields[1] (in per cent)

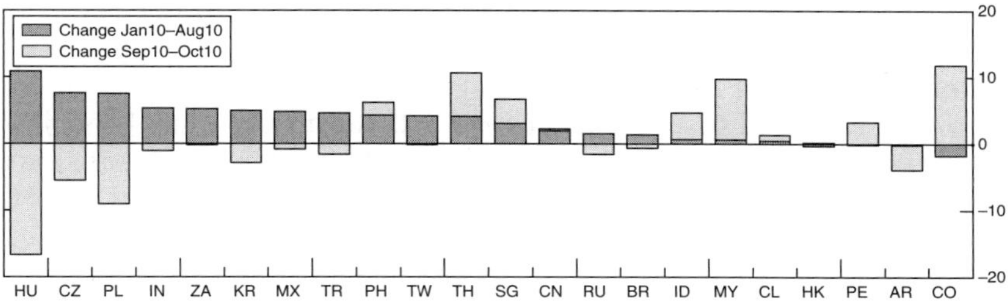

Notes:
1. US$ per unit of local currency; an increase indicates appreciation of local currency. AR = Argentina; BR = Brazil; CL = Chile; CN = China; CO = Colombia; CZ = Czech Republic; HK = Hong Kong SAR; HU = Hungary; ID = Indonesia; IN = India; KR = Korea; MX = Mexico; MY = Malaysia; PE = Peru; PH = Philippines; PL = Poland; RU = Russia; SG = Singapore; TH = Thailand; TR = Turkey; TW = Chinese Taipei; ZA = South Africa.

Sources: Bloomberg; Datastream; national data.

Figure 9.6 Changes in nominal exchange rates[1] (in per cent)

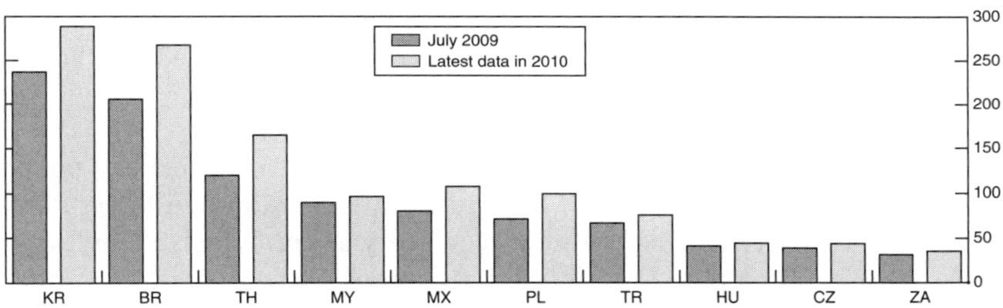

Sources: CEIC; Datastream; IMF, International Financial Statistics; national banks.

Figure 9.7 Reserve accumulation (US$ billion)

much more substantial than that in CEE (or South Africa). Looking at something like this, one is immediately drawn to asking how long it can continue.

Regardless, we can see that policy makers are in a real bind. Even if foreign exchange intervention and capital controls limit the pace and extent of currency appreciation, they cannot alleviate the inflationary pressures arising from the expansion of banking sector balance sheets. The natural response is to raise interest rates, but this will tend to attract additional inflows, making the problem worse. The pressure for adjustment of the macroeconomic policy mix is increasing.

REGULATORY REFORMS AND CREDIT SUPPLY

I would be remiss if I neglected to mention the implications of regulatory reform in this context. For emerging Europe, the impact could be limited credit supply as foreign-owned banks adjust. Given the changes that are being put in place, these banks are reconsidering their business models after years of extremely rapid credit growth in this region.

How are the new liquidity and capital standards likely to affect international banks active in CEE? Regarding liquidity, banks have already put greater emphasis on local deposit gathering. One can also discern a trend toward centralizing wholesale funding activities on the parent level. Regarding capital adequacy, major European banking groups active in CEE had relatively high capitalization levels before the crisis. Banking systems in CEE are also generally well capitalized, with levels well above those mandated by the new Basel III standards. Some banks could nevertheless change their credit policies, turn to their well-capitalized subsidiaries in CEE for help in meeting the new requirements, or dispose of some business units in CEE.

IMPLICATIONS FOR CEE MONETARY POLICY AND FINANCIAL STABILITY

Against this background, what are the implications for monetary policy in CEE of an extended period of low global interest rates and the gradual transition of parent banks to new regulatory requirements? Currently, most CEE countries are experiencing a gradual recovery, with low inflation, weak credit demand and therefore low domestic policy rates. Unlike their peers in emerging Asia and Latin America, CEE countries have lowered their policy rates by 25–100 basis points since the beginning of this year.

Banks are consolidating their operations and repairing their balance sheets – in fact, peak levels of non-performing loans are expected in 2011. At the same time, central banks in the region are assessing how their monetary policy frameworks performed during the crisis, and how to adjust these frameworks in the future, with a view to combining monetary policy and financial stability objectives. As a consequence, monetary policy in the region is simply waiting to see what happens next.

Looking at policy frameworks, there is a clear sense that they served countries well during the crisis. Both inflation targeting central banks and those operating fixed exchange rate regimes avoided currency collapses and banking crises. In both groups, central banks attributed good performance in large measure to the combination of sound banking systems and the presence of non-standard elements in their frameworks, including various macroprudential tools.

The Vienna Initiative was, of course, instrumental in protecting several CEE economies from currency crises. The few near misses have also highlighted the need to elaborate better contingency plans for emergency foreign currency liquidity provision in the future and to reduce the vulnerabilities that have led to currency mismatches in private sector balance sheets in the first place.

However, rather than just looking backward, monetary policy must concentrate on the challenges ahead. Here that means focusing on the familiar issues of capital inflows, asset price increases and catching-up. In particular, CEE countries are destined to grow faster than the euro area. Looking at Figure 9.8, we see that current projections envisage slower growth than before the crisis, mostly in the 3–5 per cent per annum range over the next five years. But *slower than before* for this region is still 2–3 percentage points faster than growth is expected to be in the euro area. Moreover, this more modest pace is likely to be more sustainable than what was happening before the crisis.

That is the silver lining. The cloud is that with positive growth differentials come interest rate differentials, as shown in Figure 9.9. And these interest rate differentials are destined to attract capital. As we have seen, such inflows have already returned to Russia, Turkey and, to a lesser extent, Poland.

It seems unlikely that this inevitable new round of capital inflows will create a new round of real estate price appreciation. While that is surely a good thing, the reason is not. Many households in CEE are saddled with high mortgage debt, and countless apartments and commercial properties remain unsold. We know from numerous property busts in the past that it takes years before the real estate demand and supply normalize around longer-term trends.

Instead, given the large financing needs of the public sector, a high share of the inflows could end up in sovereign bonds and bank credit to the government. As Figure 9.10 shows, as local banks have become more risk averse, we have already seen a big increase in bank lending to these governments.

The problem with such inflows is that easy access to credit weakens the incentives of governments to implement structural fiscal reforms; something that is sorely needed in most CEE countries. Not only that, but in these circumstances large public sector borrowing requirements are particularly prone to crowd out investment in the non-financial corporate sector; something that is surely not good for long-term growth.

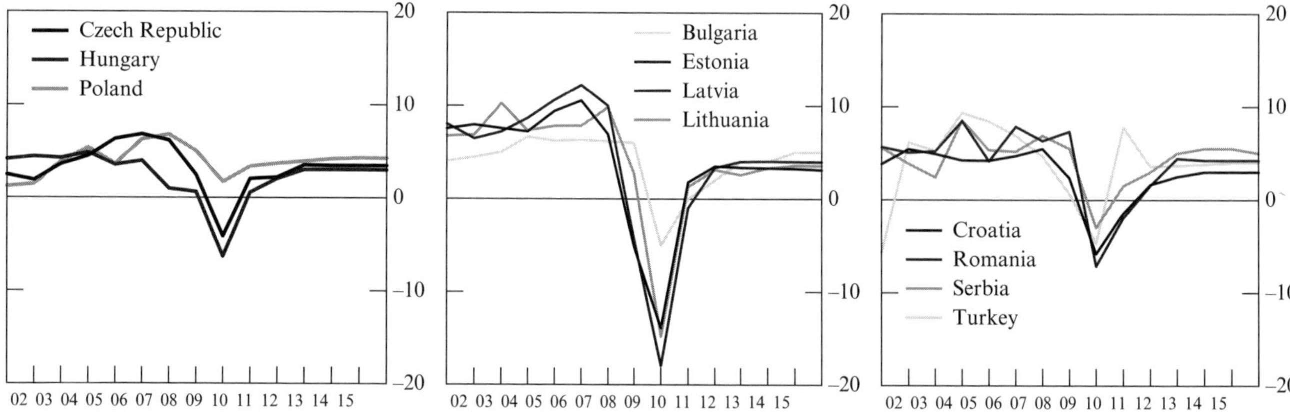

(*a*) *Czech Republic, Hungary, Poland* (*b*) *Bulgaria, Estonia, Latvia, Lithuania* (*c*) *Croatia, Romania, Serbia, Turkey*

Source: World Economic Outlook (September 2010).

Figure 9.8 Real GDP growth (annual percentage changes)

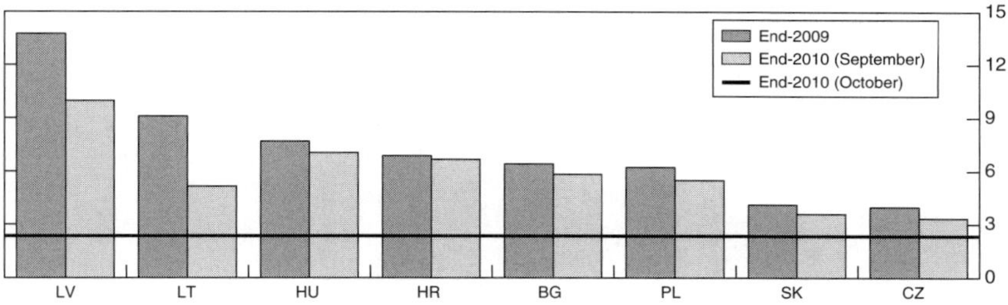

Notes:
1. Long-term domestic currency government bonds; the horizontal line refers to the 10-year German benchmark bond; in per cent.
   BG = Bulgaria; CZ = Czech Republic; HR = Croatia; HU = Hungary; LT = Lithuania; LV = Latvia; PL = Poland; SK = Slovakia.

Sources: ECB; Datastream; national data.

Figure 9.9 Long-term interest rates[1]

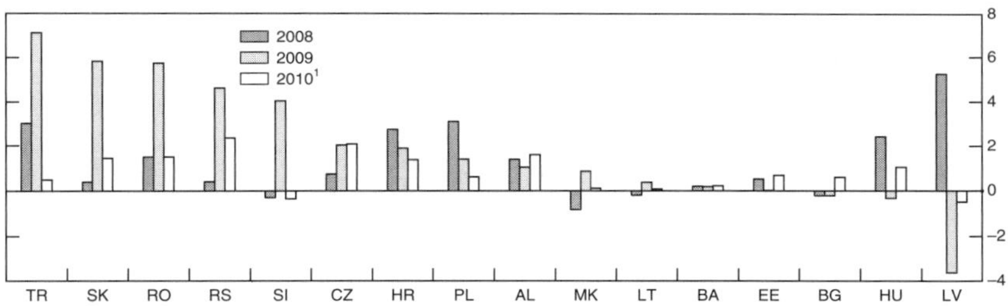

Notes:
1. Latest available.
   AL = Albania; BA = Bosnia-Herzegovina; BG = Bulgaria; CZ = Czech Republic; EE = Estonia; HR = Croatia; HU = Hungary; LT = Lithuania; LV = Latvia; MK = Macedonia; PL = Poland; RO = Romania; RS = Serbia; SI = Slovenia; SK = Slovakia; TR = Turkey.

Sources: IMF; national data.

Figure 9.10 Bank credit to the government (annual changes, as a percentage of 2008 GDP)

Finally there is the risk that capital inflows could lead to a rise in equity prices and a fall in domestic bond yields that are disconnected from underlying fundamentals. The exchange rates could also start appreciating – as happened before the crisis (Figure 9.11) – reducing the debt burden on households that borrowed in euros or Swiss francs, and increasing the

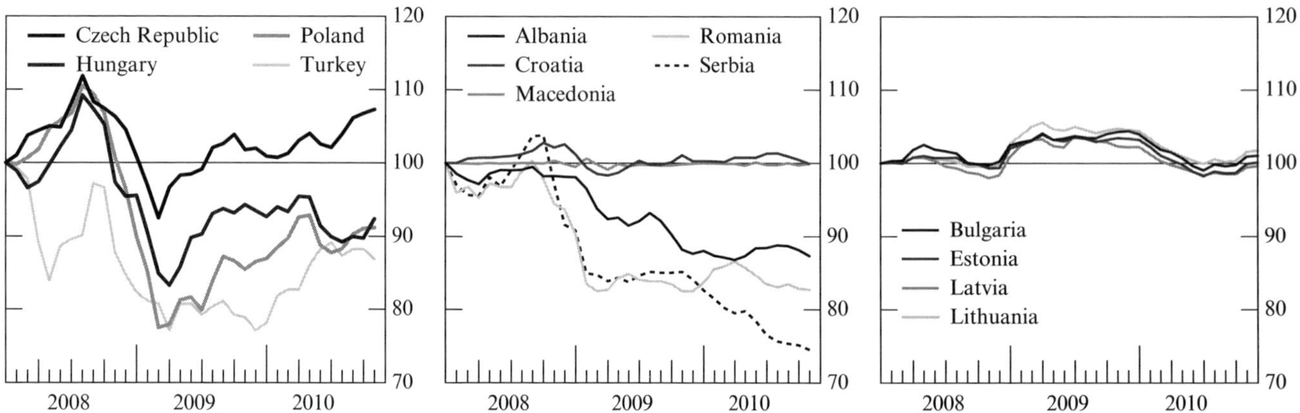

Note: 1. December 2007 = 100; euro per unit of local currency (nominal effective exchange rates for Bulgaria, Estonia, Latvia and Lithuania). An increase indicates an appreciation; monthly averages.

Sources: ECB; Datastream; national data; BIS.

Figure 9.11 Exchange rates[1]

incentives for new borrowing in foreign currencies. This would undermine the ongoing efforts of several central banks and institutions such as the EBRD to develop local currency capital markets. But, at the same time, allowing exchange rates to appreciate would avoid the problems that other emerging market countries resisting this trend are currently facing.

CONCLUSION

In conclusion, monetary policy in Central and Eastern Europe finds itself at a transition point. And, it is at times like this that there is the greatest potential for errors.

Existing monetary policy frameworks served countries in the region well during the crisis, and do not seem to require significant modification to incorporate required financial stability objectives. And, since central banks in this region in fact have considerable experience with the use of macroprudential tools, incorporating them into a new inflation targeting framework should be more or less straightforward.

At the same time, however, central banks need to get ready to confront the challenges created by capital inflows, asset price inflation and catching-up issues. In doing this, it will be essential to retain focus on traditional monetary policy and financial stability objectives, resisting spillovers from policies pursued by other EMEs. Maintaining exchange rate flexibility – or, in countries with fixed exchange rates, labour market flexibility – will be of key importance.

Furthermore, CEE countries need to be encouraged to maintain free capital flows and to continue to pursue domestic financial liberalization, avoiding a return to financial repression. These policies have been instrumental in the rapid financial and economic convergence accomplished thus far, and should not be abandoned under pressure from short-sighted populist policies.

NOTES

1. I would like to thank Dubravko Mihaljek and Agne Subelyte for their assistance. The views expressed here are those of the author and do not necessarily reflect those of the BIS.
2. On the other hand, if the central bank lowers policy rates in an attempt to limit the inflows sensitive to interest rate differentials, the inflows seeking to exploit the higher return on capital might still occur. This dilemma was first identified in the mid-1990s by then Czech National Bank Governor Josef Tošovský; it has subsequently been referred to as the 'Tošovský Dilemma' (see Lipschitz et al., 2002).

REFERENCE

Lipschitz, L., T. Lane and A. Mourmouras (2002), 'Capital flows to transition economies: master or servant?', IMF working paper no. 02/11, January.

10. Central banking for the 21st century: an American perspective

Paul A. Wachtel[1]

Central banks are peculiar institutions with one foot in the private sector and one foot in the government.[2] In the United States, in particular, the central bank stands out as the extra-constitutional fourth branch of the federal government. It has considerable power which it can exercise without any significant formal review or interference from Congress, the President or any elected officials.

Indeed, modern thinking about central banking gives enormous emphasis to the notion of central banking independence. Only a central bank that is independent of the political sphere will be able to maintain a consistent anti-inflationary policy stance. So, central bankers should not be subject to regular political review or oversight and should hold office for a long period of time. Some central banks were set up with this independent quasi-governmental status, such as the Federal Reserve System.[3] Some evolved in that direction, such as the Bank of England, which was a private institution until it was nationalized by the post-war Labour government and then was not granted its policy independence until 1997.[4]

Towards the end of the 20th century, it seemed to many observers that a consensus view had emerged regarding the proper functions of a central bank. However, as is often the case, just when this happens something comes along to upset the consensus. And the recent financial crisis has thrown the issue wide open once again. A fresh examination of the history of central banks shows that our understanding of the role of central banks has always been changing.[5] Most importantly, at present the long shadow of the financial crisis has left large elements of uncertainty regarding the proper role of central banks. In this chapter I categorize the historical roles of central banks in an effort to determine what the 21st-century role of central banks should be.[6]

Central bank functions fall into three areas: monetary policy, the supervision and regulation of individual financial institutions, and systemic regulation of the financial sector as a whole. The third function includes both the traditional concern for the functioning of the payments system and a new set of concerns about system-wide (or macro-prudential) risk arising from the increased complexity and interconnectedness of financial institutions and markets. We will argue here that the relationships among these three areas have been widely underappreciated. The predominant view in the 20th century was to deal with the first two functions independently and the third not at all. Central banking in the 21st century will have to develop ways of dealing with all three functions simultaneously.

MONETARY POLICY

Very few would argue with the idea that monetary policy aimed at economic stabilization should rest in the hands of an independent central bank. Economists have shown that independent central banks achieve lower and less volatile inflation rates than those that are beholden to governments in power, and that they do so at no long-run cost to economic output.

In the United States, the Federal Reserve has a dual mandate to maintain stable prices and full employment. Many other central banks – the European Central Bank (ECB) is a notable example – have price stability as their primary mandate. A central bank uses its policy tools to influence interest rates and the growth of money and credit in order to attain its specified goals. An independent central bank can pursue these goals without concern for an election cycle that might tempt elected policy makers to pursue short-term goals such as unsustainably high employment and real growth with little concern for longer-run inflationary implications.

Some argue that the function of a central bank should begin and end with the macro objectives of monetary policy, and that any other obligation would distract the central bank from achieving its primary goal of economic stabilization (or specifically, price stability). However, this approach ignores important links between monetary policy making, financial regulation and prudential supervision that favour a wider role for a modern central bank. In addition to its macroeconomic effects, monetary policy can affect the behaviour of financial institutions and may create weaknesses in the financial system.

A good example of this is the monetary policy pursued by the Federal Reserve in the early 2000s. The Fed began reducing its target for the funds rate even before the economy started contracting and it fell rapidly from 6 per cent to 1.75 per cent during 2001. Although the expansion began in November 2001, the funds rate target was reduced again at the end of 2002 and in mid-2003. It reached a record (at that time) low of 1 per cent in June 2003 and was held at that level for 12 months. Thus, the first increase in the funds rate target occurred 29 months after the end of the recession. By one measure the real Fed funds rate was negative for five years.[7]

It is interesting to read the Federal Reserve Board's own (2003) description of its thought processes and considerations around the time that the funds rate target reached its lowest value:

> To provide more specific guidance about its views, the FOMC [Federal Open Market Committee] included in its [May 2003] announcement separate assessments of the risks to the outlook for economic growth and inflation. . . . The Committee viewed the upside and downside risks to economic growth as balanced, but it perceived a higher probability of an unwelcome substantial fall in inflation than of a pickup in inflation from its current low level. That said, members concluded that there was only a remote possibility that resource utilization would remain so low that the disinflation process would cumulate to produce a declining overall price level for an extended period.
>
> [At the June meeting] [w]ith inflation already low and inflation expectations subdued, the Committee judged that it would be prudent to add further support for economic expansion, and it lowered the target for the federal funds rate 25 basis points, to 1 percent. The FOMC continued to view the risks to economic growth as balanced and again noted that the minor probability of substantial further disinflation exceeded the probability of a pickup in inflation from its current low level. But because of the considerable amount of economic slack prevailing and the economy's ability to expand without putting upward pressure on prices, the Committee indicated that the small chance of an unwelcome substantial decline in the inflation rate was likely to remain its predominant concern for the foreseeable future.

The Fed funds rate was kept very low for a very long period because of concerns about deflation and weakness of a recovery that was almost two years old. The report does indicate an awareness of issues that became more important in later years – mortgage refinancing, accounting practices at the GSEs (government sponsored enterprises) and 'buoyant growth' of the broad money supply, M2. Policy seems to carefully weigh the upside and downside risks regarding both macro goals but (easily said in retrospect) seems blithely unaware of any longer-term implications for behaviour in credit markets or by financial institutions.

A particular macro policy, like that in 2003, is not necessarily going to imply that systemic problems will arise but the emphasis on macro conditions and policy meant that no one within the Fed or elsewhere was even asking whether monetary policy might have such systemic consequences. Experience in the intervening years has surely shown that 21st-century central banking should avoid this disconnect between macro monetary policy and its other functions.

SUPERVISION AND REGULATION

It is important to remember that central banks started as banks with important lending activities, both on a regular basis and as the lender of last resort. The monetary policy function of central banks grew out of their lending activities as early central banks discovered that their lending influenced credit availability, interest rates and gold flows even before macroeconomic policy became an acknowledged function. As a regular lender to the financial system and sometimes the lender of last resort when special liquidity problems threatened the operation of the banking system, the central bank had a clear interest in knowing the viability of its customers. It is only logical that such a lender should have sufficient information about borrowers to be able to make sound loans. Thus, it is no accident that the lender of last resort also played a role with bank regulatory and supervisory functions. However, the supervisory function of the central bank is only significant if it maintains an active lending role.[8]

The regular lending activities of the Federal Reserve System became less significant in the late 20th century as the threat of banking panics retreated once deposit insurance was introduced and as other means to obtain liquidity developed. Some economists have suggested that the lender of last resort role for central banks is obsolete. In the modern world, well-developed financial markets with liquid securities markets and an active interbank market, there should be no such thing as an illiquid but solvent firm and no need for central bank lending functions. Solvent firms should always be able to arrange financing on the interbank market or the repo market.

Anna Schwartz (1992) examined the history of discount lending by the Federal Reserve and concluded that it had moved irreparably away from Bagehot's conception. She argued that the distinction between lending to provide liquidity and lending to prop up insolvent institutions had become unclear, although the Fed never acknowledged as much. Further, she was concerned (perhaps with prescience) with the use of central bank funds to provide capital loans to non-banks. Her recommendation was that the Fed's discount window be abolished. She argued that any systemic liquidity needs could always be satisfied with open market operations. The need for targeted lending responses when failing institutions can create a systemic problem was simply not entertained.

The discount window was not closed down although it virtually disappeared in the late 20th century. However, central bank lending came back with a vengeance in 2008 when the Fed utilized emergency lending powers that were hardly known and little understood because they had not been used after the 1930s.

The Fed had extensive lending powers under the 1932 amendment of the Federal Reserve Act (section 13(3)) and revised later on (see Fettig, 2002) to lend to non-banks in 'unusual and exigent' circumstances. On several earlier occasions there were suggestions that the Fed use these lending powers to provide funds to non-banks, such as at the time of the Chrysler bankruptcy in 1970, the New York City bankruptcy in 1975 and when the US airlines faced serious problems after 9/11. However, the Fed resisted such suggestions (although there was a short loan to the FDIC bank insurance fund in 1991) until March 2008. It reversed precedent when it arranged the sale of Bear Stearns to Morgan Chase. By the end of that year 2008, there were US$600 billion in section 13(3) loans outstanding. From August to December, the Fed's balance sheet increased by more than two times. The Fed quickly adapted its lending activity to cope with the crisis. Nevertheless, there was considerable public backlash against the Fed's lending, which was characterized as a bailout of Wall Street firms. As a result, the Dodd–Frank financial reform bill passed in 2010 circumscribes the Fed's ability to use emergency lending powers to assist individual institutions.

The crisis experience demonstrated the continuing 21st-century relevance of central bank lending capabilities. As long as lending of last resort continues to be an important central banking role, it is crucial that the lender be able to obtain timely information about any potential borrower. This is a key ground of the argument that the central bank should have a role in bank supervision and regulation. The central bank needs to know its customers.

Conceivably, the supervision and regulation of individual banking institutions need not be a central bank function. In some countries, it is housed in other government agencies. For example, in the United Kingdom all bank supervision was moved from the Bank of England to the FSA (Financial Services Authority) in 2000. The ECB has no direct role in bank supervision, which is done at the national level. And in the United States the Fed has always shared these functions with state and national agencies responsible for chartering banks, as well as with the deposit insurance agency.

One might argue that the real issue is effective communication between the central bank and any other agencies with supervisory authority. In practice, however, instances where the roles of supervisor and lender of last resort have been separated – such as in the United Kingdom, where the Bank of England acts as lender of last resort and the Financial Services Authority oversees the potential borrowers – have highlighted how difficult it is to communicate effectively in a crisis. As a result, the Conservative Party in the UK has proposed eliminating the FSA and returning bank supervision to the Bank of England.

The benefits of linking the lender of last resort and the role of supervision go beyond the advantages of rapid communication. The skills and expertise developed in the course of regulation and supervision may help the lender of last resort to innovate when necessary in a liquidity crisis. For example, the rapid introduction of new Fed lending facilities during the crisis under conditions of extreme stress would have been difficult in the absence of extensive hands-on experience in the financial system on the part of the Fed. Similarly, experience in regulation and supervision may be critical for the development of effective systemic risk regulation, which we will discuss below.

Thus, the thrust of our argument is that the central bank should have a role in the supervision, regulation and examination of financial institutions so that it is well informed about its potential borrowers. Further, the knowledge gathered in the regulatory process leaves the lender of last resort prepared to respond when crises emerge. We have not discussed here the parameters of supervision that keep the regulator well informed. Perhaps most important is the regular examination of banks and the setting of accounting and valuation standards. In addition, the determination and enforcement of capital adequacy and liquidity standards is essential to prevent individual institutions from becoming insolvent.

The scope of bank regulatory activities is well known. A more complex issue is determining which types of organizations should be supervised. The lender of last resort role probably is of greatest relevance in dealing with institutions whose instability would pose a direct threat to the financial system as a whole. The experience of the recent crisis suggests that large complex financial institutions (LCFIs) are more likely to be sources of systemic disruption. For this reason, there would appear to be a stronger case for linking the lender of last resort to the supervision of LCFIs than to the supervision of other financial institutions.

Nevertheless, it is possible for a wide array of small financial institutions to pose such a systemic threat if they face a common exposure that makes them collectively vulnerable. In the US, the thrift crisis of the early 1980s is the usual example although it really did not present the truly systemic risks that we faced in 2008–09. The best-known problems in the recent crisis were the LCFIs such as Lehman and AIG. However, the most dangerous aspects of the crisis were the meltdown of the commercial paper market and the run on money market funds, both examples where common shocks to many small entities had systemic implications.

The set of institutions that can present systemic risks includes financial institutions other than banks. The fact the Fed had little connection with the shadow banking system was a contributory factor to the panic that occurred at the height of the crisis. The legal authority to support lending to non-banks was at times unclear and lack of knowledge of their activities made intervention to lend or support shadow banks in both the US and Europe uncertain.

The Federal Reserve and its district Reserve Banks are naturally reluctant to give up their supervisory role over any banks, including smaller ones. Bank regulation is a major activity for the district banks. Ensuring the soundness of banks large and small is viewed as integral to the economic health of the regions they serve. Confidential information obtained in the course of supervising banks can be of use in evaluating monetary policy, especially when it helps policy makers to anticipate demand for and supply of credit. Nevertheless, the case for Fed supervision of smaller banks is less compelling than the case for supervision of large, potentially systemic financial institutions – including non-banks.[9]

Thus, we see that the central bank has a role to play in the regulation and supervision of any potential borrower. It should be party to regulation that monitors risk taking so that financial institutions remain individually solvent and do not need to turn to the lender of last resort. As long as we are thinking of risk taking by individual institutions, the central bank does not have to be principally involved in setting standards and conducting oversight; good communication could be adequate. However, the argument for central bank involvement is compelling when we consider financial institutions that might be part of a systemic failure.

SYSTEMIC RISK REGULATOR

Although systemic risk is not a new idea, the notion of an explicit systemic risk regulatory function is new. Addressing systemic threats was an implicit function of the Fed because its lender of last resort facility was the only tool available to respond to systemic risk problems. When clearing failures, Y2K concerns or the terrorist attacks of 9/11 threatened the operation of the financial system, the Fed's discount window was the tool available to address the problems. The availability of the discount window for emergency lending made it the central bank's tool for responding to systemic risks.

It is often hard to make a clear distinction in advance between lending that might be needed by an individual institution and lending that might be needed to prevent systemic problems. In some instances, support of a single institution (such as the Fed's use of the discount window to ameliorate the effects of operational problems) can prevent systemic problems. In other instances, lending to a specific institution such as AIG or a set of institutions such as the commercial paper market is needed to maintain the functioning of the financial system.

Emergency lending does take the central bank's focus away from monetary control and there are still some who would argue against any other role for central banks. However, the recent crisis demonstrated the importance of having an institution that can respond quickly and broadly to systemic risks.

A tool for responding to systemic risks is not the same thing as a macro-prudential regulator with the authority to monitor systemic risks and take regulatory actions to reduce them before they erupt into crisis. The fact that the central bank has the tools to respond to emergencies does not mean that it must also be the macro-prudential regulator. It is well suited to do so because of its existing connections with the financial system and, as the recent crisis highlighted, it is valuable to have one authority unambiguously responsible for responding to systemic risks. Interestingly, the recent financial reform legislation in the US (the 2010 Dodd–Frank bill) partially removes the Fed from that role by setting up an interagency Financial Stability Oversight Council as the systemic regulator.

A systemic risk regulator should have influence that stretches out in multiple directions. First, the systemic regulator needs to augment the oversight and supervision of institutions that are so large and interconnected that any insolvency would create systemic problems.

Second, it must be able to address systemic problems that can arise from smaller institutions facing a common vulnerability. For example, the 2008 run on money market funds, none of which was individually sufficiently large or interconnected to present a systemic risk, threatened the financial system. These funds, part of the so-called shadow banking system, lacked deposit insurance and automatic access to the lender of last resort and therefore were vulnerable because funds can be withdrawn at face value with little or no notice and assets are not always liquid.

Third, the systemic regulator must have authority over the shadow banking system, including any new institutions or instruments that may create new systemic risks. Important contributors to the crisis were shadow bank institutions – such as broker-dealers – that are dependent on the collateralized repo market.[10] The systemic regulator should have the authority to regulate such risk-laden market funding practices, in addition to the behaviour of any institution that can generate systemic risks.

Fourth, economic conditions can give rise to systemically risky activity. Rapid credit expansion, the deterioration of credit standards and asset price bubbles are all macro problems that can give rise to systemic weaknesses. For example, the extended period of low interest rates in the early 2000s promoted rapid credit expansion and some of the excesses, particularly in the mortgage markets, that generated the crisis. Thus the phrase 'macro-prudential regulation' arose to reflect the post-crisis realization that monetary policy needs to stay cognizant of the systemic stability implications of policy.

For these reasons, systemic risk and the regulation, supervision and oversight of individual financial institutions are closely linked. The monitoring of each financial institution individually is not sufficient for avoiding systemic problems. Thus, the systemic risk regulator should be a powerful entity. It should have explicit regulatory authority over systemically important institutions (the LCFIs). In addition, it should be able to rein in the systemically risky activities of all kinds of financial institutions – shadow banks, hedge funds, insurance companies, for example – including ones that are not otherwise subject to regulatory oversight. If the behaviour of any financial institution creates systemic threats, the regulator has reason to be concerned.

In the Greenspan–Bernanke era the Fed's narrow focus on macroeconomic monetary policy led to a policy culture that eschewed any concern about the potential for systemic problems. This is well illustrated by the debate that started in the late 1990s concerning whether asset price bubbles should be a concern of monetary policy (see Wadhwani, 2008). The issue is whether monetary policy should respond to sharp rises in asset prices and take action to prevent the growth (and the burst) of bubbles. Greenspan and Bernanke both argued against any role for asset prices in policy setting. In regard to bubbles, Greenspan (1999) told Congress that policy should 'mitigate the fallout when it occurs'. This has led famously to the notion that the role of the central bank is to mop up after the bubble bursts. Similarly, Bernanke (2002) said '"leaning against the bubble" is unlikely to be productive in practice'. Other central bankers seemed to agree that the policy tightening needed to prick a bubble would have to be large enough to push an economy into recession. The danger of false positives – tightening when there really was not a bubble – was viewed as too great to warrant any concern ex ante about bubbles.

In retrospect the debate had important implications that were not adequately appreciated. Monetary policy analysis broadly concerned with asset market conditions would have been paying closer attention to the role of financial institutions and the amounts of leverage. The policy discussions often took too simple a view by asking whether asset prices should be a macroeconomic target. The emphasis on bubbles in asset prices was misplaced because policy makers seemed to argue that asset prices only mattered when a bubble occurred. Bubbles are only identifiable as such when they burst. To my knowledge, no one articulated the view that policy makers should watch and evaluate asset price movements before a bubble bursts, or is even expected, because of their potentially important implications for systemic stability.

Central bankers emphasized inflation targeting and chose not to pay attention to potential bubbles. As a consequence, little attention was paid to the implications of asset prices for financial stability. Thus, policy makers paid little attention to significant developments such as increased lending, increasing leverage ratios and weakening financial institutions that are often associated with increasing asset prices. By choosing to ignore asset price inflation, the Fed chose to ignore these other developments as well. The narrow view of macro targets weakened any connection between monetary policy making and the systemic health of financial institutions.

Thus, experience tells us that central banks are well advised to be concerned with systemic stability; however, it is not self-evident how this concern should be expressed. There are two distinct dimensions of macro-prudential regulation. First is the one given the most attention in the recent crisis: crisis management, or the ability to respond in a timely and comprehensive manner to systemic problems. The Federal Reserve's use of section 13(3) lending authority and other innovations in the recent crisis are examples and there has been much discussion of whether these crisis response tools should be expanded or circumscribed because they were abused. As long as the central bank has the authority to lend in emergency situations, it should, as we argued above, have a role in the regulation of institutions that might present systemic risks. The second and more challenging aspect of macro-prudential regulation is how to set systemic risk standards for the financial sector as a whole: macro-prudential policy. Little is known about the tools for measuring systemic risks and the instruments to regulate it.

Central banks do not have a clear idea yet of what are appropriate measures of systemic risk or what they should be targeting in order to conduct macro-prudential risk management. The modestly named BIS Committee on the Global Financial System (CGFS) is addressing the issue. In a recent paper (CGFS, 2010) it acknowledges that its definition of systemic risk is vague because of 'its dependence on time- and economy-specific circumstances' (p. 2) and, further, that 'In most countries, macro prudential policy frameworks are at an early stage of development' (p. 8). Systemic risk may not be a new idea but systemic risk management is. Twenty-first-century central banks need to develop the tools for systemic risk measurement and management that are needed for crisis avoidance.

Experience has taught us how, for example, to set minimum capital requirements for an individual institution operating in a normal environment. We can determine the appropriate capital stock buffers that an institution needs to maintain in order to withstand a negative shock. But we have little experience in determining the buffers that individual institutions and the system as a whole need to maintain in the presence of a systemic shock or crisis.

Monetary authorities in both the US and Europe quickly introduced some efforts at prudential management in the immediate aftermath of the crisis in the form of 'stress tests'. These tests postulate a macroeconomic shock and simulate its effect on the balance sheets of financial institutions in order to determine whether the banks have sufficient capital to cope with the hypothesized stress. The Federal Reserve's initial stress tests were conducted on the 19 largest bank holding companies in the US. The results, announced in May 2009, had a calming effect on financial markets because the capital shortfalls were less than had been feared. The Committee of European Banking Supervisors along with other authorities conducted stress tests on a large number of European banks in both 2009 and 2010.

These stress tests are based on macroeconomic scenarios but are in the end examinations of individual banks rather than tests for systemic weakness. The appropriate systemic risk standards for both capital held by each bank and the aggregate amount of capital in the banking system (and hence overall leverage levels in the financial industry) are yet to be developed. Vice Chair of the Board of Governors of the Federal Reserve System Janet Yellen (2010) acknowledges that many of the tools of macro-prudential supervision are the same as those traditionally used for micro-prudential supervision. The standards to be used to measure systemic risks are missing and the responses to be used in the presence of systemic risks need to be defined. Yellen (2010, p. 3) further argues that 'Monetary policy cannot be a primary instrument for systemic risk management.' That is, a monetary tightening would not have been the only appropriate response to the developing systemic risks in the US in the years before the crisis. There are a few suggestions of what the appropriate tools might be, such as countercyclical capital requirements and contingent capital arrangements. However, much more needs to be done both to develop the means of measuring the presence of systemic risks and to put in place the tools to respond to it.

Thus, monetary policy, regulation of financial institutions and macro-prudential regulation are tightly linked together. As a result an argument can be made for giving the central bank a role in all three. Even if we view macro policy to be the primary function of the central bank, it needs to monitor financial institutions because no macro policy can succeed without financial stability. And since economic stability goals cannot be attained without a modicum of financial stability, the macroeconomic and macro-prudential roles are tied together. The micro-regulatory role is tied in as well since large complex institutions as well as panics among smaller institutions can have systemic implications.

These broad roles for the 21st-century central bank do not come without risks. The emergency responses to crisis, such as those put in place in 2008–09, may cross the line into fiscal policy and involve political judgments which might compromise the independence of the central bank and its ability to pursue its primary role, macroeconomic monetary policy. Goodfriend (2010) warns that central bank bailouts are politically contentious fiscal decisions that will destroy the central bank's independence. The Fed had never stepped over this line before and the 2010 Dodd–Frank bill will result in power sharing with other regulators and the Treasury. Broad oversight of the financial system should be a concern of the central bank but also, appropriately, a concern shared with other agencies.

CONCLUSION

As the 20th century drew to a close there seemed to be a consensus view of central banking. A central bank was a politically independent entity that was responsible for monetary control. Other functions were peripheral at best. For example, discount lending was a useful emergency facility but really just a remnant of the central bank's historical banking functions. Bank supervisory activities were also peripheral and could just as easily be located elsewhere. The crisis of 2007–09 changed these views forever by bringing the prudential and regulatory roles of central banks to the forefront and showing the interdependence of the roles.

I have made, I hope, a reasonably compelling case for a central bank with broad interrelated functions. First, a central bank should be able to conduct monetary policy without political interference; second, it should serve as the lender of last resort to provide liquidity in emergency situations; and third, it should have a role in monitoring systemic risks and responding when they might emerge. That is a rather large remit for one government agency. But it is inevitable due to the connections among these functions.

As a result, central banking is pulled into the realm of politics as the border between monetary policy and fiscal policy becomes blurred. Consider the following. In 2008, the Federal Reserve sold billions of dollars of government securities from its portfolio and used the funds to finance some new corporations – the Maiden Lane corporations (the New York Fed is located on Maiden Lane), which bought assets from Bear Stearns, AIG and so on – and to create new funding facilities such as those used to support the commercial paper market. Is this a proper role for the central bank or has it crossed the line into the realm of fiscal policy, the legislation and appropriation of funds? If Congress wants to buy a bank or nationalize a corporation or bail out GM or funnel funds to the commercial paper market, it has the right to do so. It passes legislation and appropriates funds. The government would have to fund such expenditures and, of course, it would do so by selling bonds – a fiscal activity. Indeed, buying GM was a fiscal activity by the US government. But, that is exactly what the Fed did when it 'bailed out' Wall Street. Has the central bank, in the name of the lender of last resort to the financial sector and the sceptre of systemic risk, usurped the role of Congress and the President to conduct fiscal policy – decide how much the government will spend, what it will be spent on and how expenditures should be financed? These are hard questions to answer. They deserve more attention from economists and politicians.

The recent crisis suggests that a broad role of the central bank that encompasses macro policy, supervision and regulation of banks and systemic risk (or macro-prudential) oversight is warranted. Although everyone agrees that monetary policy is a central bank concern, there are wide differences of opinion regarding the extent to which the central bank should also have responsibility for the supervision and regulation of individual financial institutions and for systemic regulation of the financial sector as a whole. Further, there is wide disagreement regarding the border between appropriate central bank crisis responses and fiscal actions.

The complexity of these issues does not obviate my contention that the strong linkages among the three functions of a central bank are sufficiently compelling to warrant giving the central bank broad authority in all three of them. As a consequence, central banks may be more political institutions than before.[11] Policy makers were aware that their innovative responses to the crisis increased the political involvement of the central bank. At the height of the crisis, in March 2009, the Fed and the Treasury issued a statement outlining their respective roles and the distinction between them. Goodfriend (2010) suggests that a new 'accord' is necessary to formally define the boundaries of Federal Reserve credit and lending policies.

It is fascinating how little attention has been addressed to these issues in the past. They just did not seem to warrant the bother. But, the questions will linger for a long time – the role of central banks warrants a lot more attention. For sure, the late 20th-century view of central banks is gone forever. The notion of an independent agency with the remit of monetary control is much too limited to be realistic. Inevitably, the central bank has other functions which drag it back into the political arena. Exactly how the 21st-century central bank ought to be designed is an open question worthy of more attention.

NOTES

1. Thanks are due to Stephen Cecchetti, Thomas Cooley, Dubravko Mihaljek, Kermit Schoenholtz, William Silber and Richard Sylla for helpful discussions, though the responsibility for all the opinions and errors found here is entirely mine.
2. Perhaps it is only of symbolic importance but only the Board of Governors of the Federal Reserve has a '.gov' web address while the regional Federal Reserve banks are private banking corporations with '.org' addresses.
3. Nevertheless, the Fed did not always maintain an independent approach to policy. Notably, starting in World War II the Treasury essentially set interest rate policy, an arrangement which only ended with the Treasury Accord in 1951.
4. Perhaps Gordon Brown's most triumphant moment as Chancellor of the Exchequer was in May 1997 when he granted the Bank its independence. He announced that the Chancellor would no longer meet monthly with the Governor of the Bank of England to determine interest rate policy, saying: 'I want to set in place a long term framework for economic prosperity . . .'.
5. Goodhart (2010) identifies three historical eras regarding the role of central banks: the real bills doctrine of the Victorian age, a mid-century period of government control and the market-oriented era that ended with the crisis.
6. The discussion draws on Chapter 2 ('The power of central banks and the future of the Federal Reserve System' by T. Cooley et al.) in Acharya et al. (2010).
7. The monthly average effective fund rates less the percentage change from a year ago in the seasonally adjusted CPI-U was negative from April 2001 until September 2006.
8. Of course it is also common for legislation to explicitly make the central bank the agency responsible for bank regulation and examination. The Federal Reserve has primary regulatory responsibility for bank holding companies and state chartered members of the Federal Reserve System.
9. Alan Blinder (2010, p. 132) agrees that Fed supervision of small banks is less than compelling and 'peripheral to its core mission'.
10. For an explanation of how the shadow banking system engaged in banking see Gorton (2010).
11. Meltzer (2010) argues that the Fed has always been subject to political influence. The idea of an independent insulated central bank was to some extent a caricature favoured by advocates of mechanical monetary policy rules.

REFERENCES

Acharya, V. et al. (eds) (2010), *Regulating Wall Street,* John Wiley & Sons.

Bernanke, Ben (2002), 'Asset price "bubbles" and monetary policy', 15 October.

Blinder, Alan S. (2010), 'How central should the central bank be?', *Journal of Economic Literature*, **48** (1), 123–33.

Committee on the Global Financial System (2010), 'Macroprudential instruments and frameworks: a stocktaking of issues and experiences', CGFS Papers No. 38, Bank for International Settlements, May.

Federal Reserve Board (2003), 'Monetary policy report to the Congress', 15 July, http://www.federalreserve.gov/boarddocs/hh/2003/july/FullReport.txt.

Fettig, David (2002), 'Lender of *more than* last resort', Federal Reserve Bank of Minneapolis, *The Region,* 14–19 December, 44–7.

Goodfriend, Marvin (2010), 'Central banking in the credit turmoil: an assessment of Federal Reserve practices', April.

Goodhart, C.A.E. (2010), 'The changing role of central banks', BIS Working Papers No. 326, November.

Gorton, Gary B. (2010), *Slapped by the Invisible Hand: The Panic of 2007,* New York: Oxford University Press.

Greenspan, Alan (1999), Testimony to US House of Representatives Committee on Banking and Financial Services, 22 July.

Meltzer, Alan (2010), 'Politics and the Fed', Carnegie Rochester Conference 'The future of central banking', April.

Schwartz, Anna (1992), 'The misuse of the Fed's discount window', Federal Reserve Bank of St. Louis *Review*, September/October, 58–69.

Wadhwani, Sushil (2008), 'Should monetary policy respond to asset price bubbles? Revisiting the debate,' *National Institute Economic Review,* 206, October, 25–34.

Yellen, Janet (2010), 'Macroprudential supervision and monetary policy in the post-crisis world', Board of Governors of the Federal Reserve System, 11 October.

11. Monetary policy challenges in the CESEE region: architecture for an earthquake zone[1]

Bas B. Bakker and Leslie Lipschitz

In 2002, one of the present authors was talking repeatedly in Europe about the imminence of potentially overwhelming capital flows to the newly emerging market economies, about the criticality of risk pricing and the complications from seemingly erratic risk premia, and about the impossible dilemmas for monetary policy. At one seminar – at the ECB – he described the challenge for monetary policy as being akin to that of architecture in an earthquake zone. At the time he was chastised for being alarmist. Others said there was little evidence of such problematic capital flows. His response at the time was: 'Just wait and watch.'

In 2006, the other author warned that large capital inflows into emerging Europe were generating imbalances and vulnerabilities similar to those seen in emerging Asia prior to the Asian crisis. He was told not to worry: 'Europe was different', capital flowing from rich to poor countries should be celebrated rather than be worried about, and the risk of a sudden stop in capital flows was very small.[2]

Before embarking on prescriptions it is helpful to undertake a diagnostic review of the recent history – a sort of ex post waiting and watching. The review below is conducted with a very broad brush. The objective is to cull useful generalizations, not to cover all the particulars of the individual economies. Clearly, of course, our appreciation of this history is influenced strongly by our earlier writing on the economic mechanisms at work.

THE HISTORY: A CRUDE SKETCH

The problems in much of the region had to do with very large capital inflows that financed rapid credit expansion and booming domestic demand. In many respects the mechanisms involved were clearly understood well before the crisis, at least as long ago as the Asian crisis of 1997–98, but really even before this.

The theoretical argument goes as follows. The emerging European economies had (and still have) lower capital–labour ratios than the advanced economies. Therefore, with converging institutions and technology levels, their notional 'closed-economy' equilibrium real interest rates should be significantly higher than those of the advanced countries. At the same time, for a variety of reasons (including Balassa–Samuelson effects), they would probably face trend real appreciations of their currencies. This combination – higher interest rates and real appreciation – would elicit very large capital inflows and impose a serious policy dilemma (the Tosovsky dilemma) on policy makers. The dilemma is as follows. If interest rates were kept low enough to discourage arbitraging capital inflows, they would be well below the marginal product of capital – so investment would far exceed saving and there would be a substantial current account deficit. If, however, interest rates were allowed to rise significantly above those abroad, there would be large capital inflows and (again) a substantial current account deficit.[3] The dilemma could only be resolved through risk premia that increased steadily with the current account deficit and/or other indicators of vulnerability, but the evidence suggested that risk premia were not that well behaved.[4]

Insofar as interest rates were above those in the advanced economies, countries with floating exchange rates would be subject to large nominal appreciations that might undermine competitiveness and slow growth; those with fixed rate regimes would have an even more difficult time dealing with the effects of capital inflows on credit expansion and domestic demand. The issue of whether to fix or float was not a matter of whether the latter would provide effective monetary autonomy; in either case the economy and monetary policy would be buffeted by external forces. Thus the choice was couched in different terms than in the early literature on the subject. Now the question was this: did a regime that fixed the exchange rate (or one that limited movement to some pre-established band) create moral hazard and encourage carry trade by providing an effective exchange guarantee to domestic agents who borrowed in foreign currency (or foreign investors who took on local currency exposure)? In any event, to the extent that risk premia were erratic – and much of the evidence suggested that they were influenced by events exogenous to the individual economies – all of the countries, whether fixing or floating, could face high volatility and extreme difficulties for stabilization policy.

Another strand of this argument went as follows. If the 'shock' of a closer association with Western Europe (through actual or prospective EU membership and perhaps eventual euro adoption) was, in effect, a drop in risk premia and thus both lower interest rates and a surge of capital inflows, there would be a considerable danger of this distorting the allocation of resources and creating asset price bubbles. Lower interest rates and easier credit conditions influence asset prices – perhaps most importantly housing prices – almost immediately. Rising real estate prices combined with easier credit conditions and incentives for speculation and leverage risked a dangerous bubble. At the same time, the rise in the relative returns in the non-traded sector – primarily real estate – would shift resources out of traded goods to the detriment of exports and the external current account.

These theoretical propositions, developed initially in response to ructions in the Czech foreign exchange market in the spring of 1997, became much more relevant for Europe after 2003.

It is useful to review what happened in the crisis in somewhat stylized form.

In the period before the crisis (1995–2007) per capita growth in the CESEE region was very strong – surpassed only by India and China (Figure 11.1).

The period until 2003 was one of rapid real economic integration with Western Europe: producers in the CESEE region became part of the European production chain as Western European manufacturers subcontracted out intermediate production to lower-cost CESEE countries. Growth was driven to a significant extent by exports. Much of the capital inflow went into traded goods' production.

From 2003 until the crisis of 2007–08, however, growth was attributable primarily to a boom in domestic demand (Figure 11.2), reflecting very rapid credit expansion (financed in large part by capital inflows from abroad) (Figures 11.3 and 11.4), booming asset prices (Figure 11.5 shows real estate prices), and pro-cyclical government spending. Of course, as we will stress below, this generalization does not apply equally to all of the countries in the region: the Czech Republic, Poland and the Slovak Republic would not fit this characterization. Countries with fixed exchange rates and deep cross-border financial integration were much more affected by capital inflows and, even if they recognized the vulnerabilities that were being built up, they struggled to find instruments to contain these developments.[5] Thus, for a number of countries, the capital inflows and corresponding current account deficits were extraordinarily large, and, increasingly, the financial flows were funding spending in the non-traded sector. Even FDI flows were going more and more into financial services, real estate and construction (Figure 11.6). Risk premia seemed impervious to the obvious vulnerabilities reflected in housing price booms and wide current account deficits.[6] Consider the incentives behind

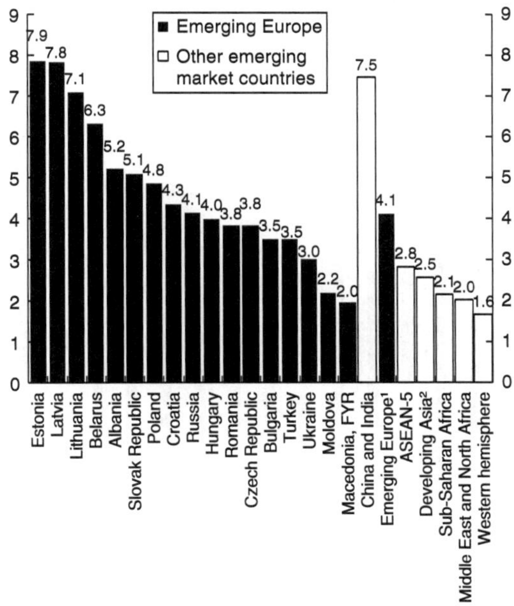

Notes:
1. Includes Czech Republic and Slovak Republic.
2. Excludes China and India.

Source: IMF, World Economic Outlook database.

Figure 11.1 Emerging Europe and selected regions: real per capita GDP growth, 1995–2007 (annual percentage change in PPP terms)

the flows. In 2006, nominal lending rates in the Czech Republic were 5.5–6 per cent with wage inflation of 5–6 per cent, so that real interest rates were generally slightly positive. In Latvia, on the other hand, nominal lending rates were 7 per cent with wage inflation at 23 per cent – a hugely negative real interest rate domestically. Clearly the demand for credit must have been very strong at these real rates – and Latvia's exchange regime severely constrained its ability to set interest rates more appropriate to its circumstances. From the perspective of a foreign investor there was a higher return to be made in Latvia – both because of the higher interest margin and because of the stronger demand for credit. But most of the new loans in Latvia were given in euros: this allowed foreign banks to lend large amounts without having an open foreign currency position. Borrowers

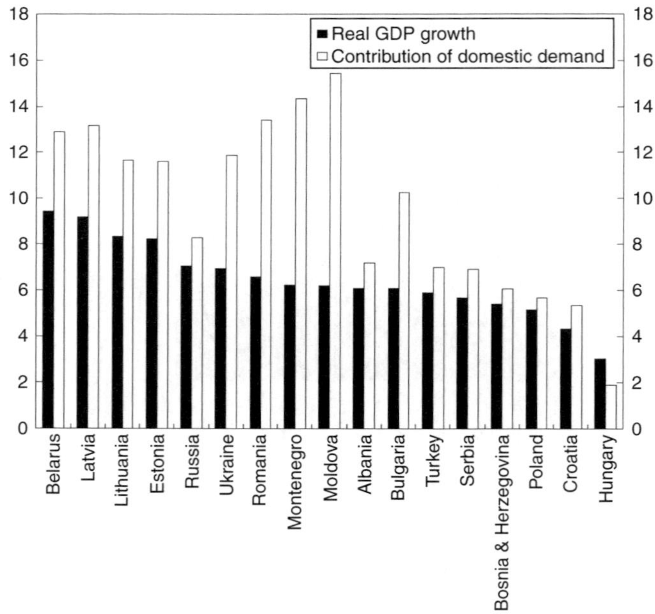

Note: 1. As the boom in the Baltic states ended in 2007, data for the Baltics refer to 2002–07.

Sources: IMF, World Economic Outlook database, Haver Analytics and IMF staff calculations.

Figure 11.2 Emerging Europe: pre-crisis real GDP growth and contribution of domestic demand (average 2003–08,[1] in per cent)

were induced to borrow in euros by a lower interest rate – and, with the exchange rate peg (an implicit exchange rate guaranty from the government), there did not seem to be much exchange risk. Given these incentives there was a plausible argument that any policy to constrain domestic bank lending would simply have led to disintermediation and direct borrowing from foreign banks.

From this history all the predictable results flowed: huge indirect foreign currency exposure and maturity transformation by banks; and a consequent fear of floating by those countries with fixed exchange rates lest depreciation lead to crippling balance sheet losses.

It is interesting to look at how the crisis has played out in the different countries. Consider, for example, Bulgaria, Estonia, Latvia,

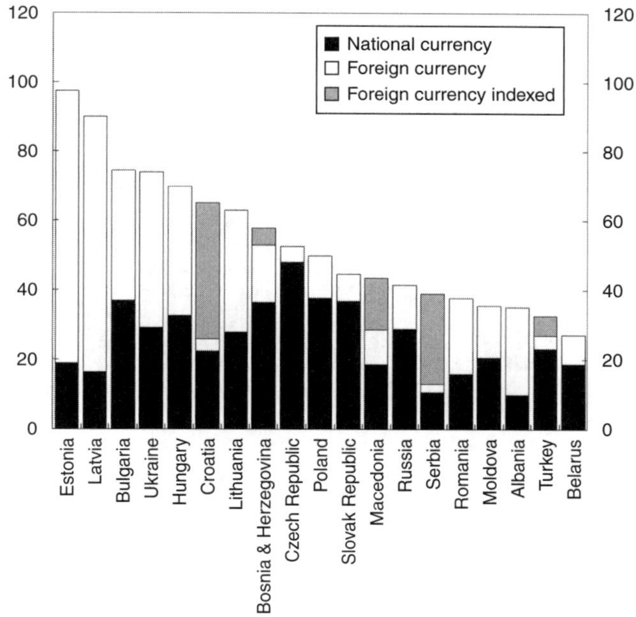

Sources: National authorities and IMF, International Financial Statistics.

Figure 11.3 Emerging Europe: total private sector credit by currency, 2008 (stock in per cent of GDP)

Lithuania and Ukraine (which only partly fits this picture) – countries with wide pre-crisis current account deficits, rapid pre-crisis domestic demand growth, large capital account inflows, and high real estate price inflation. These countries, which saw massive reductions in net capital inflows during the crisis, have suffered most severely, with GDP still well below the level of the third quarter of 2008 (Figure 11.7). (Others, most notably Poland and the Czech and Slovak Republics, are now above or not much below their third-quarter 2008 levels.) While exports have recovered in most CESEE countries (Figure 11.8), these most-affected countries have not yet seen much of a recovery in domestic demand (Figure 11.9) – hence the much weaker GDP. Most of these countries had rigidly fixed exchange rates (conventional pegs or currency boards); this explains the salient facts in the pre-crisis history and the weak subsequent recoveries as domestic demand has had to bear the brunt of the adjustment.

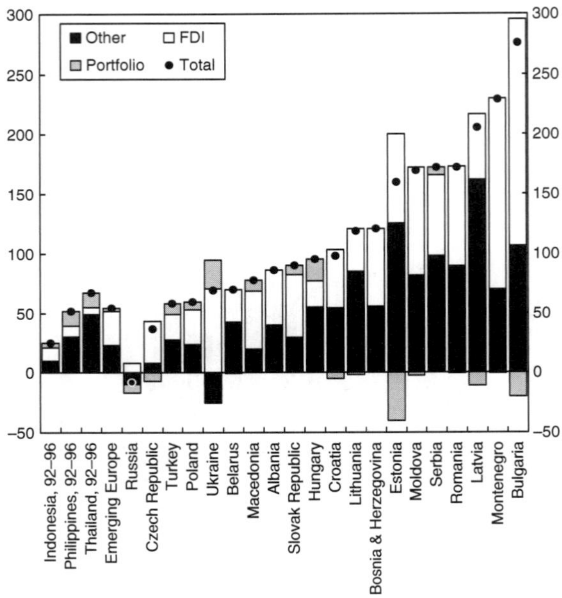

Note: 1. As the boom in the Baltic states ended in 2007, data for the Baltics refer to 2002–07 (in per cent of GDP).

Source: IMF, World Economic Outlook database.

Figure 11.4 Emerging Europe: cumulative net capital inflows, 2003–08[1] (per cent of 2003 GDP)

THE LESSONS FOR MONETARY POLICY

The European context limits the monetary policy options – particularly for countries committed to less exchange rate flexibility en route to euro area membership.

In theory, given the underlying mechanisms and incentives, countries with fixed exchange rates should see large capital inflows, asset inflation, current account deficits, price inflation, and a reallocation toward non-traded goods – the whole set of developments exemplified by the history of, for example, the Baltic countries. For countries with flexible exchange rates, incipient capital flows should force a nominal appreciation with similar real effects, albeit lower inflation. Yet the exchange guaranty implicit in the commitment to a fixed exchange rate and the disincentive created by a degree of exchange rate volatility seems to have had real

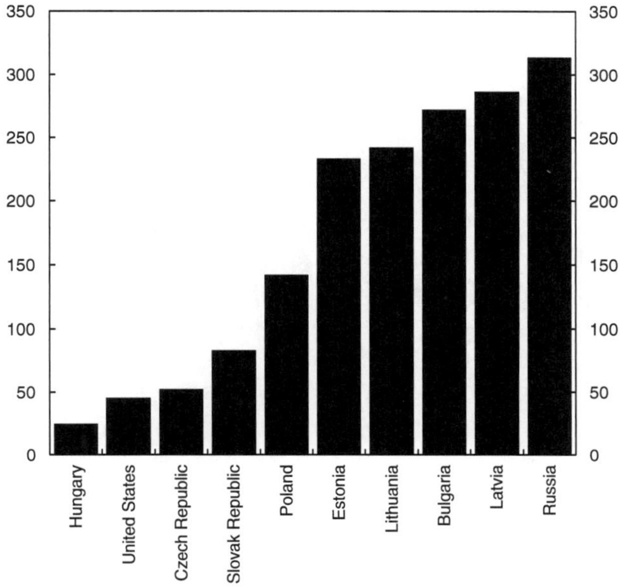

Note: 1. As the boom in the Baltic states ended in 2007, data for the Baltics refer to 2002–07.

Sources: Haver Analytics and country statistical offices.

Figure 11.5 Emerging Europe: change in real estate prices, 2003–08[1] (percentage change)

effects. So one piece of advice would be to behave like Poland or the Czech Republic – that is, focus on inflation and let the exchange rate float (and, of course, complement monetary policy with serious micro- and macro-prudential policies for the financial sector).

But this monetary policy advice is useless if a country is bent on limiting its exchange rate flexibility en route to the goal of euro adoption. Here the advice must be less simple and more eclectic. But perhaps it can be summed up as follows: do everything possible to avoid excess – excessive capital inflows, excessive credit expansion, excessive inflation of either conventional price indices or of asset prices, and excessive current accounts deficits – and use all the tools available.

This prescription is easier to state than to put into practice. For a start, what is excess? And if a situation is characterized by excess, won't market forces effect a change through, for example, higher risk premia? If we have learned anything from the experience of the last few years, it is that we

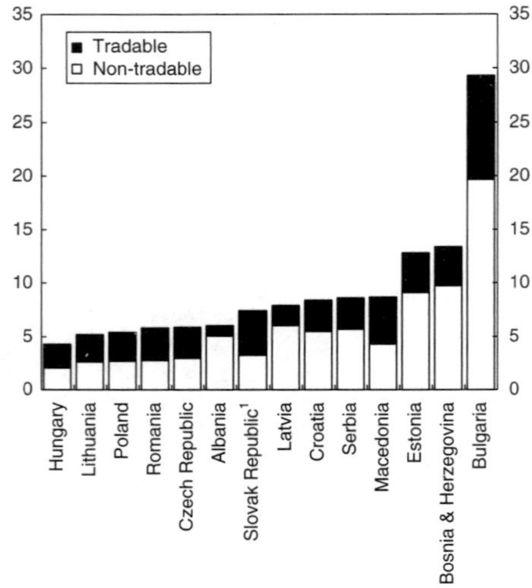

Notes:
1. Data refer to 2006.
2. The tradable sectors consist of manufacturing, agriculture, mining, retail, hotels and restaurants, while the non-tradable sectors are construction, electricity, transport, communication, real estate and financial intermediation.

Sources: IMF, World Economic Outlook database, and WIIW database on foreign direct investment.

Figure 11.6 Emerging Europe: foreign direct investment flow in tradable and non-tradable sectors,[2] 2007 (per cent of GDP)

should take a conservative view of excess and that we should be very sceptical of market forces, especially as regards the pricing of risk.

So, in practice, policy makers should scrutinize all of the variables mentioned. If, for example, there is a significant increase in the rate of credit expansion, and especially if this is correlated with capital inflows and asset price inflation, they should take pre-emptive action to dampen these developments. It is unlikely that monetary policy will suffice – indeed higher interest rates may simply exacerbate inflows – so that the armoury required must include serious micro-prudential, macro-prudential and fiscal instruments. Credit surges might sensibly elicit increases in bank capital requirements and liquidity requirements to limit maturity transformation (especially in foreign currency). Limits on lending (or borrowing) in foreign currency will require foreign financiers to shift to domestic currency loans and hedge the exchange risk: the limits on liquid markets for hedging will probably constrain such lending. There are circumstances where marginal reserve

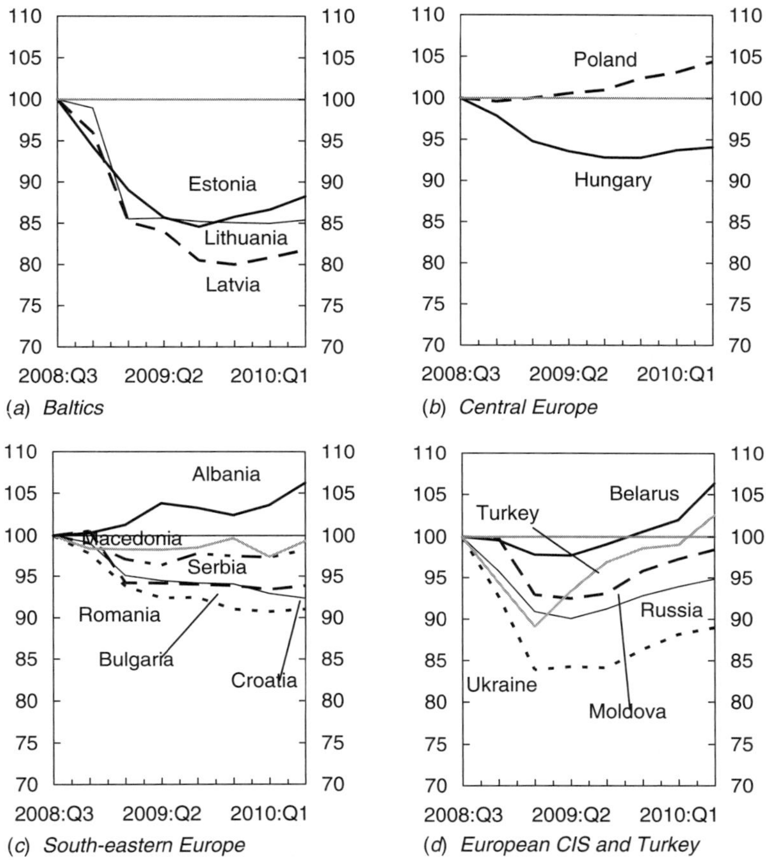

Sources: Eurostat, Haver Analytics and IMF staff calculations.

Figure 11.7 Emerging Europe: real GDP 2008:Q3–2010:Q2 (seasonally adjusted, index 2008:Q3 = 100)

requirements or other, more explicit, taxes on bank lending, or certain types of lending, may be warranted. Among fiscal instruments, higher taxes on short-term real estate capital gains, or transaction taxes on mortgage lending (beyond the first house) or on high loan-to-value loans may be worth considering. In sum, a highly eclectic policy is what we would favour.

Eclectic policies of the type described fall into two categories: blunt instruments, aimed at discouraging huge inflows, and more targeted instruments that seek not to discourage the inflows per se, but rather to

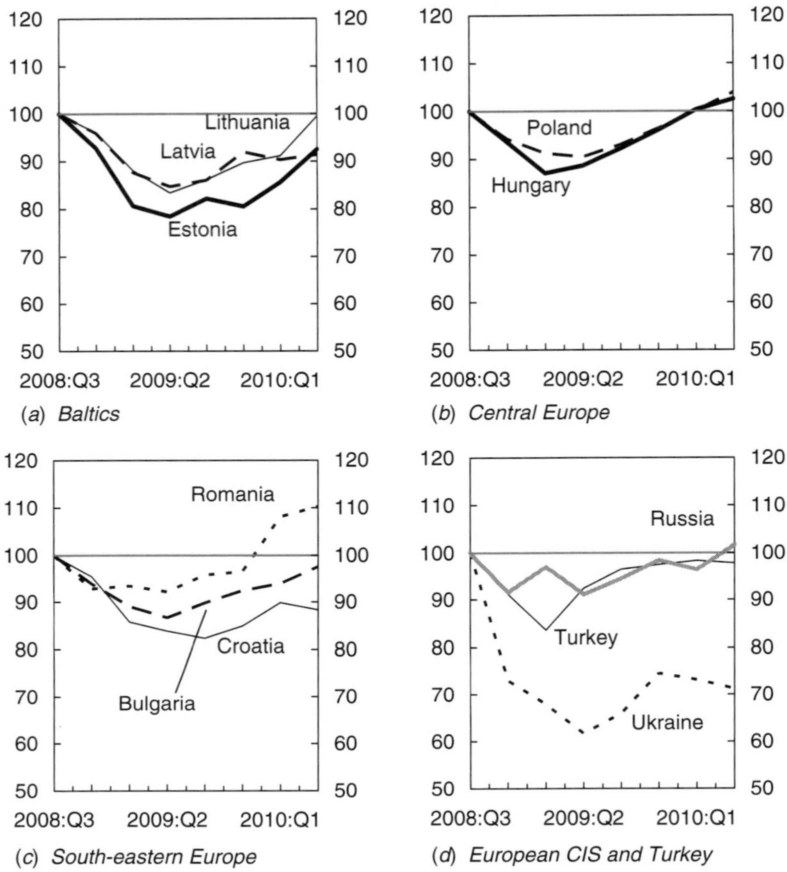

Sources: Eurostat, Haver Analytics and IMF staff calculations.

Figure 11.8 Emerging Europe: real exports 2008:Q3–2010:Q2 (seasonally adjusted, index 2008:Q3 = 100)

limit their being directed into areas likely to distort allocation or create bubbles. This second type of instrument, though perhaps more politically palatable in some circumstances, may be more difficult to make effective in the face of creative financial innovation.

One final point should be stressed. The costs of crises are borne by the citizens of both creditor and debtor countries, though clearly not in equal measure. The onus of preventing damaging carry-trade flows cannot be on recipient countries alone. Unless central banks and financial regulators in

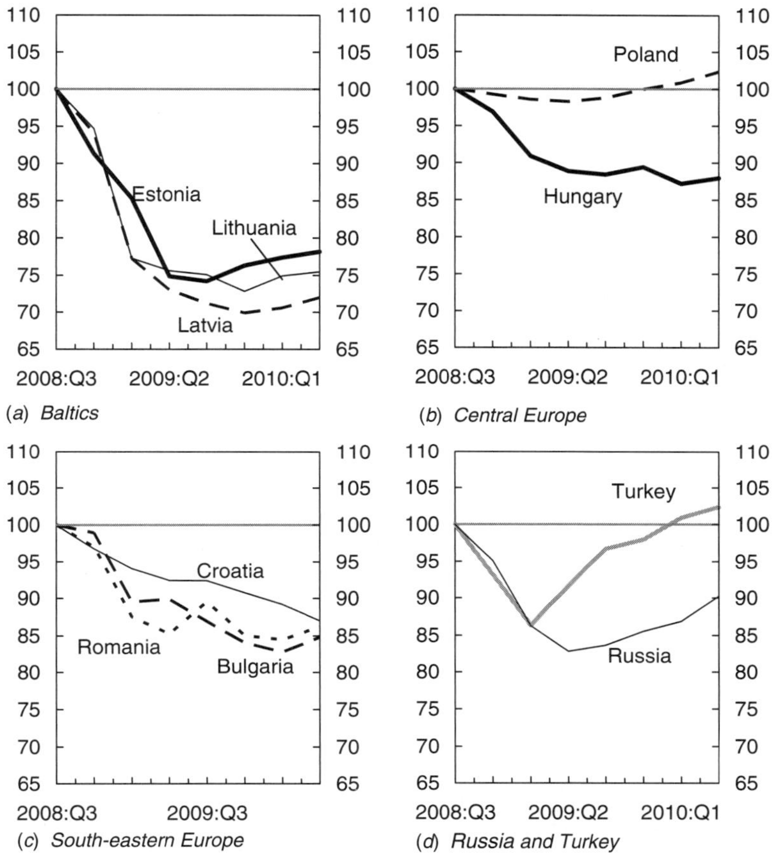

Sources: Eurostat; Haver Analytics and IMF staff calculations.

Figure 11.9 Emerging Europe: real domestic demand, 2008:Q3–2010:Q2 (seasonally adjusted, index 2008:Q3 = 100)

creditor and debtor countries work together, the huge incentives for such ultimately destabilizing capital flows may prove too difficult to contain.

NOTES

1. The authors are grateful for comments from Ales Bulir and Susan Schadler. This presentation draws heavily on the IMF's October 2010 Regional Economic Outlook for Europe, but errors of fact or analysis are attributable solely to the authors. The views

expressed herein are those of the authors and should not be attributed to the IMF, its Executive Board, or its management.
2. See Bakker and Vladkova-Hollar (2006) and Sorsa et al. (2007).
3. While both cases would entail large capital inflows, in the first case the current account imbalance would be primary and in the second case the capital inflows would drive the process.
4. Lipschitz et al. (2002a, 2002b, 2004, 2005) argued in a series of papers that huge capital inflows into the emerging countries of Europe were inevitable and would pose an extraordinarily difficult dilemma (the Tosovsky dilemma) for monetary policy and stabilization policy more generally. But well before this Schadler et al. (1993) examined the issue of capital surges in the early 1990s – of the six countries examined, three experienced crises in the five years after the study.
5. See Bakker and Gulde (2010) for a discussion of policy challenges in the run-up to the crisis.
6. See Luengnaruemitchai and Schadler (2007), who show that risk premia in emerging European countries were reduced by EU membership and were lower than would have been predicted by fundamentals.

REFERENCES

Bakker, Bas B. and Anne-Marie Gulde (2010), 'The credit boom in the EU new member states: bad luck or bad policies?', IMF Working Paper 10/130, 1 May, Washington, DC: International Monetary Fund.

Bakker, Bas B. and I. Vladkova-Hollar (2006), 'Asia 1996 and Eastern Europe (2006), Déjà-vu all over again?', mimeo, International Monetary Fund.

Lipschitz, Leslie, Timothy Lane and Alex Mourmouras (2002a), 'The Tosovsky dilemma: capital surges in transition countries', *Finance & Development*, **39** (3), September.

Lipschitz, Leslie, Timothy Lane and Alex Mourmouras (2002b), 'Capital flows to transition economies: master or servant?' IMF Working Paper 02/11, International Monetary Fund, October (subsequently, *Czech Journal of Economics and Finance* (2006), **56**, 5–6).

Lipschitz, Leslie, Timothy Lane and Alex Mourmouras (2004), 'How capital flows will influence the EU accession countries of Central and Eastern Europe in supervisory systems, fiscal soundness and international capital movement: more challenges for new EU members', Vienna: SUERF, The European Money and Finance Forum, SUERF Studies 2004/1.

Lipschitz, Leslie, Timothy Lane and Alex Mourmouras (2005), 'Real convergence, capital flows, and monetary policy: notes on the European transition countries', in Susan Schadler (ed.), *Euro Adoption in Central and Eastern Europe: Opportunities and Challenges*, Washington, DC: International Monetary Fund.

Luengnaruemitchai, Pipat and Susan Schadler (2007), 'Do economists' and financial markets' perspectives on the new members of the EU differ?', IMF Working Paper 07/65, March, Washington, DC: International Monetary Fund.

Schadler, Susan et al. (1993), 'Recent experiences with surges in capital flows', IMF Occasional Paper No. 108, Washington, DC: International Monetary Fund.

Sorsa, P. et al. (2007), 'Vulnerabilities in emerging Southeastern Europe – how much cause for concern?', IMF Working Paper, 07/326, 1 October, Washington, DC: International Monetary Fund.

12. A policy recipe for successful convergence of CESEE countries in the post-crisis world

Júlia Király, Attila Csajbók and Mihály András Kovács[1]

The financial crisis is not something that will fade away quickly; its effects will most probably stay with us for several years. Our impression is that the crisis clearly changed the rules of the game for emerging countries with the intention to converge to developed countries. This road will be much bumpier compared to what it looked like in the past, therefore it requires a very conscious strategy in policy making. This chapter explores what lies ahead for Central, Eastern and South-Eastern European (CESEE) countries regarding their convergence process in this new post-crisis environment.

First, we sketch the new rules of the game in the post-crisis world. Then monetary policy options and macro-prudential challenges in the years ahead will be outlined. Finally, we make a few remarks on euro area accession. Most remarks will be general, that is, valid for all CESEE countries. Others will be more relevant for countries with a high foreign currency debt burden.

1 CRISIS AND CONVERGENCE IN THE CESEE COUNTRIES

The financial crisis brought a reassessment of the riskiness of debt financing. Those countries where real convergence was accompanied by current account deficits and excessive debt flows had to face deeper recessions (see Figure 12.1).

The reliance of CESEE countries on foreign funding depended on two key elements of the macroeconomic framework: fiscal and exchange rate policies. First, countries with *tight fiscal policies* and low government debt ratios (for example, the Czech Republic and Poland as opposed to

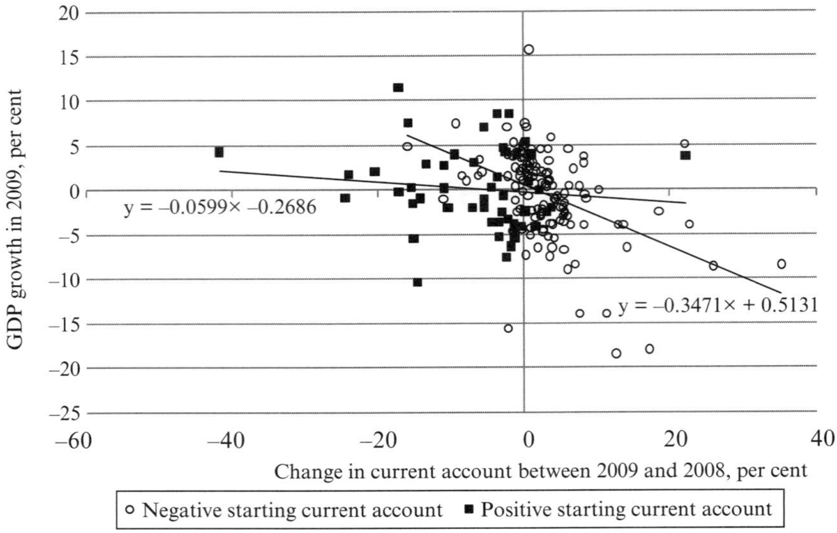

Source: IMF WEO database.

Figure 12.1 Relationship between the initial current account and economic growth in the financial crisis

Hungary) ceteris paribus had lower external imbalances. Second, *flexible exchange rate systems* (flexible inflation targeting versus currency board regimes) ceteris paribus helped prevent large credit booms. Naturally, these two parameters do not capture all the relevant information on whether a country became fragile in macroeconomic terms prior to the crisis. However research has shown that they were instrumental for the resilience of countries with respect to excessive capital inflows and sudden stops (see, for example, Bakker and Gulde, 2010). In addition, differences in macro-prudential policies in controlling capital flows helped to some extent to mitigate excessive capital flows, but their effectiveness was very far from perfect.

Though financial markets started to consolidate somewhat in the second half of 2009, we believe that lower risk tolerance compared with pre-crisis levels will prevail in the next few years. This is a natural consequence of global deleveraging, which takes several years after a financial crisis (Tang and Upper, 2010). As is shown in several papers (and illustrated in Figure 12.2), deleveraging means that CESEE countries in the post-crisis world might rely on external financing to a lesser extent than previously (Atoyan, 2010; MNB, 2010). Unless these countries find more domestic savings to finance the catching-up process, real convergence will slow down.

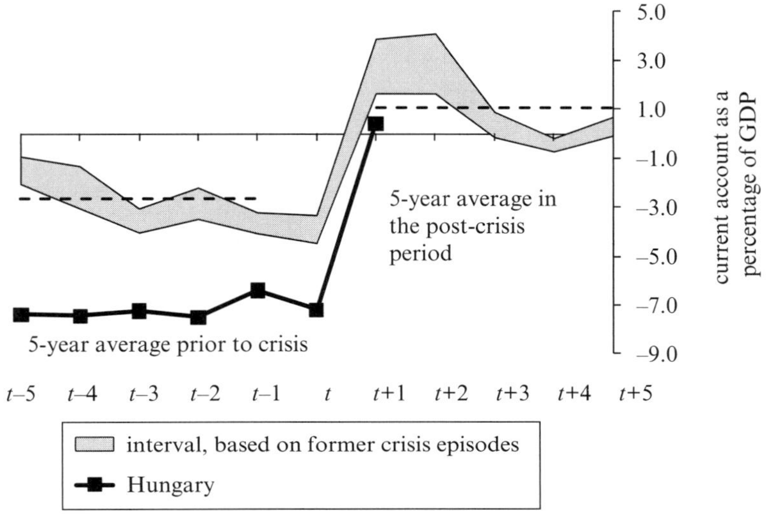

Note: The band is based on the min-max range of different crisis episodes; *t* refers to the start of the crisis.

Source: Annual data, using the database of Laeven and Valencia (2008).

Figure 12.2 Current account adjustment in crisis

Lower risk tolerance at the end of the day might lead to higher uncertainty, and higher volatility. Lower risk tolerance means that economic sustainability had become a key issue and there are very few, if any, countries among the CESEE group that are firmly on a sustainable path. The closer a country is to a point where the sustainability of its economic policy is questioned, the more sensitive it becomes to both global and country-specific economic news. In Hungary we had to learn this lesson several years ago. We need economic policies that push countries towards sustainability.

On the *fiscal* side sustainability requires tight policies, that is, we have to decrease indebtedness to levels where countries do not become excessively reliant on external financing sources. As CESEE countries are less developed than core Europe, the same level of government debt cannot be afforded, contrary to what traditional macroeconomics would suggest. As lower GDP per capita implies lower household wealth, the same level of government debt as, for example, in Germany would require much more external financing, hence external debt. This is also a lesson that can be learnt from the Hungarian case (see Figure 12.3). Tight fiscal policy also

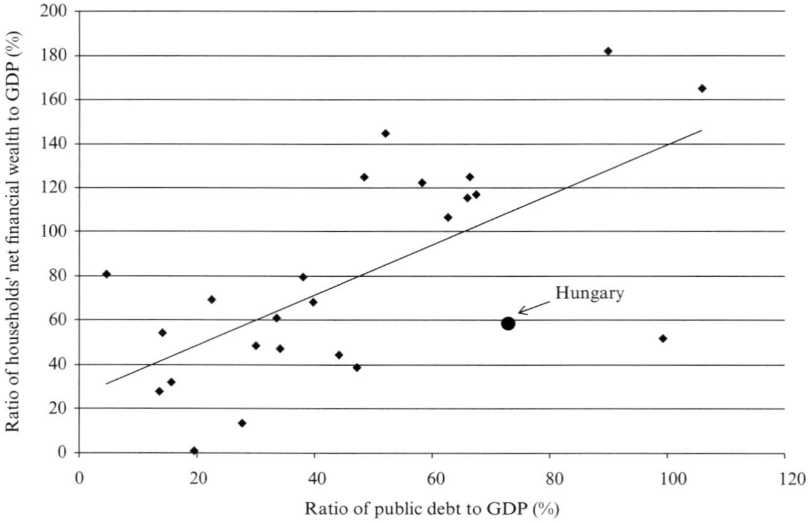

Source: Eurostat.

Figure 12.3 Household net wealth and government debt in Europe, 2008

helps private savings to finance private investments and hence we can avoid a slowdown in real convergence in a period of scarce external financing.

However it is clear that most problems among CESEE countries, perhaps apart from Hungary, were caused by excesses in the private sector rather than by excessive government spending. Though as it was shown during 2010 in the case of 'peripheral Europe', this picture can change quickly; that is, systemic risk in the private sector can easily turn into government debt.

Regarding private sector imbalances, the issue is even more complex, as we cannot identify a single actor that would be responsible for the behaviour of a whole sector. Here we have two options for policy intervention: monetary and macro-prudential, and one should not forget about their interaction. Let us look at each of them in turn.

2 MONETARY POLICY AND POST-CRISIS UNCERTAINTY

As we argued before, the crisis brought a reassessment of risk, resulting in the reassessment of sustainable external balances. Foreign investors are not the only actors to change their opinion regarding the most likely path of future variables. Households, corporates and all economic actors should reassess the sustainability of their consumption and investment paths. With forward-looking agents, this means that they react now more strongly in output, expenditures and prices compared with how they did in the past. All this means an extreme level of uncertainty.

In such an environment, we need a robust monetary strategy that provides a solid framework for life under higher uncertainty. We need a transparent framework flexible enough to absorb risk premium shocks, which at the same time ensures price and financial stability in the long run. Flexible inflation targeting might be considered a system that can facilitate this. Inflation targeting as a framework can give a firm nominal anchor but also the flexibility to (1) avoid reacting to excessive risk premium volatility with interest rate policy and (2) incorporate other policy considerations, like macro-prudential ones.

It is also obvious however that one instrument, namely interest rate policy, cannot be sufficient to achieve both price and financial stability. One of the most important lessons from the financial crisis is that there can be conflicts between these two goals. Empirical evidence suggests that increasing price and macroeconomic stability gives extreme incentives to financial risk taking, as risk aversion declines due to observed stability (see Csermely and Szalai, 2010, for a survey).

Like almost every other problem, the conflict of price stability and financial stability among small open emerging economies is mostly linked to the volatility of *capital flows* (De Gregorio, 2009). During 'good times' excessive capital inflows drive up the exchange rate and, as a consequence, overheating does not necessarily appear in inflationary pressure but rather in rising external imbalances and credit booms. During 'bad times', on the contrary, capital outflows cause depreciation and inflationary pressure, when financial sector imbalances are closing. From a financial stability point of view, traditional inflation targeting seems to be too loose when imbalances are building up and too tight when financial imbalances are closing. Macro-prudential policies can help to tackle this problem, though their effectiveness largely depends on whether they are implemented internationally or only nationally. National policies can easily be circumvented in a world of globalized capital markets and a multinational banking sector.

We also know, however, that CESEE countries are not uniform regarding the fragility of their financial systems. In fact the countries in the region that relied on excessive foreign funding prior to the crisis outnumbered those which did not. Hungary is one of the countries whose external deficit was relatively large prior to the crisis, though it did not reach the

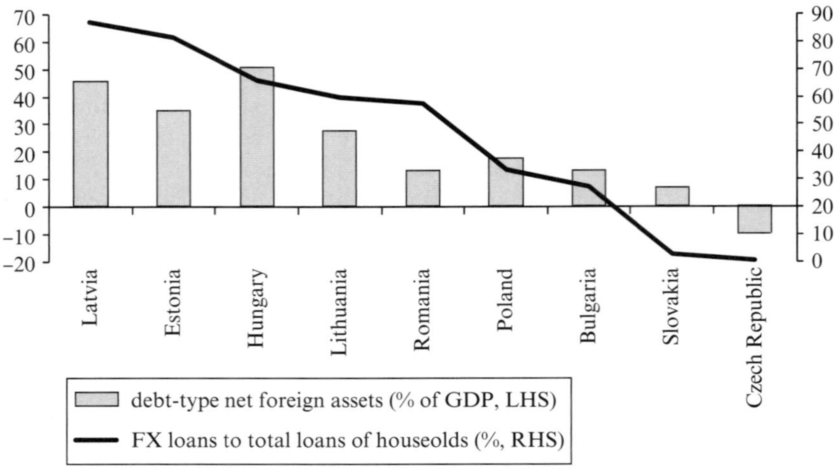

Sources: Csajbók et al. (2010); Eurostat.

Figure 12.4 Net foreign debt and the share of FX loans in the household sector

level of fixed exchange rate countries. These countries could only run these sizeable deficits absorbing foreign exchange (FX)-based capital flows as foreign investors were reluctant to take the FX risk associated with quick debt accumulation (see Figure 12.4). In other words, the 'original sin' syndrome created sizeable currency mismatches in them.

There is an increasing complexity of the monetary transmission mechanism (MTM) in countries moving from a sizeable external deficit to a more sustainable path. The first element of change is a strengthening of the interest rate channel on new flows. Prior to the crisis the domestic interest rate channel was circumvented by FX borrowing, which meant that only the exchange rate channel of the monetary transmission mechanism did really work. Following the crisis macro-prudential regulation has been implemented in several countries to constrain FX lending (in Hungary FX mortgage lending is already legally prohibited), and it is also true that observed exchange rate volatility has induced a reassessment of risk associated with FX lending. In the future these factors should mean that on new credit flows the domestic interest rate will be the dominant price, contributing to a strengthening of the traditional interest rate channel. However we cannot estimate the exact magnitude of these new parameters, as a sufficient amount of data for the new regime is not yet available.

A second point is related to the inheritance of the past: we have to live with the unhedged FX loan stock for several years, as there is no possibility of a quick redenomination (Balás and Nagy, 2010). This would require transferring the FX risk to the foreign sector, which is obviated by the problem of *original sin*.

Due to these factors, the stock and flow channels of monetary policy might offset each other. While the effect of monetary loosening/tightening on output and hence inflation might increase if we consider only new flows, the unhedged FX debt stock effect works in the opposite direction. A given change in the exchange rate has a smaller effect on output and hence on inflation than in the past. A weakening of the Hungarian forint increases household indebtedness, which causes a drop in domestic demand, weakening the effect of stronger net exports. The exact magnitude of different channels, notably the FX stock channel, varies over time, depending on exchange rate levels. As a consequence, monetary loosening may have a perverse (negative) real growth effect. On the other hand it means that disinflation entails a lower growth sacrifice than in 'normal times'.

3 CROSS-BORDER MACRO-PRUDENTIAL COORDINATION

The crisis made it clear that in order to achieve long-lasting macroeconomic stability, striving for price stability is not enough: stable prices need to be reinforced by a stable financial system. These two goals often conflict with each other, therefore monetary policy alone is not capable of continuously facilitating both of them. Macro-prudential regulation can be such an additional policy tool for mitigating systemic risk inherent in or stemming from volatile capital flows.

Macro-prudential tools are generally categorized into two types according to their primary aims, which can be (a) enhancing systemic resilience or (b) leaning against the financial cycle (reducing pro-cyclicality). *Systemic resilience* tools are typically micro-prudential instruments recalibrated for macro-prudential purposes. These may include the regulation of various ratios, such as loan-to-value (LTV) or payment-to-income (PTI), or forbidding 'toxic' products. Hungary deployed such tools in 2009–10 in order to discourage unhedged FX lending, which proved to be a major source of systemic risk. Regulation may be stricter in the case of systemically important (for example, too-big-to-fail) financial institutions. Typical examples of *counter-cyclical tools* are dynamic provisioning (for instance, as implemented in Spain even before the crisis) or a counter-cyclical capital buffer (for instance, as proposed in the new Basel III regulatory standards).

Similarly to monetary policy, macro-prudential policy can be tight or loose. In other words macro-prudential policy may be characterized by its *stance*, just like monetary policy.

As we mentioned earlier, an important factor in the effectiveness of macro-prudential policies is cross-border consistency (for a detailed discussion about macro-prudential coordination issues, see Csajbók and Király, 2010). Cross-border coordination in the end should boil down to coordination of macro-prudential stances. The key motives for cross-border coordination are to avoid regulatory arbitrage on the one hand and to provide a level playing field for financial institutions on the other. We believe that this is especially true in the case of the CESEE region as these countries are deeply integrated in the European banking system, with the branches and subsidiaries of Western European banks being dominant players in the CESEE domestic financial systems. Home–host coordination is therefore of primary importance.

If macro-prudential policy stances substantially differ in home and host countries, this may encourage regulatory arbitrage. Regulatory arbitrage stems from the feature of the globalized financial system that many financial transactions between two parties in the same country can in fact be executed in another country (through, for example, subsidiaries/branches of internationally active financial institutions). In a home–host setting, for example, tightening the macro-prudential stance in the host could be circumvented if the home stance is loose and allows for a redirection of intermediation through, for example, branches.

The flipside of this story, which gets less attention, is that a cross-border rechannelling of financial activity from a country with a tougher regulatory regime to a more lightly regulated one increases the potential for contagion to the more disciplined country (think of the decline in share prices of the large internationally active Austrian banks when the markets started to focus on their Eastern European exposures).

While regulatory arbitrage seems to be a home–host issue, the 'level playing field' argument for macro-prudential coordination is probably more relevant in host–host relations. This stems from the fact that the financial systems in CESEE countries often share the same parent banks. As a result they are to some extent competitors in the cross-border allocation of funds from parent banks. In such a situation, loosening the macro-prudential stance in one host country might channel intermediation activity from another host. In addition to violating fairness, such beggar-my-neighbour regulatory policies can lead to a mutually detrimental 'race to the bottom' regarding regulatory standards (Goodhart, 2010), driving up region-wide systemic risk.

In a nutshell, the case is strong in the CESEE region for a cross-border coordination of macro-prudential policies both in the home–host and in host–host directions in order to avoid regulatory arbitrage and to create a level playing field. While bilateral coordination may be sufficient in certain home–host issues, multilateral coordination seems to be superior in most of the cases and certainly in host–host coordination. At the time of writing, however, the institutions for such coordination are not in place. Supervisory colleges may come close, but they do not have a macro-prudential angle. It remains to be seen whether the European Systemic Risk Board (ESRB) can serve as an effective coordination vehicle for CESEE macro-prudential policies.

Having said all this, we would make a precautionary warning against relying on macro-prudential policies only in facilitating financial stability. In our opinion, although they are necessary, they certainly are not sufficient in themselves for this purpose. First, without sustainable macro policies (fiscal in particular) and price stability, the financial system may easily find itself in trouble or may intermediate insufficiently. Secondly, although its aim is to reduce system-wide risk, macro-prudential policy in the end is a set of particular tools targeting particular problems in particular parts of the financial system. In other words it is not as general as monetary policy, which affects virtually all economic agents. If, for example, there is a long-lasting general tendency of increased (and excessive) risk-taking in the economy, macro-prudential policy in itself can at best slow it down but cannot offset it permanently. In such situations support from monetary policy, for example, in the form of leaning-against-the-wind behaviour, is necessary.

4 EURO ENTRY: OUR ULTIMATE SAFE HARBOUR OR A COMPULSORY TASK?

Prior to the crisis it seemed a safe bet to assume that euro entry brings stability and prosperity in the region, especially in Central Eastern Europe. Arguments in this respect were based on three main results. First, there is a deep economic integration with core European countries (especially with Germany): a high trade share with high intra-industry components and a high level of FDI in the traded sector. Second, there is a deep financial integration with core European countries, mainly due to a high level of foreign ownership in the financial sector. Finally, institutional similarity and convergence also made it probable that most of the region forms an optimal currency area with the euro area (see Csajbók and Csermely, 2002).

In Hungary, with probably the largest swings in fiscal policy in the past decade, we soon realized that we should, at least in fiscal terms, ‘put our house in order', before euro area entry. We also carefully watched the performance and sustainability of some Mediterranean euro area member countries.

However, relatively small care was taken when analysing the institutional weaknesses of the euro area set-up. The unexpectedly large shock of the crisis revealed these institutional weaknesses of the euro: the enforceability of the Stability and Growth Pact, and imbalances with fixed exchange rates in the private sector. With the hope that recent reform efforts tackle area-wide problems, we still cannot sit back and relax. We have to draw conclusions regarding the criteria for successful euro area membership from a small acceding country point of view. This is all the more important given that the weak economic performance of some countries became obvious only after several years of entry and that prevention seems much cheaper than crisis resolution.

The first lesson is that formal convergence criteria are necessary but more attention is necessary with respect to the sustainability of fulfilling them, and a careful monitoring of general economic sustainability. Unsustainable fiscal policies and private sector imbalances are hard to correct inside the euro area, as countries have fewer policy tools to adjust after giving up exchange rate flexibility. Though it is also true that, with a high FX debt burden, the room for exchange rate adjustment is limited, too.

Second, it turned out that deep economic and financial integration without monetary integration raises coordination issues: the exchange rate is not just an adjustment tool, but a source of shocks as well. Thus, from this point of view, new member states should enter the euro area as soon as possible, because outside countries are more vulnerable. However, this is only an option if policies are sustainable.

Finally, we have to admit that being a sustainably successful country in the euro area is going to be an extremely challenging task. It is like a labyrinth, and it is easy to lose the way at every step. First we need disciplined public finances, to keep fiscal reserves for bad times. Second, we need anchored inflation expectations, to avoid artificially low interest rates fuelling a credit boom in the private sector, and to minimize the possibility of wage competitiveness problems. Finally we need flexible prices and wages, so that they can adjust relatively easily inside the monetary union if corrections in the real exchange rate become necessary. If we have all of these, we can probably exploit all of the benefits of a single market. In our view, however, we should not pretend that staying outside in the long term is a feasible solution. For a small open economy in an increasingly globalized world domestic policies have an ever decreasing role in controlling the domestic economy, so integration and effective coordination is probably the only suitable long-term strategy.

NOTE

1. The views expressed in the chapter do not necessarily reflect the official view of the Magyar Nemzeti Bank.

REFERENCES

Atoyan, R. (2010), 'Beyond the crisis: revisiting Europe's new growth model', IMF Working Paper, 10/92.

Bakker, B.B. and A.M. Gulde (2010), 'The credit boom in new member states: bad luck or bad policies?', IMF Working Paper, 10/130.

Balás, T. and M. Nagy (2010), 'Re-denomination of FX loans', *MNB Bulletin*, October.

Csajbók, A. and Á. Csermely (2002), 'Adopting the euro in Hungary: expected costs, benefits and timing', MNB Occasional Paper, 24.

Csajbók, A. and J. Király (2010), 'Cross-border coordination of macroprudential policies', forthcoming in a Chicago Fed–IMF conference proceedings volume.

Csajbók, A., A. Hudecz and B. Tamási (2010), 'Foreign currency borrowing of households in new EU member states', MNB Occasional Paper, 87.

Csermely, Á. and Z. Szalai (2010), 'The role of financial imbalances in monetary policy', *MNB Bulletin*, June.

De Gregorio, J. (2009), 'Monetary policy and financial stability: an emerging markets perspective', *International Finance*, **13** (1), 141–56.

Goodhart, C. (2010), 'How should we regulate the financial sector?', in Adair Turner et al., *The Future of Finance: the LSE Report*, pp. 165–86.

Laeven, L. and F. Valencia (2008), 'Systemic banking crises: a new database', IMF Working Paper, 08/224.

Magyar Nemzeti Bank (2010), 'Analysis of the convergence process, from the point of view of the financial crisis', MNB.

Tang, G. and C. Upper (2010), 'Debt reduction after crisis', *BIS Quarterly Review*, September.

13. Monetary policy challenges in the CESEE region – the case of Poland

Marek Belka[1]

INTRODUCTION

Recent decades have witnessed a substantial rise in financial integration, which has increasingly encompassed also emerging economies. Although substantial benefits may be derived from increased access to international financial markets, rising financial integration also brings about risks to the macroeconomic and financial stability of emerging economies. In particular, developments in a number of emerging European economies (predominantly the Baltic countries, Hungary and Ukraine) in the run-up to and during the recent global financial crisis provide an illustration of the destabilizing potential of large and volatile capital inflows, that is, their potential to fuel unstable credit and asset price booms resulting in excessive indebtedness and vulnerability to economic and financial shocks.

These experiences, together with the rebound in capital flows to emerging economies in the aftermath of the crisis, reignited the debate on risks related to financial integration and the constraints it puts on macroeconomic management in small open economies, including monetary policy making – the debate that was also vivid in the aftermath of the financial crises that affected a number of emerging economies throughout the 1980s and 1990s (for example, the Mexican crisis, the Asian crisis).

Preserving macroeconomic and financial stability in an environment of highly integrated financial markets remains an important concern for economic authorities in emerging Europe, including Poland. From the Polish central bank's perspective, two issues related to growing financial integration are of particular importance, both of which will be tackled more extensively in the following sections. First, trade-offs faced by monetary policy in an environment of strong capital inflows will be discussed. Second, the issue of foreign currency lending to households and its consequences for monetary policy conduct will be addressed.

CAPITAL INFLOWS AND MONETARY POLICY TRADE-OFFS

In principle capital inflows are desirable in savings-constrained catching-up economies as they allow for expanding investment frontiers and for consumption smoothing, thus supporting higher economic growth and facilitating the real convergence process. However, ample evidence, including the recent experience of some catching-up European economies, points to the destabilizing tendency of large and/or persistent capital flows, including their potential to induce overheating, loss of competitiveness and increased vulnerability to shifts in risk perception in global financial markets and capital reversals. Episodes of substantial capital inflows tend to be associated with real effective exchange rate appreciations, worsening current account balances, amplified boom–bust cycles and asset bubbles, including the housing market bubbles (Sá and Wieladek, 2010). When a capital influx leads to a persistent misallocation of resources, that is, their excessive shift towards the low-productivity non-tradable sector (for example, banking, construction, real estate), it may also negatively affect potential output growth and hence the sustainability of external debt. Indeed, empirical evidence shows that economies experiencing large capital inflows face a substantial risk of external debt crises (Reinhart and Rogoff, 2008) as well as banking and currency crises (Reinhart and Reinhart, 2009). In the two decades up to 2006 over one-third of identified episodes of large capital inflows ended abruptly and/or with a currency crisis (Cardarelli et al., 2009).

Given the above-mentioned risks associated with capital inflows as well as their pro-cyclicality, it is no wonder that capital inflows remain an ongoing concern for policy makers in many emerging economies (for example, De Gregorio, 2010; BIS, 2010), including the National Bank of Poland (NBP). The global financial crisis brought only a short-lived slump in net private capital flows to emerging economies. Since the second half of 2009 a recovery in financial flows to emerging markets has occurred, reflecting a combination of 'push' and 'pull factors' that is expected to persist also in the coming years. The global factors that were an important determinant of capital inflows to emerging economies during previous episodes of 'capital flow bonanzas', namely sluggish growth and low interest rates in advanced economies (Reinhart and Reinhart, 2009), are once again in place. Interest rates in major advanced economies are running at record low levels and may be expected to remain low as highly accommodative monetary policy is to support the recovery in an environment of continuing adjustments in the balance sheets of economic agents. Expectations of sustained low interest rates together with ample global liquidity, which had already exceeded the pre-crisis levels, induce the search for yield and risk-taking, thus 'pushing' capital to flow to emerging markets. In the case of many emerging economies the 'pull' factors are also there, both for short- and longer-term capital inflows: favourable interest rate differentials and expectations of exchange rate appreciation as well as robust growth prospects together with solid economic fundamentals. The factor that may periodically weaken capital inflows to emerging markets or even lead to capital outflows is unexpected spikes in risk perception.

Catching-up European economies, which prior to the crisis were the largest recipient of financial flows among all regional groupings of emerging economies, in its aftermath have received only a small share of total capital flows to emerging markets – except for Poland. The scale of capital inflows to Poland has resumed quickly to the record high levels observed in the run-up to the crisis. The composition of these inflows has changed substantially, however. In the past the bulk of net capital flows to Poland consisted of foreign direct investment, which typically proves much more resilient in the capital reversal episodes (Cardarelli et al., 2009) and tends to be more growth-enhancing than other types of capital inflows.[2] A substantial part of these inflows was also in the form of other investment, mainly cross-border bank lending, which was used to finance credit expansion. In the aftermath of the crisis portfolio flows, predominantly to the market of government bonds, have become the dominant form of capital inflows. Given the high volatility pertinent to such flows, their large scale relative to the size of the domestic market may increase the country's vulnerability to shocks which trigger the reassessment of risks on the global financial markets.

Such developments raise the question of appropriate monetary policy making under surging capital inflows. The monetary policy framework of the National Bank of Poland, that is, inflation targeting under a floating exchange rate regime, may provide a good buffer against the consequences of surging capital inflows. Exchange rate appreciation fuelled by capital inflows may even be helpful in reducing inflationary pressures in the economy, including those induced by the inflowing capital. There is, however, a risk that an appreciating currency could further strengthen capital inflows as short-term (carry trade) investors will seek a return not only on domestic assets but also on the strengthening currency. A prolonged period of nominal appreciation due to persistent capital inflows may also be conducive to households' misperception of risks related to foreign currency lending. Such a self-propelling mechanism may easily result in excessive exchange rate volatility.

Risks related to overly strong or rapid currency appreciation may constrain monetary policy making. Monetary authorities may be wary of interest rate hikes if they fear that such increases may attract excessive capital inflows. Delayed monetary policy tightening may, however, not be feasible if there are significant risks of overheating fuelled by a credit and asset price boom in the economy. Imposing capital controls on short-term financial flows could create more room for manoeuvre for domestic monetary policy but such a policy option is not possible for an EU member state such as Poland. This shows the need for other policies, including fiscal and regulatory policies, to complement monetary policy in dealing with excessive short-term capital inflows. The way forward to tame the short-term capital inflows is bank regulations aimed at reducing the scale of banks' wholesale external financing.

THE CHALLENGES OF FOREIGN CURRENCY LENDING

Developments in emerging Europe during the global financial crisis have also strengthened concerns over the risks related to foreign currency lending. The potential of excessive indebtedness in foreign currencies to generate financial and macroeconomic instability has put the issue of foreign currency lending at the forefront of the discussion on challenges to financial stability in Poland.

Foreign currency lending to unhedged borrowers (predominantly households) may be a source of four main types of risks to macroeconomic and financial stability.

First, excessive use of external wholesale funding by the domestic banks can accelerate credit growth well above the rate of GDP growth, which may create a growing credit risk within the banking system.

Second, sudden hikes in the costs of servicing the foreign currency debt due to exchange rate depreciation or devaluation may negatively affect the balance sheets of unhedged borrowers and their ability to service such debt, posing risks for both economic growth and the stability of the banking system. Although these risks did not materialize in Poland during the recent crisis despite the zloty's significant depreciation, the conclusion that such risks are limited in general is not justified. It has to be kept in mind that the rise in debt servicing costs due to the zloty's exchange rate depreciation was mitigated by interest rate cuts abroad (in particular in Switzerland as the bulk of foreign currency mortgage loans to households was denominated in Swiss francs).

Third, increased foreign currency lending may raise banking sectors' vulnerability to international financial market tensions as banks use foreign financing (for example syndicated loans or credit lines from parent institutions) and FX swaps to close the gap between foreign currency loans and deposits. Such vulnerability became apparent during the recent crisis. The seizing-up of the FX swap market rendered it difficult for Polish commercial banks to obtain Swiss franc and other currency funding in the market. To help meet commercial banks' demand for foreign currency funding, the National Bank of Poland set up swap facilities and arranged swap lines with the Swiss National Bank and the European Central Bank. The NBP's action complemented the funding offered by foreign parent banks and helped to mitigate the risks to the banking sector related to the FX-swap-market breakdown.

Fourth, to the extent that interest rates and exchange rate policies exert significant influence on the demand for foreign currency debt, foreign currency lending may also pose challenges to monetary policy making. Empirical studies suggest that interest rate differentials were an important determinant of foreign currency borrowing in Poland and in other emerging European economies in the period preceding the crisis (Basso et al., 2007; Brzoza-Brzezina et al., 2010; Rosenberg and Tirpák, 2008). Households were willing to trade off the principal risk on loans stemming from the potential exchange rate shocks against lower interest rates.[3] Because domestic interest rate hikes may widen the interest rate differential, an attempt by the monetary authority to tighten monetary conditions may be counteracted to some extent by raising demand for foreign currency loans (Brzoza-Brzezina et al., 2010). This weakens the stabilization function of monetary policy and can make it very costly, if not impossible, to prevent a credit and demand boom through the interest rate channel. A response to negative economic shocks may also be constrained by the high level of unhedged foreign currency denominated debt, as stability considerations may put a limit on resorting to interest rate cuts to stimulate the economy and using the exchange rate as a shock absorber. Risks related to the zloty's sharp depreciation, including those stemming from a large stock of foreign currency indebtedness, were among the factors determining the scale of monetary policy easing in Poland during the crisis.

Addressing the risks associated with foreign currency lending warrants limiting its supply to unhedged borrowers by appropriate financial supervision and regulation. Under existing legislation the supervisory powers are placed outside the National Bank of Poland, within the Polish Financial Supervision Authority. Hence, dealing with challenges and risks to financial stability, including the issue of foreign currency lending to unhedged borrowers, requires close cooperation and coordination between the two institutions.

The first step towards mitigating risks related to foreign currency lending was taken in Poland as early as 2006 when Recommendation S was enforced. It induced more restrictive creditworthiness assessment for foreign currency loans. The effectiveness of this measure is, however, hard to judge. On the one hand, increased foreign currency lending continued after its introduction – over the two following years the stock of foreign currency loans in Poland increased by 83 per cent (Komisja Nadzoru Finansowego, 2010). On the other hand, the quality of the foreign currency mortgage loans remained relatively stable despite the zloty's significant depreciation during the global downturn, which might suggest that the tighter lending standards imposed by Recommendation S had at least been helpful in limiting credit risk.[4]

Given the limited impact of previous regulations on the supply of foreign currency loans, additional measures may be required – all the more so if foreign currency lending to households, which was significantly limited during the crisis, picks up again, supported by record low interest rates in the external environment of the Polish economy. This may complicate monetary policy making because a conflict between the medium-term price stability orientation of domestic monetary policy and financial stability is very likely to arise. An attempt to raise domestic interest rates to stabilize inflation at the NBP's target over the medium term may be conducive to increasing demand for foreign currency loans. This conflict can best be resolved if the supply of foreign currency loans to households is restricted by additional well-tailored regulation.

CONCLUSION

Large, possibly volatile, portfolio capital inflows and foreign currency lending to unhedged borrowers may significantly constrain monetary policy options and weaken the ability of monetary policy to stabilize the economy. Given the potential large macroeconomic costs associated with these aspects of financial integration, it is important that monetary policy be supplemented with other macroeconomic policies, predominantly regulatory and supervisory policy, in managing the surging capital inflows and unhedged foreign currency lending.

NOTES

1. The author would like to thank Anna Małgorzata Kosior from the National Bank of Poland for assistance in drafting this chapter.
2. A caveat here is that the composition of foreign direct investment in a catching-up economy may be an important determinant of the growth-enhancing effects of FDI inflows. Excessive foreign-financed investment in the non-tradable sector (banking,

construction, real estate) may result in resource misallocation to the detriment of the tradable sector, denting the country's competitiveness and hence its ability to keep the external debt at sustainable levels.
3. In fact, this risk might have often been misperceived. The persistent nominal appreciation of the zloty exchange rate since Poland joined the European Union could have created expectations of the zloty's further appreciation or at least an impression of relatively small exchange rate risk related to foreign currency borrowing.
4. In 2009 the Polish Financial Supervision Authority introduced an enhanced version of Recommendation S and in 2010 it approved Recommendation T on good practices with regard to risk management of retail credit exposures that also partly related to foreign currency borrowing.

REFERENCES

Bank of International Settlements (2010), 'Post-crisis policy challenges in emerging market economies', *BIS Annual Report* 2009/2010, Basel.
Basso, H.S., O. Calvo-Gonzalez and M. Jurgilas (2007), 'Financial dollarization: the role of banks and interest rates', European Central Bank Working Paper No. 748.
Brzoza-Brzezina, M., T. Chmielewski and J. Niedźwiedzińska (2010), 'Substitution between domestic and foreign currency loans in Central Europe: do central banks matter?', Working Paper Series 1187, European Central Bank.
Cardarelli R., S. Elkdag and M. Ayhan Kose (2009), 'Capital inflows: macroeconomic implications and policy responses', International Monetary Fund Working Paper No. 09/40.
De Gregorio, J. (2010), 'Tackling the capital inflow challenge', speech at the Bank of Spain, http://www.bis.org/review/r100527c.pdf.
Komisja Nadzoru Finansowego (Polish Financial Supervision Authority) (2010), Information on risks related to foreign currency lending (Polish version only), http://www.knf.gov.pl/opracowania/sektor_bankowy/raporty_i_opracowania/analizy_opracowania/index.html.
Reinhart, C. and V. Reinhart (2009), 'Capital flow bonanzas: an encompassing view of the past and present', in *NBER International Seminar on Macroeconomics 2008*, National Bureau of Economic Research, Inc.
Reinhart, C. and K.S. Rogoff (2008), 'This time is different: a panoramic view of eight centuries of financial crises', NBER Working Papers 13882, National Bureau of Economic Research, Inc.
Rosenberg, C.B. and M. Tirpák (2008), 'Determinants of foreign currency borrowing in the new member states of the EU', International Monetary Fund Working Paper No. 08/173.
Sá, F. and T. Wieladek (2010), 'Monetary policy, capital inflows and the housing boom', Working Paper No. 405, Bank of England.

14. Monetary policy challenges in the CESEE region – the case of Romania

Cristian Popa

The aim of this chapter is to illustrate both challenges going forward and things that Romania has had to deal with from the onset of the crisis and even before that. Perhaps contrary to first impressions, the pre- and post-crisis periods are not disconnected, there being both commonalities and idiosyncratic events that characterize each. Let me reiterate the context, and that is of Romania, quite like Poland, Hungary and Croatia, being a small, open economy, which has two things that interest us at this point, amongst many others; one is the sensitivity to the volume, direction and yield of external financing flows, and the other is the realization that full capital mobility for such an economy, and especially for one undergoing fast growth, is a fact of life and one has to take that into the configuration of one's policy decisions and realize that there are limitations to one's actions.

My first point is about a need that arose, to some extent was met, but will continue to be a challenge for the period ahead: the capacity for monetary policy embedded in the policy mix to be able to execute smooth turns in policy response to shifts in the business cycle phase. What do I mean by that? Initially, going out of the boom period – which obviously meant that monetary policy was more than pulling its weight, being counter-cyclical and trying especially to limit demand growth by limiting growth in foreign exchange lending – we shifted after late 2008 to a policy where the initial, short-run phase was an attempt at stabilization, understood by us as being the orderly unwinding of imbalances. There was not only a massive reduction of capital inflows but also a shift from more than 8 per cent growth in 2008 to Q3, and, indeed, close to 7 per cent as an average of the previous five years, to something that for Romania was in 2009 minus 7.2 per cent. And that was a considerable shift.

The consequence of that shift from rapid growth to contraction was obviously that interest rate setting had to not only account for transmission problems, where commercial banks before had been competing domestically for market share and now they were trying to accentuate the deleveraging process, in a bid to reduce vulnerabilities. The existence of a sizeable stock of foreign exchange denominated loans (about 62 per cent of total non-government credit, even if the latter is quite low by international peer country comparisons, standing at 40 per cent) had to be taken into account, via the generation of potentially sizeable balance-sheet and wealth effects for borrowers in the real sector. One of the immediate consequences of such a feature in Romania's banking system is also the fact that one cannot necessarily look at depreciation (besides exchange rate movements resulting from a rebalancing of economic fundamentals) as the be-all and end-all tool of stimulating an economy in deep recession, in the textbook sense that net exports would be expected to be increasing as a result: the above-mentioned balance-sheet and wealth effects will be considerably higher than the provided net export stimulus (over and above the fact that Romanian exports include a hefty import content). Obviously, in such a context there may be not only further challenges to financial stability but also a major challenge to something that we continue to see as our main objective, which is price stability.

While exchange rate volatility has been quite low for the entire year 2010, episodes of high volatility in end-2008 to first quarter 2009 and in late 2009, tied mainly to a significant reduction in capital flows and a correction of the current account deficit from 11.8 per cent of GDP in 2008 to 4.2 per cent in 2009, form a background against which, together with the balance-sheet and wealth effects, also may explain why we started to cut interest rates with a delay and were quite mindful of the signalling effect of those interest rate changes. We managed to accumulate 400 basis points of reduction and then stopped because of the temporary but significant shock provided by the VAT rate increase during the first half of 2010.

The third element, and this is, I believe, of crucial relevance for many more countries than just the peer group, is that there is now a need to even further merge inflation targeting – or other 'activist' monetary policy regimes – with issues of financial stability as an ongoing concern. I think this is something that not only we have seen is motivating academics in research but also will be the main challenge for central banks. And it is not necessarily limited to inflation-targeting central banks. The National Bank of Romania was a pioneer, but also controversial, in merging price stability and financial stability concerns in its manner of conducting flexible inflation targeting even during the boom period. We came out as early as 2006 stating that we were seeking lasting disinflation over the medium term instead of temporarily achieving an annual inflation target, and, in particular, that we did not see nominal appreciation as something that was useful in combating inflation in the durable way spoken of before, when that nominal appreciation was unsustainable, given that it was achieved at the cost of accelerating inflation pressures, ever deeper external deficits, and the growing risk to financial stability, because of asset liability mismatches. We also made the point that the reversal and disorderly correction of such unsustainable nominal appreciation (with annual real wage growth running significantly above productivity growth) was likely to have considerably stronger inflationary effects compared with the disinflationary effects provided by nominal appreciation (the latter being milder if economic agents saw appreciation as temporary and did not lower prices in proportion).

The second issue where we were innovators, together with Croatia – who, in a candidate-country context, had relatively larger room for manoeuvre – was trying to stem rapid credit growth in foreign exchange. I think we were the ones who, within the context of the new EU member states, wrote the book on how to try to limit foreign exchange lending. We also tried to ensure that capital adequacy, as a proxy for prudent regulation, stayed high and that was very, very useful in entering the crisis with a solid capital base, since requests to banks to increase their capital had been made by us prior to the collapse of Lehman Brothers. Even now, despite non-performing loans having risen to almost 12 per cent in an internationally comparable definition, and with high provisioning requirements, with the capital increases that we have continued to – gradually and where appropriate, but pro-actively – request from banks, capitalization is still, according to the more stringent Romanian accounting standards, about 15 per cent. Therefore I think that Basel III will not require a lot of additional effort going forward, if the current standards are being maintained, even as the Romanian banking system will be moving to international financial reporting standards (IFRS) from 2012. But again, this reasoning in terms of financial stability will have to become part and parcel of the way inflation targeting is implemented. I do not think it was possible to consider them separately even before – indeed, this was probably an illusion during the boom period – but it is certainly not going to be possible to separate financial stability and inflation targeting and pursue them as independent goals. And this obviously poses problems as to how policies are configured and implemented and also how governance is organized within central banks.

Fourth, there is the problem of the inter-temporal consistency of the macro-policy mix and the fact that monetary policy was over-burdened; it did more than it probably should have, had fiscal policy and wage policy been appropriately prudent and counter-cyclical. Unfortunately for us, the fiscal policy loosening happened in structural terms, as well as nominal terms, towards the end of the boom period and therefore complicated existing problems and made the correction of the imbalances more pressing and the need to fiscally consolidate that more stringent. Romania's deficit reduction efforts in 2010 were worth about 4 per cent of GDP, which is quite a large amount; despite that, we at the central bank see that there is further need to continue fiscal consolidation and reduce the deficit to below 3 per cent at end-2012. In terms of the stance of monetary policy itself, the prudent nature of policy is something we have maintained throughout and will continue to pursue, not only with respect to the monetary policy rate of interest but especially in the more encompassing context of broad real monetary conditions. We remain cognizant in terms of the need for maintaining prudence at all times.

A few final words on new things that are more technical in terms of monetary policy transmission. One thing that I do not recall hearing about before the crisis was liquidity. Nobody was concerned about it, possibly because there was altogether too much liquidity. And I think the fact that it evaporated in the context of the post-Lehman period and then came back again is a worthy policy-making and academic preoccupation. It is no wonder that in Basel III and other contexts we hear a lot about this. Obviously, with us it was always a question of supplying enough liquidity for the appropriate functioning of interbank and other markets, domestically, without a view to pouring additional pressure on top of exchange rate volatility, even though public debt to GDP was lower in Romania than in peer countries, and a smaller proportion of that relatively lower debt was held by non-residents. The other items we must be aware of, which are connected to turns in the business cycle, are, first, the possibility that growth rates, while still exhibiting some real catching-up, will be lower and by a pretty large degree lower than before the crisis; and second, the fact that potential GDP may remain quite depressed for a prolonged period due to the effects of the crisis, as gross fixed capital formation in Romania dropped about 25 per cent in 2009, and the drop in the first half of 2010 compared with the first half of 2009 is about 18 per cent. Admittedly, a part of this impact is likely to be removed in the medium term, but I expect that in many countries – the difficulties for meaningful comparisons arising from structural breaks notwithstanding – there will be a significant gap between pre- and post-crisis estimates of potential GDP, which will further challenge output gap and structural fiscal deficit forecasts. It seems that central banks and macroeconomists everywhere will not want for issues of policy relevance in their day-to-day work. These are major issues for the profession and – especially conducting monetary policy with a price stability objective that includes financial stability considerations – they will remain challenging for a number of years to come.

15. Monetary policy challenges in the CESEE region – the case of Croatia

Boris Vujčić

In terms of monetary policy challenges, this chapter will look into three things, the first being price stability, that is, a constitutional primary mandate that the central bank has to fulfil. After the financial and economic crisis of 2008, price stability was not a big concern. Times of crisis have quickly removed our primary goal from the list of our main preoccupations. Inflationary pressures were subdued due to the recession, which came with a sharp decline in both foreign and domestic demand. So, central banks focused on reigniting demand, while price developments were not really a challenge. However, it could well be that crisis has only temporarily interrupted a trend of inflationary pressures that will continue once the recovery of the (world) economy accelerates. I remember that, just as the crisis was starting, in 2008, I participated in two conferences that dealt with the question of rising inflationary pressures and renewed concern about price developments. There was much worry that we might see a resurgence of high inflation, particularly in countries with a high weight of food and energy prices in the Consumer Price Index (CPI) basket (see IMF, 2008). In Croatia we also experienced a sharp increase in CPI inflation during 2008 (Figure 15.1).

The fact that we dropped into a deep recession and stopped worrying about inflation immediately after this episode might well turn out to be just a temporary phenomenon. A potential danger in the medium term is the resurfacing of higher commodity and food prices, as the world economy recovers, which could easily restart inflationary pressures, particularly in countries with a high share of food and energy prices in their CPI baskets. As this will mostly be an imported inflationary pressure, the monetary policy response will not be easy. Some inflation-targeting countries might find two-thirds of their inflation goals consumed by food and/or commodity price increases in the world market, which leaves little room for manoeuvre.

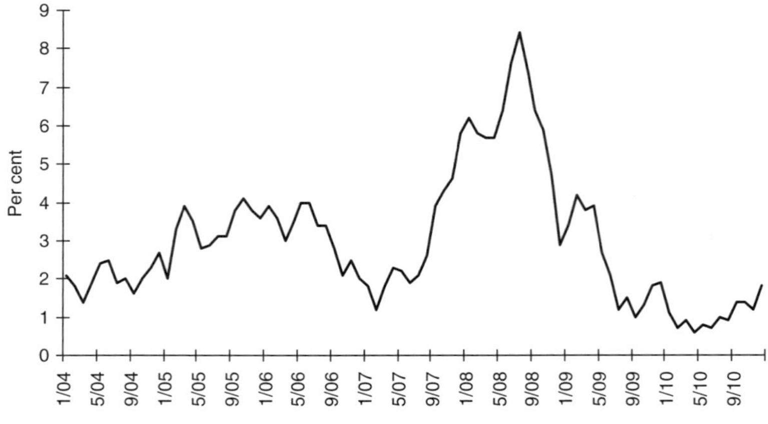

Source: Croatian Bureau of Statistics.

Figure 15.1 CPI year-on-year change

The second thing, which is stated in our mandate, is that, to the extent that it is not compromising the primary goal, namely price stability, the central bank should help the growth prospects of the country as such. At the time when growth disappeared and price pressures with it, monetary policy refocused on stimulating growth. And, obviously, there is not much credit growth these days, which is something that monetary policy should be able to influence in one way or another. Up until the financial crisis had started, the Croatian National Bank (CNB) employed many, often unconventional, instruments to slow down what we considered excessive credit growth. In spite of the heavy criticism levelled at the unconventional measures that we used, like capital inflow tax, credit growth tax, and high foreign exchange liquidity requirements, these measures have proven to be successful in curbing excessive credit growth (Figure 15.2).

That became particularly clear in the light of the subsequent crisis. In 2009, however, the policy-making landscape changed completely as we were faced with rapidly disappearing credit growth. In order to address the issue, again counter-cyclically, we scrapped capital inflow and credit growth taxation, and lowered minimum foreign exchange liquidity requirements and the overall reserve requirement, thus creating a large supply of additional liquidity. In the wake of the crisis, we basically created new liquidity equivalent to 10 per cent of GDP. Unfortunately, much of this amount is still sitting in our overnight deposits at the time of writing. So, the old saying is clearly valid still, namely that monetary policy is much like a rope; it is much more easily pulled than pushed. We did what needed to

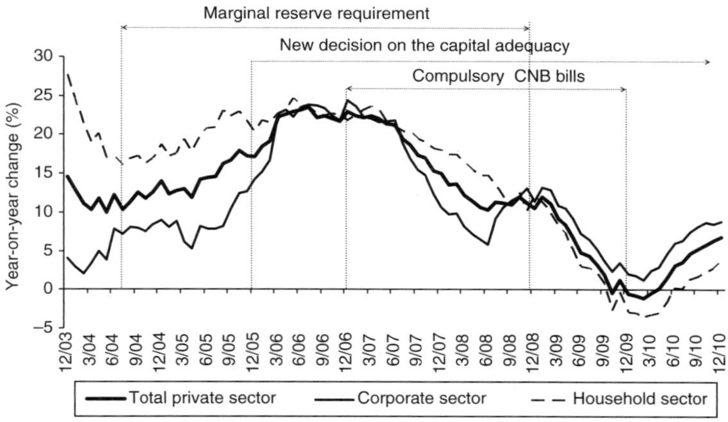

Source: Croatian National Bank.

Figure 15.2 Credit growth in Croatia

be done, created a lot of liquidity and brought money market interest rates to historical lows, but that was not enough to see this liquidity being transformed into credit growth nearly at the rates experienced prior to the crisis. Risk aversion in 2010 was still too high, contrary to the situation prior to the crisis, when the risk management departments of the commercial banks were basically saying: 'Everything is fine, there are no risks. You can grow credit by 30 per cent or more. You can do Swiss francs, you can do yen, all is fine!' When crisis had struck, the same risk managers said to the credit officers: 'Everything is dangerous!' So, from one extreme, the risk management departments' pendulum swung to the other.

Now, how to deal with risk aversion? We thought, maybe, if we can create some kind of a risk-sharing scheme that could help re-ignite credit growth. So, what we did is that we created a scheme in which the government-owned development bank is syndicating loans, conditionality attached, together with commercial banks. Through that scheme, government, basically, shares the risk in the loans extended by the commercial banks.

While contributing to a moderate growth of credit to the corporate sector (+6.6 per cent in 2010), the scheme has not been a total success, and it ran out of steam towards the end of the year. At the same time, households were still deleveraging in 2010, a development that we expect to come to an end, and we shall see positive credit growth to households in 2011. Overall, the government sector absorbed most of the liquidity created during the crisis and was, thus, also the prime beneficiary of the monetary easing.

The third thing that I would like to touch upon is financial stability, both from the macro and the micro perspective. Financial stability is on everybody's mind these days. Central banks only have a partial role in maintaining financial stability, but in the end, often the crucial one. Where do we see the risks to financial stability today?

First there is the debt burden. With corporate debt-to-GDP and household debt-to-income levels of close to 90 per cent and with a total foreign debt-to-GDP level close to 100 per cent, of which two-thirds is the debt which is not due to either parent banks or parent companies, one has to be cautious. These are not the levels that one would worry that much about if the growth potential was high. But, as argued in previous chapters of this book, the potential growth rates have come down. So, in that context, the debt levels that might not have looked that worrying when the potential growth rate was 4–5 per cent, for example, in pre-crisis Croatia, look worse now, when the potential growth rate has come down. The issue at hand really is what needs to be done to increase the potential rate of growth of the economy, and, equally important, how to do it on a sustainable basis, as we have learned that much of the growth that we saw prior to the crisis was not built on solid grounds. This question is, however, not so much a challenge for monetary policy as it is for other policies. So, I would say that the key things now are in the hands of government: structural policies and fiscal policy. And I often have a feeling, not only in Central and Eastern Europe but overall, that too much faith is being put in monetary policy, the powers of which are limited.

Next, a few remarks about another risk to financial stability – foreign currency lending. Interestingly, the public, policy makers and international financial institutions homed in on this risk only after the crisis, although it surfaced a lot earlier (see, for example, EBRD, 2010; ECB, 2010). But, like some other risks, it has been underestimated. I have many times before encountered neglect or underestimation of the extent of the risk that foreign currency lending introduces into a financial system. Now that problem awareness is high, I would like to emphasize that in dealing with the problem it is crucial to clearly distinguish between two different cases. One is where foreign currency lending is coming from simple carry trade. Marek Belka writes (in Chapter 13 of this volume) that, basically, the interest rate differential is currently the only incentive for the continuation of foreign currency lending in Poland. But Poland has less than 10 per cent of the deposits in foreign currencies. So, the liability side of the banks' balance sheet is not dollarized (or euroized). In Croatia, for example, on

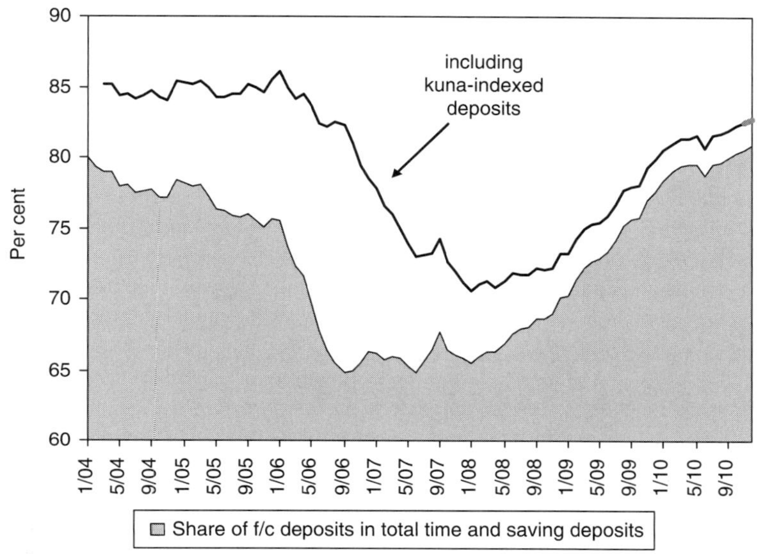

Source: Croatian National Bank.

Figure 15.3 Share of foreign currency deposits in total time and savings deposits

the liabilities' side of the banks' balance sheets over 80 per cent is foreign currency deposits (Figure 15.3).

That is actually more than the amount of credit extended in foreign currency, or indexed to a foreign currency. So, looking at the currency composition of banks' balance sheets in Croatia (Figure 15.4), one can say that it is more a case of hedging the FX position than a case of carry trades. If banks have low deposits in foreign currency, and a lot of assets, that is, if they engage in a pure carry trade, then it is much easier to tell them that they cannot extend foreign currency (indexed) loans. If, on the other hand, they do it as a way of hedging the liability side of their balance sheet, then it is much more difficult to ban foreign currency lending. If one does so, without at the same time changing the currency composition of the liability side of the balance sheet, one is effectively forcing banks to take large open currency positions, which, as a regulator, one should actually limit. So, we should be very careful about the kind of policies we adopt. Any policy should be tailor-made to different circumstances, that is, the level of currency substitution, in different countries.

For example, in Croatia we introduced, as early as 2006, additional

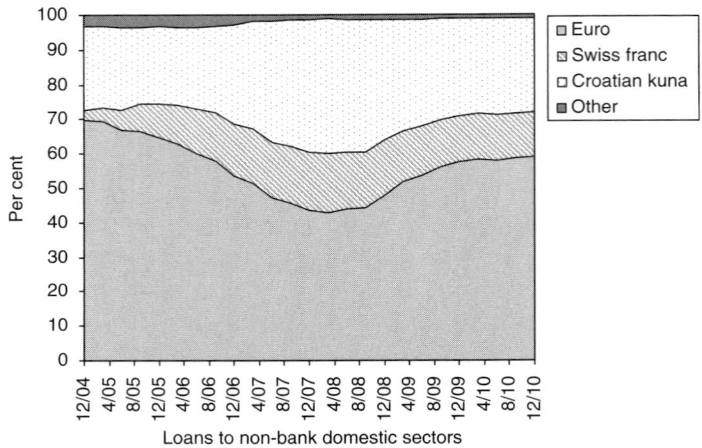

Source: Croatian National Bank.

Figure 15.4 Currency composition of loans in Croatia

capital adequacy rules, basically saying to the banks: 'If you extend foreign currency loans to unhedged borrowers, these are more risky loans, so, for those loans you should put aside more capital.' So, in Basel terms, we did not ban the product, but rather assigned higher capital weights for a riskier product. And that worked well. Banks reduced the extent of outstanding foreign currency (indexed) loans from 85 per cent to 60 per cent. But they did so gradually by, at the same time, reducing the liability side of the euroization of their balance sheets also to 60 per cent.

Unfortunately, the crisis has, in a matter of months, reversed this multi-year effort as depositors swiftly reverted to euro deposits as the crisis emerged at end-2008. So, we are now again at over 70 per cent of euroization on both the liability and asset sides of the balance sheet. And I would guess that, at least in Croatia, because of the long history of euroization, dating back more than 40 years (it used to be 'deutsche-markization'), of the liability side of the banks' balance sheets, this is something that is largely here to stay until we adopt the euro. Transactions in Swiss francs, on the other hand, have really declined. Loans outstanding in Swiss francs, mostly car loans, are now at approximately 14 per cent of total loans, which is much less than prior to the crisis.

The final risk in terms of financial stability that I want to touch upon here is the market reappraisal of risks. It is obvious that first post-Lehman, second post-Greece, or subsequently post-Ireland or whatever, there has been a clear reappraisal of risks (Figure 15.5). Also, it seems that, this time

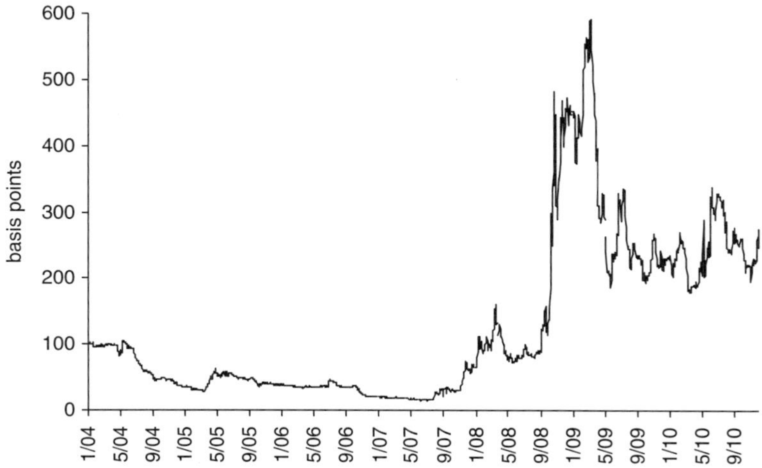

Source: Croatian National Bank.

Figure 15.5 Five-year credit default swap spread for Croatia

around, this reappraisal is here to stay for the foreseeable future. That also poses a risk to financial stability, as some countries have already bitterly experienced. The usual vulnerability indicators all affect risk perception, but, on the other hand, might also be easily affected by a change in risk perception.

Let me end on a positive note, though. Some things have started to look less risky. First, we find the real estate price bubble to have been less pronounced in Croatia than in many other countries which experienced boom–bust cycles. Neither the level of price adjustment nor the degree of exposure of the banking sector were such that they might have created problems in the order of magnitude that we see in some other European countries; far from it. Second, the decline in economic activity automatically started to quickly bring down the external deficit. Now, the challenge is how to get back to the pre-crisis growth rates of GDP without pushing up the external deficit excessively. And that is a tough challenge, which requires changes in the growth model, that is, a reorientation of drivers of growth from domestic more towards foreign demand. Also, the interest rate environment abroad is benign, actual to optimal international reserves look fine, and the dynamics of debt growth have improved significantly as a result of a quick external adjustment.

Even more importantly, the capital adequacy ratio of Croatian banks was 19 per cent at end-2010, and stress tests show that the system is resilient to a negative scenario. If we stress banks with still negative growth rates in 2011 together with a modest depreciation, the capital adequacy ratio still remains in the mid-teens.

Having said that, challenges in terms of near-term inflation developments, growth prospects and financial stability remain equally present. The worst has been avoided ever since the crisis broke in 2008, but bringing the potential rate of growth back to the pre-crisis levels, while at the same time maintaining price and financial stability (particularly at the macro level) in a new, post-crisis, environment, will not be an easy task.

REFERENCES

European Bank for Reconstruction and Development (EBRD) (2010), *Transition Report 2010: Recovery and Reform*, London.
European Central Bank (ECB) (2010), 'Financial stability challenges in EU candidate countries', Occasional Paper Series, no. 115, Frankfurt, July.
International Monetary Fund (2008), World Economic Outlook (WEO) update, Washington DC, July.

16. Challenges for monetary and exchange rate policy in CESEE created by the crisis: back to square one?

Peter Mooslechner

> Many ask what fundamental rethinking will be necessary to save macroeconomic theory. Some answers may lie with models that have applied to fit the realities of emerging markets, models that are at home with the financial market imperfections that have now unexpectedly turned up in industrialized countries as well. Purists will be reluctant to seek salvation from this direction. But they should not fear. (Frankel, 2010)

The CESEE region's traditional growth model proved unsustainable in the crisis and – following the severe downturn in the industrialized world – CESEE countries slipped into deep recessions as well. While the drought is over, the recovery in the CESEE region is partly still fragile and surrounded by various risks. In a medium-term perspective, economic growth will not only be weaker than before the crisis but probably also more volatile. This background will set the scene for monetary policy in the coming years, which will be confronted with challenges not realized before.

One of the central challenges will be to continue safeguarding both financial and monetary stability, while at the same time contributing to economic recovery and sustainable long-term growth. The success of this undertaking obviously depends on external factors, such as global economic prospects and the financial position of parent banks from developed countries, but definitely also on local factors. Those include, for example, the speed of debt restructuring by different economic sectors, the time horizon needed to overcome the problem of non-performing loans and banks' willingness to restart lending. However, in order to avoid a re-emergence of the financial vulnerabilities seen before the crisis, ensuring a sustainable path of future lending seems of the utmost importance. It requires effective mechanisms and timely action with a view to:

1. restraining excessive developments and addressing unsustainable trends
2. decreasing the dependence on foreign funding by fostering domestic savings and deposit financing
3. encouraging lending in domestic currencies with the main purpose of reducing foreign exchange risks.

These issues, from a financial markets perspective, call for developing long-term local currency capital markets, but also for intensified cooperation between home and host supervisory authorities of foreign bank subsidiaries. At the same time, they will complicate the conduct of monetary policy and also have an adverse impact on capital flows to the region. Such flows have been important building blocks in CESEE countries' growth models, but they can also cause distortions when volatile and add to widening external imbalances when excessive. In sum, these closely interrelated and highly sensitive factors ask for particular attention in the analysis of the CESEE region and, in particular, in the formulation of appropriate macroeconomic policies (IMF, 2009a).

MORE THAN A CRISIS: A GROWTH MODEL UNDER STRESS

Although CESEE financial markets were severely hit and virtually the whole region plunged into deep recession, a twin currency and banking crisis was avoided. But unlike in other emerging markets, the longer-lasting impact of the crisis hardly seems to be over in the CESEE region. The immediate effects of the crisis on the economy and the financial markets have faded out, but the second-round effects are becoming visible in weak domestic demand, decreasing corporate profits, rising unemployment, deteriorating fiscal positions, a significant rise in non-performing loans and insolvencies, and rising pressure on bank capital.

In addition, the exit from the significant fiscal and monetary policy easing implemented in 2010 has not really taken place. Medium-term adjustment to growth with less capital inflows, financing of elevated public debt, fiscal consolidation and dealing with the burden of write-downs on bank loans have yet to be tackled.

Central and Eastern European countries have enjoyed rapid growth for a long period of time fuelled by substantial net capital inflows. The region benefited from various types of external financing sources: direct investments, portfolio investments, financial derivatives, bank loans and others. It is evident why the region was very popular for international investors:

capital was scarce, the level of human capital was relatively high, and actual and potential EU and euro area membership anchored expectations. Western European banks invested heavily, aiming at developing new markets. At the same time, euro area interest rates and risk sentiments played a role in determining capital flows to CESEE.

During the boom years, massive capital inflows were considered largely to be part of the catching-up process (BIS, 2005). However, already before the global financial crisis hit the region, there were concerns with regard to the sustainability of such immense external financing. Some countries recorded large external imbalances making these countries vulnerable to a sudden reversal of foreign capital flows.

At the beginning of the financial crisis, it was assumed that many countries in CESEE were sheltered from the turmoil. But as the financial crisis went on, economic troubles also spread to these countries. However, the impact was by no means homogeneous: countries with larger imbalances tended to be affected more severely and the crisis had a major impact on the capital flows to the region. Fortunately, a fully-fledged financial meltdown did not take place.

The main source of external financing in Central and Eastern Europe, foreign direct investments, resisted the global turmoil better than other forms of capital flows. The deep integration of CESEE banks in the European banking system also had a stabilizing effect. For parent banks under pressure it proved to be difficult to maintain the level of funding prior to the crisis. External finance has become much more difficult and expensive.

The recent global experience has strikingly demonstrated that large capital inflows bear major risks to catching-up economies. Now there is a need to address the question how a more sustainable financing model can be established. One obvious step towards more sustainable growth financing would be to shift the focus from external to internal financing. To strengthen local capital markets is one of the important measures in this respect, which obviously takes time and is difficult to achieve.

INTENSIFIED CHALLENGES OF INTEGRATION

Despite the almost common crisis experience, the effects of monetary integration will impact CESEE countries with varying degrees of intensity. This creates two problems, perhaps more from a political than an economic point of view, that may be important as the process of integration proceeds.

A major problem is the gap between existing expectations and future developments. If the integration runs smoothly and there are no additional disturbances, monetary integration should generate positive benefits, but it will not solve all the problems. The requirement to satisfy pre-specified criteria to participate in monetary union can serve as a powerful policy instrument to address a wide number of policy issues. But flexibility must be maintained. In both the medium and long term, the programme to join monetary union should not be treated as a 'deus ex machina'. To do so may lead to a dangerous underestimation of policy needs and create a large gap between expectations and the reality of monetary union, which may lead to disappointment and a weaker commitment from the population.

The important benefit of creating/joining a monetary union comes from the 'dynamic effects' on investment and growth (Baldwin, 1992). Unfortunately, these large effects are uncertain and depend on how a country creates opportunities. Empirical estimates of these effects vary widely and are sometimes close to zero. As yet, we understand little about the size of the long-term net benefits, or how long it will take for these benefits to materialize.

This is particularly true for the effects of a common currency on trade and growth, which is a highly contested issue. There is considerable debate about the magnitude of these effects in the case of the European Monetary Union (EMU), as kicked off by Rose (2000) and summarized early by Skudelny (2003). On the other hand, the magnitude of the static and dynamic benefits from transaction cost savings is clearer but relatively moderate. In any case, the potential benefits of integration are not automatic and will take time and effort to develop.

A further problem is that the risk of asymmetric shocks may be much more pronounced than usually expected. Under these conditions, much more effort and flexibility will be needed to adjust economic structures. Care must be taken in analysing the differences between countries and in drawing general conclusions from this about the integration process. A useful approach to further explore the monetary integration challenges of current and prospective EU accession countries is to ask where the common ground is in the discussion on these matters and what the open issues are.

An additional issue relates to the implications of monetary integration for output volatility. Does a flexible nominal exchange rate help smooth output variability or does it add to this variability? There is some evidence for the larger acceding countries that exchange rate flexibility has helped stabilization. Based on Granger causality tests, real exchange rate flexibility, promoted by nominal exchange rate flexibility, has therefore tended to act as a buffer in these countries and has thus helped smooth output variability. Furthermore, the results show that shock absorption is more efficient under a flexible exchange rate regime than under an inflexible one.

While the evidence at this stage is limited, it underscores that it can be a viable and – with a particular view on stabilization issues – potentially beneficial option for countries that operate a flexible exchange rate regime to retain such a regime over the medium (and perhaps even longer) term. At the same time, a flexible exchange rate regime is not a reasonable option for all acceding countries, as it presupposes the existence of sufficiently liquid financial markets. Moreover, it is not an attractive proposition for countries that have well-functioning and credible fixed exchange rate regimes in place (Calvo and Reinhart, 2000).

A further interesting subject is the implication that a high degree of de facto euroization has for monetary policy and monetary integration. While a high degree of de facto euroization does not necessarily complicate a programme for successful disinflation, it entails some specific financial stability risks. It creates systemic solvency risks arising from a sharp depreciation of the local currency. In addition, there are also liquidity risks, as the lender of last resort role of the central bank is constrained if the financial system is characterized by a high degree of foreign exchange-based financial intermediation. Tight prudential regulation can reduce these risks but at the cost of impeding financial intermediation (in the extreme case, it may come close to 'financial repression'). While the adoption of the euro will eventually do away with these problems, it should not be seen as a tool for achieving this objective. Rather, the challenge for highly 'euroized' countries is to design and implement a comprehensive set of policies that reduce the risk of using local currency and enhance the attractiveness of local currency-based financial intermediation, thereby lessening the incentives to use foreign currencies in domestic transactions.

The crisis has shown that CESEE countries can successfully master serious hardships (for example, Slovakia and Estonia). Joining the euro area at some point in time, however, is obligatory for almost all EU members and timing accession well is a demanding task. Certainly, it depends on the underlying economic structure of the respective country and the advances made on the integration path. It also needs to be mentioned that giving up the exchange rate instrument and resorting to the euro as a policy anchor might be a more attractive option for small and more flexible countries. Other countries, however, may find that they fare well with a flexible exchange rate (as the example of Poland has shown in the crisis) and might want to stick to this policy tool for some time longer – to gain leeway for executing necessary structural adjustments.

RETURN TO SMOPEC?

Despite a number of common features, CESEE economies are highly different from other emerging markets in other instances. First, they tend to be small economies. Consequently, export-led growth is a straightforward way toward economic convergence. Second, external debt is only a problem for some countries of the region and not for the others. Third, European integration provides an economic and political anchor for a large number of CESEE countries and euro adoption is an (expected) exit strategy from existing monetary policy strategies.

Of course, the whole framework of macroeconomic policies is relevant for successful economic policies and smooth monetary integration in particular, but some elements have proven to be of specific importance by historical experience. Among these are some of the most basic challenges of the macroeconomic framework, such as the challenges created by the so-called policy trilemma.

Perhaps the most important element to be considered in this respect is the so-called SMOPEC (small open economy) characteristic that gained particular importance in the discussions following the Mundell–Fleming model of fundamental open-economy characteristics, introduced at the time mainly to allow for differences concerning optimal currency area (OCA) preconditions between large and small countries. Essential elements of this perspective are that small countries are price-takers on international markets and that they are characterized by a high share of constant return industries, a high concentration of product/industry specialization and a high geographic concentration of production as well as an overall high share of foreign trade in GDP. As a result small countries typically face a higher likelihood of asymmetric shocks.

A different set of criteria is based on the concept of a nominal anchor (Bordo, 2004). In an environment of high inflation, as was the case in most countries in the 1970s and 1980s, pegging to the currency of a country with low inflation was viewed as a pre-commitment mechanism to anchor inflationary expectations. In a SMOPEC a pegged exchange rate may promote such a pre-commitment device, at least as long as the political costs of breaking the peg are sufficiently large (Krugman, 1989).

According to Frankel (2010) some models of monetary policy originally designed for (larger) industrialized countries apply even more strongly to (smaller) developing countries, especially in light of the credibility problem. But because most developing countries are price-takers on world markets, the SMOPEC model, with non-traded goods, is more often useful than the two-country two-good model. Contractionary effects of devaluation are far more important for small open emerging countries, particularly because of the balance sheet effects that arise from currency mismatch.

THE CENTRAL ROLE OF FINANCIAL MARKETS AND (FOREIGN OWNED) BANKING

Financial markets in CESEE have not performed as well as other emerging markets. They have not yet fully recovered from the global financial crisis. Local equity markets improvement has been driven by global factors rather than by the strengthening of fundamentals. The improvement in other markets has also been limited: spreads on credit default swaps (as well as sovereign eurobonds) remain above the pre-crisis levels; and despite some gains, many local currencies are still weak.

It is also clear that international banks and their subsidiaries in CEE cannot go back to 'business as usual' and continue to finance the rapid credit expansion in CEE, often in foreign currencies, with funds borrowed in international wholesale markets, or with 'excess' savings from western European home markets. Both of these sources have become much harder to tap after the crisis, and are not likely to return to the previous size of flows soon. This raises the question how international banks might rebalance their business model and how this might affect macroeconomic developments and financial stability (IMF, 2009b).

Banking profitability, credit demand and credit supply in the region are all likely to remain subdued, while banks restructure their balance sheets. However, the long-term potential of the CESEE banking industry remains intact. Economic convergence of the region is expected to continue, and the gap in terms of banking penetration and financial deepening will prevail, for at least another two decades.

Clearly, on the positive side, western European parent banks have not abandoned their subsidiaries during the critical phase of the crisis. Most parent banks generally consider these operations as belonging to their 'core' activities, and have also demonstrated their commitment through financial support. Together with the maintenance of credit lines, these measures underline how closely the reputation of parent banks has become aligned with that of their CESEE subsidiaries.

With respect to the institutional framework and reforms, CESEE has advanced substantially in terms of overall banking system transformation. The privatization of large parts of the banking sectors was a characteristic feature in the region. Institutional reforms and ownership transformation contributed significantly to the deepening of financial intermediation; at the same time, the growth of credit to the private sector, in particular to households, has been fairly strong.

HOW VOLATILE WILL THE POST-CRISIS CONTRIBUTION OF CAPITAL FLOWS BECOME?

Emerging markets and developing countries still face specific challenges in developing their own financial sectors and a credible and legitimate regulatory environment, and need more voice in international financial reforms, policy decisions and actions to help overcome these challenges. The recent global financial crisis has exposed weaknesses in economic policy and financial architectures on a national and international scale. The policy and reform agenda is large and much remains to be done.

One of the main lessons to emerge is that prevention is better than cure. While interventions have been effective at maintaining short-term stability, policy makers must remain vigilant about the need for appropriate regulation to establish a sustainable and effective financial architecture.

Many emerging countries are at a serious disadvantage relative to developed economies in that they lack an effective lender of last resort. The economy's fragility may not be noticeable in normal and tranquil times, but its fault lines are revealed during turbulent periods, even in the absence of a major crisis (South African Reserve Bank, 2009). Although the policy interest rate is the instrument of choice for developed economies, in the case of emerging countries it could become uncomfortably weaker during periods of high volatility. Thus, it may be advisable to switch to more robust instruments to ensure the overall effectiveness of the framework.

In general, developing countries experienced two shocks early in the crisis: a 'sudden stop' of capital inflows driven by global deleveraging and a collapse in export demand as a result of the global downturn. In the literature several types of relevant shocks are distinguished. A *current account reversal* is defined as a reduction within one year of the current account deficit of a certain percentage of GDP. A *sudden stop* is typically defined as a substantial unexpected reduction in net capital inflows. A *speculative attack* means a discrete increase in demand for foreign currency, in exchange for domestic currency, by speculators.

The macroeconomics of developing countries is a field of its own. The specific characteristics of developing countries include: greater exposure to supply shocks than industrialized countries in general and trade volatility in particular, procyclicality of international finance, lower credibility with respect to both price stability and default risk, procyclicality of fiscal policy, and – perhaps first of all – imperfect institutions.

MONETARY POLICY UNDER MULTI-DIMENSIONAL PRESSURE

All these analytical elements dealt with above show up as framework conditions and determinants of monetary policy in the end (Calvo, 2009). The importance and sensitivity of these became uncomfortably visible in the course of the crisis. Most central banks in the CESEE region reacted to declining price pressure and low medium-term inflation risks by lowering their policy rates. Those decisions were also supported by the stabilization of financial markets. With economic conditions improving, a core question will concern the design and the timing of exit strategies from monetary easing. This is especially challenging as energy and commodity prices have started to rise, thereby exerting pressure on inflation – much earlier than justified from a purely macroeconomic policy point of view.

After the most acute phase of the crisis, chances improved that the countries in the region would avoid extended currency and banking crises. Because of this, monetary policy shifted its attention from crisis management to longer-term challenges (Hammond et al., 2009). With inflation temporarily off the agenda, the policy response has focused on cuts in interest rates, extended liquidity and exchange rate support measures, and prudential policies aimed at financial stability. Countries with fixed exchange rate regimes were more limited in the use of interest rates, but they did make use of non-standard and prudential tools.

Central banks and governments in the CESEE region have implemented extended liquidity and exchange rate support measures to counter the impact of the crisis on their economies. The aim of this was to stabilize financial markets and to minimize spillovers on the real economy. Most central banks thus took domestic liquidity easing measures, but unlike advanced economies they took only a limited range of non-conventional monetary policy measures.

Monetary policy is typically the first weapon to counteract internal and external shocks. However, emerging market economies face a number of difficult challenges in designing monetary policy frameworks that work well with respect to monetary and financial stability. Many emerging market economies still have relatively underdeveloped financial markets and institutions. This puts a number of constraints on the effective formulation and implementation of macroeconomic policies. Even if economic theory provides lessons for designing effective monetary policy frameworks, each country has specific institutional features that determine how monetary policy decisions are taken and implemented. Perhaps the overriding institutional setting in the case of emerging countries is the concrete exchange rate regime in place.

BACK TO SQUARE ONE: THE (UNPLEASANT) CHOICE OF AN EXCHANGE RATE REGIME

The choice of exchange rate regime is no more clear-cut for emerging market countries than it is for advanced countries. On the one hand, a small size, openness and less developed financial markets point would call for fixed rather than flexible exchange rates. On the other hand, terms-of-trade volatility and the experience with speculative attacks would call for flexible rather than for fixed exchange rates.

Standard theory suggests that the choice between fixed and floating exchange rate regimes should be governed by the desire to minimize output and employment volatility. Hence, the nature of the shocks hitting an economy is primordial. If an economy is exposed to nominal shocks due to money supply or demand, choosing a fixed exchange rate regime seems natural, as the fixed rate acts as a shock absorber for nominal shocks. If shocks are real, due to productivity for instance, a flexible exchange rate performs better. However, standard theory is not very appealing to emerging market economies because 'no exchange rate regime can prevent macroeconomic turbulence' (Calvo and Mishkin, 2003, p. 13).

Notwithstanding these arguments, both types of exchange rate regimes have their merits and shortcomings. Generally, pegs are thought to be a disciplining device for fiscal policy. At the same time, pegs reduce exchange rate premiums that open the way to financing public spending at cheaper rates, a possible recipe for disaster. Importantly, pegs may provide a usual nominal anchor to inflation expectations in the wake of high inflationary periods and can even import anchor currency credibility. Fixed exchange rate regimes help in reaping the gains of economic integration by eliminating the detrimental effects of exchange rate fluctuations on trade (Frankel and Rose, 2002). Fixed exchange rates are more useful than floats for developed countries if they engage in economic integration and if adjustments due to asymmetric shocks can be adjusted by factor mobility, labour market flexibility or increasing intra-industry trade.

Floating exchange rate regimes facilitate an autonomous domestic monetary policy if capital flows are fully liberalized. Floats require no international reserves, and large external imbalances can build up more easily under a peg if exchange rate misalignments become persistent. They can be handled not only via internal adjustment but also through the external adjustment channel (Calvo and Mishkin, 2003).

Obstfeld et al. (2004) forcefully restated the argument that policy makers in open economies face a macroeconomic trilemma of pursuing three typically desirable yet contradictory objectives. The trilemma consists of stabilizing the exchange rate, enjoying free international capital mobility and employing monetary policy for domestic goals at the same time. With liberalized international capital flows generally considered a basic precondition for participating in international markets, whether or not to fix the exchange rate and at which level of development to decide on the issue become fundamental questions for a small country's policy orientation.

Relating this to the situation of countries at an earlier stage of economic development or real convergence, it becomes immediately clear that one of their permanent and ultimate policy-making objectives is to balance the needs of domestic development goals and international monetary integration. In an unstable environment and a situation in which it is difficult to establish internationally acknowledged institutions and to enforce sound decision-making, perhaps the biggest challenge for economic policy – and for monetary policy alike – is how to gain and preserve credibility.

A particular problem in this respect is the move from one currency regime to another (Dornbusch, 1980). Countries which at some point set out on the road towards a particular exchange rate regime for specific – and possibly well-justified – reasons are largely 'tied' to this particular choice because of market pressure as well as potentially bad expectation formation and consequent exchange rate instability. Although the choice of an exchange rate regime may certainly be seen as an outstanding economic policy challenge, the transition from one regime to another one – for example, from a well-established currency board to managed floating – obviously means a multiplication of problems, with unclear results.

Long-term historical tendencies may suggest that an increase in capital mobility tends to make intermediate exchange rate regimes disappear, in favour of the extremes of currency boards or monetary union on the one hand and freely flexible exchange rates on the other. But one has also to take a view on whether the abandonment of intermediate exchange rate regimes is the result of voluntary choice or whether countries are forced to exit, for example because of a speculative attack. But if a forced exit involves a sort of choice between alternative regimes, then both elements would be present at the same time. Therefore, forced exit – even preventive strategies of exit – could lead into a situation of new equilibrium if the right choice is made at the right time and if the respective framework conditions allow for implementing such a choice. No doubt, explaining transitions between exchange rate regimes and their consequences is the central challenge, and a very real challenge at the time of writing, for some countries of the CESEE area given their ultimate perspective of joining monetary union (Backé and Mooslechner, 2004).

Taking into account that countries have to choose their exchange rate regimes for a variety of international and domestic reasons, one obvious requirement is that all actors surely understand the properties of alternative – or potential – regimes. There are some important trade-offs in the choice of the exchange rate regime. On the one hand, an exchange rate regime can promise to impose policy discipline, thereby stabilizing expectations and creating confidence in the currency. On the other hand, no exchange rate regime can substitute for sound macroeconomic management, leaving the burden of doing the right things to policy makers again.

CONCLUSIONS

The crisis in CESEE peaked in early 2009. Central and Eastern Europe was particularly vulnerable at the time because it had (re)financed its long expansion to a considerable extent with capital inflows, leaving the region exposed with large accumulated external and internal imbalances. These vulnerabilities were multiplied in the hot phase of the financial turmoil, when it seemed likely that the region would become another case in a long series of emerging market currency and banking crises.

On their way into the EU, the countries in CESEE are to a large extent free in choosing their monetary and exchange rate policy strategies, indeed. This is clearly reflected in the variety of exchange rate regimes in place across the region, which range from currency boards to lightly managed floats, as well as in the variety of monetary policy strategies and, last but not least, in the variety of crisis measures adopted.

In general, the confidence and stability-enhancing effect of hard pegs was followed in several of the countries; but this does not preclude other monetary strategies – notably inflation targeting and a loose float – from being effective as well. Overall monetary and economic policy soundness, credibility and perseverance remain the key to success under both approaches. In particular, general policy discipline, possibly favoured by peer pressure, EU and IMF surveillance and EU as well as EMU membership aspirations have assisted the central banks in pursuing their goals.

But is there clear-cut advice on which exchange rate regime is appropriate for which country? Despite the extensive academic literature on this important basic question, real-world uncertainty leaves us with a substantial range of indeterminateness when trying to find a straightforward answer on this point. Potentially sustainable exchange rate regimes can be divided into four different groups (Crockett, 2004): (i) fully fixed rates, in particular if they come close to abandoning the individual exchange rate of a country; (ii) pegging regimes, when they are supported by appropriate economic policies or framework conditions; (iii) managed floating regimes, when market expectations concerning exchange rate 'moves' or 'instability' never become too strong; and (iv) free floating regimes, where countries have to accept the potentially real economic consequences of this choice. In any case, the main burden of implementation will lie with monetary policy, supported by or in confrontation with the overall policy setting of a country. As the whole region will have to search for a new type of growth model at the same time, substantial policy challenges as well as ongoing institutional adjustment pressures can be expected to shape CESEE economic development over a considerable period of time.

REFERENCES

Backé, P. and P. Mooslechner (2004), 'From transition to monetary integration: Central and Eastern Europe on its way to the euro', *Comparative Economic Studies*, March.

Baldwin, R. (1992), 'Measurable dynamic gains from trade', *Journal of Political Economy*, **100** (1), 162–74.

BIS (2005), 'Globalisation and monetary policy in emerging markets', Monetary and Economic Department, BIS Papers No. 23, May.

Bordo, M. (2004), 'Exchange rate regimes for the 21st century: a historical perspective', in *60 Years of Bretton Woods*, Proceedings of OeNB Workshops, No. 3, Oesterreichische Nationalbank.

Calvo, G. (2009), 'Monetary policy challenges in emerging markets: sudden stop, liability dollarization and lender of last resort', NBER Working Paper 12788.

Calvo, G.A. and F. Mishkin (2003), 'The mirage of exchange rate regimes for emerging market economies', NBER Working Paper No. 9808.

Calvo, G.A. and C.M. Reinhart (2000), 'Fear of floating', NBER Working Paper No. 7993.

Crockett, A. (2004), 'Exchange rate regimes in theory and practice', in P. Mizon (ed.), *Monetary History, Exchange Rates and Financial Markets*, Cheltenham, UK and Northampton, MA, USA: Edward Elgar.

Dornbusch, R. (1980), 'Exchange rate economics: where do we stand?', *Brookings Papers on Economic Activity*, **1**, 143–85.

Frankel, J.A. (2010), 'Monetary policy in emerging markets: a survey', NBER Working Paper 16125.

Frankel, J. and A. Rose (2002), 'An estimate of the effect of common currencies on trade and income', Harvard University, John F. Kennedy School of Government, Working Paper Series rwp01-013.

Hammond, G. et al. (eds) (2009), *Monetary Policy Frameworks for Emerging Markets*, Cheltenham, UK and Northampton, MA, USA: Edward Elgar.

IMF (2009a), 'Lessons of the global crisis for macroeconomic policy', Washington, DC.

IMF (2009b), 'Lessons of the financial crisis for future regulation of financial institutions and markets and for liquidity management', Washington, DC, February.

Krugman, P. (1989), *Exchange Rate Instability*, Cambridge, MA: MIT Press.

Obstfeld, M., J. Shambaugh and A. Taylor (2004), 'The trilemma in history: trade-offs among exchange rates, monetary policies, and capital mobility', *Review of Economics and Statistics*, December, 423–38.
Rose, A. (2000), 'One money, one market: the effect of common currencies on trade', Economic Policy: a European Forum, London: Centre for Economic Policy Research.
Skudelny, F. (2003), 'Exchange rate uncertainty and trade: a survey', Mimeo.
South African Reserve Bank (2009), *Challenges for Monetary Policy-makers in Emerging Markets*, South African Reserve Bank Conference Series 2008.

PART III

The new role of financial integration, growth financing and exports

17. Policy perspectives on financial integration after the crisis

Ignazio Angeloni[1]

Among the many consequences of the crisis on the European economy, on financial stability, growth and employment, sovereign debts and risks, and so on, less frequently emphasized is the impact it had – and continues to have, in spite of the time elapsed – on European financial integration. Financial integration is the degree to which the financial sector within a given geographical area is capable of functioning as a single entity, guaranteeing broadly uniform borrowing and lending conditions to its residents wherever located, after risk and other relevant characteristics are accounted for. After making steady progress for several years, financial integration in the euro area has deteriorated markedly since 2007. Financial integration is a necessary feature of a well-functioning currency area, hence this development is a worrisome signal that should not be underestimated.

Most of the deterioration occurred in the money and the bond markets, the areas where progress towards integration used to be most visible in earlier years. These markets are central to the proper functioning and the transmission of monetary policy. Recent developments suggest that these losses will not easily be reverted; return to normality will be slow. The actions by central banks and other authorities to preserve the functionality of markets and to reform European financial regulation and supervision, though helpful also from the viewpoint of financial integration, are unlikely to be enough. As I shall argue, it is essential that national governments cooperate, refraining from actions that protect national markets or intermediaries while hampering cross-border integration. Beyond this, attaining sustained euro area financial integration will involve more time and effort than optimistically believed prior to the financial crisis. It will require further reform of euro area financial markets and enhancements in its policy architecture. Some of these changes are underway, also under the stimulus provided by the crisis, but the restoration of well-functioning and integrated markets is far from completed.

It is helpful to start by examining the recent developments in euro area financial integration on the basis of some statistical evidence, and then reflect on the implications for the future. In Section 1, I will recall why and how, shortly after the start of the monetary union, the European Central Bank (ECB) and the Eurosystem made financial integration in the newly created currency area a central policy goal, to be achieved in collaboration with other European authorities. Section 2 presents some evidence, drawn from recent ECB analyses, that illustrates the setback financial integration has suffered as a result of the crisis – unquestionably, the most serious one since the launch of the EU internal market for capital and financial services in the late 1980s. Finally, Section 3 concludes with some reflections on how our perspectives on financial integration have changed as a result of recent events, and on some future policy directions.

1 EUROSYSTEM INVOLVEMENT IN FINANCIAL INTEGRATION

The Eurosystem started early to focus on financial integration as a central bank policy objective. A search on the ECB website section listing press releases and official statements reveals a sequence of Executive Board statements on this subject as early as 1999. Some of these statements focused on the Eurosystem responsibilities in the area of payment systems, seeing the strengthening of payment and settlement infrastructures as a technical condition to achieve financial integration more generally.[2] In a few cases, a broader perspective was taken, examining how integrated finances in the EU or the euro area could contribute to the ECB's ultimate function and goal – conducting monetary policy aimed at price stability – or help foster European integration.[3] In some instances, the emphasis was on the ECB's cooperation with other European authorities, notably the Commission and the Council, then engaged in implementing the Financial Services Action Plan.[4]

In these early documents, the lack of financial integration was at the time seen essentially as a historical legacy, reflecting the multi-country and multi-currency origin of the euro area. As such, financial integration could be attained, it was felt, essentially by removing legal or technical barriers preventing smooth cross-border payments, capital flows and arbitrage, erected at a time when financial markets were organized following a national logic. Financial integration was regarded as a *structural* phenomenon, typically slow-moving and not easily reversible. One finds little or no recognition, in these early documents, of the fact that financial market integration could suddenly reverse as a result of unexpected shocks, for example to financial stability. Financial stability, in turn, was typically seen as a by-product of price stability, at least in the long run.

These initial debates generated in the ECB a momentum for a more systematic reflection; first and foremost to agree on a definition of financial integration, and to consider whether and to what extent it should feature among the central bank objectives and why, and what actions would be necessary to achieve it. This was all the more necessary since the Treaty and the annexed ECB statutes do not mention financial integration at all. They do, however, refer to a number of activities – such as providing support to national authorities in safeguarding financial stability, preserving the smooth operation of payment systems, and supporting the Community's economic policies – where the central bank is heavily involved and that directly or indirectly relate to financial integration or imply it.

In the ECB such reflection started around the years 2002–03, prompted essentially by the then Executive Board members Tommaso Padoa-Schioppa and Sirkka Hämäläinen. The result was a series of studies leading, among other things, to the following formal definition of financial integration: 'a situation whereby there are no frictions that discriminate between economic agents in their access to – and their investment of – capital, particularly on the basis of their location'.[5] The ECB/Eurosystem's role in pursuing financial integration was explicitly recognized and a new set of research-based statistical indicators was developed to analyse and monitor the phenomenon. Financial integration was made part of the Eurosystem mission statement with the following wording: 'Acting also as a leading financial authority, we [the central banks of the Eurosystem] aim to safeguard financial stability and promote European financial integration'.[6] Note that the relevant geographical area is taken to be the European Union, not the euro area alone.

The new set of statistical indicators, periodically refined and updated, offered the basis for introducing a new annual report focused on financial integration, launched in 2007: *Financial Integration in Europe*. Typically, the report contains comments on recent developments in the integration indicators, thematic essays analysing specific aspects relevant to financial integration, and a detailed concluding description of Eurosystem activities. Concerning the last of these,

> The Eurosystem generally distinguishes between four types of activity through which it contributes to the enhancement of financial integration: (i) giving advice on the legislative and regulatory framework for the financial system and direct rule-making; (ii) acting as a catalyst for private sector activities by facilitating collective action; (iii) enhancing knowledge, raising awareness and monitoring the state of European financial integration and (iv) providing central bank services that also foster European financial integration.[7]

The report includes a technical appendix, targeted mainly at analysts and scholars, describing the methodologies used for constructing the statistical indicators and the underlying sources of data. The indicators, regularly updated, are available on the ECB website, hence providing also a valuable source of statistical material for students and analysts.

2 DEVELOPMENTS IN MONEY AND BOND MARKET INTEGRATION DURING THE CRISIS

We concentrate our attention on money and bond markets; information on other market compartments is available in the annual ECB Report on Financial Integration already mentioned.

Money markets are of obvious importance for the transmission of monetary policy; they are the markets where the central bank directly intervenes and which transmit the first impulses to the financial sector and to the rest of the economy. The transmission from money markets runs through various channels; for example, several financial contracts (mortgages, indexed loan and deposit rates, floating rate certificates, and so on) are directly linked to money market rates. Even in the absence of explicit indexation, money market rates enter crucially into the decision rules and portfolio strategies of financial intermediaries and private as well as institutional investors. Money market integration is a key requirement for a proper functioning of monetary policy, because it ensures that policy actions are transmitted to the euro area economy in a balanced and uniform way.

Figure 17.1 shows cross-sectional standard deviations of Euribor and Eurepo rates, at two maturities (1 and 12 months) from 2007 to 2010. This and the following figures are drawn, with minor further elaboration and update, from the ECB (2010a) Report, *Financial Integration in Europe*. The figure shows the within-country and the cross-country standard deviation, as well as the difference between the two. Euribor is the rate at which euro interbank term deposits are being offered by one prime bank to another within the EMU zone, while Eurepo is the corresponding rate on interbank loans backed by general collateral. The key difference between Euribor and Eurepo is that in the latter the transaction carries a dual guarantee, by the counterparty and by collateral chosen from a commonly agreed pool.[8]

Several indications emerge from the figure. The crisis (in August 2007, but much more in the autumn of 2008, with the demise of Lehman Brothers) led to a dramatic divergence of market rates relative to the

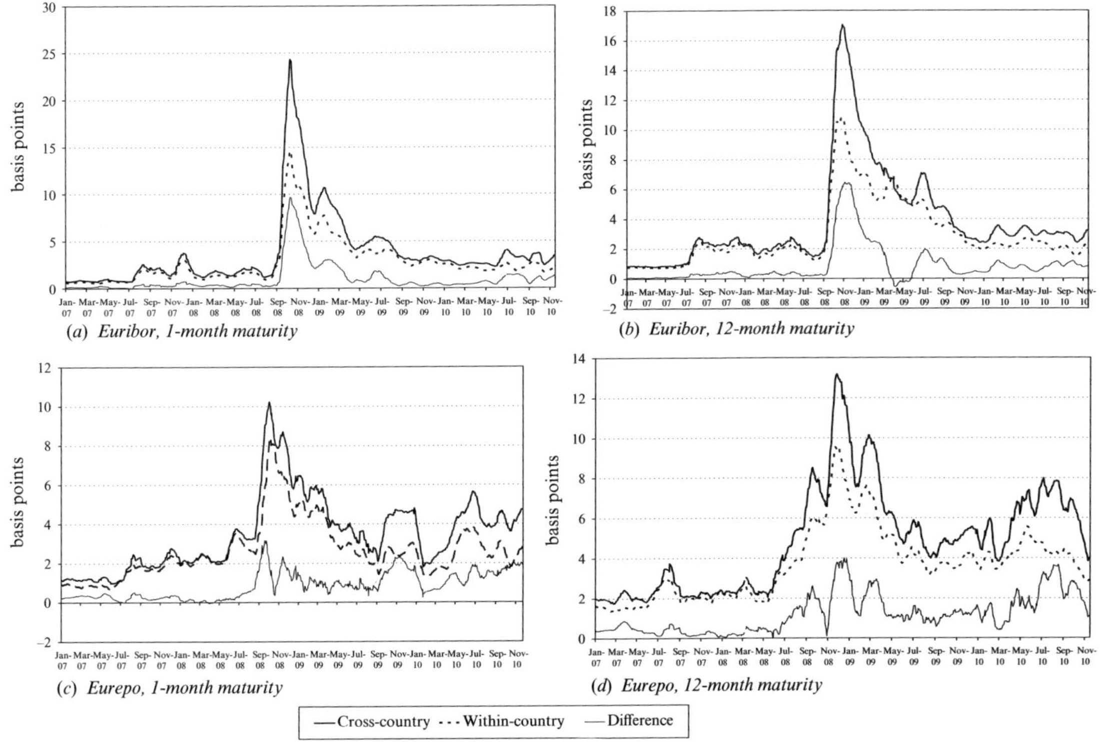

(*a*) *Euribor, 1-month maturity*

(*b*) *Euribor, 12-month maturity*

(*c*) *Eurepo, 1-month maturity*

(*d*) *Eurepo, 12-month maturity*

Sources: EBF and ECB calculations.

Figure 17.1 Standard deviation of the Euribor and Eurepo rates

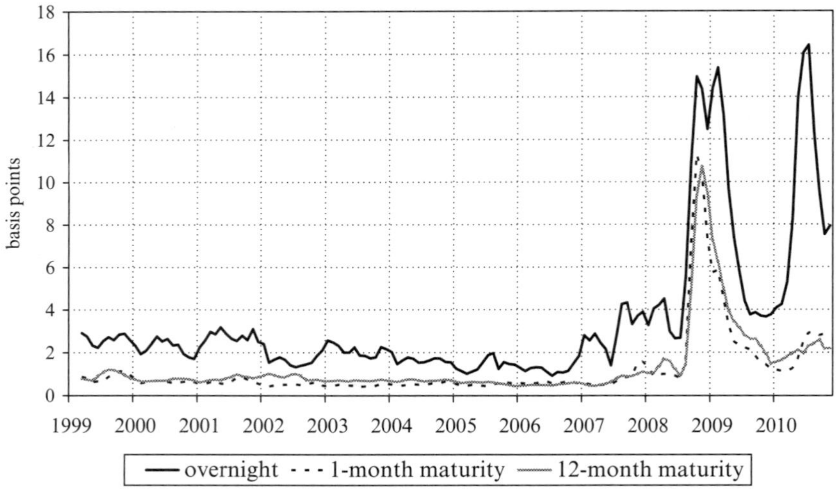

Sources: EBF and ECB calculations.

Figure 17.2 Cross-country standard deviation of Eonia and Euribor rates

preceding period, where the standard deviation had been constantly in the order of 1 basis point. The divergence was, from September 2008 onwards, much greater across countries than within countries. This reveals that risk premia, induced by uncertainty about the solvency of the counterparties (counterparty risk), were systematically greater for transactions involving parties resident in different countries within the euro area. Moreover, while in the Euribor segment the *gap* in the standard deviations between cross-border and domestic transactions gradually declined in recent months, in the Eurepo segment it remained high and actually tended to increase. This reflects the further element of uncertainty linked to the quality of collateral – generally consisting in government bonds – in an environment increasingly dominated, in recent times, by uncertainties about the solvency of sovereign issuers.[9]

Figure 17.2 shows similar calculations for the Eonia rate, that is, the overnight rates applied to actual transactions conducted by a panel of reporting banks, in comparison with Euribor rates on longer maturities. The pattern is similar to that of the previous figure but the fluctuations are much larger, as one would expect due to the one-day maturity of Eonia. In 2010, a sharp increase in the standard deviation occurred only in the overnight segment, a sign that the phenomenon was perceived as short-lasting.

The standard deviation shown in the figure is an average calculated over all transactions, regardless of the location of the borrower and lender. If one excludes the transactions involving countries that experienced the most visible fiscal strain in 2010, the standard deviation tends to decrease, even sharply. This suggests that unlike in the earlier period, in 2010, and specifically after the Greek rescue, fiscal uncertainty was the major driver of money market dis-integration. Remarkably, *unsecured* transactions were also strongly affected in those countries – albeit less so – illustrating the presence of a negative spillover from the dis-integration of the sovereign sector to that of money markets. The fact that sovereign risks affected *all* money market transactions, not only those backed by government bonds as collateral, is noteworthy because it illustrates the role that sovereign issuers play, at least in the perception of markets, as guarantors of the viability of the respective banking systems.

This evidence demonstrates that money market integration is closely linked to bond market integration, to which we now turn. There are several ways of measuring financial integration in securities markets; some of them are based on quantitative data (amount invested, portfolio shares, and so on), others on relative yields or spreads. The two sources of evidence are complementary and, in this case, mutually reinforcing. Quantity data indicate that the degree of 'home bias' (the propensity of asset holders to invest in domestic securities being a higher share than optimality considerations would suggest) declined markedly in the euro area until 2007. From 2008 it has increased again for debt instruments, while continuing to decline for equities (ECB, 2010b, box n. 54).

In the market for sovereign bonds, a commonly used measure of integration based on returns data is the comparison of yields on benchmark instruments of equal maturity, typically ten-year government bonds. Figure 17.3 shows the extraordinary increase in yield spreads in the euro area in 2009 and 2010. Current sovereign yield spreads are unprecedented in EMU times, and approach levels experienced previously in the mid-1990s. Note that in the more recent period the German yield declined, reflecting a 'flight to quality' effect.

Yield spreads are, however, a potentially misleading measure of integration. As noted already, market integration presupposes that all borrowers and lenders face equal opportunities and conditions once account is taken of their risk characteristics. Market returns can diverge in perfectly integrated markets, if the discrepancies between yields reflect credit risk premia, generated by the proper assessment and pricing of the underlying risk. In practice, however, when markets are stressed and risk premia

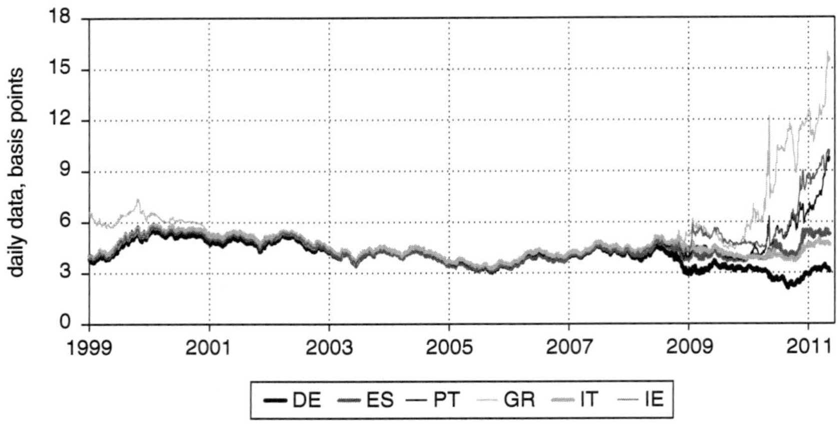

Sources: Thomson Reuters Datastream and ECB.

Figure 17.3 Selected ten-year sovereign bond yields

reach unprecedented levels, as they have in recent times, the pricing process is likely to be hampered. In these conditions, markets may become dysfunctional and rationing and segmentation phenomena can play a significant role, giving rise to additional liquidity risk premia that effectively reduce market integration.

One way to disentangle the credit risk component from other components of risk is to compare yield spreads with the corresponding spreads on credit default swaps (CDS). CDS are derivative instruments used to separate credit from other components of risk. If yield spreads reflected credit risk alone, their movement should be matched by comparable spreads between CDS rates. Figure 17.4 shows, for the same group of countries as in Figure 17.3, the CDS-bond basis, that is, the difference between the CDS premium relative to a benchmark and the bond yield spread relative to the same benchmark. The benchmark chosen is this case is the ten-year OIS (overnight indexed swap).

For Germany and, until end-2010, also for Italy and Spain, the CDS-basis oscillates moderately and tends, in stressed market conditions, to rise above pre-Lehman levels. For the countries where the fiscal risks were highest (Greece, Ireland, Portugal), it oscillates much more widely and tends instead to fall below historical levels. The decline in the CDS-basis reflects the stronger increase in yield spreads relative to CDS premia, and hence is a measure of the extra premia not attributable to credit risk.

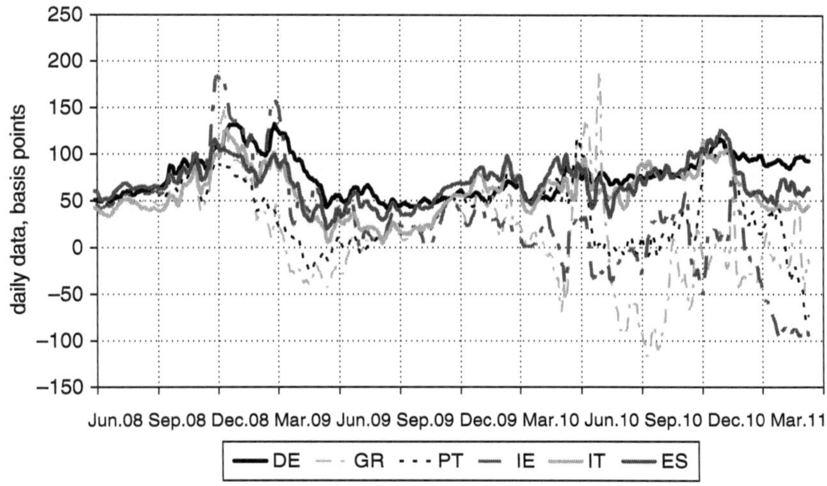

Note: The benchmark is the OIS rate.

Sources: Bloomberg, Thomson Reuters Datastream and ECB.

Figure 17.4 CDS-bond basis (CDS premium – bond spread) for selected countries

3 LOOKING AHEAD

The above evidence illustrates clearly – in spite of some ambiguities in interpreting the statistics – the sharp loss of cross-border integration experienced by euro area money and bond markets as a consequence of the crisis. The massive interventions undertaken by the ECB (enhanced liquidity provision to offset the decline in bank intermediation, securities market purchases) ensured the essential intermediation function in the economy, but could not prevent a sharp deterioration of the functionality and integration of these markets, let alone restore the pre-crisis levels of integration.

One striking aspect is the speed with which the market retrenchment occurred, in contrast with the steady process of integration that had taken place in the preceding years. The indicators reveal that almost all money markets essentially froze immediately after the Lehman failure, particularly in cross-border business. Financial integration showed its cyclical and disruptive aspect rather than the presumed structural qualities.

A key lesson of this experience is the close link (indeed, multiple two-way linkages) between financial integration, financial stability, macroeconomic conditions and sovereign risks. It all started with a banking crisis, originating from risky and opaque financial instruments hidden in equally opaque bank balance sheets. This fuelled counterparty risk and eventually resulted in a gridlock of interbank markets, particularly across frontiers. Bank risks quickly spilled over to the macroeconomy, generating a recession from the aggregate demand side. This, together with the bank rescues, led to ballooning fiscal deficits and debts. The sovereign debt crisis, highly differentiated across countries reflecting country-specific initial conditions and reactions of the fiscal authorities, in turn fed back to financial integration, both by creating segmentations in the collateral used to guarantee interbank transactions and by exacerbating uncertainty about the viability of banking sectors. Clearly, the risks stemming from vicious cycles between the macroeconomy and micro-finance, and between private and public finance, were vastly underestimated in both academic and policy-making circles in the preceding years.

The conditions and policies to put the euro area financial sector durably back in shape are likely to be as complex as the forces at play. Financial integration, financial stability, macroeconomic stability and fiscal discipline appear, in this phase and in prospect, inextricably linked.[10] Many policy areas will need to contribute: regulatory and supervisory reform, fiscal consolidation at the domestic level, stronger fiscal and macroeconomic governance rules for the euro area. In all these areas reform is partly underway and many ideas are discussed; no specific comments are needed here. We conclude, instead, with two remarks more directly focused on our central theme, financial integration.

First, financial authorities in the euro area are likely to remain focused, in the foreseeable future, on the goal of strengthening national banking sectors, through regulatory reform and direct support. Predictably, measures will be geared to domestic conditions and needs. To the extent that such actions, even uncoordinated, effectively improve market confidence, they should help improve cross-border integration as well. There is a risk, however, that some of them may effectively support national intermediaries and markets to the detriment of their cross-border integration. Experience shows that the domestic retrenchment observed recently in many banking activities (not only interbank and securities market transactions but also to some extent retail customer lending and deposit taking) was stimulated also by prudential measures at the national level. Such effects are counterproductive and should be avoided; surveillance by the Commission, in the areas of internal market and competition particularly, will be important.

Secondly, a key lesson of the recent months, as illustrated in the preceding section, is that the dishomogeneity of the government bond market in the euro area entails significant threats for the area's financial integration. Hidden most of the time, the disruptive potential constituted by fragmented euro area sovereign bond markets reappears, with disruptive force, when market tensions arise.

In this context, the establishment of a market for pan-European securities would be of considerable help. A liquid market for standardized official supranational instruments would constitute a useful benchmark for market transactions, offering, more than anything existing at present, something close to a 'riskless rate', comparatively robust even in times of stress. It would also enrich the pool of attractive collateral for private and central bank transactions. As such, it could reduce, perhaps dramatically, the cross-border spreads observed in money markets.

The many arguments against an uncontrolled issuance of European sovereign bonds need to be taken carefully into consideration. These objections are particularly compelling since Europe is not ready, institutionally and politically, to pool taxpayers' resources into a common fiscal policy. Embracing the issuance of such bonds indiscriminately, while fiscal decisions remain national, would create incentives for budget laxity. But from a technical standpoint, the establishment of a Eurobond market in itself would not necessarily open the way to moral hazard if adequate safeguards are introduced.[11] The advantages of such instrument for financial integration, a vital good for the euro's future, should not be disregarded.

NOTES

1. Shortly after I wrote this chapter Tommaso Padoa-Schioppa prematurely passed away. I dedicate these pages to him, for the vision and inspiration he left us also in the area of European financial integration. I am grateful to Francesco Papadia, Roberto de Santis, Alexander Popov and Stefano Borgioli for helpful comments and information. The views expressed here are personal and should not be attributed to the ECB or the Eurosystem.
2. See, for example, Padoa-Schioppa (1999).
3. See, for example, Hämäläinen (2000).
4. See, for example, Padoa-Schioppa (2002).
5. See ECB *Monthly Bulletin* article titled 'The integration of Europe's financial markets', October 2003 p. 153. In practice, a financial market is considered to be integrated when all potential market participants are subject to the same set of rules, have equal access to the market and are treated equally when they operate in it.
6. http://www.ecb.europa.eu/ecb/orga/escb/html/mission_eurosys.en.html.
7. ECB (2010a).
8. See www.euribor.org for details.
9. Eurepo is defined as the rate at which prime banks offer funds in euro to other prime

banks in exchange for the best collateral in terms of rating and liquidity within the Eurepo general collateral basket. In practice, such 'best' collateral may not always be used, and market participants may adjust the terms and conditions of repo operations depending on the perceived quality of collateral.
10. On the linkages between financial integration and financial stability see ECB (2010a), special feature D, 'Stability implications of financial integration and development'.
11. See, for example, the discussion in the Monti report (2010) on the Single Market.

REFERENCES

ECB (2010a), Financial Integration in Europe, April.
ECB (2010b), *Monthly Bulletin*, May.
Hämäläinen, Sirkka (2000), 'The single currency and European integration', speech delivered at the seminar, 'EMU experience and prospects', Institute of European Affairs, Dublin, 16 October.
Monti, Mario (2010), 'A new strategy for the Single Market', Report to the President of the European Commission, May.
Padoa-Schioppa, Tommaso (1999), 'Payments and the Eurosystem', speech, Sibos, Munich, 13 September.
Padoa-Schioppa, Tommaso (2002), 'Remarks at the roundtable: mid-term review of progress towards European financial integration', Brussels, 22 February.

18. The need for an enhanced role of local supervisors and shareholder oversight

Andrzej Stopczyński[1]

INTRODUCTION

The integration of financial markets in Europe is fuelling economic growth as it gives banks extended access to wholesale funding and enables them to transfer capital and liquidity through fast channels. Yet this very positive impact can turn into a source of enormous risk if the above-mentioned phenomena get out of control. Lessons learned from the last crisis have changed the minds of supervisors and forced them to look beyond oversight structures that remain limited to single banks and bank groups.

NEW SOURCES OF RISK

One of the most visible effects of financial integration is the rapid development of securities markets. The growing market for corporate bonds gave corporates the option of meeting their funding needs by issuing bonds. As this narrowed banks' possibilities of extending loans to large companies, they were forced to seek other sources of revenues. The financial liberalization of the 1980s and technological progress made it possible for banks to shift towards mortgage lending (Green and Wachter, 2007). However, mortgage loans were financed not only by households' deposits but also by wholesale funding, which produced a gap between the rate of growth in loans and the rate of growth in deposits. On top of that, globalization enabled the massive use of external wholesale financing, and thus helped turn wholesale funding into one of the factors behind the global banking crisis (Hume and Sentence, 2009).

REFOCUSING BANKING SUPERVISION

If we take into consideration that banks are institutions of public trust and have decisive influence on financial stability both at the local and at the global level, and if we take into consideration that, unlike investment and pension funds, banks take risks on their own account, the obvious conclusion would be to keep the banking industry among the most heavily regulated industries on the local as well as global level. Preserving the long-term stability of the banking system is the primary task of supervisors apart from fulfilling national and European legal obligations. Recent experiences of many countries illustrate that banking supervision should be refocused on shielding banks and economies against the risk of boom–bust cycles (Brunnermeier et al., 2009). Following this idea it is clear that the common framework focused on current capital adequacy ratios and liquidity measures is not enough to safeguard the long-term stability of the banking system. The same experiences also show that the evolution of bubbles is usually determined by local conditions (Regling and Watson, 2010) so the measures should be applied predominantly at local level and put into the hands of local regulators and supervisors who are well placed to use these powers. All this supports the conclusion that capital and liquidity management should remain at the local level.

SHAREHOLDERS AS SUPERVISORS' POTENTIAL ALLY

Are the supervisors alone in the battle against boom–bust cycles? If we take into account the interests of all actors, we find banks to be seeking short-term profit at the cost of excessive risk against the interests of shareholders (Jansen, 2004). Therefore the shareholders could be natural allies of supervisors, supporting their efforts in building up banks' real (long-term) value. Some form of an alliance between supervisors and shareholders could eliminate at least some banking activities that may have damaging effects on the local markets (as was the case with massive foreign exchange lending). Such cooperation could support organic growth financed mainly by domestic savings, as is the case in many Latin American and Asian countries (Canales-Kriljenko et al., 2010).

The proposed alliance could promote a new 'risk management culture' within the banking system. Some forms of cooperation between supervisors and shareholders would be in accordance with supervisory targets, despite the difficulty that might appear in creating institutional platforms for cooperation that would protect supervisors' independence.

HOST AND HOME COUNTRY SUPERVISORS: A COMMONSENSE SOLUTION

Now, is it in the interests of host countries to put more 'power' into the hands of local supervisors while the home countries are expected to support the idea of group-level supervision (UniCredit Group, 2009)? The answer is as follows. The recent Ireland experience is a striking example of the phenomenon that, given spillover effects, unstable local markets pose a threat to global stability. The other example is the threat of a full-fledged currency crisis that was averted thanks to IMF loans and the Vienna Initiative (Allen, 2010). Therefore, preventing unstable credit booms is in the interests of both home and host countries, and all local supervisors, be they home or host country supervisors, need to have sufficient powers.

CURRENT TRENDS

Unfortunately, the share of loans extended to the corporate sector is decreasing in emerging Europe at the time of writing. Banks have become more and more focused on consumer and mortgage loans. This produces a potential threat to emerging Europe, as is evidenced by a statement on recent developments in some euro area countries by Fernando Ulrich, chief executive of the Portuguese Banco BPI: 'We cannot afford to invest any more money in cement for the next ten years. We have to spend all our available funds on improving the competitiveness of the export sector' (*Financial Times*, 2010). The housing sector is important for the economy but it is characterized by low productivity growth. Thus the situation in which construction absorbs the growing share of economic resources may hamper the economy rate of growth and its long-term competitiveness. Figure 18.1 illustrates this process in Poland.

The other challenge for banks and economies in emerging Europe is the necessity to develop the domestic markets that would mobilize local savings and channel them into the domestic banking system (Kamil and Rai, 2010; Sławiński, 2010).

CONCLUSIONS

Micro-prudential supervision of banks cannot protect the banking sector against systemic risk and it cannot mitigate the risk of boom–bust

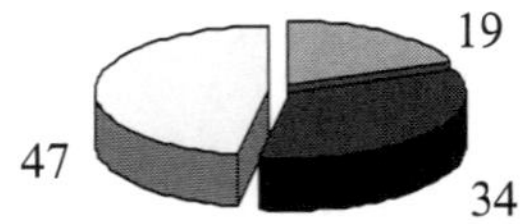

(a) Current loan portfolio structure

(b) Loan portfolio structure at the end of 2008

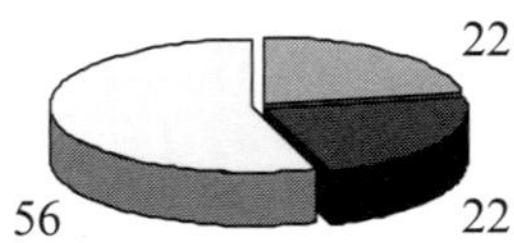

(c) Loan portfolio structure at the end of 2006

Source: Polish Financial Supervisory Authority (KNF).

Figure 18.1 The loan portfolio structure of Polish banks

cycles. In order to do that, supervisors would need to go beyond their previous practices and find new ways of motivating banks to support stable economic growth and avoid unstable booms in consumer and mortgage lending. Local supervisors would need to have at their disposal effective tools to avert local lending booms. A long-term perspective in banking could be provided by an alliance of supervisors and banks' shareholders; such an alliance seems very promising given the extended set of common targets it embraces. Of course, the first step toward achieving this goal would be to create the necessary institutional solutions.

NOTE

1. Special thanks to Professor Andrzej Sławiński, Director of the Economic Institute in the National Bank of Poland, for his useful suggestions.

REFERENCES

Allen, M. (2010), 'The Vienna Initiative', Polish Financial Supervisory Authority, Conference on Households' Foreign Exchange Lending, 20 October.

Brunnermeier, M. et al. (2009), 'The fundamental principles of financial regulation', Geneva Reports on the World Economy, 11/2009, London: ICMB.

Canales-Kriljenko, J.I., B. Coulibaly and H. Kamil (2010), 'A tale of two regions: foreign-bank lending to emerging markets during the global crisis different from continent to continent', *Finance & Development*, **47** (1), 35–6.

Financial Times (2010), 'Portugal: peripheral nerves', 7 November.

Green, R.K. and S.M. Wachter (2007), 'The housing finance revolution', prepared for the 31st Economic Policy Symposium: Housing, Housing Finance and Monetary Policy, Jackson Hole, Wyoming.

Hume, M. and A. Sentence (2009), 'The global credit boom: challenges for macroeconomics and policy', Discussion Paper No. 27, Bank of England.

Jansen, M. (2004), 'The agency costs of overvalued equity and the current state of corporate finance', *European Financial Management*, **10** (4), 549–65.

Kamil, H. and K. Rai (2010), 'The global credit crunch and foreign banks' lending to emerging markets: why did Latin America fare better?', IMF Working Paper WP/10/102, April.

Regling, K. and M. Watson (2010), 'A Preliminary Report on the Sources of Ireland's Banking Crisis', Dublin: Government Publications.

Sławiński, A. (2010), 'Joining the euro zone: from the perspective of emerging Europe countries', Folia Oeconomica, no. 239/2010.

UniCredit Group (2009), 'Cross-border banking in Europe: what regulation and supervision?', Discussion Paper, UniCredit Group, Forum on financial cross-border groups, 01/2009.

19. Firms' patterns of trade and access to finance

Jože P. Damijan and Črt Kostevc

1. INTRODUCTION

Vast empirical research conducted since the mid-1990s on the issue of international trade has documented significant differences between exporters and firms serving domestic markets only. At the same time, both empirical and theoretical work on trade has been quite ineffective in establishing a convincing mechanism for learning-by-trading. In other words, evidence is still limited on how firms' foreign trade participation feeds back into their performance. One of the primary reasons is that much of the literature has focused solely on exports. Here, the existing theoretical models with heterogeneous firms and randomly assigned productivities in the tradition of Melitz (2003) fall short of explaining why some firms are initially 'better', enabling them to start exporting.

Studies dealing with the impact of imports on firm performance are rather scarce, but importers have been shown to have a larger productivity premium than exporters (Altomonte et al., 2008). The notion of imports has traditionally been a source of increased competition in the local markets, impacting firms' productivity through increased competitive pressures. Only recently have studies started to focus on other aspects of imports as a source of corporate productivity growth, such as lower input prices and larger input varieties. Amiti and Konings (2007) document the effects of import liberalization on the productivity of Indonesian firms, which imply that access to cheaper intermediates might have a much larger impact on firm productivity gains than that of increased import competition. Goldberg et al. (2011) demonstrate the impact of trade liberalization in India on manufacturing productivity growth through a broader variety of intermediate inputs. These findings suggest that input tariff liberalization may have relaxed the technological constraints for local firms, and thus enhanced their performance, by giving them access to new imported inputs and by lowering the input price index.

In addition, Goldberg et al. (2011) document that larger input varieties have also impacted firms' innovation in terms of new products they launched. This echoes findings of some previous studies documenting a sequencing of firm trade participation. Based on Spanish micro data, Damijan and Kostevc (2010) demonstrate that sequencing goes from imports through innovation to export decision.

Another issue that has recently surfaced is the role of finance for exporting firms. Firms' own cash flow and their access to bank finance and to internal credit markets have been found to be a trigger factor in their decision to start exporting, and a crucial factor in enabling them to survive in export markets and expand along the intensive and extensive margins of trade. Access to external finance is in particular important for small firms and during financial crises. Exporters are likely to be affected more adversely by financial turmoil than firms serving only local markets, given higher working capital requirements and longer time lags in payments. Recent empirical evidence shows that small exporters are hit harder when bank finance dries up. The striking evidence of recent empirical literature highlights the stabilizing effects of foreign direct investments as inter-firm finance does not appear to dry up at times of crisis. Hence, exports of firms that are part of the networks of multinational firms are more stable during financial crises.

This chapter summarizes recent advances in the empirical research on firms learning from trade participation and the role of finance in both starting to trade and surviving in export markets as well as expanding along intensive and extensive trade margins. Section 2 below discusses new findings about how firms learn from trade. Section 3 discusses factors hampering expansion in export markets, while Section 4 documents the role of financial constraints for participation in trade. Section 5 documents the role of finance during the financial turmoil and identifies factors that help firms withstand crises more successfully. Section 6 concludes.

2 HOW DO FIRMS LEARN FROM TRADE?

Empirical research starting with Bernard and Jensen (1995, 1999) and Roberts and Tybout (1997) has documented substantial differences between exporting and non-exporting firms. Exporting firms are shown to outperform non-exporters in terms of productivity, capital intensity, wages and size. A wide body of cross-country evidence (see Greenaway and Kneller, 2007, and Wagner, 2007, for an overview of empirical studies) documents a quite substantial productivity premium of exporting firms, ranging between 20 and 30 per cent when measured by ordinary least squares (OLS) and between 7 and 10 per cent when taking into account firm fixed effects (see Table 19.1).

Table 19.1 Average productivity premia for exporters (value added/employee, in %)

	Pooled OLS	Fixed effects
Average 14 countries *(ISGEP, 2008)*	22.4	7.0
US *(Bernard et al., 2007)*	29.7	10.5
France *(Mayer & Ottaviano, 2008)*	31.0	

Note: Pooled OLS – estimates obtained by using the ordinary least squares method and pooled over all years. Fixed effects – estimates obtained by accounting for firm fixed effects.

Two competing hypotheses, which are not mutually exclusive, have been examined by economists all over the world in order to explain this productivity premium of exporting firms. The first hypothesis stresses *self-selection* of firms into exporting status; that is, only more productive firms can afford to pay the extra export cost. The second hypothesis actually points towards reverse causality: the *learning-by-exporting* hypothesis claims that exporters become 'better' once they have started to export, as more intense competition and knowledge flows from foreign buyers have improved their post-entry performance. Broad empirical evidence, however, unanimously points towards self-selection of initially better performing firms into exporting and not vice versa. Table 19.2 gives an overview of pre-entry and post-entry performance of new exporters for a set of European countries, China and the US. Pre-entry premia of future exporters over non-exporters three years before starting to export are found to be around 10 per cent on average (and slightly less in the US). Post-entry growth premia of new exporters three years after starting to export, however, have been found to be very meagre – on average only around 2.5 per cent and insignificant (zero per cent) in the US.

The observed large pre-entry productivity premia of new exporters compared with non-exporters imply that the decision to start exporting has to be determined by factors that affect the productivity of firms before they start exporting. While empirical studies document substantial heterogeneity in firm productivity within and between industries (Bartelsman and Doms, 2000), the theory on firm dynamics still does not provide a convincing explanation of what generates this firm heterogeneity and divergent growth dynamics of firms. Some explanation for this can be found in endogenous growth theory, which associates productivity with decisions such as to invest in R&D and innovation. Romer (1990) stresses that innovative activity is central to corporate technological progress and productivity growth. Ericson and Pakes (1995) analyse the behaviour of

Table 19.2 Pre- and post-entry growth premia (value added/employee, in %)

	Pre-entry premia *t-3*	Post-entry growth difference *t+3*
Austria	0.1	0.1
Belgium	6.1	19.3
Chile	12.1	1.9
China	20.8	−4.5
Colombia	15.9	−0.1
France	7.5	−0.2
Western Germany	4.7	0.0
Eastern Germany	5.6	−2.2
Ireland	16.1	−1.4
Italy	17.4	4.3
Slovenia	−1.2	6.2
Spain	24.1	5.2
Sweden	−1.2	2.1
UK	10.9	3.9
Average	9.9	2.5
US	8.7	0.4

Sources: ISGEP (2008) for 14 countries; Bernard and Jensen (1997) for US.

firms exploring profit opportunities in the world of uncertainty arising from investment in R&D-type processes and derive firm optimal policies, including entry and exit. Costantini and Melitz (2008) present a model that shows that anticipation of trade liberalization may cause a firm to bring forward the decision to innovate in order to 'dress up' for future participation in the export market. Similarly, Atkeson and Burstein (2008) model the interdependence between the choices of exporting and investing in R&D on the one hand and firm productivity on the other hand.

Recent empirical studies find some support for the link between innovation, productivity premia and export decisions. Exploring micro data, Aw et al. (2008) and Lileeva and Trefler (2007) show that exporting is correlated with firm investment in R&D and innovation. Aw et al. (2009) find that both R&D and exporting have a positive direct effect on future productivity, which reinforces the selection effect. They find that the productivity effect of R&D is larger, but that fewer firms opt to innovate than to export, given higher costs. Cassiman and Golovko (2007) find that the productivity premia of exporting firms disappear when controlled for product innovation. In a related paper on a sample of Spanish firms, Cassiman and Martinez-Ros (2007) find that engaging in product innovation significantly increases the probability to start exporting. Similarly, Becker and Egger (2007) find after controlling for the endogeneity of innovation that product innovation at German firms plays an important role in increasing the propensity to export, while they find no such evidence for process innovation. Finally, Damijan et al. (2010a) find for a sample of Slovenian firms that both product and process innovations increase the likelihood of becoming an exporter. At the same time they find evidence that exporting increases the probability of becoming a process but not a product innovator, and that exporting leads to productivity improvements. These findings suggest that participation in trade may positively affect firm efficiency by stimulating process innovations, which can also make a case in favour of the learning-by-exporting hypothesis.

On the other hand, importing has attracted much less attention in empirical studies as a source of important knowledge spillovers. Recently, studies by Altomonte et al. (2008) and Damijan and Konings (2011) using micro data for Hungary and Slovenia demonstrate that the impact of imports on firm performance is several times more important than the impact of a firm's engagement in exporting. Amiti and Konings (2007) study the channels through which imports can boost firm productivity. By using the Indonesian micro data, they find that benefits arising from lower tariffs on intermediate inputs might have an impact that is ten times larger than that of increased import competition on firm productivity gains. This finding has been strengthened recently by Goldberg et al. (2011) who study the impact of trade liberalization in India on productivity growth of manufacturing firms. They find that trade liberalization facilitates imports of new varieties of intermediate inputs, which lowers the import price index for intermediate goods on average by an additional 4.7 per cent per year. In addition, they show lower input tariffs to account on average for 31 per cent of the new products introduced by domestic firms. These findings suggest that input tariff liberalization may have relaxed technological constraints for local firms through firms' access to new imported inputs and hence boosted their better performance after trade liberalization. Similarly, Halpern et al. (2009) show imported inputs in the period 1992–2003 to have increased Hungarian firm productivity on average by 11 per cent, with new varieties of imported intermediates accounting for 60 per cent of this effect.

This evidence suggests that firms' trade participation may be sequenced in a particular way. A firm starts out to venture abroad by importing capital goods or intermediates that are either not available at home or less expensive abroad. Exporting starts later, after a firm has 'dressed up' sufficiently in terms of productivity to bear the fixed entry cost of foreign markets. In the meantime, investment in R&D and innovation helps firms to start producing new varieties suitable for sale in foreign markets. A recent study by Damijan and Kostevc (2010) using Spanish micro data finds a clear sequencing pattern in how firms learn from trade, proceeding from (1) engagement in imports, through (2) the decision to start product or process innovation, to (3) the decision to start exporting. Therefore, there is a complexity of channels through which firms benefit from trade, whereby the export decision may well come very late in the sequence.

3 WHY IS EXPANSION IN FOREIGN MARKETS SO SLUGGISH?

Recent empirical research on export activity of individual firms broadly focuses on the causes and consequences of the gap between exporters and non-exporters. Much less attention has so far been paid to the heterogeneity of exporters themselves and the evolution of export activity. With access to more detailed information on all dimensions of exporting activity, the research focus has shifted partly towards explaining the patterns of exporting growth. There is a growing number of recent empirical studies using transaction-level data that focus either on the number of exporting markets or on the dynamics of the exported product mix (Eaton et al., 2004, 2006; Damijan et al., 2011; Eaton et al., 2008). A study by Eaton et al. (2008), employing transaction level data for Colombia, offers a rare glimpse into the evolution of exporting activity of first-time exporters. They tend to be small firms starting off tentatively with only one initial export market, with most first-time exporters ultimately managing only a short stint in this market. Their future expansion and survival depends crucially on the choice of that initial export destination.

Recent studies provide evidence on the existence of destination-specific sunk costs of market entry. Studying the dynamics of the export product mix on a sample of Mexican firms, Iacovone and Smarzynska Javorcik (2010) confirm the existence of within-firm product heterogeneity. They also find that new exporters test the foreign markets with a single variety and very small volumes relative to their total sales. While most exported varieties do not survive in a given foreign market any longer than a year, their survival rate is shown to increase with a variety's tenure in the export market. This suggests that exporters are facing great uncertainty in the foreign markets, making the strategy of experimenting with a small number of varieties, small sales volumes and/or different partners in the export markets a likely choice for first-time exporters.

A recent paper by Albornoz et al. (2010) provides a theoretical rationale for the observed export patterns of new exporters incurring sunk costs of entry into the initial foreign market in spite of the high failure rates. Namely, by proposing that export profitability is positively correlated over time and across exporting destinations, they show that a firm has the option, upon realizing its true exporting productivity, of entering new export destinations or, alternatively, upon realizing a less favourable 'profitability', of exiting the foreign markets after the initial period. It is the potential of profitable expansion in terms of both intensive and extensive margins which prompts surviving exporters to try out new destinations and new varieties.

Yet this mechanism still does not offer a satisfactory explanation for the generally sluggish expansion of new exporters. Having paid a fixed entry cost, firms do not adjust instantaneously in export markets in terms of volumes, varieties and destinations, as is implicit in Melitz's (2003) workhorse model of trade with heterogeneous firms. Among the questions remaining unanswered are therefore: why do new exporters not start by exporting all available varieties to all prospective markets and why do they not adjust instantaneously in the second year of exporting or in subsequent years once they have realized their exporting profitability?

A recent paper by Damijan et al. (2011) sheds new light on the evolution of exporters by proposing that the process of adjustment in foreign markets is delayed above all by demand uncertainty and financial constraints. Studying the export dynamics of Slovenian new exporting firms, they find extremely slow expansion along both of the extensive dimensions of exporting. While average first-time exporters typically start by exporting a single variety to one foreign market, the most productive new exporters can only serve up to two foreign markets with up to four varieties. Following initial entry, export expansion – controlled for survival – is very protracted. The surviving exporters add new varieties to existing export markets very gradually, while expansion to new destinations happens at an even slower rate. This suggests that adding a new variety to an existing exporting destination is less costly than entering a completely new foreign market. Damijan et al. show that the slow pace of expansion, on the one hand, reflects the cost of serving foreign markets, which increases with the dimensionality of the pattern of export products and markets. The more complex a firm's product-market space becomes, the higher the 'aggregate cost of exporting'. On the other hand, exporting is associated with the demand uncertainties a firm faces for each variety in every single foreign market. Although markets and products may smooth overall risks, more complex exporting patterns generally increase the 'aggregate uncertainty' faced by the firm. The aggregate cost of exporting a firm can bear and the magnitude of uncertainty it can cope with, however, are related not only to its size and productivity but also to its access to either internal or external sources of finance.

The issues of export expansion fit into a more general question about the fundamentals of firm dynamics. Foster et al. (2008) explore the reasons for the slow growth of small firms. Exporting markets can be viewed as only another layer of added complexity in a firm's choice set. This view is consistent with a recent unified model of firm growth by Arkolakis (2009), who assumes that firm growth is balanced across all markets in which a firm has to pay a market penetration cost. In general, recent firm growth literature shows that growth dynamics depend decisively upon market uncertainties (Luttmer, 2007) and firm heterogeneity in terms of access to finance (Cooley and Quadrini, 2001; Cabral and Mata, 2003). Therefore, sluggish export expansion can be attributed to inherent financial constraints. As financing a complex product-market export pattern is costly, each firm's export expansion is limited by its internal finance, that is, its equity, as well as by its access to external finance.

Such financial constraints, along with the aggregate fixed cost of exporting and the associated aggregate uncertainty in foreign markets in a multi-product/multi-destination setting, imply that firm size is the single most important determinant of the speed of export expansion. The amount of equity raised directly and indirectly through profit accumulation and external debt may hence explain the variation of export margins across firms. Ceteris paribus, smaller firms will find export growth, both in terms of geographical expansion and in terms of number of exported varieties, a much slower process.

Damijan et al. (2011) provide empirical evidence for Slovenian exporting firms that adding new varieties to existing export markets and expanding to new foreign destinations is positively associated with firm size, productivity and access to finance for both new and incumbent exporters. Interestingly, though, as demonstrated in Table 19.3, they find that – when controlled for firm size and skill intensity – firm equity, return on assets and access to bank finance and to internal credit markets (within multinational firms' networks) play a more important role for export expansion than firm productivity (as measured by total factor productivity, TFP). New exporters who face positive demand shocks in foreign markets that also translate into positive cash flows will not only be more likely to decide to expand at a faster rate, but will primarily have the means to finance expansion themselves or be able to get external finance. This suggests that, other things being equal, a firm's ability to finance a costly and risky export expansion might be essential for understanding why some firms expand faster than others.

Table 19.3 Expansion dynamics and survival in foreign markets – evidence from Slovenia

	Pr[Survival]	Markets_*t*	Products_*t*
Equity_*t-1*	0.111***	0.058***	0.074***
Employment_*t-1*	−0.039	0.021***	−0.001
Return on assets_*t-1*	0.554***	0.154***	0.277***
TFP_*t-1*	0.042	0.012	0.022
High school_*t-1*	−0.015	0.104***	0.053
Capital per employee_*t-1*	−0.027	−0.011**	−0.026***
Debt-to-Assets Ratio_*t-1*	0.407***	0.255***	0.415***
Foreign Ownership_*t-1*	0.376***	−0.013	0.092***
Time fixed effects	Yes	Yes	Yes
Industry fixed effects	Yes	Yes	Yes
Observations	19084	19084	19084

Note: Standard errors omitted from the table; *** p<0.01, ** p<0.05, * p<0.1.

Source: Damijan et al. (2011).

4 EXPORTS, FIRM SIZE AND FINANCIAL CONSTRAINTS

A large body of literature suggests that access to financing is an important determinant of firm investment (Stiglitz and Weiss, 1981; Fazzari et al., 1988; Evans, 1987; Bond, 1994; Dixit and Pindyck, 1994; Hubbard, 1998). Cabral and Mata (2003) argue that the expansion of small firms is hampered by financial constraints resulting in observed right-skewed firm size distribution. Financial factors are also shown to be important in explaining the patterns of international trade. Chaney (2005) has theoretically shown that, given large fixed costs of exporting, access to financing may explain part of the variation in the foreign market participation. Greenaway et al. (2007) confirm this prediction for a set of UK manufacturing firms. Further, Zia (2008) reports that the removal of subsidized credit causes a significant decline in the exports of privately owned Pakistani firms, while the exports of large, publicly listed, and group network firms remain unaffected.

In a similar vein, Bellone et al. (2009) demonstrate that less financially constrained Italian firms are more likely to start exporting earlier, but that exporting per se does not improve the financial health of exporters. Taking export intensity as a proxy for serving a large number of destinations, they also find a negative relationship between access to financing and export intensity. The reasoning for the latter is straightforward. The further expansion of exporters to new foreign markets, as well as the introduction of new products to the existing markets, is associated with significant sunk costs. Financial constraints will therefore provide an important barrier both to export market entry and to the dynamics of expanding in foreign markets. Damijan et al. (2011) show that Slovenian firms with higher debt-to-asset ratios tend to export a greater number of products to a greater number of markets. In both cases, firm size is shown to be positively correlated with the new exporters' expansion dynamics.

These findings suggest that the patterns of export expansion may vary for exporters of different size. While large firms are likely to experience monotonic expansion due to their larger internal funds and better access to external finance, this pattern might be non-monotonic for small exporters for a number of reasons. First, small exporters may have weaker access to external finance or have to pay higher finance premia. The speed of foreign market expansion is therefore constrained by the internal funds available to them. Second, as famously argued by Knight (1921), bearing risk is one of the essential characteristics of entrepreneurship. As noted by Bond et al. (2008), households with a lower relative risk tolerance shy away from business ventures in times of excessive macro volatility. Small firms are in general more risk averse and will shy away both from taking excessive risks in foreign markets and from taking on excessive external debt to finance export ventures. Studying financial constraints affecting new French firms, Bonnet et al. (2005) found that there is a non-negligible share of firms which do not ask for a bank loan even when facing financial constraints. This self-imposed constraint produces a vicious circle, squeezing their intensive and extensive export margins even more than their smaller size would imply.

The lower intensive and extensive export margins of small firms in combination with their necessary larger exposure to external debt, however, affects also their survival in export markets. where small firms are poorly insured against the risk of failure. While large firms can use the extensive geographic dispersion of export markets and a variety of products exported as insurance against the risk of failure in a single foreign market or in a single product exported, any failure in export projects can be terminal for small firms. They may have to exit the export market, or excessive debt might even drive them out of business altogether.

This means that, for the same levels of external financing, small firms will export a smaller share of their total sales. Furthermore, small firms may expand to a lesser extent than large firms even if they are not liquidity constrained. A smaller size of internal funds and the risk of failure will cause smaller exporters to be more cautious in terms of taking additional risks associated with increased export intensity. At the same time, small firms willing to risk tapping into external finance may well use the additional funds more efficiently. Bond et al. (2008) show that households with promising business opportunities and modest wealth would be the main beneficiaries of better-functioning credit markets.

Drawing a correlation between the level of external debt and export intensity, large firms are more likely to display a monotonic relationship, while an inverted U-shape will be more common among small firms. The right tail will consist of firms that have failed in their exporting endeavour because they have taken on excessive debt. As a consequence, their export share diminishes and their debt-to-asset ratio rises significantly.

In a recent paper Damijan et al. (2010b) analyse this relationship between the extent of liquidity constraints and the intensive margin of exports for firms of different sizes for a set of Slovenian firms for the period 2001–08. They take corporate cash flows as firms' main internal source of liquidity and use outstanding short- and long-term bank loans as well as intra-group borrowing as external sources of finance. Table 19.4 reveals a positive correlation between the lagged debt-to-asset ratio and export intensity for both small and large firms, implying that access to external financing improves the scope of firm exposure in foreign markets. The impact on mid-sized firms is ambiguous as it is not significantly different from zero. On the other side, own cash flow relative to sales (*EBITDA/sales*) is shown to increase export intensity in small firms only. For small firms, the share of loans from associated firms also increases their export shares. For mid-sized and large firms this relationship to borrowing from associated firms in the group is not significant, while firm size (*Sales*), productivity (*VA/emp*) and lagged interest rates (*Int_rate*) and lower variation in sales (*Variance_sales*) positively impact the export share.

The above estimates show only average responses of export intensity to different measures of firms' access to finance. Damijan et al. (2010b), however, also provide an econometric test to determine whether, for the same expected debt-to-assets ratio, small exporting firms experience a different pattern of export expansion from those of their medium and large-sized counterparts. They use a continuous matching technique based on the generalized propensity score and the relevant dose response functions in order to test how additional bank debt impacts a firm's export share.[1] As shown by Figure 19.1, the response of export intensity to relative indebtedness is not linear. This is particularly evident for small and medium-sized firms, while for large firms a linear response of export intensity to relative financial constraints seems to be in place. Secondly, firm size crucially impacts the dose response function, which gradually becomes flatter as

Table 19.4 Impact of financial constraints on firms' intensive margin: evidence from Slovenia (dependent variable: export share)

	small firms	medium firms	large firms	small firms	medium firms	large firms
EBITDA/sales_t-1	0.046**	−0.128**	−0.115			
Debt_assets_t-1				0.054***	−0.003	0.142***
Va_emp_t-1	0.000	8.731e-06***	0.000	−6.794e-07*	9.785e-06***	6.557e-06**
Sales_t-1	9.6e-08***	3.286e-08***	5.403e-09***	9.122e-08***	3.139e-08***	4.212e-09***
Int_rate_t-1	0.014	0.503***	0.552***	0.014	0.511***	0.273**
Collateral_t-1	−0.028*	0.007	−0.092	−0.027	−0.006	−0.078
Sh_assoc_t-1	0.070**	−0.023	−0.007	0.066**	−0.021	−0.033
Variance_sales_t-1	4.370e-16**	−1.305e-16***	−2.267e-18***	4.960e-16***	−1.278e-16***	−1.792e-18***
Constant	0.997***	−0.599	0.765	−0.191	−0.033	0.335
Observations	8170	2096	1051	8399	2113	1060
R-squared	0.164	0.386	0.66	0.162	0.383	0.662

Note: Standard errors omitted from the table; *** p<0.01, ** p<0.05, * p<0.1. Size classes are defined as: small firms (at most 50 employees), medium-sized firms (from 51 to 200 employees) and large firms (more than 200 employees).

Source: Damijan et al. (2010b).

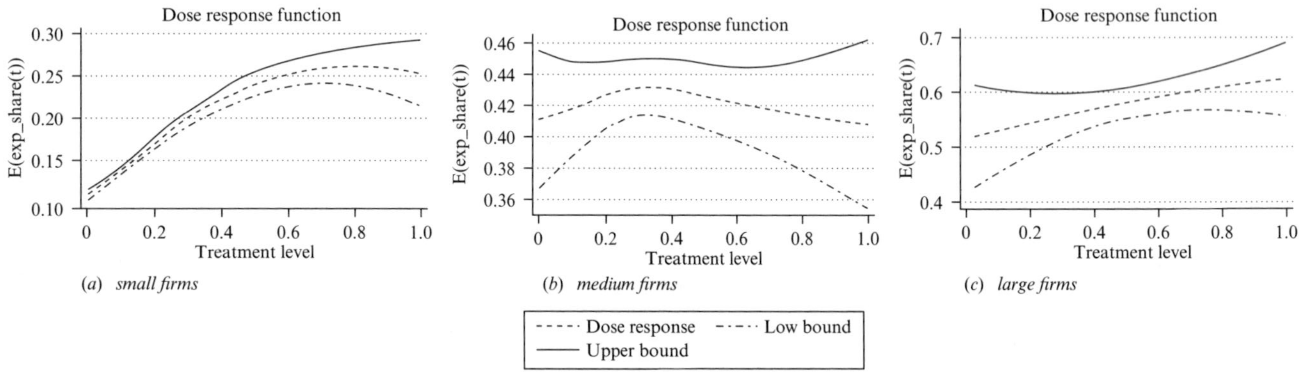

Note: Size classes are defined as: small firms (at most 50 employees), medium-sized firms (from 51 to 200 employees) and large firms (more than 200 employees).

Source: Damijan et al. (2010b).

Figure 19.1 The impact of relative debt-to-asset ratio on export intensity of Slovenian firms in 2000–07 firm size increases. This is particularly evident for large firms where the dose response function appears linear, but less so for medium-sized firms that still exhibit a more concave response. In any case, this evidence suggests that improving access to finance does not necessarily monotonically translate into higher export intensity. It is only generally valid for large firms, while for small and mid-sized firms export shares only increase with better access to finance up to a certain range of debt-to-asset ratio.

5 CREDIT CRUNCH AND EXPORTS

Given the results on the importance of access to finance for firms participating in exports and expanding along either the intensive or the extensive margin of exports, one may expect that the global financial crisis has had a negative impact on exporting firms, in particular on small firms. Dried-up finance may affect exporters more severely. The reasoning is straightforward. Exporting is costly and more risky too, hence exporters are exposed to higher default risk and higher working capital requirements, which requires additional trade credit. As pointed out by Amiti and Weinstein (2010), the need to insure against credit default risk arises because exporters usually do not have the capacity to evaluate default risk and usually turn to banks to provide payment insurance and guarantees. In addition, exporters need more working-capital financing than firms engaged in domestic transactions because of the time lags inherent in international trade. Hence, if banks limit trade finance, exports are likely to be affected more adversely than domestic sales.

Several empirical studies conducted to analyse either past crises or the global financial crisis that emerged in 2008 demonstrate that the drying-up of credit finance adversely affects exporters. Iacovone and Zavacka (2009) studied banking crises and exports in 23 banking crisis episodes between 1980 and 2000 and found negative and significant effects of banking crises on export growth. They found that the credit crunch-induced impact of 'supply-side' shocks is additional to and independent of that of 'demand-side' shocks (especially in sectors producing durable goods). These effects are found to be stronger for deeper crises and in countries with a less developed financial system. Interestingly, unlike bank finance, inter-firm finance does not appear to dry up at times of crisis and sectors characterized by a higher share of tangible assets are affected significantly less by the crisis (due to collateral). Amiti and Weinstein (2010) studied Japanese financial crises of the 1990s and found a causal link from shocks in the financial sector to exporters. They found that limiting trade credits (fewer letters of credit) results in exports declining much faster than output. The size of these bank-induced export declines accounts for about one-third of the drop in Japanese exports. These effects are found to be smaller for large firms, for multinationals and, interestingly, for firms that export mostly by air (due to shorter time lags in payments).

Bricongne et al. (2009) studied the impact of the current crisis on French exporters by exploiting monthly firm-level export data. They found that drops in French exports are mainly due to the declining intensive margin of large exporters, which reduced the size of their shipments. However, small and large firms are evenly affected when sectoral and geographical specializations are controlled for. At the same time, firms in sectors structurally more dependent on external finance are found to be most affected by the crisis. Similarly, Chor and Manova (2009) studied the collapse of international trade flows during the recent global financial crisis using detailed data on monthly US imports. They showed that adverse credit conditions were an important channel through which the crisis affected trade volumes. Countries with higher interbank rates and thus tighter credit markets exported less to the US during the peak of the crisis. These effects were especially pronounced in sectors that require extensive external financing, have few collateralizable assets, or have limited access to trade credit. As in the Bricongne et al. (2009) study for France, they found that exports of financially dependent industries were more sensitive to the cost of external capital and that this sensitivity rose during the financial crisis.

Empirical studies related to credit crunches and exports unanimously point out that a sound financial system is essential for promoting exports as exporters are more prone to dried-up finance. Hence, fixing financial sectors will facilitate the catching-up of exports. At the same time, firms with better access to internal credit markets (that is, firms within a multinational affiliates network) are less affected by financial crises. FDI seems to have a remarkable positive 'stabilization effect' on exporting.

6 CONCLUSIONS

This chapter gives an overview of recent empirical studies on exporters by focusing on factors that affect the decision of firms to start to export, how firms learn from trade and expand along the intensive and extensive margins, and what helps them survive in export markets. Evidence on firms' learning-by-exporting has been shown to be very scarce by the vast majority of cross-country studies. Instead, imports are shown to precede the decision to start exporting and to have a strong effect on efforts to dress up in terms of pre-export-entry productivity growth. Moreover, evidence suggests that the process of trade participation is sequenced in a particular manner.

Usually, a firm will start out to venture abroad by importing capital goods or intermediates. This step affects its productivity by increasing the variety of goods it can offer on the home market and/or by lowering the price index of inputs. Exporting starts only later, after a firm has dressed up sufficiently in terms of productivity to bear the fixed entry cost of foreign markets. In the meantime, investments in R&D and innovation may help a firm start producing new varieties suitable for sale in foreign markets.

Sound finance and access to external finance are crucial both for firms' export decisions and for their export dynamics. Firms with larger internal cash flows and better access to bank credits and to internal credit markets are shown to export broader varieties and to expand to new export markets at a higher rate. The same is found for firm expansion along the intensive margin. Access to external finance is particularly important for small firms and during financial crises. Evidence shows that exporters are likely to be affected more adversely than firms serving only local markets. In particular, exports of financially dependent industries are shown to be more sensitive to the cost of external capital, while sectors characterized by a higher share of tangible assets are affected significantly less by the crises. One of the most striking findings in the empirical literature is that inter-firm finance does not appear to dry up in times of crisis and that exports of firms that are part of the networks of multinational firms are more stable during financial turmoil.

NOTE

1. Given that the continuous matching technique requires that the treatment variable is continuous on the relevant interval, we constructed a measure of a relative debt-to-asset ratio on an interval between 0 and 1. For that purpose relative values of the debt-to-asset ratio are calculated by relating absolute values to the year–industry–size class-specific maximum debt-to-asset ratios. The resulting relative debt-to-asset ratios therefore span in the interval between 0, which implies no debt, and 1, which is the highest debt-to-asset ratio achieved by a firm of that size class in the relevant year and industry.

REFERENCES

Albornoz, F. et al. (2010), 'Sequential exporting', CEPR Discussion Paper No. 8103.

Altomonte, Carlo, Gabor Bekes and H. Murakozy (2008), 'Trading activities and productivity: evidence from Hungary', Bocconi University, mimeo.

Amiti, Mary and Josef Konings (2007), 'Trade liberalization, intermediate inputs, and productivity: evidence from Indonesia', *American Economic Review*, **97** (5), 1611–38.

Amiti, Mary and David Weinstein (2010), 'Exports and financial shocks', NBER Working Paper No. 15556.
Arkolakis, Costas (2009), 'A unified theory of firm selection and growth', CESifo Working Paper No. 2679.
Atkeson, A. and A. Burstein (2008), 'Innovation, firm dynamics, and international trade', Department of Economics, University of California, Los Angeles, working paper.
Aw, Bee Yan, Mark J. Roberts and D.Y. Xu (2008), 'R&D investments, exporting, and the evolution of firm productivity', *American Economic Review*, Papers and Proceedings, **98** (2), 451–6.
Aw, Bee Yan, Mark J. Roberts and D.Y. Xu (2009), 'R&D investment, exporting, and productivity dynamics', NBER Working Paper No. 14670.
Bartelsman, Eric J. and Marc Doms (2000), 'Understanding productivity: lessons from longitudinal microdata', *Journal of Economic Literature*, **38** (2), 569–94.
Becker, S. and Peter Egger (2007), 'Endogenous product versus process innovation and a firm's propensity to export', CESIFO Working Paper No. 1906.
Bellone, F.P. Musso, L. Nesta and S. Schiavo (2009), 'Financial constraints and firm export behavior', GREDEG Documents de travail, 2009-01.
Bernard, Andrew B. and J. Bradford Jensen (1995), 'Exporters, jobs, and wages in U.S. manufacturing: 1976–1987', *Brookings Papers on Economic Activity: Microeconomics*, 67–119.
Bernard, A.B. and J.B. Jensen (1997), 'Exporters, skill upgrading, and the wage gap', *Journal of International Economics,* **42** (1–2), 3–31.
Bernard, Andrew B. and J. Bradford Jensen (1999), 'Exceptional exporter performance: cause, effect, or both?', *Journal of International Economics*, **47** (1), 1–25.
Bernard, Andrew B. et al. (2007), 'Firms in international trade', *Journal of Economic Perspectives*, **21** (3), 105–30.
Bond, E., J.R. Tybout and H. Utar (2008), 'Credit rationing, risk aversion and industrial evolution in developing countries', NBER Working Paper No. 14116.
Bond, S. (1994), 'Financial constraints and company investment', *Fiscal Studies*, **15** (2), 1–18.
Bonnet, J., S. Cieply and M. Dejardin (2005), 'Financial constraints on new firms: looking for regional disparities', Discussion Papers on Entrepreneurship, Growth and Public Policy No. 3705.
Bricongne, Jean-Charles et al. (2009), 'Firms and the global crisis: French exports in the turmoil', Banque de France, Documents de Travail, 265.
Cabral, Luis M.B. and Jose Mata (2003), 'On the evolution of the firm size distribution: facts and theory', *American Economic Review*, **93** (4), 1075–90.
Cassiman, Bruno and Elena Golovko (2007), 'Innovation and the export-productivity link', IESE Business School, mimeo.
Cassiman, Bruno and Ester Martinez-Ros (2007), 'Product innovation and exports: evidence from Spanish manufacturing', IESE Business School, mimeo.
Chaney, T. (2005), 'Liquidity constrained exporters', mimeo, University of Chicago.
Chor, Davin and Kalina Manova (2009), 'Off the cliff and back? Credit conditions and international trade during the global financial crisis', Stanford University, mimeo.
Cooley, Thomas F. and Vincenzo Quadrini (2001), 'Financial markets and firm dynamics', *American Economic Review*, **91** (5), 1286–310.

Costantini, J.A. and M.J. Melitz (2008), 'The dynamics of firm-level adjustment to trade', in E. Helpman, D. Marin and T. Verdier (eds), *The Organization of Firms in a Global Economy,* Cambridge, MA: Harvard University Press.

Damijan, Joze and Jozef Konings (2011), 'Does import of intermediates promote exporting?', University of Ljubljana, mimeo.

Damijan, J. and C. Kostevc (2010), 'Learning from trade through innovation: causal link between imports, exports and innovation in Spanish microdata', LICOS Discussion Papers 264/2010, LICOS – Centre for Institutions and Economic Performance, K.U. Leuven.

Damijan, Joze, Črt Kostevc and Saso Polanec (2010a), 'From innovation to exporting or vice versa?', *The World Economy*, **32** (2), 374–98.

Damijan, Joze, Črt Kostevc and Saso Polanec (2010b), 'Firm size, financial constraints and non-monotonic export intensity', University of Ljubljana, mimeo.

Damijan, Joze, Črt Kostevc and Saso Polanec (2011), 'Export strategies of new exporters: why is export expansion along the extensive margins so sluggish?', LICOS Discussion Paper No. 277/2011, LICOS – Centre for Institutions and Economic Performance, K.U. Leuven.

Dixit, A.K. and R.S. Pindyck (1994), *Investment under Uncertainty*, Princeton: Princeton University Press.

Eaton, Jonathan, Samuel Kortum and Francis Kramarz (2004), 'Dissecting trade: firms, industries, and export destinations', *American Economic Review*, **94** (2), 150–54.

Eaton, Jonathan, Samuel Kortum and Francis Kramarz (2006), 'An anatomy of international trade: evidence from French firms', *Meeting Papers* 197, Society for Economic Dynamics.

Eaton, J. et al. (2008), 'Export dynamics in Colombia: transaction-level evidence', in E. Helpman, D. Marin and T. Verdier (eds), *The Organization of Firms in a Global Economy*, Cambridge, MA: Harvard University Press, pp. 231–72.

Ericson, R. and A. Pakes (1995), 'Markov-perfect industry dynamics: a framework for empirical work', *Review of Economic Studies*, **62**, 53–82.

Evans, D.S. (1987), 'The relationship between firm growth, size and age: estimates for 100 manufacturing industries', *Journal of Industrial Organization,* **35** (4), 657–74.

Fazzari, Steven, R. Glenn Hubbard and Bruce Petersen (1988), 'Financing constraints and corporate investment', *Brookings Papers on Economic Activity*, **19** (1), 141–95.

Foster, Lucia, John Haltiwanger and Chad Syverson (2008), 'Reallocation, firm turnover, and efficiency: selection on productivity or profitability?', *American Economic Review*, **98** (1), 394–425.

Goldberg, P. et al. (2011), 'Imported intermediate inputs and domestic product growth: evidence from India', *Quarterly Journal of Economics*, forthcoming.

Greenaway, D. and R. Kneller (2007), 'Firm heterogeneity, exporting and foreign direct investment', *The Economic Journal*, **117** (February), 134–61.

Greenaway, D., A. Guariglia and R. Kneller (2007), 'Financial factors and exporting decisions', *Journal of International Economics*, **73** (2), 377–95.

Halpern, László, Miklós Koren and Adam Szeidl (2009), 'Imported inputs and productivity', CeFiG Working Papers, No. 8, Center for Firms in the Global Economy.

Hubbard, R. Glenn (1998), 'Capital-market imperfections and investment', *Journal of Economic Literature*, **36** (1), 193–225.

Iacovone, Leonardo and Beata Smarzynska Javorcik (2010), 'Multi-product exporters: product churning, uncertainty and export discoveries', *The Economic Journal*, **120** (May), 481–99.

Iacovone, Leonardo and Veronika Zavacka (2009), 'Banking crises and exports: lessons from the past', World Bank Policy Research Working Paper 5016, Washington, DC: World Bank.

ISGEP (International Study Group for Economic Performance) (2008), 'Understanding cross-country differences in exporter premia: comparable evidence for 14 countries', *Review of World Economics*, **144** (4), 596–635.

Knight, F.H. (1921), *Risk, Uncertainty and Profit*, Boston: Houghton Mifflin.

Lileeva, A. and D. Trefler (2007), 'Improved access to foreign markets raises plant-level productivity for some plants', NBER Working Paper No. 13297.

Luttmer, E.G.J. (2007), 'Selection, growth, and the size distribution of firms', *Quarterly Journal of Economics*, **122** (3), 1103–44.

Mayer, T. and G. Ottaviano (2008), 'The happy few: the internationalisation of European firms', *Intereconomics: Review of European Economic Policy*, **43** (3), 135–48.

Melitz, Marc J. (2003), 'The impact of trade on intra-industry reallocation and aggregate industry productivity', *Econometrica*, **64** (6), 1695–725.

Roberts, Mark J. and James R. Tybout (1997), 'The decision to export in Colombia: an empirical model of entry with sunk costs', *American Economic Review*, **87** (4), 545–64.

Romer, Paul Michael (1990), 'Endogenous technological change', *Journal of Political Economy*, **98** (5), 71–102.

Stiglitz, J. and A. Weiss (1981), 'Credit rationing in markets with imperfect information', *American Economic Review*, **71**, 393–410.

Wagner, J. (2007), 'Exports and productivity: a survey of the evidence from firm level data', *The World Economy*, **30** (1), 60–82.

Zia, B.H. (2008), 'Export incentives, financial constraints, and the (mis)allocation of credit: micro-level evidence from subsidized export loans', *Journal of Financial Economics*, **87** (2), 498–527.

20. Financing for growth in CESEE

Joachim Nagel and Corinna Knobloch

INTRODUCTION

A couple of years after emerging markets were hit by the financial crisis in 2008 seems the right time to discuss 'Catching-up Strategies in CESEE Economies'. It is the right time because good policies have to be forward-looking. Although we are still heavily engaged in the challenges of surmounting the financial crisis, new business opportunities will emerge as soon as these problems are overcome. Therefore we should, even at this early stage, raise the issue of what Eastern Europe needs to do to reap the benefits of its underlying growth potential in the years to come. In this chapter, we will look into the issue of growth financing in CESEE countries after the crisis. We will focus on the following issues.

First, we will briefly analyse the imbalances inherent in pre-crisis growth financing in CESEE that led to the unprecedented contagion in the region during the global financial crisis. Second, we will elaborate on the need to rethink the hitherto prevailing model of growth financing. Third, we will raise some important issues and questions with regard to the elements needed to ensure the future financing of sustainable growth and the challenges this entails.

PRE-CRISIS GROWTH FINANCING MODEL

On the first issue, the pre-crisis growth financing model, we would like to draw attention to the relationship between massive capital inflows and the build-up of internal imbalances in emerging Europe. Growth during the (post-)transition period was mainly financed by large capital inflows. A significant wage differential compared with Western Europe, high levels of human capital and low capital–labour ratios attracted foreign direct investment. In addition, FDI inflows were boosted by economic transition, convergence with the EU and the prospect of joining the euro area.

Heavy investment by Western banks in Eastern European markets led to increasing inter-linkages with other European banking sectors. Credit flows surged and replaced foreign direct investment as the main driver of capital inflows.

These capital inflows resulted in varying degrees of vulnerability. Most Central European countries channelled a large part of the investment into the tradable sector and enhanced export capacity. This helped to prevent a build-up of major imbalances. In the South-Eastern European countries and the Baltics, however, capital inflows were associated with high credit growth (often in foreign currency). In many of these cases, fixed exchange rate regimes contributed to an underestimating of exchange rate risk associated with loans denominated in foreign currency. Funds were largely channelled into real estate and construction, boosting consumption and fuelling asset price bubbles. Real estate prices surged and stock prices gained sharply. As a result, internal and external imbalances grew dramatically. Imports surged, unprecedented current and capital account deficits emerged and economies overheated.

As a consequence of the global financial crisis, capital flows ground to a halt. It was not the sudden stop – the complete loss of access to international capital markets – we had experienced in traditional emerging market crises. In Eastern Europe, contagion was triggered by the fall of Lehman Brothers through financial and trade channels. Parent banks continued to roll over outstanding credit lines to subsidiaries. Funding for additional activities, however, was no longer available. Other capital flows to the region declined as well, albeit to a lesser extent. The drop in capital flows induced a sharp decline in consumption as new credit dried up. In parallel, the slump in global trade curtailed export earnings and exacerbated the recession.

A full-blown crisis was avoided by the Vienna Initiative and the support provided by the international financial institutions. These were vital in preventing a large-scale withdrawal by European banks and in stabilizing the region. However, slow but steady deleveraging can still be observed in the region.

NEED TO RETHINK THE MODEL OF GROWTH FINANCING

Although we are not yet out of the woods at the time of writing, it is the right moment to think about the post-crisis world. This leads us to the next issue, the need to rethink the model of growth financing. The legacy of the crisis will be more expensive financing and more difficult access to financing. Two sets of factors are likely to act as future constraints on growth financing: changed external circumstances and internal adjustment needs.

First, emerging Europe will have to cope with an altered external environment: large capital inflows driven by an extraordinarily benign external environment are a thing of the past. As a result of the crisis, the region will be confronted with tighter financing conditions than other emerging markets. Now that the previous under-pricing of risks in Eastern Europe has been corrected and as long as vulnerabilities continue to weigh on sectoral balance sheets, these conditions are likely to reflect a new normality. Higher spreads are therefore here to stay.

In addition to generally higher financing costs, CESEE countries face further pressures from deleveraging in European banking systems. European parent banks are struggling to rebuild their balance sheets. Moreover, risk-adjusted returns in Eastern Europe presumably will not reach pre-crisis highs. In this context, the need to re-assess pre-crisis business models and make financial institutions more resilient is also likely to have an impact on the Eastern European financing model, which is dominated by funding through parent banks. In the real economy, a potential drop in trend growth in important European export markets may weigh on export revenues.

Furthermore, the developments in Greece and the market's increased vigilance regarding weak fundamentals that this has brought about will enhance consolidation pressures. Perceived vulnerabilities will lead to higher refinancing costs and difficulties in securing funding.

Second, not only will the different pattern of capital flows be a drag on growth financing but internal adjustment needs will also affect future sources of growth financing. Consumption-based growth has proven unsustainable. Now, adjustment to a new normality is needed. Extraordinary accumulation of FX debt (in the period of plenty) has undermined households' financing position in many parts of Eastern Europe. Moreover, exchange rate fluctuations could further aggravate debt levels in the case of foreign-currency-denominated debt. This points to the need for continued deleveraging in the household sector. Therefore, subdued consumption could act as a drag on the internal growth trend.

In addition to that, pro-cyclical fiscal policies are likely to be a thing of the past. The availability of public funds for stimulus will be limited by a deterioration of governments' fiscal positions. While the risk of a double-dip scenario has receded, a lower growth scenario for the recovery would entail lower incomes and lower consumption with negative effects on tax revenue.

ENSURING THE FINANCING OF SUSTAINABLE GROWTH

The risks associated with the unbalanced financing model of the past and the likelihood of more subdued capital inflows imply that some adjustment will be necessary with respect to sources of financing. Rebalancing growth financing to a more sustainable path will require changing the composition of external flows and strengthening internal sources of financing.

With regard to capital flows, less dependence on portfolio and credit flows would lead to a more sustainable structure. This would imply strengthening FDI flows at the expense of credit flows. Changing the composition of external flows towards FDI would enhance growth potential (by increasing knowledge transfer).

Yet, in order to profit from higher levels of FDI, it will also be vital to channel FDI into key growth sectors, develop the tradable sector and ensure a more efficient use of funds. Competitiveness gains in the tradable sector could enhance income generated from exports and help to improve the current account through the trade balance.

Attracting FDI is not an easy task as emerging Europe competes with many other potential receiving countries. Further structural and regulatory reforms will be necessary in a number of countries to attract stable FDI flows and cope with less external financing.

Internal sources of growth financing could also play a more prominent role in Eastern Europe despite the large presence of Western European banks. A greater reliance on local refinancing could mitigate the financial stability risks associated with the previous dependence on cross-border financing through foreign parent banks. Thereby, it could also reduce the incentives for banks to provide foreign-currency-denominated credit to unhedged borrowers.

Local refinancing could be improved through different channels: in this context, stepping up deposit financing plays an important role in creating a more stable and longer-term refinancing base. This would mitigate the vulnerabilities associated with the extraordinarily high loan-to-deposit ratios in a number of countries. If accompanied by a reduction of the traditionally large savings–investment gap in the private sector, this would also create new sources of internal financing on a macroeconomic level.

Certainly, this would have to be accompanied by a higher household propensity to save. This in turn could potentially be helped by the ongoing process of balance sheet repair. Yet, scarcity of private savings has traditionally been a problem in the region. Raising private savings to a level sufficient to finance future growth is therefore likely to be one of the major challenges in the CESEE region.

Another avenue to strengthen local financing would be the development of local capital markets. Fostering local capital markets is important as greater recourse to local refinancing would help to mitigate risks stemming from over-reliance on cross-border financing by parent banks. However, it entails far-reaching implications: these range from the relatively small size of Eastern European markets to potential vulnerabilities associated with insufficiently deep and liquid markets.

One important lesson from the crisis is that countries that managed to avoid a build-up of vulnerabilities associated with asset price bubbles fuelled by external credit were more resilient. Hence, macroprudential policies aimed at slowing unsustainable credit growth and preventing the build-up of asset price bubbles associated with large capital inflows are likely to play a more prominent role in preventing future crises.

To sum up, it will be one of the major challenges for the region to address the questions related to new sustainable sources of financing in the wake of the global crisis. There are certainly no easy solutions, but imbalances have to be dealt with. In addition to that, an important challenge is re-launching the stalled private sector credit while at the same time ensuring improved regulatory standards. A more sustainable financing model will hopefully result in a slower but more sustainable financial deepening process and enhance macro-financial resilience in the region.

21. Capital inflows, exports and growth in the CESEE region

Jarko Fidrmuc and Reiner Martin[1]

1 INTRODUCTION AND MOTIVATION

Most of the countries in Central, Eastern and South-Eastern Europe (CESEE)[2] are seen as good examples of the growth-enhancing effect of downhill capital flows, that is, capital flows from relatively capital-rich to relatively capital-poor countries. In addition, they are good examples for an export-led growth strategy, although especially more recent papers on growth in the region often emphasize that growth in the years immediately preceding the recent economic and financial crisis had been too much consumption driven (EBRD, 2010).

These two facets of the CESEE region's recent growth experience – substantial capital inflows and a very strong export performance – are closely interrelated and need to be seen in the context of the region's gradual EU integration, which culminated in the EU accession of ten CESEE countries in 2004 and 2007. First, a large share of the capital flows into the region originated from the EU. These inflows, in particular inward FDI, arguably helped to build up the capital stock in the CESEE countries, which was expected to facilitate export growth. Second, EU integration provided a major boost for the CESEE exporting industries by opening up a large market at the region's doorstep.

The economic and financial crisis which started in 2007 (or 2008 for most of the CESEE region) had a major impact on these two facets of the CESEE growth model.[3] First, capital inflows into the region took a severe hit – although the worst-case scenario of a financial meltdown did not occur. Second, import demand in Western European countries, the region's main trading partners, dropped significantly with strong repercussions for trade in the CESEE countries (Francois and Wörz, 2009; Keppel and Wörz, 2010), although external demand picked up again in 2010. Taken together, these developments led to a rise in uncertainty regarding the region's medium- and long-term growth prospects. In particular, a possible permanent decline of capital flows (Jevčák et al., 2010) was generally seen as a potential cause of concern for the long-term growth prospects of the region. In addition, there is considerable uncertainty about the long-term prospects of external demand.

In this chapter, we approach the issue of medium-term growth prospects for the CESEE region. We estimate the long-run relationship between FDI, exports and growth. Trade and FDI are often mentioned in the literature as the most important elements of the CESEE growth model. However, to the best of our knowledge, they have not been analysed jointly. Therefore, we believe that a rigorous quantitative cross-country examination of the interlinkages between capital flows, exports and industrial production can help in assessing the possible long-term implications of the economic and financial crisis for the countries in the region.[4]

The chapter is organized as follows. Section 2 reviews the relevant literature. Section 3 provides stylized facts on the key variables we are using, and Section 4 describes the estimation strategy as well as the empirical results. Section 5 concludes and presents some policy recommendations.

2 LITERATURE OVERVIEW

2.1 Foreign Activities and Economic Growth

There is a long tradition of economic theories relating exports and other foreign activities to economic growth. Basically, these arguments go back to mercantilism and classical trade theories as presented by Adam Smith and David Ricardo. The importance of economic openness for growth gained popularity again when a number of South-Eastern Asian emerging market economies (EMEs), for example, Hong Kong, South Korea, Taiwan and Singapore, posted very rapid growth, especially between 1960 and 1980.[5] This was generally seen as a result of these countries opening up their economies, reducing trade barriers and attracting FDI. More generally, these explanations for rapid growth in a number of very open economies resulted in the development of the export-led growth hypothesis (Balassa, 1978; Marin, 1992). This theory, in turn, was also one of the intellectual arguments in favour of a rapid economic opening-up of the CESEE countries after the end of the cold war and their integration into the EU.[6] Similarly, Herzer et al. (2008) discuss FDI and growth in developing countries. For Eastern European countries, the relationship between FDI and growth is often addressed in earlier literature. Damijan and Rojec (2007) show that FDI contributed to the catching-up in CESEE countries. Campos and Kinoshita (2002) show that FDI was an important channel of technology transfer. Correspondingly, FDI had a significant and positive impact on growth in CESEE countries. Badinger and Tondl (2002) stress also the importance of capital accumulation and technology transfers for catching-up in Eastern Europe.

Nevertheless, the theoretical explanation of the export-led growth hypothesis remained rather weak. Several authors proposed models including learning-by-exporting effects (Krugman, 1980; Grossman and Helpman, 1991; Bernard et al., 2003; Damijan and Kostevc, 2006), but the empirical evidence supporting these models remained limited.[7]

More recently, foreign trade theory based on heterogeneous firms (Melitz, 2003; Helpman et al., 2004) has stressed the relationship between productivity and different modes of international activities. In this strand of the literature, the productivity of firms at the domestic level is regarded as a major determinant of activities abroad. Once a firm achieves a certain productivity threshold, it starts to export to foreign markets. The most productive firms also set up subsidiaries abroad, which in turn inherit the high productivity from their parent companies.

This link between activities abroad and the relative level of productivity is due to the relationship between transport costs or the fixed costs of market entry and the variable costs of serving foreign markets from the home location. Only firms with a sufficiently high productivity level can export and compete with local firms. The productivity differential must be so high that products are competitive although they are subject to transport costs. Furthermore, only the most productive firms can afford to invest abroad, which is the microeconomic explanation why such inward investment flows increase the aggregate productivity level in the receiving country. This 'self-selection channel' (Wagner, 2002) between foreign activity and productivity is referred to as the extensive margin of trade and FDI in the new trade literature. At the macroeconomic level, the access of the most productive firms to foreign markets causes a link between foreign activity and growth, which is at the core of the export- and investment-led growth hypothesis.

2.2 Capital Inflows and Growth

The second facet of the CESEE growth model that we address in this chapter – the substantial capital inflows in recent years – triggered a large amount of research that focused on its determinants and economic implications. Starting with the determinants for downhill capital flows, Lane (2008) emphasizes that EU accession implied lifting all capital controls at the time of accession at the latest and resulted in a range of institutional provisions that arguably fostered capital inflows. In addition, the region's increasing financial integration with the EU, in particular the widespread foreign ownership of the CESEE banking sector, also contributed to capital inflows (Herrmann and Winkler, 2008).[8]

Turning to the economic implications of capital inflows into the region, Mileva (2008) finds that during the period 1995–2005, FDI into 22 transition countries added to the capital stock and stimulated additional investment in the host countries, at least in the less advanced transition economies. By contrast, loans (often from parent banks to local subsidiaries) are found to have had a significant positive effect on other investment only in advanced transition economies, notably the new EU member states and candidate countries. Mileva finds no significant effect for portfolio capital inflows. In another cross-country study, Gheeraert and Malek Mansour (2005) use a structural econometric model based on earlier work by Islam (1995) and find a significantly positive relationship between private capital flows and economic growth in 45 EMEs, including five CESEE countries as well as Russia. The results for FDI are, however, considerably more significant than for portfolio and equity investment.

Generally speaking, the academic debate on capital inflows into CESEE tended to be less sceptical of possible negative effects than it was for other emerging market regions (von Hagen and Siedschlag, 2008). This was partly because a relatively large share of capital inflows was FDI, which is seen as less volatile and more beneficial for economic development than short-term capital flows (Abiad, Leigh and Mody, 2009). Lane and Milesi-Ferretti (2006), for example, argued that the large capital inflows to the CESEE countries had a positive impact on convergence and stressed that FDI provided 'attractive risk-sharing and technological benefits'. Yet other authors emphasized that the sustainability of the rapid convergence process in these countries depends also on the use of capital inflows. For instance, Bems and Schellekens (2007) argued that the recent rapid financial deepening process in emerging Europe disproportionately benefited the non-tradable sector including real estate and construction rather than exports.[9] Following the same line of reasoning, Atoyan (2010) maintains that future growth in the CEE countries should rely more on exports rather than domestic demand and more on domestic savings rather than foreign capital. Another hotly debated issue related to recent capital inflows into the region is whether credit growth is still an equilibrium phenomenon. Zumer et al. (2009) argue that the ratio of private sector credit stocks to GDP reached and in a few cases surpassed its estimated equilibrium level by early 2009 in most countries of the region.

Looking at EMEs outside the CESEE region, Sethi and Patnaik (2007) find long-run equilibrium relationships between private capital inflows into India, its economic growth and its exchange rate for the period 1995–2006. More specifically, they find that FDI and, to a smaller extent, portfolio investment are positively affecting economic growth, while foreign institutional investment (FII) has a negative effect.[10] The BIS Committee on the Global Financial System (BIS, 2009) finds cross-country evidence that equity flows, especially FDI, are beneficial for growth because they diversify risk abroad and are often linked with a transfer of valuable expertise. By contrast, the benefits from debt flows are found to be more ambiguous. In fact, the report suggests that the opening up of capital accounts only exerts a positive impact on the level of real income via the broadening and deepening of domestic financial markets, the strengthening of local financial institutions and the improvement of macroeconomic policies. The liberalization of capital flows is actually found to entail economic dangers if these elements are absent. Saborowski (2009) looks at the appreciation of the real exchange rate due to capital inflows and the resulting possible destabilization of the macroeconomic situation. In line with the BIS report, he argues that this effect can be partly mitigated by developing a deep financial sector. Moreover, he finds that flexible exchange rate regimes help to reduce the negative impact of capital inflows on the real exchange rate.

The long-term implications of the crisis for the growth prospects of the region have been widely discussed since the global economic and financial crisis started to affect the CESEE region, *inter alia* via a slump in capital imports and in export demand. Furceri and Zdzienicka (2010), looking at 11 European transition economies, find a stronger negative long-term effect on output in smaller transition countries with a relatively higher dependence on external financing. They also find that this negative effect is much stronger in transition countries than in more advanced EU economies.[11]

To what extent external financing will resume remains to be seen, however. In the autumn of 2009, the IMF (2009) assumed that FDI inflows to emerging Europe would decline by 49 per cent in the 2008–14 period compared with 2004–07. Based on this and other assumptions, the IMF predicted a substantial drop in medium-term growth for emerging Europe. By spring 2010, capital inflows to some – but not all – of these countries had resumed, and the focus of the debate shifted back to making the best use of capital inflows, and notably to finding an appropriate balance between the tradable and non-tradable sectors (IMF, 2010).

3 STYLIZED FACTS

In this section, we provide some stylized facts about the key variables used in the empirical analysis conducted in Section 4 of the chapter, namely exports, industrial production (excluding construction) and the stock

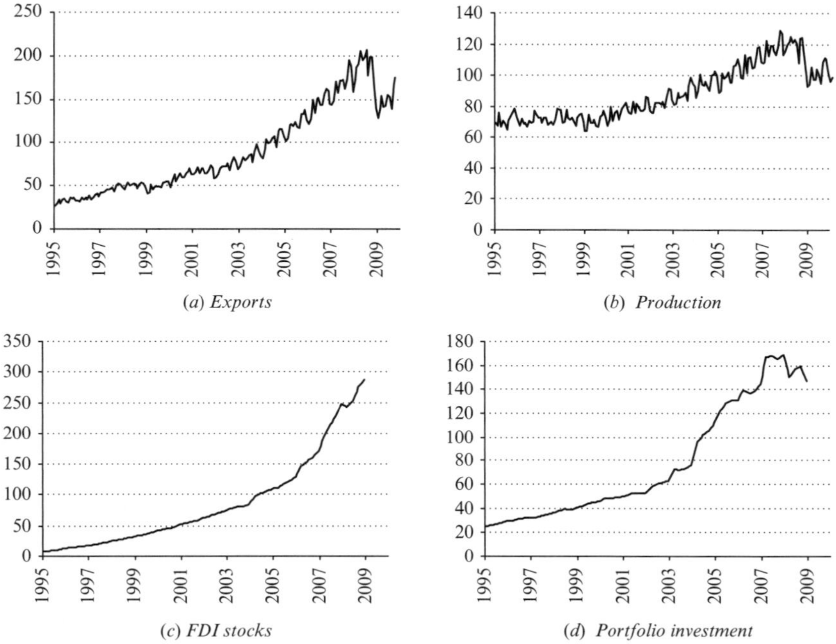

Note: Unweighted average of 11 CESEE countries, May 2004 = 100.

Sources: IMF, ECB, OeNB.

Figure 21.1 Stylized facts on exports, production and capital flows

of FDI and portfolio investment in the CESEE countries for the period 1995–2009. Looking first at exports, the (unweighted) CESEE aggregate shows an upward trend over time until the international economic and financial crisis hit the region in 2008 (Figure 21.1a). The rate of growth for the regional aggregate accelerated around 2003, that is, just before the EU accession of eight CESEE countries. A country-level analysis of exports shows some country-specific differences, for example with regard to the severity of the impact of the 2008 crisis, but the overall picture is fairly homogeneous.

Turning to the index of industrial production (excluding construction) (Figure 21.1b), a rather steady increase can be observed both in the CESEE aggregate and country by country. In addition, the impact of the 2008 crisis is also clearly visible in almost all countries under review. Yet the growth rate of industrial production remained significantly below that of exports. Whereas a number of countries in the sample, for example, Bulgaria, Croatia, Lithuania, Latvia and Romania, managed to increase their exports from around 50 per cent of the 2004 level to almost 300 per cent of that level just before the crisis, the corresponding growth pattern for industrial production seems much more modest and ranges generally from around 80 per cent of the 2004 level in the late 1990s to around 150 per cent of that level before the start of the crisis. The differences in the relative development of these indicators suggest that the CESEE economies became substantially more open over time.

The development of the stock of FDI (Figure 21.1c) and portfolio investment (Figure 21.1d) also shows a strong increase over time. Given that this is a stock variable, the impact of the 2008 economic and financial crisis is, however, less visible than for exports and industrial production. By contrast, the step change in growth around the time of EU accession in 2004 is more noticeable for the stock of FDI and portfolio investment than for the other two indicators. A country-specific analysis shows that cross-country differences are also more pronounced than for the other two variables. Using May 2004 as the base level again, the FDI stock in some CESEE countries, such as Bulgaria, Hungary and Romania, had increased by a factor of around five to six by 2009.

Overall, the stylized facts for the three key variables we will be using in the analysis below suggest some strong similarities, in particular a dynamic growth pattern up until the outbreak of the economic and financial crisis in the CESEE region in 2008, the (more or less pronounced) positive change in the rate of growth around the time of EU accession and different degrees of heterogeneity across countries.

4 EMPIRICAL ANALYSIS

4.1 Tests of Export- and FDI-led Growth

In this section we analyse the determinants of industrial production. We are aware that the theoretical literature concentrates on the relationship between trade, FDI and productivity. However, productivity growth is generally associated with growth of industrial production. Moreover, we use levels of production in order to distinguish between productivity and efficiency changes. The latter, also referred to as jobless growth (Onaran, 2007), have played an important role in CESEE countries. By using growth of industrial production, we adjust productivity growth for employment reductions in industry.

A major problem for the empirical analysis relates to the availability and quality of the necessary data. Because standard quarterly time series are relatively short, we use monthly proxies including industrial production and exports. Stocks of FDI are interpolated into monthly data because there are no monthly proxies for these time series. Given the high persistence of FDI stocks, this is not likely to bias the results. All variables are in logs and are seasonally adjusted using the standard X12 seasonal filter. Standard unit root tests confirm that all variables can be regarded as integrated variables.[12]

The modern literature on trade, FDI and productivity concentrates on the analysis of individual firm data, thus introducing several limitations on empirical analysis. Most importantly, consistent microeconometric data are usually not available for longer periods and for comparative countries, and in the case of CESEE countries they are often not reliable, either. Therefore, we concentrate on aggregate data for industrial production, exports and FDI for 11 CESEE economies (Bulgaria, the Czech Republic, Croatia, Estonia, Hungary, Latvia, Lithuania, Poland, Romania, Slovakia and Slovenia). For most countries, the data start in 1995, but for some they are not available before the end of the 1990s.

We use the stock of inward FDI, because outward FDI is generally not important in CESEE. On the one hand, this corresponds with the investment-led growth hypothesis. On the other hand, outward FDI may have ambiguous effects. In particular, it can support domestic production by supplying cheap intermediate materials. It can also increase the demand potential for domestic products. However, outward FDI can also have a negative effect on domestic production if it is related to outsourcing of labour-intensive processes. Thus, the CESEE countries are especially attractive for testing the investment-led growth hypothesis, because only a few large firms in the region are also active as investors abroad.

Output, exports, and the stock of FDI are expected and found to be non-stationary. We therefore estimate the following vector error correction (VEC) model:

$$\Delta X_t = \alpha\beta X_{t-1} + \sum_{i=1}^{p} A_i \Delta X_{t-i} + \varepsilon_t \qquad (21.1)$$

where vector X includes output and the selected variable of foreign activity (exports or FDI). Furthermore, the long-run relationship includes also the deterministic components (intercept and – if necessary – a trend). Moreover, we include several dummy variables which cover special factors. While the early reform periods were often characterized by a worsening of the economic performance, growth improved in nearly all countries after EU accession in 2004 or 2007. The recent financial crisis likewise lowered growth in nearly all CESEE countries. The Russian crisis of 1998–99 lowered growth especially in the Baltic States, Poland and the Czech Republic. In addition, there was a country-specific financial crisis in the Czech Republic in 1997. Finally, the introduction of the euro in Slovenia and Slovakia in 2007 and 2009 respectively is expected to have had an impact on economic developments in these countries.

4.2 Empirical Results

We start with the estimation of the export-led growth hypothesis in Table 21.1. Panel B shows that a robust co-integrating relationship between industrial production and exports can be found for all selected countries, that is, the null of no co-integration is clearly rejected by both co-integration tests shown here. Panel A reports the estimated co-integration relationships. In general, we can see a strong relationship between exports and production. The coefficients are very close to unity in all countries with the exception of the Czech Republic and Slovenia. In turn, we find a surprisingly high coefficient for Estonia only (1.9). The co-integration tests confirm that the estimated relationship is a co-integrating relationship for all countries.

When we compare these results with the results for the relationship between industrial production and FDI (see Table 21.2), we can see that the latter relationship is slightly weaker. In particular, the co-integration tests present weaker evidence on the existence of a co-integrating relationship between industrial production and FDI for Bulgaria, the Czech Republic and Slovakia. This outcome may, however, also reflect data restrictions, given that the stock of FDI relates to the whole economy and not only the industrial sector.

Despite these problems, we get co-integrating relationships between FDI and industrial production in all countries. FDI seems to be a highly significant determinant of industrial production in all CESEE countries (and particularly so in Lithuania and Slovakia), which broadly confirms the FDI-led growth hypothesis for the countries in the region.

In contrast, the results for portfolio investment were rather weak (see Table 21.3). This is not really surprising, also in view of some empirical studies mentioned above, because portfolio investments are less related to technology transfers than FDI. More specifically, a co-integration relationship appears to exist only for Latvia, Lithuania and Poland. However, the coefficient for portfolio investment in the growth equation for Lithuania is negative and the coefficient for Latvia is low compared with previous FDI-based estimations.[13] Overall, the results do not provide much support for possible growth effects of portfolio investments in the CESEE region.

Table 21.1 Production and exports in selected CESEE countries

	Bulgaria	Czech R.	Croatia	Estonia	Hungary	Latvia	Lithuania	Poland	Romania	Slovakia	Slovenia
A. Estimation results											
Period	Mar.00–Dec. 09	Apr. 95–Dec. 09	Apr. 95–Dec. 09	Apr. 98–Nov. 09	Apr. 95–Oct. 09	Jan. 99–Nov. 09	Apr. 97–Dec. 09	Apr. 95–Oct. 09	Apr. 95–Dec. 09	Mar. 95–Nov. 09	Apr. 95–Dec. 09
No. of obs.	118	177	177	140	175	131	153	175	177	177	177
Exports	1.135	0.472	0.694	1.933	0.779	0.916	0.675	0.761	0.875	0.820	0.368
t-stat	*12.997*	*8.651*	*19.348*	*5.996*	*18.852*	*8.599*	*16.093*	*10.920*	*7.620*	*9.950*	*18.587*
Intercept	1.481	1.133	1.989	−3.564	−2.601	3.941	2.338	0.549	1.038	−0.775	1.688
B. Co-integration tests											
Trace statistics	18.140**	18.321**	37.734***	18.911**	28.359***	15.536**	16.507**	20.521***	24.608***	21.062***	22.695***
p-value	0.020	0.018	0.000	0.015	0.000	0.049	0.035	0.008	0.002	0.007	0.004
ME statistics	17.968**	18.174**	36.589***	16.815**	24.829***	14.669**	16.089**	20.377***	21.381***	19.312***	21.209***
p-value	0.012	0.012	0.000	0.019	0.001	0.043	0.026	0.005	0.003	0.007	0.003

Note: Dummy variables are not reported. ***, ** and * denote rejection of the null of no cointegration at the 1, 5 and 10 per cent significance levels, respectively.

Source: Authors' estimations.

Table 21.2 Production and FDI in selected CESEE countries

	Bulgaria	Czech R.	Croatia	Estonia	Hungary	Latvia	Lithuania	Poland	Romania	Slovakia	Slovenia
A. Estimation results											
Period	Mar. 00– Sep. 09	Apr. 95– Sept. 09	Apr. 95– Sep. 09	Apr. 98– Sep. 09	Apr. 95– Sep. 09	Jan. 99– Sep. 09	Apr. 97– Sep. 09	Apr. 95– Sep. 09	Jan 98– Sep. 09	Apr. 95– Dec. 08	May. 96– Sep. 09
No. of obs.	115	174	174	138	174	129	150	174	141	165	172
FDI	0.457	0.268	0.451	0.516	0.789	0.314	1.715	0.685	0.342	0.976	0.157
t-stat	*8.759*	*4.767*	*8.509*	*12.494*	*9.379*	*2.413*	*4.878*	*6.386*	*9.257*	*3.694*	*5.727*
Trend						−0.013				−0.019	
t-stat						*−5.254*				*−2.995*	
Intercept	2.138	2.010	1.933	1.142	−4.328	−4.859	−3.980	−0.737	2.302	1.614	3.107
B. Co-integration tests											
Trace statistics	15.384*	16.369**	50.073***	29.905***	54.505***	36.030***	18.493**	19.664**	29.485***	29.454**	19.508**
p-value	0.052	0.037	0.000	0.000	0.000	0.002	0.017	0.011	0.000	0.017	0.012
ME statistics	15.380**	13.598*	48.160***	27.708***	53.839***	34.136***	15.309**	19.158***	28.982***	18.987*	16.999**
p-value	0.033	0.064	0.000	0.000	0.000	0.000	0.034	0.008	0.000	0.057	0.018

Note: Dummy variables are not reported. ***, ** and * denote rejection of the null of no cointegration at the 1, 5 and 10 per cent significance levels, respectively.

Source: Authors' estimations.

Table 21.3 Production and portfolio investment in selected CESEE countries

	Bulgaria	Czech R.	Croatia	Estonia	Hungary	Latvia	Lithuania	Poland	Romania	Slovakia	Slovenia
A. Estimation results											
Period	Mar. 00–Sep. 09	Apr. 95–Sep. 09	Jun. 95–Sep. 09	Apr. 98–Sep. 09	Apr. 95–Sep. 09	Jan. 99–Sep. 09	Apr. 97–Sep. 09	Apr. 95–Sep. 09	Jan. 98–Sep. 09	Apr. 95–Dec. 08	Apr. 95–Sep. 09
No. of obs.	115	174	172	138	174	129	150	174	141	165	174
PI	0.952	1.020	−0.209	6.596	1.514	0.573	−0.031	1.829	0.703	0.028	0.193
t-stat	*2.593*	*3.832*	*−1.717*	*3.017*	*7.207*	*5.621*	*−0.506*	*6.494*	*4.151*	*0.256*	*4.315*
Trend	0.012									0.003	
t-stat	*6.091*									*2.258*	
Intercept	1.433	−3.907	5.643	−30.100	−12.066	3.729	4.527	−8.450	1.404	−4.016	2.967
B. Co-integration tests											
Trace statistics	17.640	14.349*	15.726**	12.267	14.366*	23.605***	19.954***	33.413***	12.874	9.620	24.463***
p-value	0.369	0.074	0.046	0.145	0.073	0.002	0.010	0.000	0.120	0.940	0.002
ME statistics	14.714	12.238	13.337*	9.602	13.389*	20.739***	16.886**	33.019 ***	12.787*	8.063	13.312*
p-value	0.210	0.102	0.070	0.239	0.068	0.004	0.019	0.000	0.085	0.816	0.070

Note: Dummy variables are not reported. ***, ** and * denote rejection of the null of no cointegration at the 1, 5 and 10 per cent significance levels, respectively.

Source: Authors' estimations.

5 CONCLUSIONS AND POLICY RECOMMENDATIONS

Starting in 2008, the CESEE economies were strongly affected by the economic and financial crisis, with the effects being mainly transmitted through the trade and financial channels (Gardó and Martin, 2010). All countries of the region suffered from severe declines in external demand and much lower (at times even negative) capital inflows. The growth implications for the region were dramatic. In fact, the CESEE region was more seriously affected than any other region worldwide, with performance being especially low when compared with other EMEs, notably China and India.

The main question addressed in this chapter is whether the long-term growth prospects of the CESEE countries are likely to have deteriorated as well. To answer this question – even though the prospects for external demand and capital inflows are still unknown – we look at the interlinkages between capital flows, exports and industrial production. Our results indicate that exports and the stock of FDI in the CESEE region are positively related to industrial production and thus economic growth. In nearly all CESEE countries under review, exports and FDI have a significant impact on industrial growth performance. Exports seem to be more important than the stock of FDI, but this may at least partly reflect statistical problems. By contrast, portfolio investment seems to be only weakly related to the industrial growth performance of the CESEE countries.

A number of policy implications can be derived from this analysis. First, the positive link between the FDI stock and industrial production implies that the CESEE countries should strive to remain attractive locations for inward FDI. Such efforts can include a diverse set of policy measures ranging from macroeconomic stability, including sound fiscal policy, to microeconomic (structural) reforms, for example, to create a business-friendly regulatory environment and flexible labour markets. Second, our results indicate that a reduction in portfolio investments is unlikely to have significant repercussions for the growth prospects of the region. In fact, the literature on capital inflows suggests that large portfolio inflows may at times entail economic risks. Third, countries should adopt suitable policies to enhance their export prospects, ranging from specific measures such as export promotion to more general macro- and microeconomic policy reforms, which are often closely related to those that help to support a country's attractiveness for FDI inflows.

NOTES

1. The views expressed in this chapter are exclusively those of the authors and do not necessarily reflect those of the Oesterreichische Nationalbank, the European Central Bank or the Eurosystem. We benefited from comments by Doris Ritzberger-Grünwald, Peter Mooslechner, Markus Eller, Julia Wörz, Marie Raková, Gergely Kiss, Peter Backé and participants of the OeNB conference on European Economic Integration and ECB research seminar, as well as two anonymous referees. We acknowledge language advice by Irene Popenberger. Furthermore, we would like to thank Magdalena Komzakova and Andreas Nader for excellent research assistance.
2. We focus on the following countries: Bulgaria, the Czech Republic, Croatia, Estonia, Hungary, Latvia, Lithuania, Poland, Romania, Slovakia and Slovenia.
3. On the impact of the crisis on the region, see, for example, Gardó and Martin (2010).
4. Besides addressing this important policy question, this chapter also extends the existing literature in this field by using more recent empirical approaches such as cointegration analysis and weak exogeneity tests.
5. For a critical discussion with a focus on Korea, see Rodrik (1995).
6. More recently, the dynamic growth in China and India is often also seen from this perspective (Herrerias and Orts, 2010).
7. While some authors found that exports had a positive impact on firms' productivity (Baldwin and Gu, 2003; Blalock and Gertler, 2004), others found no such impact (Bernard and Jensen, 1999).
8. On the determinants of capital flows, see also, for example, Gibson and Tsakalotos (2004).
9. Supporting this argument, Brixiova et al. (2009) find that the massive recent capital inflows into Estonia led to an excessive allocation of resources in the non-tradable sector.
10. Kim and Yong Yang (2008) find that inflows into South Korea led to a rise in stock prices but not land prices.
11. In a related analysis on a much larger sample of countries, Abiad et al. (2009) find that output tends to be substantially depressed following banking crises with no rebound to the pre-crisis trend. The recent international economic and financial crisis did not, however, result in 'classic' banking crises in the CESEE region, thus limiting the applicability of these findings.
12. Detailed results are available upon request from the authors.
13. For the remaining countries, the estimated long-run relationships are often insignificant (for example Slovakia), low in comparison with previous FDI coefficients (for example Slovenia) or negative (for example Croatia).

REFERENCES

Abiad, A., D. Leigh and A. Mody (2009), 'Financial integration, capital mobility and income convergence', *Economic Policy*, **24** (58), 241–308.

Abiad, A. et al. (2009), 'What's the damage? Medium-term output dynamics after banking crises', IMF Working Paper WP/09/245.

Atoyan, R. (2010), 'Beyond the crisis: revisiting emerging Europe's growth model', IMF Working Paper WP/10/92.

Badinger, H. and G. Tondl (2002), 'Trade, human capital and innovation: the engines of European regional growth in the 1990s', ERSA conference papers No. ERSA02P043.

Balassa, B. (1978), 'Exports and economic growth: further evidence', *Journal of Development Economics*, **5**, 181–9.

Baldwin, J.R. and W. Gu (2003), 'Export-market participation and productivity performance in Canadian manufacturing', *Canadian Journal of Economics*, **36** (3), 634–57.
Bems, R. and P. Schellekens (2007), 'Finance and convergence: what's ahead for emerging Europe?', IMF Working Paper WP/07/244.
Bernard, A.B. and J.B. Jensen (1999), 'Exceptional exporter performance: cause, effect, or both?', *Journal of International Economics*, **47** (1), 1–25.
Bernard, A.B. et al. (2003), 'Plants and productivity in international trade', *Econometrica*, **93** (4), 1268–90.
BIS (2009), 'Capital flows and emerging market economies', Committee on the Global Financial System, CGFS Papers 33.
Blalock, G. and P.J. Gertler (2004), 'Learning from exporting revisited in a less developed setting', *Journal of Development Economics*, **75** (2), 397–416.
Brixiova, Z., L. Vartia and A. Wörgötter (2009), 'Capital flows and the boom–bust cycle: the case of Estonia', *Economic Systems*, doi: 10.10167j. ecosys.2009.11.002.
Campos, N.F. and Y. Kinoshita (2002), 'Foreign direct investment as technology transferred: some panel evidence from the transition economies', *Manchester School*, **70** (3), 398–419.
Damijan, J.P. and Č. Kostevc (2006), 'Learning-by-exporting: continuous productivity improvements or capacity utilization effects? Evidence from Slovenian firms', *Review of World Economics*, **142** (3), 599–614.
Damijan, J.P. and M. Rojec (2007), 'Foreign direct investment and catching up of new EU member states: is there a flying geese pattern?', *Applied Economics Quarterly*, **53** (2), 91–118.
EBRD (2010), 'Invigorating trade integration and export-led growth', in Transition Report 2010, pp. 66–77.
Francois, J. and J. Wörz (2009), 'The big drop: trade and the great recession', in R. Baldwin (ed.), *The Great Trade Collapse: Causes, Consequences, and Prospects*, VoxEU.org.
Furceri, D. and A. Zdzienicka (2010). 'The real effect of financial crises in the European transition economies', *Economics of Transition*, **19**, 1–25.
Gardó, S. and R. Martin (2010), 'The impact of the global economic and financial crisis on Central, Eastern and South-Eastern Europe – a stock-taking exercise', ECB Occasional Paper 114, June.
Gheeraert, L. and J. Malek Mansour (2005), 'On the impact of private capital flows on economic growth and development', CEB (Centre Emile Bernheim) Working Paper 5/003, April.
Gibson, H.D. and E. Tsakalotos (2004), 'Capital flows and speculative attacks in prospective EU member states', *The Economics of Transition*, **12** (3), 559–86.
Grossman, G. and E. Helpman (1991), *Innovation and Growth in the Global Economy*, Cambridge, MA: The MIT Press.
Helpman, E., M.J. Melitz and S.R. Yeaple (2004), 'Export versus FDI with heterogeneous firms', *American Economic Review*, **94** (1), 300–316.
Herrerias, M.J. and V. Orts (2010), 'Is the export-led growth hypothesis enough to account for China's growth?', *China & World Economy*, **18** (4), 34–51.
Herrmann, S. and A. Winkler (2008), 'Real convergence, financial markets and the current account – emerging Europe versus emerging Asia', ECB Occasional Paper 88.

Herzer, D., S. Klasen, and D.F. Nowak-Lehmann (2008), 'In search of FDI-led growth in developing countries: the way forward', *Economic Modelling*, **25** (5), 793–810.
IMF (2009), Regional Economic Outlook: Europe – Securing Recovery, October.
IMF (2010), Regional Economic Outlook: Europe – Fostering Sustainability, May.
Islam, N. (1995), 'Growth empirics: a panel data approach', *Quarterly Journal of Economics*, **110** (4), 1127–70.
Jevčák, A., R. Setzer and M. Suardi (2010), 'Determinants of capital flows to the new EU Member States before and during the financial crisis', Economic Papers 425, European Commission.
Keppel, C. and J. Wörz (2010), 'The impact of the global recession in Europe: the role of international trade', in P. Backé, E. Gnan and P. Hartmann (eds), *Contagion and Spillovers: New Insights from the Crisis*, SUERF Studies 2010/5, Vienna and Brussels: Larcier.
Kim, S. and D. Yong Yang (2008), 'Managing capital flows: the case of the Republic of Korea', ADB Institute Discussion Paper 88.
Krugman, P. (1980), 'Scale economies, product differentiation, and the pattern of trade', *American Economic Review*, **70** (5), 950–59.
Lane, P.R. (2008), 'The macroeconomics of financial integration: a European perspective', IIIS Discussion Paper 265.
Lane, P.R. and G.M. Milesi-Ferretti (2006), 'Capital flows to Central and Eastern Europe', IMF Working Paper WP/06/188.
Marin, D. (1992), 'Is the export-led growth hypothesis valid for industrialised countries?', *The Review of Economics and Statistics*, **74** (4), 678–88.
Melitz, Marc J. (2003), 'The impact of trade on intra-industry reallocations and aggregate industry productivity', *Econometrica*, **71** (6), 1695–725.
Mileva, E. (2008), 'The impact of capital flows on domestic investment in transition economies', ECB Working Paper 871, February.
Onaran, Ö. (2007), 'Jobless growth in the Central and Eastern European countries: a country specific panel data analysis for the manufacturing industry', Vienna University of Economics and Business Administration, Working Paper No. 103, March.
Rodrik, D. (1995), 'Getting interventions right: how South Korea and Taiwan grew rich', *Economic Policy*, **10** (20), 53–107.
Saborowski, C. (2009), 'Capital inflows and the real exchange rate: can financial development cure the Dutch disease?', IMF Working Paper WP/09/20.
Sethi, N. and K.U.S. Patnaik (2007), 'Impact of international capital flows on India's economic growth', *The ICFAI Journal of Applied Finance*, **13** (1), 89–96.
Von Hagen, J. and I. Siedschlag (2008), 'Managing capital flows: experiences from Central and Eastern Europe', ESRI Working Paper 234, March.
Wagner, J. (2002), 'The causal effect of exports on firm size and labour productivity: first evidence from a matching approach', *Economics Letters*, **77** (2), 287–92.
Zumer, T., B. Égert and P. Backé (2009), 'Credit developments in CEE: from boom to bust or back to balance?', *Bancni Vestnik – The Journal for Money and Banking*, **58** (11), 94–101.

22. Structural components of international trade growth 1995–2009

Joseph F. Francois and Julia Wörz[1]

1 INTRODUCTION

For many years, the global trade volume expanded considerably faster than global output. From 1995 to 2009, real annual export growth was 6 per cent on average, while global GDP and production grew only half as fast in real terms, by approximately 3 per cent per annum (WTO, 2010). Similarly, trade fell by a disproportionally large amount during the crisis that emerged in 2008. The question thus arises: what factors have been driving the overshooting of the trade response, both upward and downward, over the past decades? And are these factors going to shape world trade growth in the future? In this chapter we attempt to identify the drivers of export growth by decomposing real world export growth into its regional and sectoral components. We will put special emphasis on Central, Eastern and South-Eastern European (CESEE) economies, which owe their successful catching-up performance since the 1990s not least to their export orientation, namely impressive export growth and enormous qualitative and regional shifts in export patterns. Fidrmuc and Martin (Chapter 21 in this volume) find empirical evidence for the export-led growth hypothesis in the new EU member states. Hence, the recovery of the global trading system will continue to shape future developments in the region.

Several explanations have been put forward to account for the continuously strong global trade growth prior to the recent collapse. One prominent strand of the literature focuses on the role of institutional factors, such as the dismantling of trade barriers within the GATT/WTO negotiations, the European economic integration process and similar developments in other regions (see Baldwin et al., 2001). Strong trade growth is often attributed to falling trading costs occurring through lower or abolished tariff and non-tariff barriers, improved business conditions, falling transportation costs, technological progress, and so on (see for example

Hummels (2007) on transportation costs and Jacks et al. (2008) on trade costs more generally). Another explanation refers to the increasing fragmentation of production, also called international outsourcing, and the rising importance of global value chains (Feenstra, 1998). Although vertical specialization is more frequently studied within the context of foreign direct investment, it clearly has strong implications for traditional trade flows. Finally, another strand of the literature analyses the income elasticity of trade (Baier and Bergstrand, 2001; Irwin, 2002).

The factors put forward to explain the recent 'trade collapse' are strikingly similar to those referred to as the long-run determinants of global trade. Numerous recent studies propose the following reasons for the strong negative trade reaction in the crisis: sharply rising trade costs including problems with trade financing (Auboin, 2009; Chauffour and Farole, 2009), the increased importance of vertical specialization manifested in increasing global supply chains (Escaith, 2009; Yi, 2009) and falling demand (Bems et al., 2010; Eaton et al., 2010; Freund, 2009). Others attribute the recent trade collapse to structural differences between domestic and external economic structures in connection with an asymmetric crisis impact on different types of goods. Capital and investment goods, which account for a large fraction of international trade, have clearly been affected more strongly in the crisis than non-durables and consumption goods (Francois and Wörz, 2009; McKibbin and Stoeckel, 2009).

In this chapter we take a long-term view on global trade and follow a decomposition approach to analyse the long-run growth of real world exports. Decomposing global export growth into its structural components, we find that the long-term rise in world export volumes largely reflects regional and sectoral shifts of emerging economies into more trade-intensive activities, such as machinery, electronic goods, motor vehicles, chemicals and textiles.

A novel aspect of our analysis is the use of sector-specific price indices in deflating export and domestic production data. This seems to be important since radically different price developments were observed in different industries. While for instance prices for office and accounting machinery, including computers, have fallen drastically since the 1990s, prices for chemicals, food and beverages have increased considerably.

The chapter proceeds as follows. In the following section, we describe our database and provide some descriptive statistics of world export growth in a regional and sectoral perspective. In Section 3 we develop a decomposition of export growth into a pure growth effect (abstracting from structural change) and two structural effects (the effect of initial specialization and the effect of changes in specialization patterns). Section 4 concludes with special emphasis on the CESEE region.

2 CONSTRUCTING A NEW DATA SET OF WORLD TRADE

Our focus is on analysing regional and sectoral patterns of trade and the trade response to output growth. Export data are taken from the UN COMTRADE database and aggregated to two-digit ISIC (rev. 3) industries. In total we arrive at a sample consisting of a maximum of 196 countries over the period 1995 to 2009, covering 22 manufacturing industries, ranging from ISIC (rev. 3) code 15 (food) to code 36 (other manufacturing). With some 150 exporters reporting trade data every year, we obtain roughly 40000 observations spanning 15 years.

We classify countries broadly into seven geographic regions. EU-15 comprises all EU member states prior to the 2004 enlargement. NAFTA includes the US, Canada and Mexico. CESEE economies are divided into two regions: we refer to the ten EU members which acceded to the EU in 2004 and 2007 as CEE-10, while the remaining ten Eastern and South-Eastern European countries are grouped as CIS (Commonwealth of Independent States) and the Balkans, including Russia. South-East Asia contains ten ASEAN members plus China, India, Japan and South Korea. Latin America (LatAm) consists of 14 mainland Latin American countries. All remaining countries are classified as rest of the world (ROW). A list of all countries and their grouping is given in the Appendix.

A major concern was to deflate all data in order to reflect different price developments within individual industries. Since industry-specific price deflators were not available for all countries in the sample, we use US prices as a shortcut. This implies the rather crude assumption that price developments do not vary across countries, but it does take account of the fact that certain goods were becoming constantly cheaper over the observation period (for example, computers lost dramatically in value) while others (such as chemical products and food and beverages) were subject to continual price increases. We use industry-specific US import price indices to deflate export data. Since the US imports goods from almost all countries in the world, we are confident that these price indices reflect average world price developments for traded goods. For domestic production data (value added, output and wages) we use the US producer price index.

2.1 Regional Trends in World Exports since 1995

World trade has roughly tripled since 1985 in real terms as new players asserted themselves (see Figure 22.1), notably China as well as South-East Asia, the new EU member states (CEE-10) and CIS and the Balkans (CIS). Their gains in world market shares came mainly at the expense of

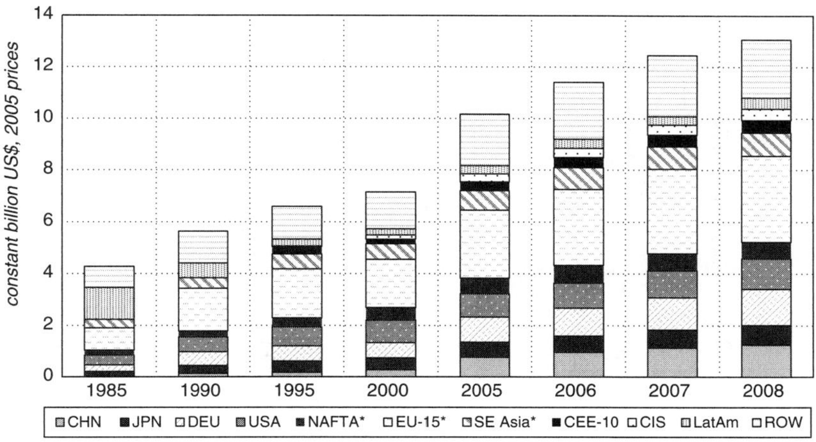

Note: Total merchandise exports are deflated using the country-specific consumer price index; see Appendix 22.1 for a list of the countries in each region; * denotes the region without the respective country displayed separately.

Source: Authors' calculations based on UN COMTRADE.

Figure 22.1 Regional composition of world exports, 1985–2008

Western Europe, NAFTA and Japan, but also Latin America, whereas Germany successfully retained its world market share, possibly because of the growing importance of intra-EU trade.

2.2 Sectoral Trends in World Exports over the Past Two Decades

The rising importance of individual players in global exports is intrinsically related to structural change within these countries. As shown in Figure 22.2, global exports are rather concentrated in a handful of economic activities. At the same time a great deal of restructuring has occurred since 1995. Measured in constant (2000) prices, the five most important industrial activities in 2009 were radio, TV and communication equipment; machinery and equipment; chemicals and related products; accounting and office machinery; motor vehicles. Together these industries accounted for 56 per cent of world manufacturing exports, whereas in 1995 their cumulative share was 44 per cent.

Rather diverse developments have been observed for each of these industries since 1995. Motor vehicle exports represented the most important category in world trade, accounting for 12.5 per cent of all manufacturing exports in 1995. This share had fallen to 8 per cent by 2009. Also

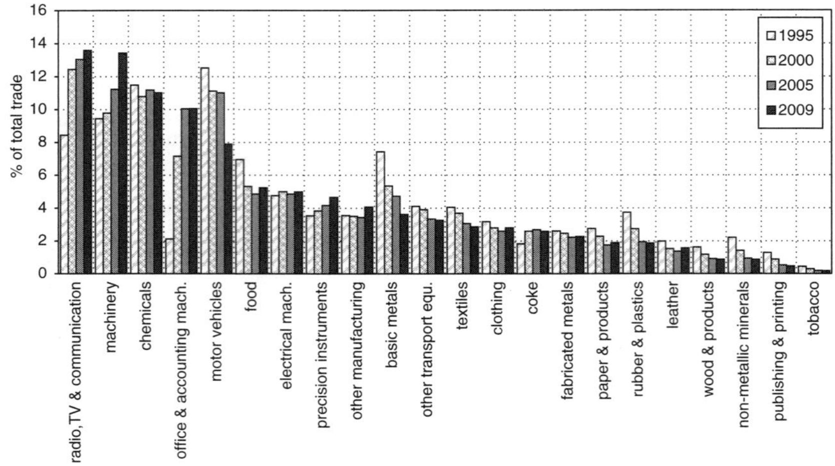

Note: Export shares are ranked by their importance in 2009; exports are measured in sector-specific US import prices of the year 2000.

Source: Authors' calculations.

Figure 22.2 Real trade shares of individual industries, 1995–2009

the share of other transport equipment has been on a moderate but continual decline, from 4 per cent to 3 per cent of real manufacturing exports. The 2008/09 crisis reinforced these developments. Among manufactured goods, motor vehicles were hit most severely during the crisis. On the other hand, real exports of office and accounting machinery have shown a tremendous increase in real terms (that is, accounting for the price decline in this category). The share of computers and related products in global export volume rose from 2 per cent in 1995 to 10 per cent in 2009. Real export shares of machinery and equipment as well as radio, TV and communication equipment also increased from 9.4 per cent and 8.4 per cent respectively in 1995 to more than 13 per cent by 2009, while the share of chemicals and chemical products remained rather constant at 11 per cent in this period.

In nominal terms, structural change appears to be less pronounced. Measured in current prices, world export flows are similarly concentrated in four activities: chemicals, machinery and equipment, radio, TV and communication equipment and motor vehicles account rather constantly for half of global exports since 1995. Again, the crisis year 2009 has reinforced longer-term trends. The share of chemical goods increased to 14 per cent in 2009 from 11 per cent in 1995, while motor vehicles dropped from a

Table 22.1 Average annual export growth rates (per cent) by regions and industries, 1995–2007

	Total manu-facturing	Machi-nery and equipment	Radio, TV and commu-nication equipment	Motor vehicles	Chemicals	Office and accounting machi-nery
CEE-10	14.5	19.8	28.8	21.6	9.8	41.6
CIS & Balkans	12.3	18.5	17.0	15.8	12.5	30.4
South-East Asia	11.2	13.1	13.1	8.0	9.3	23.4
Other	10.0	10.5	18.1	14.7	9.0	23.7
World	8.4	10.6	12.4	7.3	8.1	20.6
EU-15	6.8	9.6	10.2	6.9	8.1	17.9
Latin America	6.6	12.4	20.1	9.1	6.4	23.6
NAFTA	5.7	8.5	7.6	4.5	4.5	15.0

Source: Authors' calculations.

rather constant share of 11 per cent to 8 per cent in 2009. The most striking difference is observed for office and accounting machinery. After peaking at a world export share of 7 per cent in 2000, the nominal share dropped again to 4.3 per cent in 2009, down from 5.6 per cent in 1995.

This comparison between nominal and real trade shares illustrates the huge quantity of electronic goods being shipped globally at ever falling prices. Further, a huge part of the production of electronic goods is concentrated in Asia, reinforcing the region's rising importance in global trade in real terms. It further illustrates a longer-term decline in the share of motor vehicles in global exports which has to date been compensated by rising prices, thus leaving the total value of cars shipped globally rather unchanged (apart from the crisis). It should be noted however that, no matter how trade is measured, there is no evidence of an increasing world market share for motor vehicles. This is an important message for the Central and Eastern European EU members whose exports are heavily specialized in this industry.

This global overview points to a fair amount of structural change in world trade flows. Moreover a more detailed look reveals – rather unsurprisingly – that the regions reporting the highest real export growth rates also increase their world market share in exactly those categories. Table 22.1 lists export growth within the five most important categories. Since we want to exclude the impact of the economic crisis on global trade shares, we constrain the observation period to the years 1995 to 2007 and

Table 22.2 World market shares (per cent) in the top five export categories

	Total manu-facturing		Machinery and equipment		Radio, TV & commu-nication equipment		Motor vehicles		Chemicals		Office & accounting machinery	
	1995	2007	1995	2007	1995	2007	1995	2007	1995	2007	1995	2007
CEE-10	2.2	4.4	1.6	4.3	0.5	3.8	1.1	7.0	2.1	2.4	0.2	3.5
CIS & Balkans	1.0	1.5	0.4	0.8	0.1	0.2	0.3	0.6	1.3	1.7	0.0	0.1
South-East Asia	23.0	30.2	20.6	26.6	47.9	48.4	21.2	21.8	16.1	18.5	39.0	52.6
Other	9.8	12.2	7.4	7.5	8.4	17.5	1.5	3.7	10.8	12.3	5.6	10.1
EU-15	44.1	36.1	51.7	45.7	23.2	17.2	49.9	46.8	51.0	50.1	32.9	21.2
Latin America	2.4	1.9	0.8	1.0	0.2	0.4	1.2	1.8	1.6	1.4	0.2	0.3
NAFTA	17.5	13.9	17.4	14.1	19.7	12.6	24.8	18.3	17.0	13.5	22.1	12.4

Source: Authors' calculations.

rank industries according to their global share in 2007, again measured in 2000 US import prices. In 2007, machinery and equipment represented the category with the highest share in world exports, followed by communication equipment, motor vehicles, chemicals, and office and accounting machinery. The most dynamic export regions – the CEE-10, CIS and the Balkans and South-East Asia – show above-average growth rates in all of these categories.

Table 22.2 summarizes the changes in world market shares for all regions between 1995 and 2007. In fact, all regions with above-average export growth rates over the period have also increased their world market shares in these five categories, while those regions which exhibited below-average export growth recorded world market share losses in these categories. Latin America is a puzzling exception to this common observation with rising world market shares in the five most important categories but an overall decreasing world market share and low cumulative export growth. In particular South-East Asia is moving strongly into exports of machinery, communication equipment and computers. In the last category, this region is dominating the world market in real terms, with a world market share exceeding 50 per cent. The CEE-10 have increased their world market shares in all five globally most important categories. The increase was particularly strong in motor vehicles, where they had a market share of 7 per cent in real terms in 2007. This is nearly double their market share in total merchandise exports (4.4 per cent in 2007, up from 2.2 per cent in 1995).

Table 22.3 Importance of the top five export categories by region (in % of country's total manufacturing exports)

	Machinery and equipment		Radio. TV & communication equipment		Motor vehicles		Chemicals		Office & accounting machinery	
	1995	2007	1995	2007	1995	2007	1995	2007	1995	2007
CEE-10	6.8	13.5	2.1	11.4	6.5	18.2	10.8	6.0	0.2	7.1
CIS & Balkans	3.2	7.8	0.8	1.4	3.8	4.5	14.6	12.8	0.1	0.5
South-East Asia	8.5	12.2	17.6	21.0	11.5	8.2	8.0	6.6	3.6	15.7
Other	7.2	8.5	7.3	18.8	1.9	3.4	12.7	10.8	1.2	7.5
World	9.4	13.8	8.4	13.1	12.5	11.4	11.5	10.7	2.1	9.0
EU-15	11.1	17.5	4.4	6.2	14.2	14.7	13.3	14.9	1.6	5.3
Latin America	3.3	7.1	0.6	2.7	6.5	10.9	7.8	8.0	0.1	1.5
NAFTA	9.4	14.1	9.5	11.9	17.7	15.0	11.2	10.5	2.7	8.0

Source: Authors' calculations.

Finally, Table 22.3 illustrates structural change within each region by depicting the shares of the five globally most important export categories in the region's total exports. In 1995, industrial export patterns in the EU-15 and NAFTA clearly showed the highest correlation with the global industry structure. By 2007, the correlation between the regional and the global pattern had become equally high for the CEE-10, South-East Asia and the EU-15.[2] While all regions showed expanding shares of machinery, communication equipment and office and accounting machinery in their export patterns over the period, the dynamics towards the global top five export categories were more pronounced in emerging regions, such as South-East Asia and the CEE-10. The new EU members show a distinct export pattern characterized by a rising importance of motor vehicles. In 2007 this category represented more than 18 per cent of CEE-10 exports, clearly surpassing the global share of this category, which was 11 per cent. Contrary to the global trend, motor vehicle exports are still gaining importance within Europe.

It should be noted that, out of all regions in our sample, the CEE-10 region probably underwent the most dramatic structural change in this period. This is not surprising for transition countries. The point we want to make here is that the impressive real export growth of the region goes hand in hand with substantial structural change at the industry level. In the next section we will systematically extract the contribution of structural change to export growth.

3 DECOMPOSING GLOBAL EXPORT GROWTH

We are interested in a decomposition of the real trade growth along several dimensions, including the national and regional component of changes in trade, the sector composition of changes in trade, and finally also changes in the sector composition of regional trade. To do this more systematically below, we decompose export growth into a pure growth component, the contribution of initial industry structure and the component added by structural change.[3] We start by defining exports X_{ic} very generally as exports X in sector i by country c. Total exports of country c are then given by $X_c = \sum_i X_{i,c}$. We define export shares by country for each sector as:

$$\phi_{i,c} = \frac{X_{i,c}}{\sum_i X_{i,c}} \tag{22.1}$$

Globally, we can also define global shares by industry, that is, further summing an industry's exports over all exporters:

$$\Phi_i = \frac{\sum_c X_{i,c}}{\sum_c \sum_i X_{i,c}} \tag{22.2}$$

With this we can decompose total export growth of a country or region as follows:

$$\dot{X}_c = \frac{X_c^1 - X_c^o}{X_c^o} = A + B + C \tag{22.3}$$

A: global change in total exports $= \sum_i \Phi_i^0 \left[\frac{X_i^1 - X_i^o}{X_i^o} \right]$

B: initial deviation from global industry structure

$$= \sum_i (\phi_{i,c}^0 - \Phi_i^0) \left[\frac{X_{i,c}^1 - X_{i,c}^o}{X_{i,c}^o} \right]$$

C: shift in composition $= \sum_i \Phi_i^0 \left[\frac{X_{i,c}^1 - X_{i,c}^o}{X_{i,c}^o} - \frac{X_i^1 - X_i^o}{X_i^o} \right]$

In equation (22.3), term A captures changes in the global volume of exports and – where country c is identical in initial export structure and

Table 22.4 Structural decomposition of world export growth, 1995–2007

	X_c – cumulative export growth (%)	A – pure global growth effect (%)	B – initial specialization effect (ppt)	C – effect of structural change (ppt)
CEE-10	445	175	−678	948
CIS	283	175	−142	250
South-East Asia	260	175	36	50
Other	242	175	−90	158
EU-15	125	175	−7	−42
Latin America	115	175	−166	106
NAFTA	117	175	7	−64

Source: Authors' calculations.

in structural change to the global average – the change in export volume for country *c*. Put differently, term *A* captures the pure growth effect in the absence of changes in the underlying sector structure. Terms *B* and *C* capture reasons why country *c*'s export growth may differ from the global average, mirroring different impacts of the sector structure of trade. In other words, a large contribution of these two effects to the country's overall export growth reflects a high importance of industrial structure or structural change for the country. The second term, *B*, captures differences in the importance of various sectors *i* for country *c* – for example, if steel exports are more important for country *i* than they are for the world as a whole. This reflects the contribution of the initial export structure to subsequent export growth. A positive effect implies that the country's initial export structure is beneficial for future export growth. In contrast, a negative value would reveal that the initial industry structure has been a drag on subsequent growth. Term *C* captures differences in the change in exports at the sector level for country *s* relative to the world – for example, if steel exports fall or rise more for country *i* than they do for the world as a whole. This effect quantifies the importance of structural change for export growth. A positive value would again reveal a growing share of fast-growing industries with rising export intensity, thus improving the country's trade performance.

Table 22.4 reports the results of this decomposition analysis applied to exports. While the EU-15, NAFTA and also Latin America recorded a cumulative growth performance over the 1995–2007 period which remained below the global export growth rate of 175 per cent in the absence of structural change (that is, they were relatively underperforming), CESEE and South-East Asia showed export growth beyond the 'pure growth' effect. Structural change played only a minor role for the two most advanced regions in our sample, NAFTA and EU-15. In both regions the contribution of structural change to overall export growth was negative; that is, they were growing more slowly than the world average in those economic activities whose importance in global trade was increasing.

When looking into the two effects of industrial structure on the successful emerging regions' export growth, we find an interesting distinction between CESEE and South-East Asia. The initial export structure of the CESEE economies was not conducive to future rapid export growth. However, the new EU member states exhibited substantial structural change, showing particularly strong export growth in industries with rising global importance. Thus, they managed to change their initially unfavourable export structure. In contrast, South-East Asia shows less evidence of structural change over the period 1995–2007. The already beneficial initial export structure was compounded by favourable structural change; both effects were positive for this region and added about one-third to the above-average export performance over the period.

Latin America also showed some restructuring towards strongly growing industries, but this effect was not strong enough to offset the region's unfavourable initial export structure.

To summarize the global decomposition of real export growth over the recent past, the CEE-10 region clearly was the one characterized by the most substantial shift of export shares at the industry level. It also exhibited the strongest export growth performance in real terms – despite the region's particularly strong specialization in motor vehicles, whose share in global trade flows has actually been declining gradually (although export growth is still high in this category in absolute terms and motor vehicles are among the top export categories). At the same time, the CEE-10 moved strongly into globally fast-rising export sectors, such as machinery, communication equipment and office and accounting machinery. This longer-term trend can be attributed to the positive effects of EU integration. As observed also by Havlik (2008), the CEE-10 increasingly specialize in high-tech and medium high-tech products, whereby EU accession and FDI inflows certainly promoted the industrial restructuring process and modernization. Contrary to this development, CIS showed hardly any signs of restructuring towards higher-tech activities and reinforced their specialization in resource-intensive industries, such as metals and petroleum refineries. Havlik (2008) attributes this to a delay of policy reforms and weak performance in attracting FDI.

Given the uniqueness of the CEE-10 region, Figure 22.3 shows the

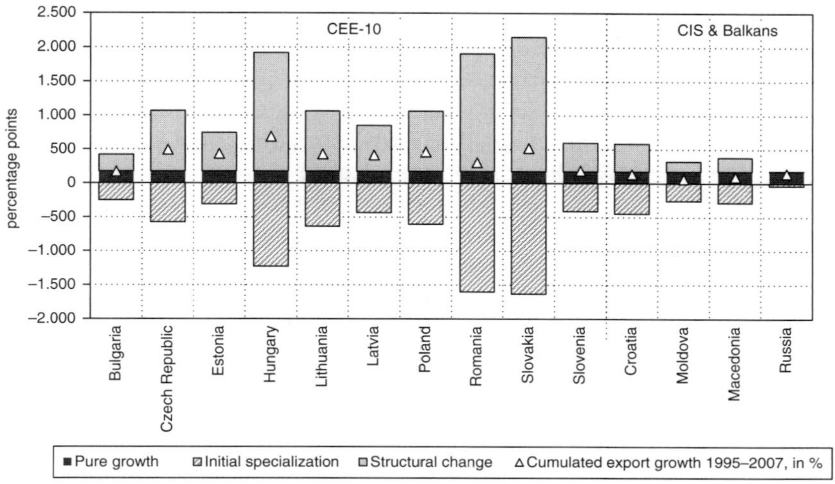

Source: Authors' calculations.

Figure 22.3 Structural decomposition of CESEE export growth, 1995–2007

contribution of all three effects to total cumulative real export growth in more detail. Hungary, Romania and Slovakia are the three countries for which structural change towards rapidly growing export sectors was most pronounced. This went hand in hand with substantial restructuring over the period, moving away from the initial disadvantageous specialization patterns prevalent in those countries in the mid-1990s. Also, Poland and the Czech Republic show significant structural change, while CIS and the Balkan countries (including Bulgaria) do not exhibit a great deal of structural change, resulting in generally lower export growth in those countries. In particular for Russia total export growth corresponds to the pure growth effect only.

4 IMPLICATIONS FOR CENTRAL AND EASTERN EUROPE AND GENERAL CONCLUSIONS

The strong historical rise and the recent deep fall of international trade have sparked a vivid debate among economists and policy makers alike in search of the reasons for and the implications of these developments. The CESEE countries were affected deeply by both developments. First, their impressive growth record since the 1990s was led by their favourable export performance (see, for example, Chapter 21 by Fidrmuc and Martin in this volume, or wiiw, 2010). Second, their strong reaction to the global financial and economic crisis is likely to have been triggered through the trade channel to a large extent. The most commonly cited factors behind the long-term rise and the crisis-related decline of international trade are surprisingly similar and relate to changes in trade costs (transportation costs, tariffs and non-tariff barriers for the rise and trade financing for the decline), increasing fragmentation of production and an increasing elasticity of trade to output. Another factor which was mentioned in the context of the recent severe drop in international trade relates to structural differences between production and export structures. Interestingly, this has not been stressed much in explaining the long-term growth of international trade. Taking a closer look at the importance of structural change in this chapter, we find that the long-term rise in world export volumes largely reflects regional and sectoral shifts of emerging and hence rapidly growing economies into more trade-intensive activities, such as machinery, electronic goods, motor vehicles, chemicals and textiles.

For our analysis, we construct a new set of trade and output data at the ISIC two-digit industry level over the period 1995–2009, using sector-specific price deflators for exports and domestic value added to account for dramatically different price developments in individual industries over the sample period. The use of sector-specific deflators affects the relative importance of individual industries in total exports. In particular, office, accounting and computing machinery exhibits a steep expansion which is not observed as strongly in traditional analyses that do not account for the relative price decline in this industry. Further, the importance of motor vehicles in total world trade shows a more pronounced decline in real terms when deflated at sector-specific prices than in traditional analyses. On the other hand, sector-specific deflators played no role for our results concerning the influence of restructuring on export growth, and our estimates of the output elasticity of exports were not affected by the form of deflation, either.

Decomposing export growth into a pure growth component and two structural effects – the growth contribution of initial industry specialization and the effect of structural change at the industry level – we find that the CESEE economies have been subject to considerable structural change with an overall positive effect on their export growth performance. This result holds only for the new EU members (CEE-10), suggesting that EU accession and related institutional and economic reforms have played a positive role (see also Havlik, 2008). The new EU members showed a successful restructuring towards globally fast-growing sectors. This has implied an increasing specialization of the region in machinery, electronic goods and motor vehicles. It should be noted that from a global perspective trade in motor vehicles is becoming less important in relative terms, although trade flows remain at a high level. In a more short-term perspective, trade in machinery and cars was severely hit in the recent crisis, corroborating the negative impact on Eastern Europe. Hence, continued domestic restructuring will remain important for the region, as global trade patterns partly move away from the current specialization patterns of the CEE-10. Substantially less structural change towards globally important trade sectors has been observed for CIS and the Balkan countries, suggesting a large potential for industrial restructuring in the region. This may also imply that we overestimate the effect of falling trading costs and global supply chains on export growth. On balance, restructuring and structural upgrading remain vital features of a successful growth and catching-up strategy for export-oriented, emerging economies such as the CESEE economies.

NOTES

1. The authors would like to thank Doris Ritzberger-Grünwald, Peter Mooslechner, Jarko Fidrmuc, Martin Schneider, Mariya Hake and Josef Schreiner as well as participants at the 12th ETSG meeting in Lausanne and the OeNB Conference on European Economic Integration for their comments and Angelika Knollmayer and Andreas Nader for their research assistance. This chapter is based on a more detailed article which will be published in *Focus on European Economic Integration*, Q3/11, OeNB, Vienna.
2. Of course, the global trade pattern is dominated by the EU-15, which is still the largest exporter in 2007. In this sense, and representing also the largest fraction of worldwide demand for manufactures, the sectoral specialization pattern in the EU-15 meets international demand and can thus be considered 'successful' (Buitelaar and van Kerkhoff, 2010).
3. Our decomposition differs conceptually from the traditional shift-share analysis or constant market share analysis which is used to decompose world market shares, that is, the changing importance of individual regions in world exports. Since we are interested in decomposing the growth of exports, we decompose here the change in export volume. In either exercise, the total change in the variable of interest (growth or market share) is decomposed into a pure growth effect and different structural components.

REFERENCES

Auboin, M. (2009), 'Boosting the availability of trade finance in the current crisis: background analysis for a substantial G20 package', Policy Insight No. 35, June, Centre for Economic Policy Research.

Baier, S. and J. Bergstrand (2001), 'The growth of world trade: tariffs, transport costs, and income similarity', *Journal of International Economics*, **53** (1), 1–27.

Baldwin, R., P. Martin and G. Ottaviano (2001), 'Global income divergence, trade, and industrialization: the geography of growth take-offs', *Journal of Economic Growth*, **6** (1), 5–37.
Bems, R., R. Johnson and K.-M. Yi (2010), 'Demand spillovers and the collapse of trade in the global recession', IMF Working Paper No. 10/142.
Buitelaar, P. and H.A.M. van Kerkhoff (2010), 'The performance of EU foreign trade: a sectoral analysis', De Nederlandsche Bank Occasional Studies **8** (1).
Chauffour, J.-P. and T. Farole (2009), 'Trade finance in crisis market adjustment or market failure?', Policy Research Working Paper 5003, July, The World Bank.
Eaton, J. et al. (2010), 'Trade and the global recession', mimeo.
Escaith, H. (2009), 'Trade collapse, trade relapse and global production networks: supply chains in the great recession', MPRA Paper No. 18433.
Feenstra, R.C. (1998), 'Integration of trade and disintegration of production in the global economy', *The Journal of Economic Perspectives*, **12** (4), 31–50.
Francois, J. and J. Wörz (2009), 'Follow the bouncing ball – trade and the great recession redux', in R. Baldwin (ed.), *The Great Trade Collapse: Causes, Consequences and Prospects*, November, http://www.voxeu.org/index.php?q=node/4269.
Freund, C. (2009), 'The trade response to global downturns: historical evidence,' World Bank Working Papers 5015, August.
Havlik, P. (2008), 'Structural change and trade integration on EU–NIS borders', in P. Havlik, O. Havrylyshyn and R. Grinberg (eds), *Transition, Restructuring and Integration*, Baden-Baden: NOMOS Verlagsgesellschaft, pp. 119–48.
Hummels, D. (2007), 'Transportation costs and international trade in the second era of globalization', *The Journal of Economic Perspectives*, **21** (3), 131–54.
Irwin, D. (2002), 'Long-run trends in world trade and income', *World Trade Review*, **1** (1), 89–100.
Jacks, D., C. Meissner and D. Novy (2008), 'Trade costs, 1870–2000', *American Economic Review: Papers & Proceedings*, **98** (2), 529–34.
McKibbin, W.J. and A. Stoeckel (2009), 'Modelling the global financial crisis', Centre for Applied Macroeconomic Analysis, The Australian National University, CAMA Working Paper 25/2009, September.
wiiw (2010), 'Will exports prevail over austerity?', wiiw Current Analyses and Forecasts No. 6, The Vienna Institute for International Economic Studies, July.
WTO (2010), *International Trade Statistics 2010*.
Yi, K.-M. (2009), 'The collapse of global trade: the role of vertical specialisation', in R. Baldwin and S. Evenett (eds), *The Collapse of Global Trade, Murky Protectionism, and the Crisis: Recommendations for the G20*, http://www.voxeu.org/reports/Murky_Protectionism.pdf#page=55.

APPENDIX 22.1 LIST OF COUNTRIES AND REGIONAL GROUPING

EU-15		**NAFTA**	
AUT	Austria	CAN	Canada
BEL	Belgium	MEX	Mexico
DEU	Germany	USA	United States
DNK	Denmark		
ESP	Spain	**Latin America (LatAm)**	
FIN	Finland	ARG	Argentina
FRA	France	BOL	Bolivia
GBR	United Kingdom	BRA	Brazil
GRC	Greece	CHL	Chile
IRL	Ireland	COL	Colombia
ITA	Italy	CRI	Costa Rica
LUX	Luxembourg	ECU	Ecuador
NLD	Netherlands	NIC	Nicaragua
PRT	Portugal	PAN	Panama
SWE	Sweden	PER	Peru
		PRY	Paraguay
CEE-10		SLV	El Salvador
BGR	Bulgaria	URY	Uruguay
CZE	Czech Republic	VEN	Venezuela
EST	Estonia		
HUN	Hungary	**South-East Asia**	
LTU	Lithuania	BRN	Brunei
LVA	Latvia	CHN	China
POL	Poland	IDN	Indonesia
ROM	Romania	IND	India
SVK	Slovakia	JPN	Japan
SVN	Slovenia	KHM	Cambodia
		KOR	Korea, Rep.
CIS and the Balkans		LAO	Lao PDR
ALB	Albania	MMR	Myanmar
BIH	Bosnia and Herzegovina	MYS	Malaysia
BLR	Belarus	PHL	Philippines
HRV	Croatia	SGP	Singapore
MDA	Moldova	THA	Thailand
MKD	Macedonia, FYR	VNM	Vietnam
MNE	Montenegro		
RUS	Russian Federation		
SER	Serbia		
UKR	Ukraine		

23. The great trade collapse and its impact on firms in Europe[1]

László Halpern

This chapter discusses recent trade developments from different perspectives: presenting, first, regional trade tendencies over time; second, national tendencies in seven particular EU countries; and third, firm-level results for this sample based on recent survey data.

The recent export collapse was larger than any other since the 1960s (see Figure 23.1). Caused by the great recession, this export contraction was sudden, severe and synchronized worldwide. This great trade collapse was mostly due to a demand shock. Commodity prices which plunged when the price bubble burst in 2008 continued to mirror the decline in world demand. The price movements and diminished demand depressed the value and volume of commodities trade.

Evidence shows that the trade collapse in 2008–09 was significantly larger than the GDP contraction in OECD countries (see Figure 23.2).

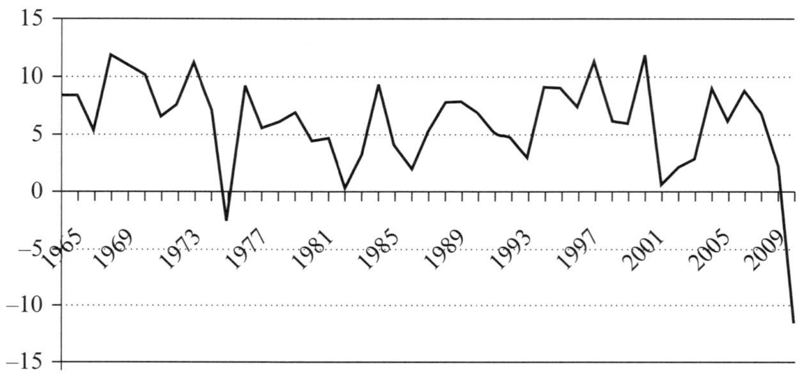

Source: OECD 'Quarterly National Accounts'.

Figure 23.1 Volume of world merchandise exports, 1965–2009 (annual percentage change)

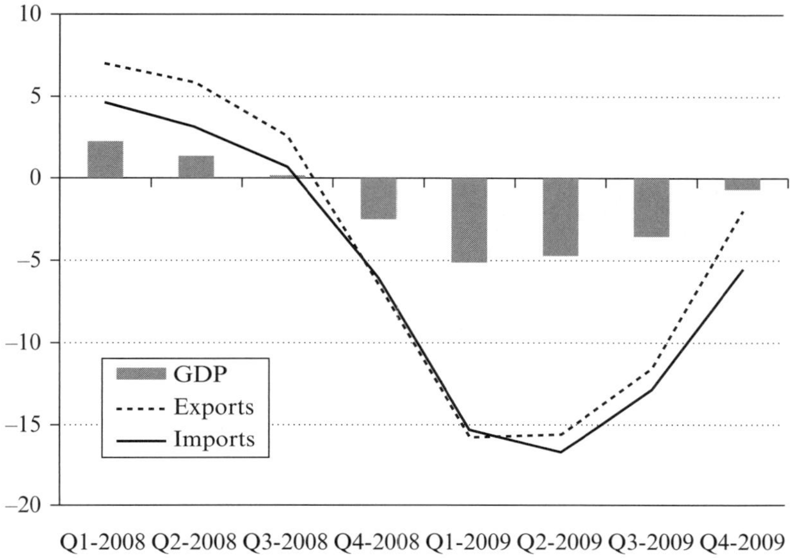

Source: OECD 'Quarterly National Accounts'.

Figure 23.2 Real GDP and trade growth of OECD countries, 2008–09 (year-to-year percentage change)

Trade fell by more than 15 per cent, while GDP declined only 5 per cent. Manufacturing output and exports collapsed as the Lehman-induced shock caused consumers and firms to retrench; private demand for all types of consumption beyond everyday use crashed. The huge gap between trade and production collapse calls for an explanation. Baldwin et al. (2009) offer some tentative explanations, based on compositional effects: they show the products with the largest contractions in consumption to represent a large share in trade but a small share in GDP. The demand shocks to GDP and trade occurred simultaneously and this coincidence was enhanced by immediate online adjustments of orders and production lines all over the world.

THE GREAT TRADE COLLAPSE AND ITS AFTERMATH

Imports and exports have fallen in all regions since Q3-2008 (see Figures 23.3 and 23.5). Imports fell by 40–60 and exports by 30–60 percentage points; only the EFIGE countries[2] fared slightly better with a drop of

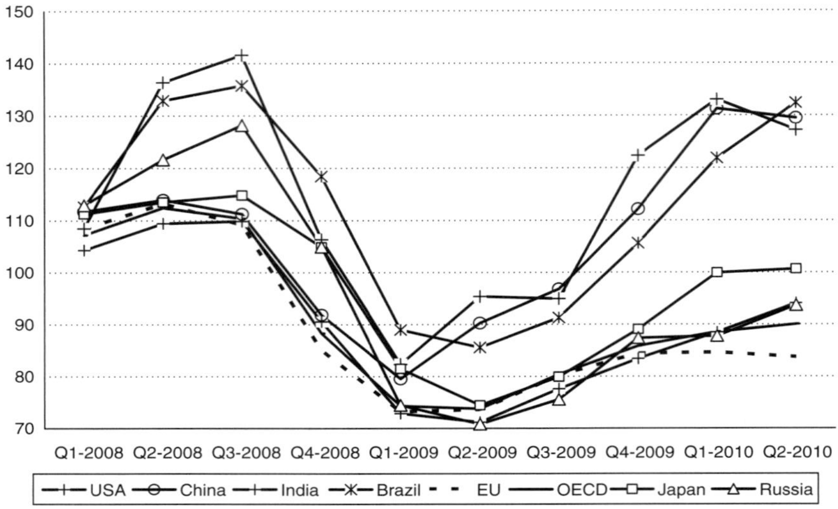

Source: Author's calculation using OECD international trade data.

Figure 23.3 Imports (Q4-2007 = 100)

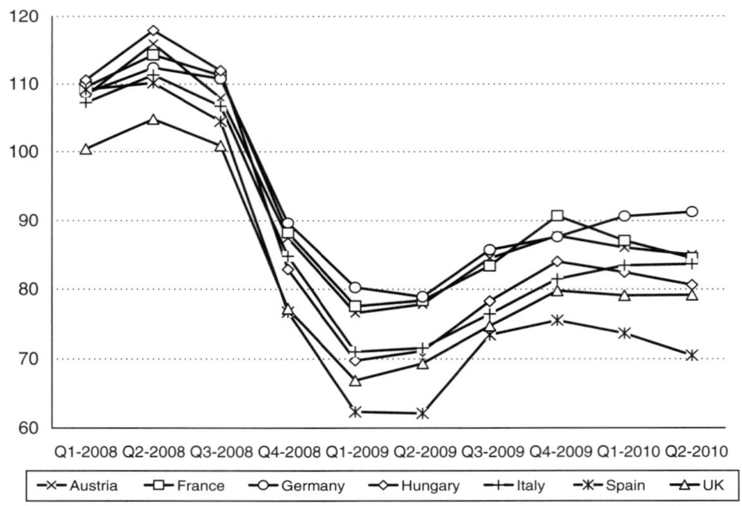

Source: Author's calculation using EFIGE survey data.

Figure 23.4 Imports in EFIGE countries (Q4-2007 = 100)

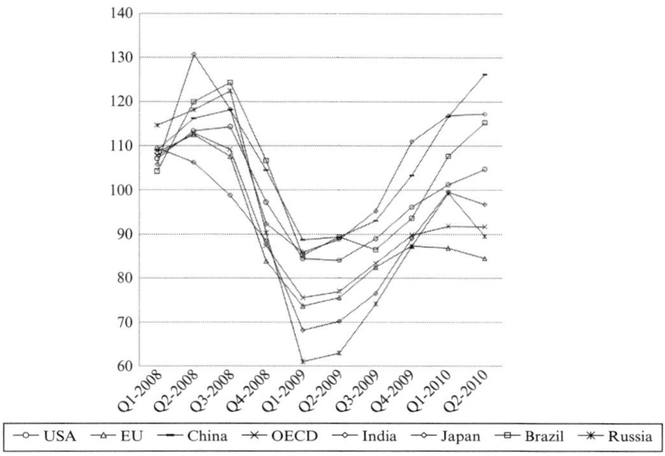

Source: Author's calculation using OECD international trade data.

Figure 23.5 Exports (Q4-2007 = 100)

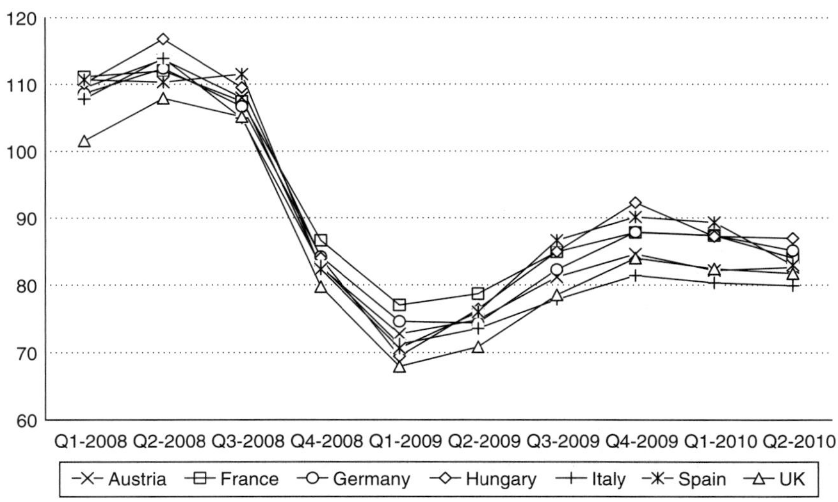

Source: Author's calculation using EFIGE survey data.

Figure 23.6 Exports in EFIGE countries (Q4-2007 = 100)

30–50 points (see Figures 23.4 and 23.6). The recovery, however, has been much more differentiated. While the return to the previous level – the U-shape – is almost complete for emerging economies (Brazil, China and India), all other regions and countries are lagging behind in the recovery, with the lag being larger for imports (around 40 points) than for exports (30 points). Moreover, Europe as a region brings up the rear in both exports and imports. Two interpretations are possible; either European economies have a different pattern of recovery, thus taking longer to rebound, or Europe has lost ground to its competitors amid a regional shift.

Our sample of European economies shows quite synchronized co-movements in both exports and imports – Spanish imports excepted, which are 10 points below those of other countries. These European economies have recovered 80–90 per cent of their end-2007 trade levels, which were already 5–15 percentage points below mid-2008 levels, though.[3]

FIRM-LEVEL PERSPECTIVE OF TRADE COLLAPSE

A few papers have looked into the causes and effects of the trade collapse at the firm level. Bricongne et al. (2010) claim that the drop in French exports mainly reflects the intensive margin of large exporters. Small and large firms are evenly affected when sectoral and geographical specializations are controlled for. Firms in sectors which are structurally more dependent on external finance have been affected most by the crisis. Fontagné and Gaulier (2009) add that firms of all sizes have been affected fairly equally by the crisis when the destination country and the sector dimensions of the decline are controlled for.

The crisis has hit firms in sectors relying on external finance more severely, regardless of firm size. The effect of external finance is robust if one controls for the fact that more globalized sectors – where intermediate imports account for a larger share of the value of final production – have also been hit more severely.

Chor and Manova (2010) study the collapse of international trade flows during the global financial crisis using detailed data on monthly US imports. They show that the adverse credit conditions were an important channel through which the crisis affected trade volumes. Countries with higher interbank rates and thus tighter credit markets exported less to the US during the peak of the crisis. These effects were especially pronounced in sectors that require extensive external financing, have few collateralizable assets, or have limited access to trade credit. Exports of financially dependent industries were more sensitive to the cost of external capital and this sensitivity rose during the financial crisis.

Table 23.1 Number of firms in the sample

	Austria	France	Germany	Hungary	Italy	Spain	UK
Firms	482	2973	2898	488	3021	2832	2142
Exporting firms	298	1578	1476	296	2086	1575	1301

Source: Author's calculation using EFIGE survey data.

The above studies deal with firms within a country. This approach should be complemented by cross-country comparisons, which requires appropriate and comparable data.

We carried out a firm-level survey for a representative sample of firms in early 2010 in order to investigate their internationalization pattern. While most questions were asked about data up to 2008, some questions also addressed the effect of the crisis on the firms' performance in three main dimensions, namely sales, exports and employment. In this respect firms were asked by how much sales, exports and employment had declined in 2009 compared with 2008. This chapter presents the results of the cross-tabulated answers across firm size – in terms of sales and employment – and export shares.

It was aimed that larger countries in this sample would have around 3000 representative firms questioned, and smaller countries around 500 (see Table 23.1). More than half of them were exporting.

Sales

The histogram of the sales size distribution is obviously skewed to the left, given the much larger number of smaller firms (see Figure 23.7). The mode is at firms with sales between EUR 2 and 10 million – Hungary excepted. The four largest size brackets have a 10 per cent share each at most. Sales by this sample of firms were hit unevenly by the crisis in 2009. In four countries – France, Hungary, Italy and Spain – the share of firms whose sales were unaffected remained below one-third (see Figure 23.8). In Austria, Germany and the United Kingdom, 37 per cent of firms reported that sales did not drop in 2009 compared with 2008. If affected, firms typically suffered a sales drop between 10 and 30 per cent in all countries.

How mixed was the sales reduction in different sub-samples of firms? Let us look at the size of the reduction in the EUR 2–10 million sales group and at the size distribution within the 10–30 per cent sales drop bracket, as opposed to the full sample, respectively, to establish the heterogeneity of the crisis impact.

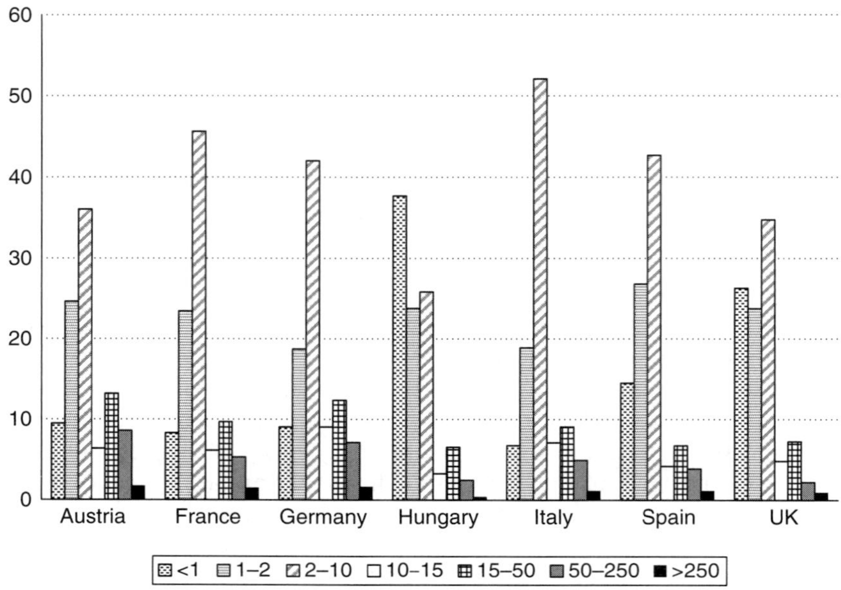

Source: Author's calculation using EFIGE survey data.

Figure 23.7 Sales size distribution of firms (per cent, million EUR)

The first perception is the conspicuous skewness to the right, that is the higher share of larger firms among firms with a 10–30 per cent drop in sales than in the full sample (see Figure 23.9). The second observation is that the country profiles are mixed; the distributions are closest for France and Italy but differ quite largely for Austria, Hungary, Spain and the United Kingdom; and Germany is somewhere in between.

For firms in the EUR 2–10 million sales group, the sales reduction distribution broadly mirrors the overall distribution in France, Italy and Spain, with a difference of less than 10 percentage points in any category (see Figure 23.10). The remaining countries report at least one category in which the difference exceeds 20 percentage points. The other sub-samples of these two dimensions are very similar in the sense that countries reveal different distribution profiles and firms in different categories exhibit different degrees of similarity.

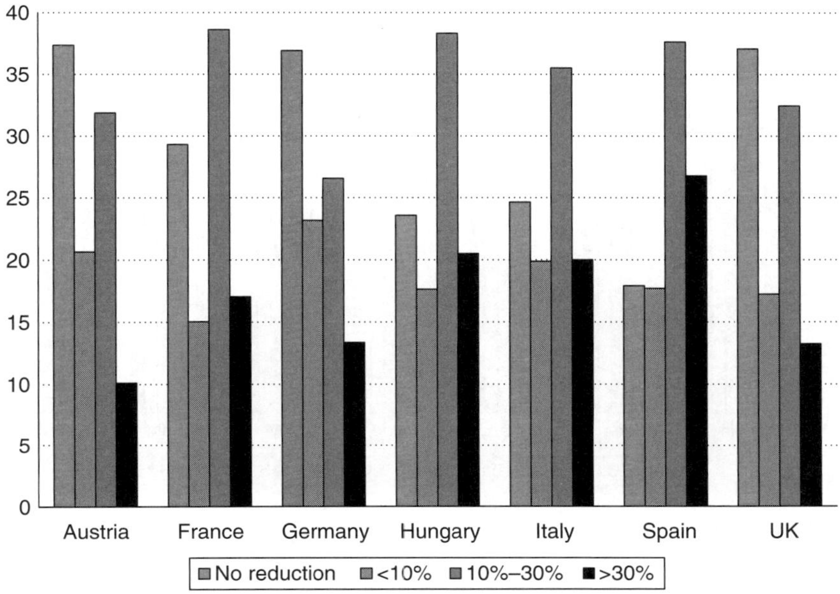

Source: Author's calculation using EFIGE survey data.

Figure 23.8 Distribution of sales reduction in 2009 for all firms (per cent)

Exports

The selection of firms in the sample was also designed to show the exposure of exports to the crisis. This feature of the EFIGE project allows us to explore the different facets of internationalization with a particular emphasis on export shares. In this respect, the export exposure should not be evaluated as such; the more meaningful information is how the country sample of firms is composed. In the all-country sample the mode is at the 20–50 per cent category with a share of no less than one-third and a maximum of 48 per cent for Germany (see Figure 23.11). The second largest category is different for smaller and larger countries; it is the 50–75 per cent bracket for the former and the 5–20 per cent category for the latter – the United Kingdom excepted, where the 'less than 5 per cent' category has a slightly larger share in the distribution.

The distribution of export growth rate is skewed to the left (see Figure 23.12). The most probable case is that exports did not change, except for France where the share of the 'no change' category is significantly smaller than that of any other category.

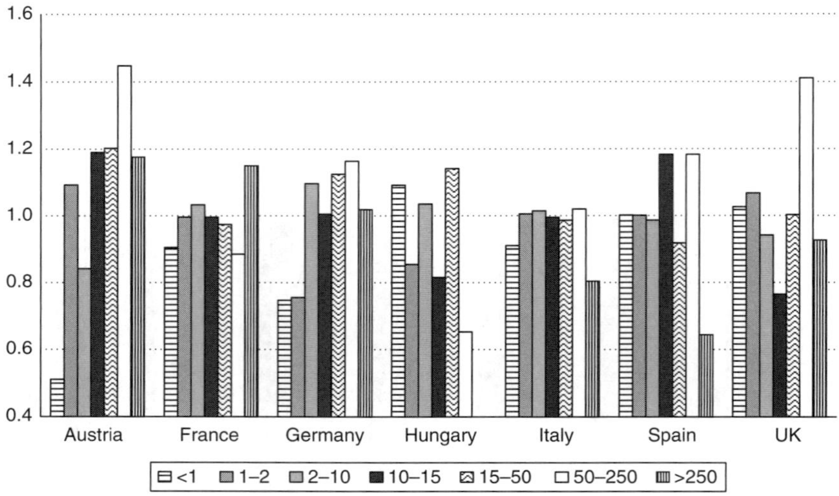

Source: Author's calculation using EFIGE survey data.

Figure 23.9 Relative sales size distribution of firms in 2008 with sales reduction between 10 and 30 per cent in 2009 (per cent, EUR million)

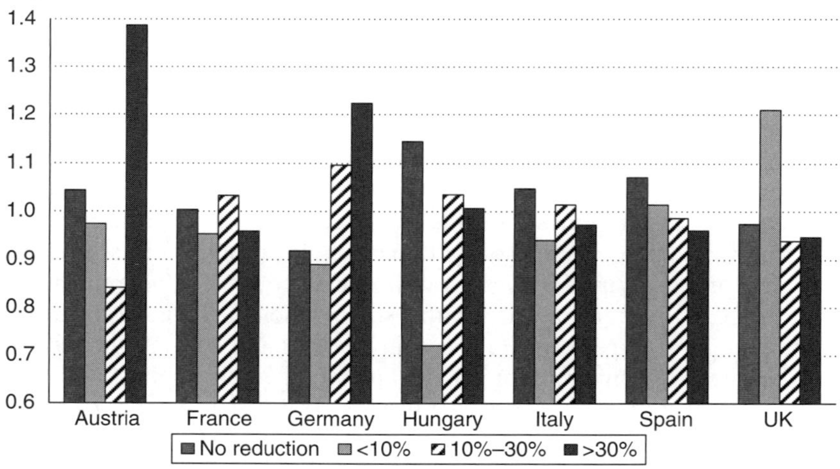

Source: Author's calculation using EFIGE survey data.

Figure 23.10 Relative distribution of sales reduction in 2009 for firms between EUR 2 and 10 million sales in 2008

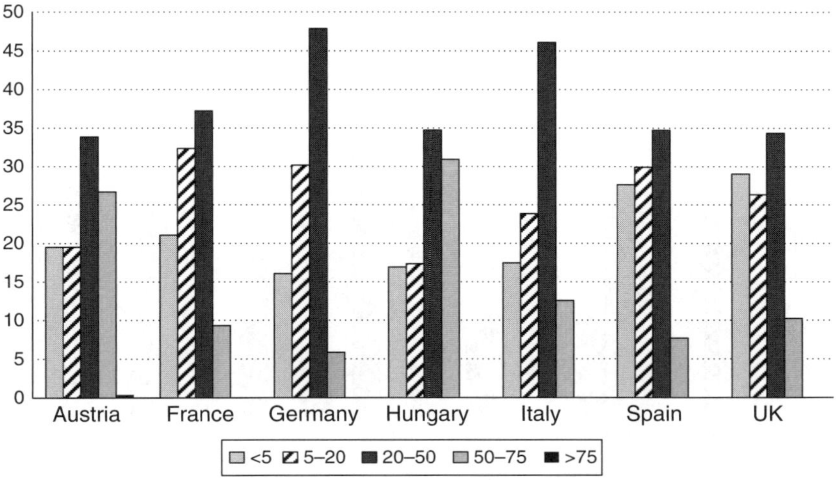

Source: Author's calculation using EFIGE survey data.

Figure 23.11 Distribution of export shares

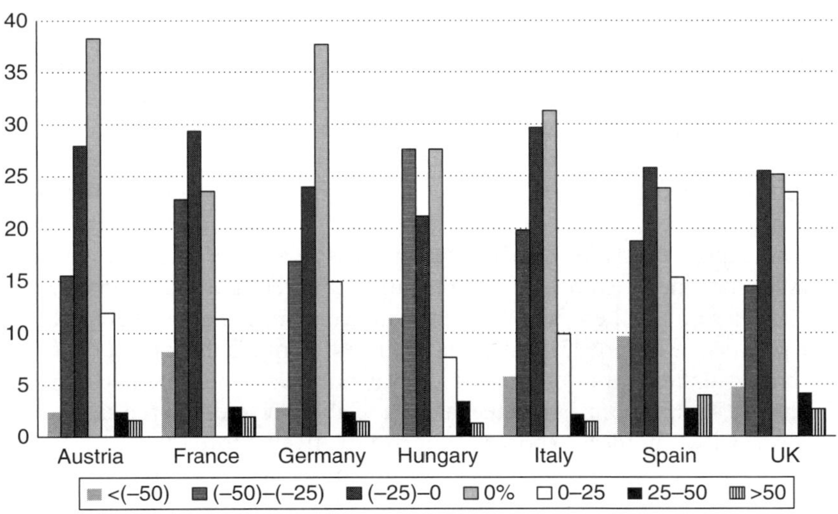

Source: Author's calculation using EFIGE survey data.

Figure 23.12 Distribution of export growth in 2009 (per cent)

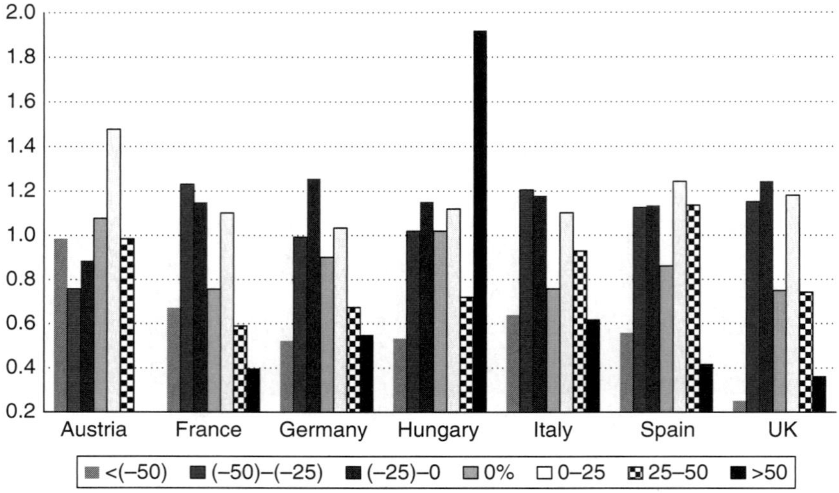

Source: Author's calculation using EFIGE survey data.

Figure 23.13 Relative distribution of export growth in 2009 of firms with export share between 20 and 50 per cent in 2008

In the 20–50 per cent export share category (see Figure 23.13), the pattern of the relative distribution is rather mixed across countries; very few categories remain within the 10 percentage point interval. The overall impression is that there is no clear visible asymmetry in the distribution across countries, though there are quite a few outliers for most countries.[4]

The export exposure distribution of the sub-sample of firms with the smallest decline in exports in 2009 is rather different from the distribution of the full sample; there is no country with a distance of at least 30 percentage points (see Figure 23.14). Actually the difference is the largest for firms with the smallest export share, which was not the least populated bracket in the full sample. One can detect a quite visible skewness to the right; that is, firms with a modest export decline are relatively more numerous in the highest export share groups. Whether this observation survives across all the categories if multiple explanatory factors are used remains for future research.

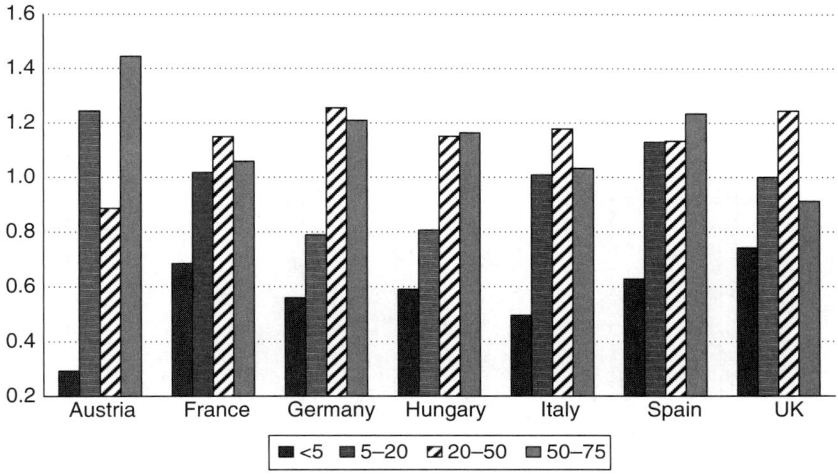

Source: Author's calculation using EFIGE survey data.

Figure 23.14 Relative distribution of export shares of firms in 2008 with export decline between 0 and 25 per cent in 2009

Employment

Firms with 10–50 employees represent the lion's share of the sample, no less than 60 per cent or even 80 per cent for Italy (see Figure 23.15). The share of micro firms is below 4 per cent. The other three remaining categories – medium and large firms – have a share of around 10 per cent each – which decreases with size – in the sample.

The distribution of the employment change is skewed to the left; job creation was dominated by job destruction during the crisis (see Figure 23.16). Spain and the United Kingdom seem to be hit hardest in this sample, with their mode being at job destruction, while 'no change' accounted for the largest share in all other countries.

The relative distribution is definitely skewed to the right for the subsample of employment declines below 25 per cent (see Figure 23.17). In other words, larger firms tended to be more successful than smaller ones in preserving staff levels. This is valid across countries – with few exceptions– and this observation deserves further and more detailed investigation in the future.

The relative distribution of employment changes at firms with a staff of 10 to 50 is quite similar among larger and smaller countries alike (see Figure 23.18). Larger countries have relatively less occurrences in the two

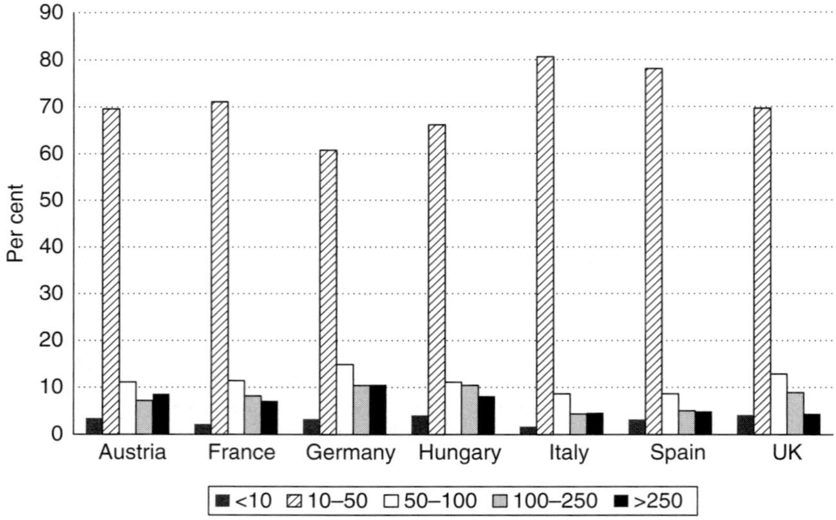

Source: Author's calculation using EFIGE survey data.

Figure 23.15 Employment size distribution in 2008

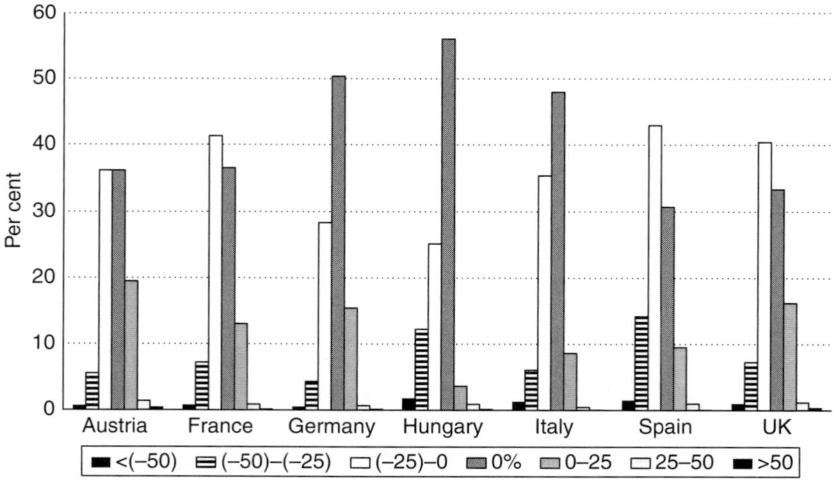

Source: Author's calculation using EFIGE survey data.

Figure 23.16 Distribution of employment change in 2009

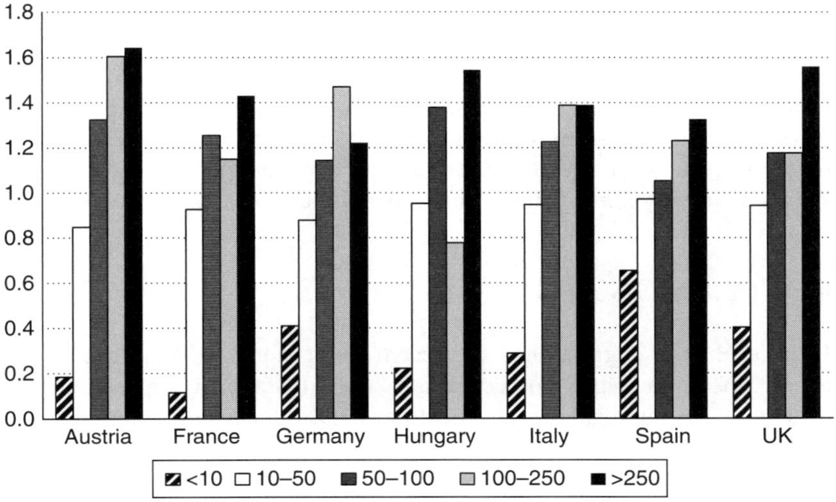

Source: Author's calculation using EFIGE survey data.

Figure 23.17 Relative employment size distribution in 2008 of firms with employment decline between 0 and 25 per cent in 2009

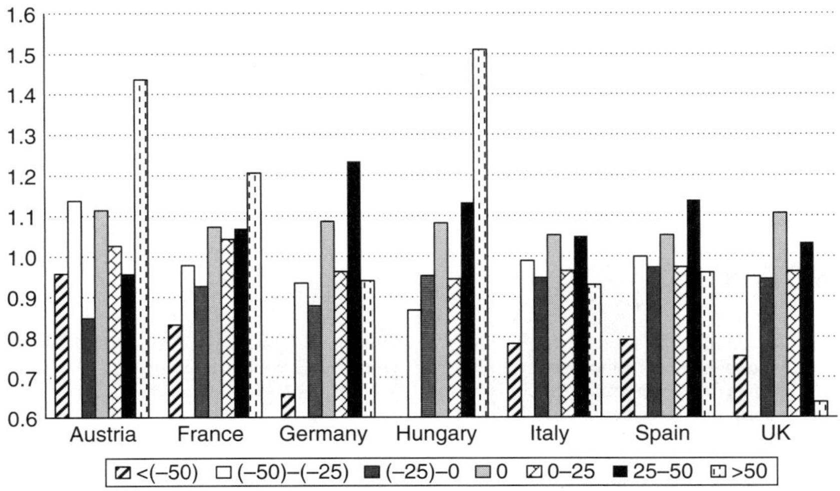

Source: Author's calculation using EFIGE survey data.

Figure 23.18 Relative distribution of employment change in 2009 of firms with a staff of 10 to 50 in 2008 extreme brackets, and the relative share of dynamic firms with a 25–50 per cent employment increase is the first or second largest. With some imagination the pattern reveals a slight skewness to the right; firms in this sub-sample seem to be net job creators. Again, this casual observation needs further scrutiny when multiple factors are used and other categories are investigated as well. Austria and Hungary have excessively high relative shares of very dynamic firms in this sub-sample.

CONCLUSIONS

Firm-level data suggest that the recent great trade collapse has had a mixed effect on European economies notwithstanding the similarities evident at the aggregate level. Put differently, intensive firm-level churning implies that firms have reacted differently in many dimensions; their performance depended on many factors. Multi-factor analysis is needed to explore whether this profound reshuffling of the industrial tissue will lead to deep restructuring, and whether this effect will move the European labour market towards more flexibility.

Successful emerging economies have increased their share in global trade, yet the European economies appear to have been at the shrinking end according to initial evidence. Whether this pattern is just a reflection of a more protracted nature of the crisis in Europe or the first sign of a re-division of global trade among different trading blocs is yet to be seen, but European firms need to revise their pattern of internationalization in order to remain competitive at home and abroad. Deeper analysis of the available survey data will give some initial indication of which side European firms are leaning towards.

NOTES

1. This chapter was prepared under the 'European Firms In a Global Economy' (EFIGE) research project, which received funding from the European Community's Seventh Framework Programme Socio-economic Sciences and Humanities (FP7/2007-2013) under grant agreement no. 225551.
2. The EFIGE project covers seven countries: Austria, France, Germany, Hungary, Italy, Spain and the United Kingdom.
3. All values used in this chapter are at current prices. Tendencies at constant prices would have shown quite similar patterns. Values at current prices give a satisfactory characterization of the trade development.
4. In certain categories a small number of firms in the full sample may imply large relative values in the sub-samples.

REFERENCES

Baldwin, Richard (ed.) (2009), *The Great Trade Collapse: Causes, Consequences and Prospects*, a VoxEU.org Publication.
Bricongne, Jean-Charles et al. (2010), 'Exports and sectoral financial dependence: evidence on French firms during the great global crisis', ECB Working Paper Series No. 1227.
Chor, Davin and Kalina Manova (2010), 'Off the cliff and back? Credit conditions and international trade during the global financial crisis', mimeo.
Fontagné, Lionel and Guillaume Gaulier (2009), 'French exporters and the global crisis', in R. Baldwin (ed.), *The Great Trade Collapse: Causes, Consequences and Prospects*, a VoxEU.org Publication.
OECD (2010), 'Quarterly National Accounts'.
WTO (2010), *International Trade Statistics 2010*.

PART IV

Challenges for banking in the CESEE region

24. After the crisis: financial sector reform in the EU

María Teresa Fábregas Fernández

The financial crisis that hit Europe in 2008 was the worst since the 1930s. But the situation would have been much worse if governments, central banks, European institutions and other international institutions had not responded forcefully. Even if the crisis is not over, we need to start rebuilding and we must reform. Financial markets were at the heart of the crisis and they cannot remain the same. Why? Global financial services regulation failed to prevent or contain the crisis. So, a profound review of our regulatory policy is needed. A safer, sounder, more transparent and more responsible financial system working for the economy, and for society as a whole, is a precondition for sustainable growth. Stricter and more comprehensive rules covering the entire scope of financial activities are therefore needed. Improved supervision is also essential; and the new supervisory structure at the European level will help to achieve this objective.

But Europe cannot do this in isolation. The crisis was international and calls for an international response. All major jurisdictions are implementing changes and we have to do it in a coherent manner. Ensuring an international level playing field is critical in this process for all players: for investors, for financial institutions, for supervisors, for everyone. And that is the reason why Europe is playing a key role in driving forward the G20 agenda. We are very active in these G20 fora, together with European Union members of the G20 group, and we are fully committed at European Commission level to implement this agenda. For this reason, the European Commission tabled several proposals in 2010, which are either under negotiation in the European Council and the European Parliament at the time of writing or have already been adopted – in the banking area and also, for instance, in the credit rating agencies' field, proposals on short selling, proposals on OTC derivatives and central counter-parties and trade repositories have already been adopted by the Commission and are under negotiation by the European Parliament and the Council.

But the work has not yet been finalized. In 2011 we will table the remaining proposals in order to complete the financial sector reform. In this context, I would like to highlight the proposals on crisis management and resolution that the European Commission plans to propose by summer 2011 in order to create a comprehensive framework in the European Union for banks. This is to equip the authorities with common and effective tools and powers to tackle bank crises at the earliest possible moment and to avoid cost for tax payers.

I mentioned the area of credit rating agencies, where at European level we already have regulation that went fully into force in December 2010. However, the work has not been finalized in this sector. With regard to the role of government bonds in the May 2010 euro zone debt crisis, government bond ratings were also put in question by some politicians and also some players in the market. This is why the European Commission published a public consultation paper in November 2010 in order to put forward suggestions for improving the work of credit rating agencies, to improve the quality of ratings concerning sovereign debt, but also to tackle issues such as the overreliance on ratings that we have currently in our regulations and usually in the banking area, the capital requirements legislation coming from Basel III discussions. And this issue is being examined not only at the European level but also at the FSB (Financial Stability Board) level, where a report has been produced in order to try to avoid as much as possible the overreliance on ratings, trying to find alternatives to this.

In the field of securities markets, we are going to propose amendments to the Market Abuse Directive and to the Markets in Financial Instruments Directive (MiFID) in 2011. We are reviewing these directives in order to cover three main objectives. The first is to close regulatory gaps. There are some areas where there is no level playing field at European level and where there is a complete lack of regulation, therefore new rules have to be introduced. The second objective is to achieve a single rulebook, in order to eliminate the divergences at national level; again, to improve integration. And the third is to be able to introduce into the legislation what we call a preventive approach. Why? Because we are producing legislation not only to fight against the current crisis but also to prevent the next one.

Concerning the first objective, closing regulatory gaps, we are looking into four specific issues. The first one would be to broaden the scope of requirements to other instruments; for instance, the MiFID legislation is mainly focused on equities, so we are looking into broadening the scope of some requirements concerning transparency to non-equities and also to tackle in particular commodity derivatives. Regarding the issue of improving transparency, it is not only to provide more data to regulators to preserve market integrity but also to provide data to regulators in order to be able to examine and tackle market stability issues.

The second element under this objective would be to achieve a level playing field between actors in the securities market, that is, both between trading venues, including also new trading venues, such as broker crossing networks, and between investors. We are trying to better protect investors, and we are trying to calibrate also better the rules for SMEs.

Concerning the second objective, we are trying to eliminate options and indiscretions in regulation, as far as possible to use the legal instrument of regulation instead of directives and also to harmonize general principles on sanctions to create a level playing field in Europe.

Concerning the third objective, the issue of introducing a preventive approach in legislation, we are trying to enhance the supervisory powers in order to also allow supervisors to take exceptional measures under exceptional circumstances, under a well-framed system and in a coordinated manner at the European level. A first example of these new powers would be the proposal on short selling that was adopted in September 2010 by the Commission. And then we have the new European supervisory authorities and in the field of securities markets we have the European Securities and Markets Authority (ESMA), which will, according to the regulation establishing this new authority, also have emergency powers.

So, all this is just to explain in broad terms what the reform of the securities market regulation will consist of. We are also in close touch with the United States authorities, because they are proceeding with similar changes on the other side of the Atlantic. So our hope is to rebuild a financial sector which is healthy and performing as it should be.

25. Banking challenges in the CESEE region from the Erste Group perspective

Andreas Treichl

Let me start with some good news. Eastern Europe, including Russia, is catching up with the other emerging markets relatively fast, and we believe that by 2012 it will be coming close to the kind of growth rates we are having in Asia or in Latin America, leaving Western Europe and the rest of the world way behind (see Table 25.1).

This leads to more good news. Emerging markets' savings rates were higher than those of the developed world in the past, and they will also be higher in the future (see Figure 25.1). Therefore, if you talk about liquidity, if you talk about potential loan-to-deposit ratios, healthy loan-to-deposit ratios, it is not the deposit base that should be the problem in the future of the CEE region: the problem may well be the growth of lending.

Let me make one point, which, I think, is incredibly serious but which is completely misunderstood by many regulators, by central bankers and by people overall. Banks have been told again and again that they have to think about capital markets. We are being told that we have to clean up our balance sheets and that we have to think about capital markets.

Table 25.1 Real GDP growth (in per cent)

	2010	2011	2012
North America	2.7	2.0	2.1
Latin America	5.2	3.6	**4.1**
Western Europe	1.6	1.1	1.4
Eastern Europe & CIS	3.1	3.6	**4.2**
Middle East & N. Africa	4.3	4.5	**4.5**
Sub-Saharan Africa	4.6	5.0	n.a.
Asia, Australia & Pacific	6.0	4.7	**5.0**

Source: EIU.

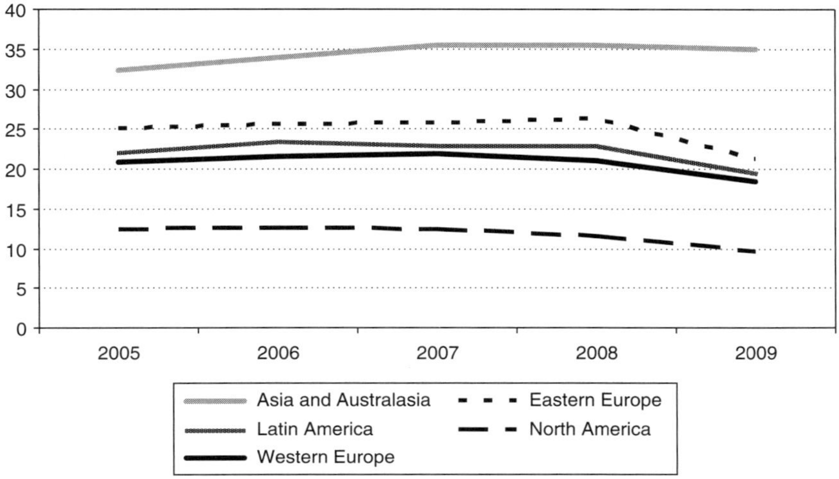

Note: 1. Amount of GDP not consumed or spent for government purchases.

Source: EIU.

Figure 25.1 Aggregated gross national savings[1] rates of different regions (per cent of GDP)

That is a very serious statement to make. At the same time we are talking about returning to the basics. Now, what is returning to the basics? Is it thinking about capital markets or the problem of Central and Eastern Europe where we just made some mistakes in basic banking? Lending, that is what banks are there for. We have made mistakes in lending for over a thousand years. That is part of our business and we will continue making mistakes in lending in the future; that will remain part of our business. For that reason we charge interest and that is why the good borrowers have to bear the costs for the bad borrowers. But are we forced to go into capital markets? Is that what the regulators want us to do now? Yes. But who in the European Commission – which is trying to clean up the securities business among other things – and who in the regulatory field is thinking about the following: where did this crisis start? Did it start with lending? Or did it start with packaging loans into funny, little, stupid securities? I think the latter was the cause of the crisis – and that is what the regulators want to get us into.

Let me explain why this concept is fraught with problems. Since there has been no bond market in Central and Eastern Europe it is going to be very difficult to develop it, as is evidenced by Figure 25.2. Now banks are

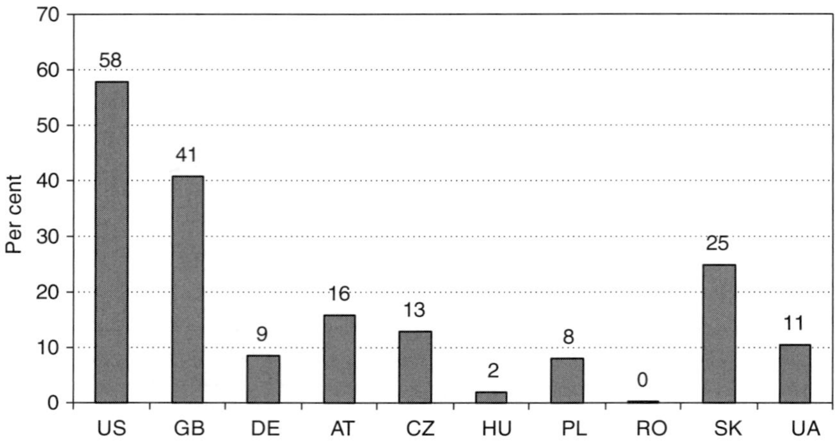

Note: 1. Securities consist of bonds, bills, certificates of deposit and similar instruments normally traded in the financial markets.

Source: EIU.

Figure 25.2 Relation of corporate securities[1] to corporate loans

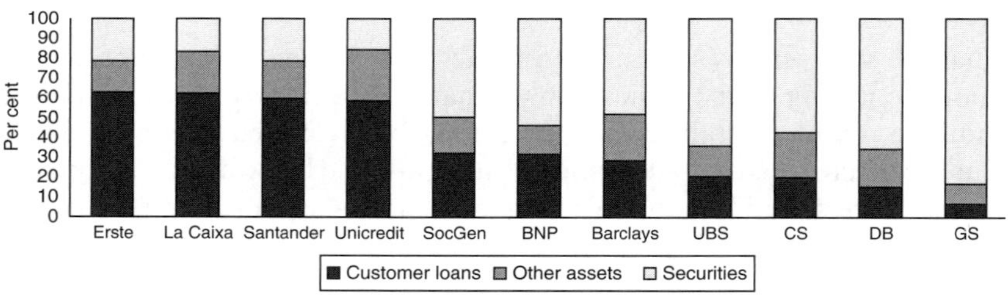

Figure 25.3 Proportion of securities business versus financing for the real economy (balance sheet structure per H1 2010)

banks, but there are very, very different banks in this world. In Figure 25.3 I show four banks that are real banks. Surprisingly, Erste Group is one of them; but also one of our competitors is one of them, which is UniCredit; so is Santander, as well as another bank that has a lot of problems with spending in Spain, La Caixa. But those are just four banks, and there are not many more banks like these in Western Europe that are predominantly in the lending business. In the business that regulators actually wanted us to do, or not? I do not know. The G20 said: 'We want banks to go back to

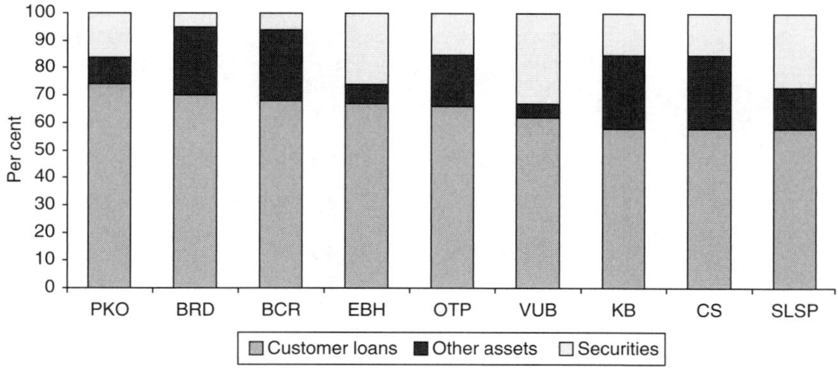

Figure 25.4 Proportion of securities business versus financing for the real economy in CEE banks (balance sheet structure per YE 2009)

their basic business, which is taking in deposits and lending.' We are a long shot from that. We are going in a completely different direction. And guess why; because all the big banks, with one mighty exception, Santander in Europe – whether it is BNP, Barclays or other banks – are not banks that are predominantly engaged in the lending business. All big banks in Europe, not only in the US, are predominantly in the securities business.

Now, look at Central and Eastern Europe (see Figure 25.4). Those are all banks active in our market. They are all real banks that have, like us, made many mistakes in lending, but there is one big difference compared with those big banks heavily engaged in the securities business: lenders in the CESEE region pay for their mistakes. If we make bad loans, we keep them on our books and we pay dearly. That is why our loan loss provisions have been skyrocketing. We are not selling them off to investors, who have no idea what they are actually buying. We are carrying our own risk. Now do regulators want us to get into a business in the future where we package Hungarian mortgage loans into securities, get Moody's and S&P to put a funny rating on it and then sell it off to pension funds in Austria? Is that what they want us to do? I do not think so, but they are forcing us to do so, because there is no bond market in Central and Eastern Europe and because there are very few companies who are actually big enough to issue bonds on their own.

And in order to show you what I mean, let me give you some of the insights of our rating (see Figure 25.5). If we issue today a bond or finance Ireland, we need one tenth of the capital we need in order to finance an SME that has 60 per cent equity and has never lost money in the past

S&P/Fitch	Corporate IRB (%)	SME IRB (%)	Sovereign STD (%)
AAA	15.31	11.98	0
AA+	24.50	19.22	0
AA	51.32	40.46	0
AA–	62.21	49.09	**0**
A+	66.62	52.57	20
A	85.43	67.27	20
A–	90.63	71.26	20
BBB+	110.77	86.21	50
BBB	132.38	100.95	50
BBB–	147.05	110.73	50
BB+	150.70	113.23	100
BB	**201.28**	152.43	100
BB–	263.75	**214.99**	100

(*a*) *Risk weights per rating class (corporate, SME and sovereign)*

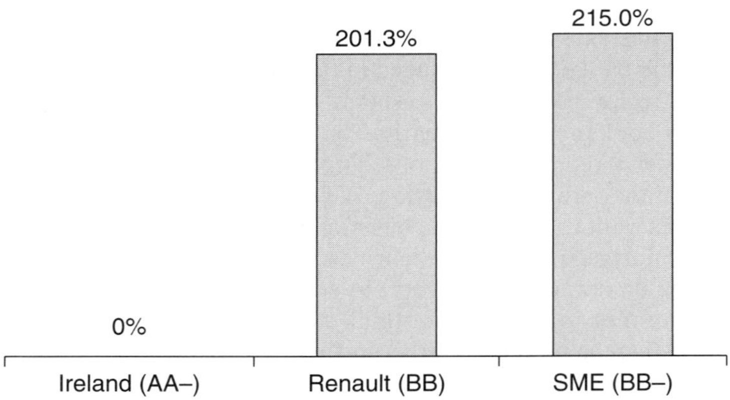

(*b*) *Risk-weighted assets*

Figure 25.5 Risk weighting

hundred years. Similarly we would require ten times more capital than if we financed some funny state which just happened to have a funny rating. And I do not mean that Ireland is funny; it is a great place with big problems at the moment. Is that going in the right direction? Is that what we want? Is that going to fuel growth? Therefore, I am going back to my opening statement. Is the claim that I made at the outset correct? Will there be growth in Central and Eastern Europe? In fact, this brings us to another question: will there be enough bank lending available? And if there is not enough bank lending available, how will we finance that kind of growth? Now that is the crucial question and I have not found one person who could give me an at least halfway intelligent answer to that yet.

26. Challenges for banking in the CESEE region – the situation in Austria and CESEE in November 2010

Michael Hysek

Economic developments in the second quarter of 2010 appeared to be much better than expected, which caused GDP forecasts for 2010 to be revised upwards. The IMF, for example, raised its GDP forecast for Austria from 1.3 per cent (forecast in April 2010) to 1.6 per cent year-on-year real GDP growth (forecast in October 2010) and for the euro area from 1 per cent to 1.7 per cent. The revision of Germany's forecast (from 1.2 per cent to 3.3 per cent) turned out to be especially pronounced, which contributed significantly to the rise in Austria's external demand: according to the Oesterreichische Nationalbank (OeNB), an increase in real exports of 4.6 per cent year-on-year is expected for 2010 following a decline of 15 per cent year-on-year in 2009.

Given this incipient economic recovery and overall improved macroeconomic conditions, the profitability of Austrian banks shows the first signs of a recovery. Based on data reported for the first half of 2010, the consolidated return on assets (after taxes) is expected to be approximately 0.4 per cent in 2010. By comparison, this ratio reached only 0.2 per cent in 2009 and a mere 0.1 per cent in 2008.

Concerning asset quality, the fast growth in the consolidated loan loss provision ratio of Austrian banking groups observed in recent years has decelerated so that the ratio reached 3.9 per cent in the second quarter of 2010. A more stable trend was observed in the Austrian market: the unconsolidated loan loss provision ratio, which primarily reflects the domestic business of Austrian banks, reached the long-term average of the last 12 years and stood at 3.1 per cent in the second quarter of 2010. Despite this evidence of improving conditions, the deteriorating asset quality will remain an important issue in 2011.

The financial crisis has clearly shown that a (too) high degree of reliance on the interbank market for refinancing purposes may create serious funding difficulties in times of crisis. Austrian banks, in contrast, generally rely on customer deposits as the primary funding source for their lending activities: the unconsolidated loan to deposit ratio in the customer business has remained at a level of roughly 130 per cent in the first half of 2010.

Austrian banks' claims on Central, Eastern and South-Eastern European (CESEE) countries and members of the Commonwealth of Independent States (CIS) amounted to EUR 212.5 billion at the end of June 2010. The Austrian exposure to the region, which represents approximately one-fifth of the CESEE exposure of the EU-15 banks, is regionally well diversified, with the EU-2004 member states accounting for 55 per cent, South and Eastern Europe for 19 per cent, the EU-2007 member states for 16 per cent and the CIS for 10 per cent.

The heterogeneity of the economic development in the CESEE region is reflected in the high variance in non-performing loan (NPL) ratios between different CESEE countries. On the one hand the NPL ratio remained below 10 per cent in the Czech Republic and Slovakia, which are two of Austrian banks' most important host countries. On the other hand, the NPL ratio reached levels between 10 per cent and 15 per cent in Hungary and Romania. Even higher levels were experienced for instance in Ukraine, where the NPL ratio exceeded 35 per cent. All in all, the growth of the aggregated NPL ratio of Austrian banks in CESEE – which stood at 12.2 per cent in the second quarter of 2010 – has decelerated so that it is expected to peak in late 2010/early 2011 in several CESEE countries.

This development is reflected by the increase in the amount of loan loss provisions, which still weigh heavily on banks' profitability. The loan loss provision rate of subsidiaries in CESEE rose at an accelerated pace by 0.5 percentage points to 6.2 per cent in the second quarter of 2010. Relating to banks' earnings, loan loss provisions of subsidiaries in CESEE amounted to almost 70 per cent of operating income at year-end 2009. For the second quarter of 2010 this share runs at slightly below 60 per cent.

Overall, the business environment remains challenging for Austrian banks. Challenging, too, are the upcoming advancements in the regulatory environment since both the legal framework and the supervisory architecture will be adjusted so as to ensure economic and financial stability.

CHALLENGES AHEAD

The financial crisis has clearly shown the need for regulatory reform. It goes without saying that a strong and resilient banking sector is vital in order to serve as a sound foundation for sustainable economic growth.

What we require to counteract future crises are stronger shock absorbers and more efficient preventive measures. Since shocks need to be absorbed on a micro- and a macro-level, proposals under revision at the time of writing include efforts both to strengthen the resilience of the individual institution and to address system-wide risks that affect the banking sector as a whole.

Generally speaking, shock absorption occurs through better risk coverage, more stringent capital requirements and higher liquidity standards.

Shock absorption through improved risk capture comprises three main factors. Firstly, the reform of the large-exposures regime will introduce a more harmonized and tighter set of measures that reduce concentration risks arising from large exposures. The second essential element relates to the capture of securitization risk. According to the new EU directive, a net economic interest has to be retained at all times by originators/ sponsors of securitized products, thus aligning risks of originators and investors. Furthermore, there will be extensive due diligence requirements so that investors should be able to monitor and control, at all times, the risk they incur when investing in securitizations. Thirdly, revisions to the market risk framework require banks to calculate an 'incremental risk charge' and a 'stressed value at risk'. These measures are expected to improve the capture of default and migration risks and should help to reduce the pro-cyclicality of the minimum capital requirements for market risk.

Another way to enhance banks' shock absorption capacity is by implementing a stronger capital base: in that respect, we will have a harmonized, principle-based recognition of hybrid capital instruments within the EU from 2011 and at a later stage a significantly higher quality and quantity of bank capital.

It is important to emphasize that the Austrian Financial Market Authority (FMA) is generally very supportive of efforts to strengthen the capital base. However, since the Basel III framework was designed with a pronounced orientation towards international joint stock banks, it is necessary to adapt this framework to European banking sector specificities. Approximately three-quarters of all banks in Austria are cooperative banks. Therefore, it can be expected that issues like the recognition of cooperative shares as core Tier 1 capital but also the deduction of minorities will remain issues at the European level in 2011. In any case, enough time should be made available for phasing in the new requirements.

One of the lessons learned from the crisis is certainly the fact that liquidity risk management is of crucial importance. So it is not surprising that the Capital Requirements Directive (CRD) II sets qualitative liquidity risk management standards, given that the existing EU liquidity standards are out of date and urgently need to be revised. Complementing these qualitative efforts, the CRD IV will introduce two quantitative liquidity risk ratios, namely the liquidity coverage ratio and the net stable funding ratio. From the FMA's point of view, a single and stricter set of liquidity standards is welcomed. The on-going negotiations of the final CRD IV will further refine this metric.

In addition to shock absorption the regulatory framework also has to provide for shock prevention: excessive leverage by banks is widely believed to have contributed to the financial crisis. To address this, the Group of 20 countries (G20) has agreed on the adoption of a non-risk-based capital measure, the leverage ratio. The underlying aim is to constrain the build-up of excessive leverage in individual institutions and in the financial sector as a whole.

While being an important step in the right direction, the leverage ratio has inherent limitations since it does not allow for the specificities of different business models. Problematic for an international level playing field are also the different accounting standards, like the US generally accepted accounting principles (GAAP), the IFRS and the national GAAP. Therefore, it is essential to adequately calibrate the nominator and denominator of the leverage ratio and to use the supervisory monitoring phase in 2011 and 2012.

Moreover, so-called 'systemically important financial institutions' should be subject to more intense supervision, and there should be an elaborated and agreed bank resolution framework in place. This would allow the orderly winding-down of a bank, reducing the moral hazard posed by systemically important financial institutions.

Coming to the new supervisory architecture, it is fair to say that the crisis has shown that the current arrangements for financial supervision in Europe are inadequate in an EU-wide integrated financial market. For that reason, the FMA welcomes the creation of the European System of Financial Supervisors (ESFS), which entails elevating the level-3 committees, currently serving as advisory bodies, to the level of European agencies with enhanced powers as authorities. The current level-3 committees, in which the FMA has seats and voting rights, include the Committee of European Banking Supervisors (CEBS), the Committee of European Insurance and Occupational Pensions Supervisors (CEIOPS) and the Committee of European Securities Regulators (CESR). These institutions will be transformed respectively into the European Banking Authority (EBA), the European Insurance and Occupational Pensions Authority (EIOPA) and the European Securities and Markets Authority (ESMA), which are – *inter alia* – going to be responsible for micro-prudential supervision at the EU level.

Moreover, to develop a European macro-prudential perspective while improving the interaction between micro- and macro-prudential analysis and to enhance the effectiveness of early warning mechanisms, an EU-wide early warning system for financial crises called the European Systemic Risk Board (ESRB) will be created.

It remains to be seen how this new supervisory architecture works in practice. So far, the FMA expects substantial benefits to materialize, for instance a quick and efficient mechanism allowing for collaborative decisions in emergency situations, a further move towards harmonized rules and powers and even stronger cooperation and trust.

DEALING WITH FOREIGN CURRENCY LOANS

While the global financial crisis has highlighted the systemic risks associated with large stocks of foreign currency loans to borrowers without matching foreign income, the OeNB and the FMA have been aware of this issue for a long time. Therefore, the OeNB and the FMA have actively raised awareness of the risks of foreign currency loans (FCLs) and repayment vehicle loans for several years. In October 2008, the FMA issued a strong recommendation to banks to refrain from granting new foreign currency loans to (unhedged) households. In March 2010, the FMA published an extension of its Minimum Standards for Granting and Managing Foreign Currency Loans and Loans with Repayment Vehicles, first released in 2003. The aim of the extension is to impose very strict criteria on the granting of new FCLs to private consumers.

The stepped-up supervisory efforts since October 2008 have already shown their effectiveness. FCLs to households have declined since October 2008: the volume of households' FCLs outstanding amounted to roughly EUR 38 billion at the end of June 2010, which means a drop of 12 per cent or EUR 4.7 billion since October 2008 on an FC-adjusted basis.

In order to address the issue of FCLs in CESEE, the FMA and the OeNB started a new CESEE FCL initiative at the beginning of 2010. The FMA very much appreciates that the 'guiding principles of the supervisory initiative on FC lending in CESEE' – which were the result of this initiative – are regarded as common reference for further attempts to reduce vulnerabilites associated with foreign currency lending in CESEE countries. The issue of FCLs in CESEE is being dealt with by the European Bank Coordination 'Vienna' Initiative under the auspices of the EBRD at the time of writing.

CONCLUDING REMARKS

A level playing field is of utmost importance. Hence, fears are understandable that the EU-wide implementation of Basel III will cause distinct disadvantages in EU banks' international competitiveness if the United States does not join in the international effort to strengthen the resilience of the banking sector. To meet these concerns, the European Commission is in close contact with the US Treasury, which has already committed itself to implementing the new capital standards at the national level by the end of 2012. At any rate, banks will need more capital and they will have to use the transition periods to raise this capital.

To conclude, the appropriate supervisory response to the challenges ahead has to comprise a combination of several measures. A clear focus has to be put on strong and independent governance and risk management practices whereby the business models of banks have to be challenged harder and a bank's management has to pass even more demanding fit-and-proper tests. Also, supervision as a complement to regulation and cross-border coordination and cooperation needs to be further strengthened. The biggest challenge, in any case, is to reach a common view and common approaches in daily supervision.

27. The CESEE experience of KBC Group

Marko Voljč

The purpose of this chapter is to give the case of a practising banker active in the CESEE region, with a view to providing an assessment about how we see the conditions for financing the future development in the region. These considerations are meant to add a practical touch to the chapters on policy-making and theoretical modelling. Specifically, I would like to address four questions from the point of view of the group that I represent: KBC, which is a Belgian group. You may ask how we came to the region given that, unlike in the case of the Austrian banks or French or Italian banks, our engagement does not seem like a natural proposition. Thus, the first question will be: how come we decided to go into a market which was terra incognita for us when the wall came down? Second, how did we weather the financial and economic crisis that hit the world in 2008? Third, what have we learned from this past period – both the pre-crisis period and particularly the crisis period itself? And the last question is: do we still believe in Central, Eastern and South-Eastern Europe? Will we stay? I will try to provide brief answers to each of these questions, maybe focusing more on the present and the future than on the past.

As a group, we were faced with the situation in the early 1990s that we were too big for Belgium and too small for Western Europe. Emerging Europe became a natural choice for expansion. We started in Hungary and we did both banking and insurance acquisitions between the early 1990s and the period immediately preceding the latest crisis. At the time of writing, we are focusing on five countries in the region, which we call our 'home market', in addition to Belgium: the Visegrad Four (namely the Czech Republic, Hungary, Poland and the Slovak Republic) and Bulgaria. And, of course, we came into those markets at different stages of development, but generally with the idea that this is a convergence play. These are countries and markets that will eventually become or have already become members of the EU and one day the EMU. They will be catching up with the more developed part of Europe, and financial services will be particularly fast-growing in areas where we felt we had a comparative advantage, given that we have had a proven and well-functioning, well-run bank insurance model in our home country, Belgium.

The early years were actually a learning experience; we had some ups and downs. We had to learn how to do business the hard way, the expensive way. We had a difficult situation in Poland some time ago and then, of course, another challenging situation in Hungary, both related to a lack of understanding of how business is done in that part of the world. But, by and large, we recovered and did quite well financially; our market shares grew, particularly in the Czech Republic, but also, quite importantly, in Hungary and more recently in Slovakia.

Then came 2008 and we felt that perhaps the crisis that was coming from the far shores of the Atlantic would not reach Central and Eastern Europe. For a while we were actually quite happy or even complacent. And then, of course, the liquidity crunch hit us in the third quarter and at the beginning of the fourth quarter of 2008 after the collapse of Lehman Brothers. And there, again, I must say that, given that we were an active participant in the region, we also wholeheartedly embraced the Vienna Initiative, which, to a certain extent, helped the economies in the banking sector deal with the crisis better, in my firm belief, than would have otherwise been the case.

Some have argued: 'But the banks, the foreign-owned banks, also contributed to the weaknesses of the banking system, mostly, of course, by allowing very high growth rates in loans, many, in some countries, foreign-denominated loans, and therefore we should also bear our share of responsibility.' I certainly agree with that and, of course, that is probably something shared with other foreign-owned banks in the region, mostly in Hungary and, to a certain extent, in Poland. But, overall, I believe the fact that the banking sector was able to adjust to the crisis reasonably well in terms of maintaining liquidity and in terms of trying to keep the risk-weighted assets unchanged, although the economies were shrinking and demand for lending has fallen quite significantly, particularly in some countries, maybe Poland being an exception there, means that the banking sector, including our group, has played a constructive role, not without losses. Yes, indeed, if you look at the risk appetite, we were part of that. We were actually benefiting from the pre-crisis period in a significant way. If you look at the profit growth rates we were all experiencing, during the decade prior to the crisis, they were quite impressive and we felt that, given that crises come and go, we would rather remain together with our partners and clients and, of course, in cooperation with the authorities in the countries where we were present.

So, I would say the crisis has been a sobering experience for all of us. I can state on behalf of KBC Group that we have learned some valuable lessons. We were actually fortunate enough to have a strong liquidity base in most countries. If you look at the loan-to-deposit ratio of the group, it has been consistently below 100, meaning that in countries like the Czech Republic, Slovakia to a certain extent, Poland and now Hungary we have a deposit base which is bigger than the loans given to non-financial-sector clients and that was a backbone of the fact we were able to actually rely on our domestically generated liquidity and not be too vulnerable to the fact that interest rates have risen significantly in the wake of the financial crisis. We were, of course, soon confronted with deteriorating portfolios, and that is something which is still going on. This is just to remind ourselves: in terms of physical output, the crisis may be over, but the quality of the loan portfolio is, to a large extent, still deteriorating. In many instances we have not seen the bottom yet. We are hoping that in the first half of 2011 we will see the worst of the non-performing loans and impairments on the loan book of the banks in the region. The non-performing loans as a share of total loans should afterwards begin gradually to decline. But, nevertheless, I think that the current quality of our loan portfolio will continue to be a cause of concern, even when the economies come to a more normal situation and we know that, of course, normal would not mean pre-crisis growth rates. So, that is one lesson we have to learn.

Risk appetite will have to be adjusted in a significant way. It is being adjusted, but it will have to be much more through the cycle type of, shall we say, awareness of what kind of risks we are confronted with in the banking business, not necessarily credit risk alone. We will have to be much more mindful of how we allocate and reallocate scarce capital. While in the pre-crisis period liquidity was abundant and capital was available for practically any type of acquisition and growth, we will, in the future, also in the wake of lower economic growth and Basel III requirements, have to be much more mindful as to how and where we deploy and redeploy capital. And, in this respect, let me add that there will be winners and losers among countries. I do not want to single out anybody here, but I am sure that countries which are able to successfully adjust to the post-crisis world will be able to attract more business and more capital. And those countries where risks of any nature will be perceived as being high, and conditions for business not conducive to a minimally accepted return on capital, profit return, whatever measure we take for capital profitability, will have to live with the consequences of that. So, I think, it is important that we bear in mind that going forward, even when the worst of the crisis is behind us, banks and their owners will be very mindful as to how capital is being used, and I would not rule out that some operations will stagnate or shrink and others will grow.

One lesson also that I draw from this crisis is that most of the players who were active in the pre-crisis period in the region, again, the Visegrad Four and Bulgaria in particular, are still here. And that means that we are likely to face fierce competition going forward, but the kind of competition that is based on different risk assessment, and there will be much less price competition than other factors that would actually distinguish losers from winners.

Yes, we still believe in the region. Yes, we will stay. The convergence play is still with us, but, of course, it is a world which will be less buoyant, and the profitability rates will be significantly more moderate than in the past. Having said that, it is still probably an advantage, once you have an established presence in those markets, to be here and benefit from the convergence, from the fact that the financial services sector will grow faster than in the more mature Europe. Therefore, despite everything, we are cautiously optimistic, and we look forward to doing more business in the region in the coming years.

28. Challenges for banking in the CESEE region – the case of Swedbank Baltic Banking

Håkan Berg

In 2010 Swedbank celebrated its 190th anniversary. Our bank has its roots in the Swedish savings bank tradition, the origins of which date back as far as the early 1820s. From a more recent perspective, Swedbank is the result of the merger of the major Swedish savings banks with the cooperative Föreningsbanken. When I entered the Swedish banking industry in the mid-1980s, banks were primarily retail banks focusing on retail and small and medium-sized clients in Sweden.

At the time of writing, Swedbank continues to be a full-service bank for both private individuals and companies. It continues to apply a traditional banking model, but it has become more international, and it has grown to serve 9.5 million private customers and 669 000 corporate customers, from 356 branches in Sweden and 222 branches in the Baltic countries. The Swedbank group is, moreover, present in Copenhagen, Helsinki, Kaliningrad, Luxembourg, Marbella, Moscow, New York, Oslo, Shanghai, St Petersburg and Ukraine. In September 2010, the balance sheet amounted to SEK 1846 billion and the number of employees totalled about 17 500.

During the financial crisis that hit Sweden at the beginning of the 1990s, Swedbank almost went bankrupt but it eventually managed to recover and was soon afterwards listed on the Swedish stock exchange. In the aftermath of the crisis huge changes were implemented as a result of which the bank developed a reputation in the market of being 'boring but safe'.

Against this backdrop, Swedbank started expanding to new markets, and by mid-2000 it was the dominant market player in the three Baltic countries, having operations also in Russia and Ukraine. At the time, the perception in the market was no longer that Swedbank was 'boring'.

When the last crisis hit in late 2007 and liquidity dried up in the market, it became clear that Swedbank unfortunately was no longer perceived as 'safe'. Swedbank had to seek support in the form of government guarantees to raise funding during the crisis, and it continues to feel the repercussions of the crisis, with the credit impairment ratio amounting to 7 per cent in the Baltic Banking segment in 2009.

In managing the downturn, Swedbank chose a rather aggressive approach. In the focus were credit management, risk control, productivity and internal structural changes. The Baltic countries, all having fixed rate regimes, have successfully performed internal devaluations. Coming from a very high-risk environment, the Baltic countries have emerged as role models for other countries still facing similar challenges in fiscal consolidation. Swedbank Baltic Banking reported a profit again in the third quarter of 2010 after six quarters in the red. The strategy going forward is to be 'safe but not necessarily boring'.

LESSONS LEARNED – INTERNAL CHALLENGES GOING FORWARD

So how can we avoid the mistakes that created the imbalances? How can we assure sustainable growth going forward?

What happened is that, essentially, risks were underestimated during the boom, and the underestimated risks were underpriced. The targets we are setting now for banks are sustainable in the long term. The loan-to-deposit ratio will support the creation of a more balanced growth. Swedbank is targeting a loan-to-deposit ratio of 130 to 150 per cent over time in the three Baltic countries. In addition, credit portfolio risk management needs to be enhanced. Understanding the concentration risk and the growth risk in the portfolio – whether it is geographical areas, industry sectors or client segments – will be critical. We will see enhanced regulation in the financial market. The regulation does not necessarily pose a threat to the industry. The effects of regulation, such as increased transparency, fair representation, controlled remuneration and proof of sustainability, will be positive effects provided that regulation is reasonable and well thought through.

The major conclusion from the lessons learned though is that it takes the contribution of all stakeholders (policy makers, regulators, supervisors, participants in the markets, customers) to create imbalances leading to bubbles. It takes all the stakeholders to join forces to avoid repeating the mistakes. It cannot and should not be the responsibility of a single stakeholder to manage sustainable growth. It is only by providing the necessary framework and acting together, sharing the responsibility, that we can build sustainable growth avoiding the traps that will lead to new imbalances.

LESSONS LEARNED – EXTERNAL CHALLENGES GOING FORWARD

We need to support sustainable growth that is built on increased exports, increased productivity, value-adding product development and innovation, and we need to support investments in those areas. At the time of writing, our feeling is that confidence in the Baltic countries is not yet at the level where people and business are starting to invest, especially in situations where external financing is needed. However, funding provided by banks alone will not be enough. One of the mistakes during the boom was that banks tended to cross the border to where financing should rather have been raised in the form of equity and risk capital. Future investments need to have access to a combination of capital and bank lending. Access to the capital market requires an attractive environment among investors where predictability, transparency and liquidity will be the important parameters.

Finally, are banks willing to lend? Lending is part of the core of banking – certainly banks will continue to lend in the future, but taking responsibility for a sustainable growth in the market also includes measures to avoid creating imbalances. Participating in a race to build volumes and market shares in lending will only lead to new unbalanced growth. It would not be in the interest of any of the stakeholders to see that happen again.

Index